BOOKS BY CHARLES REZNIKOFF

POETRY AND VERSE DRAMA

Rhythms (1918)

Rhythms II (1919)

Poems (1920)

Uriel Acosta: A Play & A Fourth Group of Verse (1921)

Chatterton, The Black Death & Meriwether Lewis, three plays (1922)

Coral & Captive Israel, two plays (1923)

Five Groups of Verse (1927)

Nine Plays (1927)

Jerusalem the Golden (1934)

In Memoriam: 1933 (1934)

Separate Way (1936)

Going To and Fro and Walking Up and Down (1941)

Inscriptions: 1944–1956 (1959)

By the Waters of Manhattan: Selected Verse (1962)

Testimony: The United States 1885–1890: Recitative (1965)

Testimony: The United States 1891–1900: Recitative (1968)

By the Well of Living and Seeing & The Fifth Book of the Maccabees (1969)

By the Well of Living and Seeing: New and Selected Poems 1918–1973 (1974)

Holocaust (1975)

Poems 1918–1936: Volume I of The Complete Poems of Charles Reznikoff (1976)

Poems 1937–1975: Volume 2 of The Complete Poems of Charles Reznikoff (1977)

Poems 1918–1975: The Complete Poems of Charles Reznikoff (1989)

The Poems of Charles Reznikoff 1918–1975 (2005)

PROSE

By the Waters of Manhattan: An Annual (1929)

By the Waters of Manhattan, a novel (1930)

Testimony (1934)

Early History of a Sewing-Machine Operator, with Nathan Reznikoff (1936)

The Lionhearted: A Story about the Jews of Medieval England (1944)

Family Chronicle, with Sarah Reznikoff and Nathan Reznikoff (1963)

The Manner "Music," a novel (1977)

Selected Letters of Charles Reznikoff 1917–1975, edited by Milton Hindus (1997)

TRANSLATIONS AND EDITIONS

Emil Bernard Cohn: Stories and Fantasies from the Jewish Past (1951)

Israel Joseph Benjamin: Three Years in America, 1859–1862 (1956)

Louis Marshall, Champion of Liberty: Selected Papers and Addresses (1957)

TESTIMONY

I

Jim went to his house

and got a pair of plow lines

and then into the stable

and put one on the jack

and led the jack out

and tied him to a fence;

and put the noose in the other line around

      the head of the jack

and began to pull.

The jack began to make a right smart noise.

Its dead body was found next morning,

fifteen or twenty feet from the stable-door;

the neck, just back of the head,

badly bruised.

II

On a Sunday--a bleak drizzling day--

Patrick Connolly, perfectly sober,

entered a streetcar.

After riding a while

without "the slightest impropriety of

behavior,"
he was suddenly | stricken
with apoplexy

Charles Reznikoff TESTIMONY

THE UNITED STATES (1885–1915):

RECITATIVE

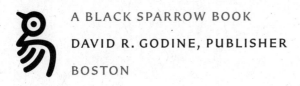

A BLACK SPARROW BOOK

DAVID R. GODINE, PUBLISHER

BOSTON

This is
A Black Sparrow Book
Published in 2015 by
DAVID R. GODINE, PUBLISHER
Post Office Box 450
Jaffrey, New Hampshire 03452
www.blacksparrowbooks.com

Book design and composition by Michael Russem
Cover design by Sarah French
The Black Sparrow Books pressmark is by Julian Waters

ACKNOWLEDGMENTS
Testimony, Objectivist Press (New York, 1934)
Testimony: the United States, 1885–1890: Recitative, New Directions (New York, 1965)
Testimony: the United States, 1891–1900: Recitative, Privately Printed (New York, 1968)
Testimony: Volume I, the United States (1885–1915): Recitative, Black Sparrow Press
     (Santa Barbara, 1978)
Testimony: Volume II, the United States (1885–1915): Recitative, Black Sparrow Press
     (Santa Barbara, 1978)

The text of the 1978 Black Sparrow edition of *Testimony*,
reprinted in this volume, was edited by Seamus Cooney.

FRONTISPIECE
From a corrected typescript of *Testimony* (undated), courtesy of
Mandeville Special Collections Library, University of California, San Diego.
Special thanks to Robert Melton, Heather Smedberg, and Colleen Garcia.

LIBRARY OF CONGRESS CATALOGING-IN-PUBLICATION DATA

Reznikoff, Charles, 1894–1976.
Testimony : the United States (1885–1915) : recitative / Charles Reznikoff.
pages cm
ISBN 978-1-56792-531-9 (alk. paper)
I. Title.
PS3535.E98T425 2015
811'.52—dc23
2014043105

FIRST EDITION
Printed in the United States

CONTENTS

Charles Reznikoff may be the most elusive poet in American poetry and *Testimony* the most elusive book-length poem of modernism. Certainly the outlines of both the poet's life and the poem's process are plain enough, but the rest tends to be filled in with negatives: all the things the poet did not do and all the things the poem isn't.

Reznikoff, born in New York in 1894, graduated NYU law school in 1916, passed the bar, but only briefly practiced, preferring to become a salesman for his father's hat business. (He much later said that law was too much work for a poet, whereas he could write his poems in the hours spent waiting in Macy's for the buyer to show up.) After that business collapsed, he held random jobs throughout his life: writer of entries for a legal encyclopedia, *Corpus Juris*; managing editor of *The Jewish Frontier*; editor of the papers of the lawyer and civil rights activist Louis Marshall; co-author of a history of the Jews of Charleston and an unfinished history of the Jews of Cleveland. His one extended stay outside of New York City—he never left the U. S.—was the three years he spent in the 1930s in Hollywood as an assistant to his old friend, the producer Albert Lewin. Given a huge office at Paramount Pictures, he had little to do and wrote poems about watching the flies on his desk.

In the late 1920s he met two younger poets, Louis Zukofsky and George Oppen. The three, all Jewish New Yorkers, shared an admiration for Ezra Pound and William Carlos Williams and the belief, along with Williams, that American modernism should be relocated from Paris and London to the U. S. Asked to edit an issue of *Poetry* in 1931, Zukofsky put them together, along with Williams, Carl Rakosi, Basil Bunting, Kenneth Rexroth, and a stylistically random collection of others (including the young Whittaker Chambers), under the rubric of "Objectivists." His manifesto in the issue was called "Sincerity and Objectification: With Special Reference to the Work of Charles Reznikoff." (Typical of Reznikoff's fate and Zukofsky's personality, when the essay was reprinted decades later, Zukofsky omitted Reznikoff entirely.) In 1934, the three poets pooled their resources to create the Objectivist Press in order to publish themselves and

Williams. The press didn't last long, but the label stuck, although the actual poetry of the three had little in common. Reznikoff may have been the only one to take the name seriously. Nearly forty years later, when asked to describe his poetry for the reference book *Contemporary Poets*, he wrote (in its entirety):

> "Objectivist"; images clear but the meaning not stated but suggested by the objective details and the music of the verse; words pithy and plain; without the artifice of regular meters; themes, chiefly Jewish, American, urban.

Until his mid-sixties, he published nearly all his books himself, setting the type for many of them on a printing press in his parents' basement. For eighteen of those years, there were no books of poetry at all. He received few reviews, most of them terrible. His first review said that he "annoys and bewilders"; his second called the poems "sordid, with an emphasis on the *sore*." The third, by Malcolm Cowley, said that he was "astigmatic," "an ecstatic with a defect in his voice, who stammers at the moment of greatest feeling." A line in Cowley's review—"He is unable to focus, and lines of splendid verse are lost to sight among heaps of rubbish"—may have led to one of Reznikoff's best-known short poems:

> Among the heaps of brick and plaster lies
> a girder, still itself among the rubbish.

It was a poem that Oppen often said ran through his mind over and over as he was trapped in a foxhole among dead and wounded comrades in the Second World War. Oppen, tellingly, always misquoted the last word as "rubble."

In 1962, New Directions, in collaboration with the *San Francisco Review* (run by Oppen's sister, June Degnan) published *By the Waters of Manhattan: Selected Verse*, Reznikoff's first visible book of poetry. It had an odd introduction by C. P. Snow, then famous as a social critic, who, "as far as a Gentile can judge," found the work had "overtones of extraordinary unfamiliarity." Three years later, the two publishers brought out the first volume of *Testimony*. In *Poetry*, Hayden Carruth—who had praised *By the Waters*—wrote: "I don't see the point in it." Surprisingly jingoistic, he claimed that the "material—all ugly, brutal, and inhumane. . . is one of relentless, absorbing, cold, bitter contempt: contempt for the society in question." Both books sold poorly; the ND-SFR collaboration ended; Reznikoff went back to printing his own books.

But in the 1960s the "Objectivists" emerged from their decades of near-total obscurity, like a council of Wise Elders suddenly among us. Oppen and Rakosi returned after their long silences; Zukofsky was published by major presses; Bunting in the U.K. produced his masterpiece, *Briggflatts*; in Wisconsin, the reclusive Lorine Niedecker was writing her best work. And Reznikoff was with them. There were readings, interviews, a prize or two. In 1974, the Black Sparrow Press began a program of bringing all of Reznikoff's poetry back into print. He died in 1976, at eighty-one, having just revised the proofs of a two-volume *Collected Poems*.

There was the legend of Charles Reznikoff, the invisible poet, walking twenty miles a day in New York City, writing down his observations in a little notebook, meeting cronies who never knew he was a writer at the Automat, publishing his own books of perfect poems for over fifty years. A sweet, elderly man who was maddeningly self-deprecating. George and Mary Oppen told me about a reading in Michigan, at the end of which the audience was on its feet, wildly cheering. Rezi, as they called him, was heard to mumble: "I hope I haven't taken up too much of your time."

And yet, because of his collaborations from the 1920s to the 1950s as editor and writer for such magazines as *The Menorah Journal* and *The Jewish Frontier*, he believed himself part of a milieu—if not exactly part of the crowd—of Upper West Side Jewish intellectuals. He had a very long marriage, though often spent apart, with Marie Syrkin, the dynamic journalist, academician, and Zionist activist; best friend of Golda Meir and a primary mentor to the young men who took over *The New Republic* in the 1970s. Reznikoff refused to accompany her on her many trips to postwar Europe, Palestine, and later Israel—explaining that he hadn't finished exploring Central Park—but happily went to the meetings and fundraising dinners, content, as he said many times, to sit at a table below while his wife sat on the dais. He was a frequent guest at the extravagant Hollywood and New York homes of the Lewins, where he is known to have dined with George Cukor, Nazimova, Djuna Barnes, and no doubt many others; he chatted with Greta Garbo on the street. He was perhaps most in his element at the Automat, but he also inhabited, however peripherally, Hollywood and Jewish high societies. Most of all, this kind, self-effacing man spent most of the last decades of his life in the systematic investigation of humanity at its worst: *Testimony* and *Holocaust*. It's too easy to call them the products of rage, inaccurate to attribute any politics or reflection on human nature to them. The fact is we will never know why these books were written, only how.

Testimony began as a book of prose in the 1930s, based on the 19th century legal documents that Reznikoff was reading for *Corpus Juris* and other historical documents. Probably inspired by Williams' *In the American Grain* (1925) and John Dos Passos' *Manhattan Transfer* in the same year and the first two volumes of his *U.S.A.* trilogy (1930 and 1932), it was written at a time when there was a preoccupation with telling the "American story" and the conviction that some kind of documentary narrative was the way to tell it. (Reznikoff's original title was *My Country 'Tis of Thee*, which was not necessarily ironic.) Given that it has only three sections—"Southerners and Slaves," "Sailing-Ships and Steamers," and "East and West"—it appears to be the beginning of a much larger panorama. Its most uncharacteristic piece, the prose poem "Rivers and Seas, Harbors and Ports," is an extraordinary reverie of the words and images of a vanished maritime world. It was unlike anything Reznikoff wrote before or after; a road not taken in his work. The book was published in 1934 by the Objectivist Press with an introduction by Kenneth Burke, and has been scandalously out of print until its inclusion here. (The copy I own came from the library of William Carlos Williams; when I bought it, the pages were uncut.)

Sometime in the 1950s, he returned to *Testimony*, this time confining himself to legal cases of criminality and negligence and writing it as poetry. The project was divided into four chronological periods (1885–1890, 1891–1900, 1901–1910, 1911–1915), in turn divided into three geographical areas (North, South, West), which contained sub-categories—some critics have read them as serial poems—such as "Machine Age," "Domestic Scenes," "Property," "Railroads," "Negroes," "Sounds and Smells," "Social Life," "Children," and so on, most of which repeat throughout the book. As far as I know, no one has investigated the structure of the book in search of determining patterns.

His research for *Testimony* was almost unimaginable. The known source for merely one of the short poems is a court transcript that runs to a hundred pages. As Reznikoff said in an interview: "I might go through a volume of a thousand pages and find just one case from which to take the facts and rearrange them so as to be interesting. . . . I don't know how many thousands of volumes I went through, and all I could manage to get out of it were these poems." (Characteristically, he adds: "And in looking through the book I might throw out some of them.") He frequently said that his original inspiration was, remarkably, Theodore Dreiser's *An American Tragedy* (1925—the same year as the Williams and Dos Passos books). But where Dreiser had expanded a single case into a massive novel, Reznikoff condensed massive documents into a brief poem.

These are notably crimes without punishment: We never learn how the judge or jury ruled in the case. The legal arguments are not represented. In some poems we have the scene of the crime without the crime itself. There is no commentary or rumination or metaphorical imagery; larger conclusions are not drawn. *Testimony*, as a cantata or mass, is a "recitative" with no chorales.

What Reznikoff liked about courtroom testimony, he said, was that what matters is the facts of the case, what the witness saw and heard, not the witness' feelings about, or interpretations of those facts. It was his ideal for poetry. He often cited some lines from the Sung Dynasty poet Wei T'ai (which he found in A.C. Graham's *Poems of the Late T'ang*): "Poetry presents the thing in order to convey the feeling. It should be precise about the thing and reticent about the feeling." His aim, in *Testimony*, was to create a "mood or feeling" by the "selection" and "arrangement" of the facts, as well as by the "rhythm of the words." (Despite Hayden Carruth's claim that "this is not poetry at all, but prose printed in irregular lines," the poems tend to have cleverly hidden internal rhymes and assonances.) Curiously, the closest thing to *Testimony* in literature—there are certainly no American poems remotely like it—may be the Icelandic sagas that Reznikoff loved: moving scenes of sheer human drama presented in the most unadorned of narratives.

Reznikoff is sometimes considered a precursor of the current vogue for "appropriated" or "found" poetry—the copying of texts, often of extreme banality, verbatim. He sometimes used a few words or a bit of local speech from the courtroom transcripts, but mainly what he "found" were the facts, which he then wrote in his own way. The poems are not pastiches; the original manuscripts of *Testimony* are covered with revisions. Reznikoff's personality bears some resemblance to Bartleby, but he was no scrivener.

Testimony is indeed an American panorama: the cases come from every state of the union and are full of things indigenous in north, south, and west. The passion of the crimes is universal; the accounts of racism (against "Negroes," Chinese, Mexicans) regional; the industrial accidents, derived from negligence lawsuits, are fixed in their historical moment. Yet there is a classicism about it: Reznikoff considered himself a Hellenist, influenced by both the lyrics of the Greek Anthology and the tragic dramas. In *Testimony*, the machines are the gods, enacting their inexplicable acts of vengeance on the hapless humans, many of them children. In the poems, the machines are usually described in detail, but the people are often nameless and nearly always featureless. They are merely actors in some unportrayed greater drama at the moment when their particular fates are sealed. And in these testimonies without judgements, their fates belong to perhaps the deepest substrata of this obsessional project: the Jewish narrative of suffering without redemption, epitomized, of course, by the *Book of Job*. From *Testimony*, Reznikoff would go on, toward the end of his life, to the transcripts of the Nuremberg Trials to create an even more devastating book: *Holocaust*.

The twenty-five-year-old Lionel Trilling, who probably met Reznikoff through his college friend Zukofsky, reviewing Reznikoff's one commercial publication—the 1930 novel *By the Waters of Manhattan*—wrote: "It has a quality of privacy which is startling. It has been written by a mind that, at once shy and unabashed, stays with itself, and, unintimidated by stale ways of seeing, makes public objects fresh in the freshness of its privacy." Reznikoff had a lifelong preoccupation with Jewish history and themes, but almost never attended a synagogue. He spent decades investigating crimes of social injustice, but expressed no political beliefs. He read very little contemporary American poetry, preferring the poets of the Greek Anthology or classical China. He once said, of something he had seen in a magazine: "When I read a poem like this, I turn the page."

ELIOT WEINBERGER

NOTE

All that follows is based on law reports of the several states.
The names of all persons are fictitious and those of villages
and towns have been changed.   C.R.

PART ONE   TESTIMONY

THE UNITED STATES (1885–1890)

RECITATIVE

Let all bitterness, and wrath, and anger, and clamour, and railing, be put away from you, with all malice.

Ephesians 4:31

THE SOUTH

I

Jim went to his house
and got a pair of plow lines
and then into the stable
and put one on the jack
and led the jack out
and tied him to a fence;
and put the noose in the other line around the head of the jack
and began to pull.
The jack began to make a right smart noise.

Its dead body was found next morning,
fifteen or twenty feet from the stable door;
the neck, just back of the head,
badly bruised.

II

On a Sunday—a bleak drizzling day—
Patrick Connolly, perfectly sober,
entered a streetcar.
After riding a while
without "the slightest impropriety of behavior,"
he was suddenly stricken
with apoplexy
and began vomiting.

The car had many passengers:
some left the car on account of this;
others called out
that he should leave.
When asked if he was drunk,
he shook his head

and said,
"I'll get out myself,"
but,
in raising himself to do so,
fell flat on the floor
and lay helpless.

The driver with the help of a passenger
lifted him
and carried him out of the car
and left him in the street—
between the car tracks and the gutter,
about two or three feet from the tracks.
Immediately afterwards,
by a convulsive movement,
he shifted his position
so that his legs were across a rail of the tracks.
A woman passing by
went to his assistance
and with the help of a man
removed him to the sidewalk. Here he remained
in the drizzle.

III
SOCIAL LIFE

1

The day had been dark and rainy,
and she and Fuller were sitting by the fire
late in the evening
in an old house on the mountain
about fifty yards from the road.
They had a bottle of whiskey between them
and had been drinking,
and Fuller was singing, "The Drunkard's Doom."

2

Della and Cliff were in a quadrille
at a party. When Cliff caught her hand
to swing her in the figure
known as "The Grand Chain,"
he tried to take her ring
from her finger. She crooked it in time.
When the figure was danced again
he succeeded in getting it.

She told her partner that she had lost her ring.
Looking Cliff straight in the face,
she said to her partner
and those helping him in the search
that they need not look on the floor:
somebody had it.

Cliff heard her,
pulled his hat down over his face
and, turning his back on Della,
began a conversation with his partner.

3

While Berry was dancing
at a public dance,
a pistol in his back pocket,
Williams pinned a white handkerchief
on the back of Berry's coat.
Berry was led out of the room
by his friends
because of his language,
and not allowed to come back
until he promised to say nothing more
about it.
But he did, and kept cursing Williams,
who told him again
that he did it only in fun;

but Berry said
that they must go out of the house
and settle the matter.

Williams left for the door
and stepped down
into the darkness—
outside of the light shining from the house.
Berry followed
but when he put his foot
on the doorstep
Williams struck him across the nose
where it joined the forehead
with a stick
the size of a walking stick—
though some said
it was a paling from the fence of a graveyard.

4
On a Sunday in May
a party of young men were bathing
in the river
when a stranger passed
and was invited to join them.
He went into the water
but soon came out angry
because someone threw water on him,
got his knife
and stabbed one of the party.
The young man stabbed
died in a few minutes.

The stranger was arrested
and, his hands tied behind his back,
carried to a store
half a mile up the river.
Here a crowd began to gather.

A cousin of the dead man—
but not one of the bathing party—
with a rifle in his hands,
calling to the crowd
to get out of the way,
faced the stranger.
His hands were still tied behind his back.
Not a word between them.
Then the dead man's cousin fired
and killed the stranger.

5

Banks and Miehle were playing a game of "pin pool"
at the Commercial Saloon in Laredo.
The game had commenced at nine o'clock on a Sunday evening
and Riverton—his name had been Reinhard—an acquaintance of
    Miehle,
was asked by Banks and Miehle to count the game.
At one in the morning a stranger came in and sat down at the pin-
    board—
someone called Douglas. He was drunk
and kept making remarks about the game from time to time.
Riverton was annoyed but Banks said: "Pay no attention."

About two in the morning, Riverton noticed that Banks was not
    playing fair.
He suggested to Miehle that they quit and go to bed,
refused to count the game any longer, went away and sat down.
At four in the morning Miehle owed Banks sixty dollars
and he said to Banks: "I will play you one more game for sixty
    dollars."
"No," said Banks, "but I will play you for fifty dollars.
I ought to have ten dollars for staying up all night."

Banks had fifteen counted on his string;
he knocked down two more pins and said: "Pool!"
Miehle said: "There must be a mistake."

He let the balls run out at the side of the table,
counted fourteen aloud and then said:
"Something is wrong."
Banks took a ball out of his pocket secretly and, hiding it in his hand,
    said:
"Are there only fourteen?"
He raked in the fourteen balls and counted all together and said:
"There are fifteen."
Miehle said "Yes, there are fifteen now.
I have had enough of his game!"
At this Douglas spoke up and said: "Banks, get your money."
"Yes," said Banks, "I want my money before you leave the house."

Miehle answered: "You will get your money."
Picking up his coat, he walked behind the bar and washed his hands.
Banks, Douglas, and Riverton followed Miehle,
and Banks asked him if he would not have a drink.
Miehle said he did not care for anything.
They were now all in front of the bar and Miehle had his side to it.
Douglas said to Banks, "Get your money before he leaves the house,"
and Banks said, "Yes, I want it before you leave the house."
Banks then said something to the barkeeper in Spanish,
and the barkeeper handed him a pistol.
Miehle looked around and saw it.
He said to Riverton: "Will you please step up to my room and bring
    me my valise?
I want to pay him what I owe him."

Riverton brought the valise to the door of the saloon.
Miehle stepped into the doorway,
opened the valise, and took out a pistol.
Douglas was standing at the bar—nearest the door.
Miehle, with the pistol in his hand
down by his side,
walked past him and up to Banks:
"You demanded this money twice before I left the house.
How do you want it?"
Douglas was leaning with his right arm on the bar.

He saw the pistol in Miehle's hand and said,
"You will see damn quick," and ran his hand into his hip pocket.
Miehle wheeled and "threw" his pistol down on him.
"My friend," he said, touching Douglas on the lapel of his coat with his
        left hand,
"this is something that does not concern you,
and I wish that you would throw up your hands."
But Douglas kept pulling at the pistol in his pocket.
Miehle waited a moment and added:
"Throw up your hands or I will have to cut you down."
Douglas made another jerk at his pistol,
and Miehle fired and shot him.
Then he wheeled on Banks and said:
"You have a gun on you:
I want it!" And "threw" his pistol down on Banks.

Banks said he was a deputy and had a right to carry a pistol.
Miehle answered: "I don't give a damn what you are.
Give up your gun!"
At that Banks made a movement to get ready to shoot
and Miehle said: "Stand up there or I will shoot your head off!"
Banks threw up his hands and Miehle reached over
and took the pistol. "Get going!" And Banks did.

6

In a small yard in the rear of a house
on a Sunday night,
twelve or fifteen Negroes were shooting dice.
The game was played on a small three-legged table,
propped up against a tree,
and lighted by a lamp
hanging from one of the branches.

Popham came in and joined the game:
he bet only small sums
until he lost sixty cents.
As the game went on,

thirty dollars were on the table;
five dollars of this King's.

Gusts of wind moved the money about,
and Popham laid his hand on it.
King at once called out:
"My bet is off!"
Popham said to him:
"Do you mean to say that I will steal your money?"
He sprang on the table
and kicked at King
but the table turned over;
then he got loose from those who held him
and started towards King.

7
A shot was fired
from the cane patch
by some person
slipping along,
bent over,
with a gun in his hands.
One of the Negroes went into the cane patch
to see who was there,
and found Coleman sitting on a log,
and brought him some chicken
from the festival.

Junius went to bed
and left some rags burning—
the mosquitoes were bad.
He had only been asleep a few minutes
when Coleman came in.
Junius asked him where his gun was.
Coleman said:
"It is half-past ten."

"I didn't ask the time.
  Where's my gun?"

The gun had been loaded when Junius left in the morning,
and had four cartridges in it.
When a gun has not been shot for a long time,
it looks white—kind of ashy—in the barrel:
the gun looked dark in the muzzle,
as if it had been shot recently.

"Coleman, what in the world is the matter with you?
  You look mighty bad."
"I feel mighty bad."
  Coleman looked as if he had run a long distance—
  all sweaty.
  His "jean pants" were wet
  and sandy about the legs.
"What time did they have at the festival?"
"A nice time—
  only that a man got shot."
"Who was shot?"
"Burley."
"Did his wife take on much?"
"Right smart,
  but no one paid much attention to her . . .

"No one ought to care for her!
  After she said that she was not going to marry Burley
  and then to go and marry him."

8

"Yellowstone Kit," as he was called,
  would come to Montgomery now and then,
  and rent a lot;
  put up a large tent
  in which he placed a stand and a number of seats around it,

and electric lights
to light up the tent at night.

In the tent he gave exhibitions of sleight of hand
and lectures on the merits of his drugs for sale,
handing them around himself or by his helpers;
and at these exhibitions there was always music by a band.

IV
DOMESTIC SCENES

1

It was nearly daylight when she gave birth to the child,
lying on the quilt
he had doubled up for her.
He put the child on his left arm
and took it out of the room,
and she could hear the splashing of water.
When he came back
she asked him where the child was.
He replied: "Out there—in the water."

He punched up the fire
and returned with an armload of wood
and the child,
and put the dead child into the fire.
She said: "O John, don't!"
He did not reply
but turned to her and smiled.

2

Late at night, their sow rooted open the door of their cabin,
and husband and wife
quarreled over driving her out.
His wife knocked him down with an iron shovel.

He started for his breeches and said,
"If I had my knife, I'd cut your throat,"
and she ran out at the door.
He shut the door after her
and propped it closed with a stick of wood.

When she was found, she was lying on her face,
frozen to death. The weather was extremely cold
and where she lay
the snow was about eighteen inches deep.

When she left the cabin, she was barefoot
and had very little clothing. The way she took
led through briers
and there were drops of blood on the snow—
where the briers had torn her legs from the knees down—
and bits of clothing that had been torn off;
at one place
she had struck her ankle against the end of a log
and it had bled freely.

3

Mrs. Farborough went into her brother's house,
leaving her husband a short distance from it—
he was the best man of the neighborhood for strength—
and, without speaking to anyone,
seized a tin cup.
Her sister-in-law said it seemed as if she took a good deal of authority
    there.
Mrs. Farborough replied she took enough to get her things,
and would also take her teakettle.
Mrs. Eller told her to take them
and get out of the house
and stay out.

Mrs. Farborough did go out
but soon returned with a stone—

as large as her fist—
which she held under her apron,
and sat down,
remarking that she intended to stay a while
just for aggravation.
Farborough then approached the house with a stone in each hand
and, when near it, sat down on a log.
After a moment or two,
he sprang into the house,
the stones still in his hands.
At this, his wife threw the stone she held under her apron
at her sister-in-law:
missed and struck the side of the house near her head.
The women clinched and fell to the floor,
Mrs. Farborough on top,
hitting Mrs. Eller in the face with her fist.

Eller went up to Farborough and said:
"Brother Martin,
take your wife out of here,
and I will take care of mine.
Let us have no fuss!"
And he started forward to part the women,
still fighting.
Farborough pushed him back:
"God damn you, stand back,
or I will kill the last Goddamn one of you!"
and lifted his right hand,
holding the stone.

He turned to look at the women,
and Eller shot him in the back with a pistol,
just where his suspenders crossed.

4
He and his wife were members of a society
known as Knights and Ladies of Honor.

The life of each member was insured for two thousand dollars—
to go to widow or widower.
He had to borrow the money to pay his dues
and had just been defeated for town marshal;
and now his wife was sick.

The Knight of Honor was seen in a saloon with a Negro
who used to work for him;
then the two were seen going into an alley.
Here he gave the Negro a quarter
and asked him to go to a drugstore
and buy him a small bottle of strychnine.
If the druggist asked the Negro why he wanted it,
he was to say to kill wolves on a farm.
The Negro asked him what he really wanted it for
and he said to poison the dogs
belonging to a neighbor where a girl was working
whom he wanted to visit at night.
The Negro brought him the bottle,
and he told the Negro that if questioned about it
he must say that he put it in the pocket of his overcoat
and left the coat hanging in a saloon,
and that the bottle was taken from his pocket
by someone.

When his wife asked for the quinine
she used as a medicine,
he went to the mantelpiece
where he had placed a package of quinine
bought the day before
and poured some of the strychnine into a spoonful of cold coffee.
She thought the powder had a peculiar look,
and tried to dissolve it
by stirring it with her finger.
He assured her it was quinine
bought where he had always bought it;
and she drank it.

V

BOYS AND GIRLS

1

A band was playing
on the excursion train;
Joe heard it
on his way home from school
and boarded the train with other boys.

A crowd waiting
to board the train.
While it was moving towards the passengers,
a man with a lantern
in one hand and a stick in the other
came through the cars,
shouting at the boys
to get off
and striking at them with the stick.

Trying to get off while the train was running,
Joe fell between the cars.

2

The railroad company's depot was between two streets:
a train had just come in,
discharged its passengers and baggage,
and was about to be switched from the main track to a side track
for the night.

Four or five little girls, eight or nine years old,
were playing around the depot
and they took a notion
to ride on the train as it was switched.
One of the girls asked permission of the baggagemaster to do so.
He was standing nearby, about to leave for home,
and nodded.

The girls entered one of the passenger coaches
and took seats at the end near the baggage car.
As the train was moved out of the main track at a pretty rapid rate,
the girls became alarmed—
afraid it was leaving the city,
and they all ran out of the car
and jumped from the train.
The youngest fell
and her foot was run over.

3

A boy of thirteen was employed in a coal mine as "door boy";
he was stationed inside the mine,
between the main track along the entrance
and its wall,
in a space only a few feet wide.

The door, hung upon hinges,
was made of thick heavy timber;
to open it,
the boy had to cross the track,
take hold of a handle on the door and return to his place,
holding the handle.

From the chambers of the mine that opened upon the entrance
the loaded cars were drawn by mules to the main track;
as each car was brought out and the mules unhitched,
the car was turned over to a "spragger"
to put a block of wood in front of the wheels,
for the main track was on a down grade.

Lights were required in the mine
to see at all, and each worker carried a light
fastened to his cap. When a train was made up
and was ready to move out of the mine,
the "train-runner" mounted the forward car,
slackened the brakes,

and signaled the switchman. He in turn
signaled the boy to open the door
and let the train pass out of the mine—
moving of its own momentum.

That morning there were brought from the chambers
seven cars loaded with coal,
put upon the main track and left standing.
The boy was absent from his station
but seen near the mouth of one of the chambers.
As the eighth car was brought out
and put upon the track,
the mule driver called to him:
"Get back to your door!"
And the boy started to do so at a run.

The eighth car moved down upon the stationary cars in front of it
with such force
as to set them in motion,
and the whole train was suddenly sent down the grade.
The boy had had time to return to his post
before the train started; he heard the approaching train
and fearing a collision between train and door—
with himself to blame—tried to open it.

The train broke through the door,
and the boy's mangled body was found under one of the cars
when the train stopped.

4

The boy was sick and went to bed just before sundown.
After supper, which was soon after dark,
his stepfather left the house to go to town.
When his mother finished clearing off the table,
she prepared to take a bath in the shed used as the kitchen.
This was next to the room where they ate
and where the boy was lying.

While his mother was still bathing,
his stepfather came back and went into the kitchen.
He heard his mother and stepfather begin to quarrel,
and then the sound of two blows
and a louder noise—a shot from a pistol.

When his mother and stepfather began talking in the kitchen,
the boy covered his head with the bedclothes.
After the shot, he heard the scraping
of his stepfather's feet on the kitchen floor,
and then his stepfather came into the room
where the boy was lying
and put out the lamp
still burning on the table.
His stepfather went back into the kitchen
and the boy heard the back door open
and close—
and then not another sound.

5

The child was about eight years old.
For some misconduct or other,
his father stripped him naked, threw him on the floor,
and beat him with a piece of rubber pipe,
crying, "Die, God damn you!"
He tried to dash the child against the brick surface of the chimney,
and flung the child again heavily on the floor
and stamped on him.

VI
MACHINE AGE

1

Forty feet above the ground on a telegraph pole,
the lineman

forced the spur he wore into the pole and,
throwing his other leg around it,
leaned over

to fasten a line with his nippers
to the end of a crossarm
by a wire around the glass cup on a pin.

The line, hauled tight
hundreds of feet ahead of him
by means of a reel,
broke,
and the crossarm
broke where it was fastened to the pole:
he fell headlong
to the stones below.

2

It was a drizzling night in March.
The street lamps flashed twice:
a break in the connection,
and all hands were looking for it.

When the policeman saw him first,
the colored man was carrying a short ladder
that the hands used
in climbing the electric-light poles.
The policeman next saw him hanging on a pole,
his overcoat flapping in the wind,
and called to him but got no answer.

They put the dead body on the counter of a shop nearby:
the skin was burnt on the inside of both his hands;
his right hand was burnt to the bone.
The insulation was off of part of the "shunt cord" he had carried
and his skin was sticking to the naked wire.

3

There were three on the locomotive:
the flagman, the fireman, and the engineer.
About two hundred yards from the man—
stone-deaf—
the flagman commenced ringing the bell;

within about a hundred yards
the engineer commenced sounding his whistle:
thirty or forty short blows.

The man did not get off the track or look around.

4

Arnold heard the blowing of the whistle:
the train was coming.
The only light was that of a small lamp
behind the shutters of the station,
and it gave at best
a weak light on the platform.

The night was dark and cloudy.
In trying to pass from the platform to the ground
where passengers boarded the train,
he could not see the steps that led from the platform:
slipped
and fell.

5

A brakeman on a freight car,
he was detailed to go out on a passenger train—
and glad to go.
"Haven't been making much this week," he said.
The brakemen were all glad to make a run of that kind.

The brakes on a freight train
are worked from the top of the cars

where there is nothing—
no railing, nothing!—
to keep a brakeman from falling off
or being thrown off
by the motion of the train;
but the brake on a passenger train is worked from the platform of a car,
and this has a railing.

The night was cold
with a fall of snow,
and the platforms of the cars
were covered with ice and slippery.
When the train reached Gainesville,
he was not on it.

A few days afterwards, his body was found
in a ditch near the railway,
where there was a steep grade
and a reverse curve in the track.
The body was frozen stiff,
and his clothes and shoes covered with shining mica
found in the embankment.
His hands were clutched
as if grasping something
but held nothing.

They dressed him in a new suit of clothes, paid for by the railway,
and at Charlotte he was provided with a suitable coffin.

VII
PROPERTY

1

They held the light very close to him,
but he could not see.
They asked him to sign the paper,

and someone put a pencil in his hand
to make his mark.
He could not take hold of it—
even feel it.

2

Her husband had been on the friendliest terms
with Mr. Bernd:
both were of foreign birth
and her husband had worked for him.
During her husband's lifetime,
she had given a note and mortgage to Mr. Bernd—
at her husband's urging—
for her husband's debt.
The mortgage was now foreclosed,
and the sheriff had advertised her property for sale
and was about to sell it.
She and her husband had been led to believe
from remarks by Mr. Bernd
that he intended to make her husband a legatee
under his will—
at least to the extent of the debt;
and upon her husband's deathbed
he had praised Mr. Bernd in the highest terms,
and had advised her
to trust in him as a faithful friend.

She was in Mr. Bernd's store one day,
and he was helping her select certain tools
which had belonged to her husband
and which she wished to keep.
The debt was mentioned,
and Mr. Bernd said to her
he would never have her property sacrificed
to pay it.
The sheriff came into the store just then
and served her with a paper to foreclose the mortgage:

she asked Mr. Bernd what the paper meant.
He told her it was about the debt she owed him.
She took the paper home
and did not read it or understand what it meant
and never heard of the matter again—
until the levy by the sheriff.

3

Early in the morning of the day of Miss Bailey's wedding,
her mother went to the home of a lawyer
and said that no marriage contract had been drawn
and one must be drawn up before the marriage,
for it would never do to let her daughter's property
go out of the family in case of her daughter's death.
She wanted the lawyer to attend to it immediately,
and the lawyer went to see the bridegroom that morning.

The bridegroom said that nothing had been said to him
by the family about the matter,
and he thought it was late and a most inappropriate time
to bring up a matter of such importance,
and he did not think it was Miss Bailey's wish
that anything of the sort should be done;
but he would think the matter over,
and see the instrument when prepared,
and then decide what to do.

Later in the day, the lawyer went to the house of the bride's mother;
and she called her daughter downstairs.
Miss Bailey looked as if she had been crying.
She asked the lawyer to tell her what was in the instrument
and she seemed impatient to get through with the interview.
She wished, she said, that she had no property at all
to be troubled about.

The lawyer then told her of the contents of the instrument,
and she asked if it contained any power to revoke it,

and told him, if it did not, she would not sign it.
The lawyer said that the instrument had no such power
but it could be added,
and the bride's mother consented that this should be done.
By this time it was about one-thirty in the afternoon.

About the middle of the afternoon, the lawyer called again with the
    instrument
and now it had a clause containing a power of revocation.
The lawyer read it to Miss Bailey's stepfather and her mother
but Miss Bailey herself was not present.
Her mother took the instrument upstairs to show to Miss Bailey,
but could not have remained long enough to have read it to her.
The lawyer took the paper to the bridegroom;
he was in his room, dressing.
He read the instrument hurriedly
and said again that he did not believe it to be Miss Bailey's wish that
    he should sign it,
that it was too important a matter to act upon at such a time as this;
and he felt that he ought to protect her interests.

The lawyer returned to Miss Bailey's mother
and told her of the interview. She called Miss Bailey downstairs.
"See there! He refuses to sign it."
Miss Bailey replied: "Oh, Mamma, my Dannie will sign it—
if I ask him to."
She then wrote a note to the bridegroom:
"I trust you fully
but I promised Mother long ago that it should be so,
and cannot refuse.
As you love me, sign this paper
and do not add to my suffering;
for I have gone through with enough to kill me.
Do as they wish us to,
and afterwards I will prove my love to you
in some other way.
You must sign."

He did, and so did the witnesses.
This was just before the wedding.

4
Alice's father was a white man,
of large estate,
and her mother a colored woman.
But her father and his wife treated Alice as his daughter—
in fact, as if she were *their* daughter;
although this, as a judge of the local court was to say,
was "revolting to the moral sense
and offensive against public policy."

She was sent to a boarding school in Washington,
and was now trying to establish herself
as a music teacher in that city.
After his wife's death, Alice's father wrote to her:
"Don't think that I will ever forget you:
I have promised this to my dear dead wife."

Alice's father had another daughter—
his child and his wife's.
When he made his will, he gave all of his large estate
to this daughter and her children;
but he had given Alice a deed to property in town that was worth
        about ten
thousand dollars.
Only her father and his lawyer, and Alice and her friends,
knew of this;
and she was advised by her friends to place the deed on record
to protect the gift—
and she did.
By this time her father was old and feeble.
He was living with his white daughter
and spent most of his time just sitting on the porch.

As soon as Alice's half sister and her husband
learned of the gift to Alice,
they were furious—
although it was only a small part of her father's property.
They sent for his lawyer. When he came,
the old man was sitting on the porch.
His daughter, holding a copy of the deed to Alice,
exclaimed: "See what Father has done!
I don't believe he knew what he was doing.
What can be done now?"

Her father finally said:
"I believe I can get Alice to reconvey the property.
I don't think she will refuse."
And he and the lawyer arranged to take an early train the very next day
to where his colored daughter happened to be staying
on a visit to a friend.

They had breakfast with Alice and her friend
and then sat on the porch together
talking about everything but the deed;
most of the conversation was about Alice's life in Washington.
The old man could not bring himself to talk
about his errand.
Finally, he and his lawyer went for a walk together
while the young women—Alice and her friend—washed up the
        breakfast dishes.
On their return, the lawyer said:
"It will be best for you
to give the property back to your father."
And her father said: "You will not lose anything by it." Tears were in
        his eyes.
The lawyer added: "His family is much disturbed
about his giving you this property,
and his son-in-law says
he would rather see him burn down all the houses on it
than convey it to you.
As it is, it would only be the land there,

and would do you no good
because the people near there have said
no colored person should live there."

Her father said: "I thought that,
as I have done a great deal for you,
you would reconvey it to me."
"Do you want me to reconvey it
without any equivalent?"
"I have no equivalent to give you."
At this he went into the yard
and began walking backward and forward.
The lawyer on the porch said: "Has he not been very kind to you
and given you a great deal?
I think that under all the circumstances
you ought to grant his request.
You will not suffer by it."
"Has my father written his will?"
"Yes, I prepared a will for him which was signed."
But he did not tell her
that in the will there was nothing for her;
nor did she ask him.

She kept looking at her father
as the feeble old man
walked backward and forward in the yard,
weeping.
And Alice said: "I can't think of causing him distress
in his old age:
he has been too kind to me.
I will let him have the property."
At that, the lawyer took the deed that he had prepared the night before
out of his pocket. "I have a deed right here and will go for a notary,"
and hurried off.

When the deed was signed, witnessed, and in the lawyer's pocket again,
he turned to Alice and said: "You have acted nobly."

VIII
NEGROES

1

One night in April or May,
his daughter saw someone's hand
make the curtain which was drawn tightly across her window
bulge
and ran into the adjoining room in her night clothes
where he and his son were sitting.
He ran around the house one way
and his son ran the other way
and they found a Negro
under a workbench
within six or eight feet of the window
holding a piece of plank before his face—
begging them not to shoot.

2

The Negro was dead
when the doctors examined him.
They found upon his belly
bruises:
he died, the doctors said, of peritonitis.

The jailer testified that the Negro had been brought to the jail
charged with burglary;
but no warrant for his arrest was produced
and the jailer did not know—or tell—
who brought him.
The Negro said that a crowd of men
had taken him from a store to the woods
and whipped him
with "a buggy trace."

He was not treated by a doctor, the jailer, or anybody:
just put into the jail and left there to die.

The doctor who saw him first—on a Monday—
did nothing for him
and said that he would not die of his beating;
but he did die of it on Wednesday.

IX

Bridget Cunningham, of King's County, Ireland,
a handsome, well-shaped lass,
with a fair complexion, dark hair and eyes,
but wild and unruly,
left Ireland with her brother when she was sixteen.
At Liverpool they parted:
Timothy went on to Boston,
Bridget to New York.

She stayed with friends for about a year
and then, one day, left her lodging
to look, she said, for "a situation."
None of her friends or relatives heard of her again.
Timothy came from Boston
to look for her
but could find no trace of Bridget.

Ten or so years later,
Kate Townsend, who had also been known as Martha Wingfield,
came from Liverpool to New Orleans
in a sailing vessel.
In time, she ran the largest whorehouse in town.
When she was stabbed to death
by her lover, Sykes—
to whom she had left all her property—
she was monstrously fat
and weighed well over three hundred pounds;
on one arm was tatooed "A. Pymm,"
and her hair, which she was always dyeing a different color,
was light brown.

Her eyes were hazel.
She had the same slight pockmarks on the side of her nose
that Bridget had,
and she was said to have told her dressmakers, hairdressers,
    chambermaids, and washerwomen
that she came from a town in King's County, Ireland,
and that her name was really Bridget Cunningham.

X

Years ago, a company procured a body of land
lying on the Gulf
and laid it off in streets, blocks, and public squares:
this was to be a great seaport
to be called Mississippi City.

The city was to be intersected by a wide street
called Railroad Street,
through which a railroad was to run to a depot and a pier—
both of which the company built—
and then it became insolvent.

Depot and pier remained, year after year:
a depot no train ever came to,
and a pier no ship ever docked at.

THE NORTH

I

1

The horse was used to the city and gentle.
He had often stood near the door of his owner
in the business part of the city, unhitched,
with drays and other vehicles constantly passing.
He had life, was restless and high-strung, fancy and stylish,
but quite sensible;
would pick up your handkerchief
and at his stall fondle you.
Under the saddle he was hard to handle
but in harness was tender of mouth
and easily managed:
he had been driven up to—and past—a locomotive
at a crossing
and had gone quietly, attached to the buggy,
with a railroad train passing from behind.

2

A Mr. Fairchild hired a horse and buggy;
when he returned in the evening
the horse had been driven sixty or more miles.
The weather was cold and sleety, the roads heavy.
Buggy and horse were nearly covered with frozen mud;
and a good deal had been thrown on top of the buggy:
in ordinary going, mud won't fly on top.
The horse could not stand for a couple of days,
lying down all the time;
and the livery-stable man could not get him up.

3

The mare, thin in flesh and a little lame
from a split in one foot,
was still a good true horse to pull
for a peddler of kindling wood.

For some reason or other, the peddler
took an iron rod out of the wagon
and whipped the mare with it;
bent the rod several times by beating her
and then would straighten it out again.

Several of the citizens came around,
but he told them it was his horse
and he would whip it as long as he pleased.
Every time he hit the mare, she grunted;
but she would not rear up
except when he struck her on the head.
When he stopped beating her
she had ridges on her
and the blood ran from her nostrils.

4

The bleating of calves
kept overnight at a slaughterhouse
to be slaughtered in the morning.

II

One of the hands on the oyster boat
was sick. He tried to work
but, unable to do so,
the captain beat him across the back and sides
with a shovel or handspike—
whatever was handy.

Next morning, too weak to wind up the anchor,
one of the other hands jerked it up,
and he fell on the deck. The captain came up to him
and kicked him; when he cried out,
pressed a foot heavily on his throat.
The captain then tied a rope about his body
and, fastening the rope to a hook on the port rail,
dragged him from side to side of the boat
until he said he would work.

But he was too weak.
Trying to turn the crank of the dredge,
he again fell flat on the deck.
The captain tied his thumbs with a rope
and, by means of a hook fastened to the rope,
hoisted his body
until his feet swung above the deck.

He was finally put into a yawl-boat
and taken ashore. As he was lying there,
the captain for good measure
stamped on his neck.
In a few hours he was dead.

The doctor, moving his head, could hear
the crackling of the bones
in the broken neck.

III
SOCIAL LIFE

1

I will be down in a few days
and want you to help me
do up the town.

Keep things still as a mouse,
and look every way
for Sunday.

2

At the party when Al asked Hattie if she would,
she answered: "We have no chance";
and when John and Jim asked her,
she merely laughed.

But when Al asked her
if Bryan had ever asked her,
she answered: "No,
he ain't got sense enough!"

3

John and Allen, young men living in the same neighborhood,
used to call on Miss English,
the daughter of a neighboring farmer. After a while,
John seemed to be in greater favor
and Allen no longer called on her.

At his last visit
he said he would kill anyone who did.
On a night in April,
Miss English invited some of her friends
to an entertainment at her father's house.
John was invited
but Allen came also:
both were members of a string band that was to play.
Allen's presence, however, was distasteful to Miss English
and she told him as much
soon after he came.
He left the house quietly
but stayed in the yard with his brother.

After they were there for an hour or so,
word was brought to Miss English's father
that Allen was making threats against John.
Mr. English went out and told him to leave:
this was not the place to settle their quarrel.

Allen and his brother went to a shed
near the road leading from the house;
perhaps to take shelter from the rain
beginning to fall
and to wait for friends
that were going their way;
perhaps to wait for John.
While they were waiting,
Allen borrowed a pocketknife
from his brother
to use, so he said, at his work next day.

At midnight the guests left the house,
and John passed the shed.
Allen came out
and soon there were angry words.
John put down the box
in which he kept his violin
and turned to face Allen;
then turned away and said
he would not fight any man who fought with a knife.
After he had gone a little distance,
he looked back at Allen,
and was struck on the forehead
by a stone
Allen threw.

John staggered
and lifted his hands to his head;
then ran towards Allen.
They scuffled
and John threw Allen down

and tried to stamp on the hand
in which he held the knife.

Allen managed to get up
and they clinched again
and this time both fell
with Allen on top.

Suddenly the fight ended.
John was badly hurt and unable
to walk.
The bystanders carried him back
to the house he had just left—
and he died
in two or three minutes.
Six wounds were found on him,
two mortal:
the blow on his forehead had fractured his skull
and the knife had been thrust into his breast
near his heart.

4
Of two second-story rooms,
both opening upon a veranda
and reached by a single flight of stairs,
Mrs. McCarthy and her son occupied one,
O'Brien and his wife the other.

O'Brien and Mrs. McCarthy's son
were in the habit of drinking together
and sometimes became boisterous.
Mrs. McCarthy complained to O'Brien about this
and they were soon unfriendly.

Sunday evening, just after the street lamps were lit,
on his way down the stairs,
O'Brien turned and said to Mrs. McCarthy—

sitting on the veranda in front of her room—
that his constant prayer was
that the curse of the Almighty might rest on her
and that she would get paralyzed.
She replied in a low voice
that she hoped he would break a leg.

O'Brien heard her
and turning at the bottom of the stairs
said: "If I hear anything more from you,
I'll come up there
and fire you over the banisters";
then, as if deciding to do so,
he darted up.

Mrs. McCarthy ran into her room
and he followed;
taking up a heavy beer glass
he struck her on the head with it—
with such force
as to drive pieces of glass into her head
and break her skull.

5
Ten or twelve colored men
were gambling in the basement of a saloon on State Street—
rolling dice,
sitting or standing on opposite sides of a table.
Scott was playing
and Luther keeping track of the bets.

Calhoun shoved a dime over to pay a man called "Kentuck";
it got mixed in with Scott's money,
and Calhoun reached forward to grab it.
Scott said: "Do you want to rob me?"
At that Luther spoke up,

lifting the little stick he held in his hand,
"Let me explain it to you, Scott."

"I don't want you to explain it to me."
"But I will explain it to you."
"I don't care for you to explain anything to me."
"I want to tell you . . ."
"I don't want you to tell me."
"Let me show you how it is."
"I don't want you to show me."
"You need not talk that way, Scott.
  I have always been a friend to you."
"And I don't give a damn for you."
  Luther leaned back in his chair
  and put his hands on the railing of the table.
"There's more people in this town cares for me
  than I do for them.
  I will show you what I care for you,"
  and he got up
  and threw the little stick down.

Scott had been picking up his money with his right hand.
  He put the money in his pocket
  and when his hand came out
  it held a pistol.
"And I'll show you how much I care for you," he said
  and shot Luther.

6

The "show" consisted of some stuffed snakes
  and some live ones in cages;
  and a contrivance upon a frame of pine wood
  in which were belts running over pulleys,
  and upon the belts little blocks of wood—
  images which would pass in review
  by turning a crank.

There was a muslin screen in front
to keep the machinery hidden,
and persons admitted to the show
looked through a small opening.
A red light was thrown upon the screen
and, at a certain point,
the machinery would touch a trigger:
fire off a little cannon
and beat a drum.

IV

DOMESTIC SCENES

1

Van Nicely with his warmest smile—
bringing presents for the children—
said: "I have just come from Trenton";
unwrapped a bottle of whiskey for Mr. Jones
and gave Mrs. Jones twenty-five dollars for Christmas;

after shaking hands with her and saying politely,
"How do you do?"
as if they had not seen each other for days
and the two of them
had not spent the afternoon together in New York.

2

The three had met at a singing society
and Schmidt engaged the music teacher
to give Mrs. Schmidt music lessons.
He himself was a dealer in lumber;
worked late and was often away on trips to buy lumber.

Schmidt was told that his wife and the music teacher
would take walks through the fields together

and that she would look into the music teacher's eyes
"as if she were his bride."
Schmidt dismissed him.

Coming home one day from one of his trips,
he found his wife and the music teacher in the parlor:
heard her running across the room
and, when he entered, she was standing near the table,
looking at some photographs,
and the music teacher was at the other side of the table.
Schmidt ordered him out of the house.
The man hesitated and was about to speak;
Schmidt added that he was "a blackguard,"
and said he would call a policeman at once
and have him put out.

When the music teacher was gone,
Mrs. Schmidt said to her husband
that in insulting him
he had insulted her;
that his own stupid face could not be compared
with the music teacher's intelligent features;
and that he was only a dwarf.
Schmidt turned away
and muttered something about "a bad woman."
At this she kicked him
and, when he turned to face her,
kicked him again
so that he doubled up with pain.

She then left the house
and caught up with the music teacher.
They went on together through the August fields.
When they sat down,
she put her arm around him
and he tapped her lap
with the newspaper he held rolled up in his hand,
and said lightly:

"How would *you* like someone to kick you there?"
And both laughed.

3

He picked up a stick of wood and said,
"By Jesus Christ, I will knock your brains out,"
and told her to leave the house.
She answered she would go when she was good and ready.
He said, "You will go before you are ready,"
and shoved her towards the door.
She caught hold of the door casing;
and their little girl began to cry.

4

They had come, man and wife, together from Italy.
Maria had been married to Antonio when she was fourteen;
now she was twenty-four.

Her second cousin got her husband a job at his trade as a mason
the very first day of his arrival in New York.
But Antonio gave it up,
said the work was too hard,
and went to shining shoes.
He wanted Maria to help him by picking up rags in the streets
but she would not:
said she would wash clothes
or do any other work suitable for a woman
but not that—
picking up rags in the street.

Antonio would beat her and kick her and spit in her face.
Finally, she left him.
Their daughter of eight was taken to a convent.
Maria had a hundred dollars when she left Italy
and only thirty remained—
not enough for a steamship ticket back to Italy.

She took rooms in a tenement and had boarders.
Antonio would come to the flat and try to get in
but she kept the door locked
and he would go away threatening her life.

That very morning he had been frightened away
by her threat to call the landlord.
He went to the butcher shop where both traded
and paid the butcher ten cents he had borrowed,
and on leaving said:
"I must see the end of my wife:
I want to spit in her face
when they lay her out as a corpse."

Later that morning, passers-by on First Avenue
saw Antonio walking along the street leisurely,
whistling,
hands in his pockets;
and Maria following him at a distance of about ten feet.
A passer-by, a few feet ahead of Antonio,
heard the report of a revolver,
and turning saw Maria with the smoking revolver in her hand,
cocking it for a second shot.
The first had struck a piece of paper and it was burning.

The man shouted to Antonio: "Run or you'll be shot!"
Maria fired again.
The second shot went into his back.
He cried out, "Holy Virgin! Holy Virgin!"
managed to run almost three blocks along the avenue
and then fell down—
dead.

Maria cocked her revolver again;
and with it in her hand
went to where her husband was lying:
walked around the crowd that had gathered
and looked between the legs of the crowd at his body.

5

He was a trunkmaker, industrious,
and had accumulated a little property by his trade
but not much. Once he left her money to pay a bill
but the bill proved to be a little more than what he had left for it
and she paid it. He pushed her out of the house,
though it was night, and threw her bonnet after her.

When she was sick and could not leave her room,
he got no one to stay with her and left her entirely alone;
put a piece of bread and some water on a chair,
and told her she ought to die and go to Heaven.
She wanted as a medicine what was called "Extract of Lettuce."
He took an empty bottle and pretended to get it
but filled the bottle instead with foul water
taken from a tub that stood outside the house.
After she had used it,
she said she was much benefited,
and he told her where he got it.

He went away on a visit to Canada;
and said nothing to her about going with him
nor did he say why he would not take her—
though she was anxious to go along.
When she saw him approaching the house on his return,
she unlocked the door and let him in,
but did not greet or speak to him,
and he did not speak to her.

She prepared breakfast for him as always,
but they did not eat together
or speak to each other.
On a Sunday evening, when they were alone in the sitting room,
she asked him if he ever intended to speak to her.
She repeated the question and he replied,
"Some time,"
left the room, went to his bedroom, and shut the door.

Finally, she wrote him a letter
and left it beside his dinner plate:
"Our lives together have indeed been unhappy,
with the exception of here and there
a ray of hope.
I could never get near enough to your heart
to understand its workings;
and have no idea what your feelings are
regarding the future.
I should like to know your mind
and have taken this method,
not knowing that it would be agreeable to you
to approach you in any other way.
Write or speak to me
as you think best."
After dinner, the letter was gone
but she received no answer.

They continued to live together in the same house,
and he did not address a single word to her,
either in anger or kindness.

6

For thirty-five years they had lived together,
treating each other kindly;
never a word of trouble.

She never said anything to her husband
about going to California
where their married daughter was living.

The neighbors told him
that she was going;
she had said that if she had a choice
of California or Heaven,
she would go to California.
Her husband answered

that he knew nothing about it,
and said nothing to his wife.
She went off while he was away cutting brush;
never bid him good-by
or left a note.

Since then they had not written to each other
and only heard from each other through their daughter.
Everything had been pleasant and nice
and your wife packs up and goes off.
How could I keep her if she wanted to go?
She was not bound to stay.
Do you think your wife would come back
if you wrote her a nice letter
and told her how much you liked her?
I hardly think so.
If you would go there,
do you suppose she would come back with you?
I suppose if I should go for her,
she would come back;
but it would be a good while before I'd go.

V

BOYS AND GIRLS

1

"Merry Margaret
as midsummer flower,"
nine years old,
was on her way along an alley
to pick up cobs and coal
alongside the track of the railroad.

One end of the sack
was wound around her arm
and she swung it to and fro.

2

Two streetcars coupled together were coming along,
and the newsboy jumped on the first one
to "halloo" his papers.

Then he stood on the bottom step of the moving car,
afraid to jump off,
for fear the wagon coming alongside
would run him over.
People at the crossing at the corner
were waiting to get on,
and the conductor shoved him off the step—
and he fell
under the wheels of the second car.

3

"In the good old summertime,"
Ellen, all of fourteen, worked in a steam laundry
as a "feeder":
put collars through the machine that pressed them.

The feeder sat on a platform,
collars on the small table in front of her;
the lower roller hot enough to iron collars as they were passed through,
while the upper roller pressed down upon them
with a pressure of two hundred pounds;
the heated roller was hollow and revolved around gas jets—
so hot that if a collar stopped on it for a minute
it would be scorched.

Ellen saw a collar with a lap on it—
the buttonhole part lapped back on the collar—
put her hand out to pull it away
and her finger was caught in the buttonhole
and she could not get it out
before her hand was drawn between the rollers—
burnt and crushed as she screamed.

4

Patrick had been hired along with other boys
to work in a coal breaker:
shove down the culm
when it accumulated in the chutes.
There were no cleats or handrails
for safety;
the chutes were small,
the position at work cramped,
and the air close.
But, when the boys had pushed down the culm,
they could go out upon a platform
near the chutes;
at least nobody stopped them.

Mr. Thrift, the foreman,
noticed that the culm was not descending
in Patrick's chute,
and went out on the platform.
Here he found him
and another boy
and called to them to shove the culm down:
they started for the chutes at a run.

In a little while the machinery stopped—
and there was Patrick's body
fallen into the wheel pit,
wedged between the belt—that ran the machinery—
and the wheel.

5

Tilda was just a child
when she began to work for the Tells.
Her mother was dead
and her father had given up their home.
When, as is the way of women,
her monthly sickness first began,

she was frightened
and told Mrs. Tell about it:
"That is bad," the farmer's wife said,
"and dangerous:
you might go crazy and die.
There is only one thing to do:
work hard!
Work as hard as you can,
and you may still get well!"

She was up at five in the morning
and on her feet
until ten or eleven at night:
milked fourteen cows daily;
carried water uphill
for forty head of hogs;
dug and brought potatoes
from the field;
and helped cook for a family of eight;
scrubbed the floors
and took care of the little ones—
did the work
two stout girls had done.

6

He was a married man in the forties
when she went to work for him;
she was fifteen,
out of an orphan asylum.

She slept on a lounge in the kitchen,
and the first thing in the morning
had to make the fire in the stove.
Later, the fire was made in the summer kitchen
ten feet from the house,
about sunup.
When the rest of the family were still in bed

he would sit down behind her
as she stooped to light the match;
and, when she started to get up,
pull her down on his lap.

He always helped her;
hugged and kissed her;
and finally she got so
she really cared for him.

7

Hank, as he was called, was between six and seven years old.
The year before, his mother had married Jeff Shallow.
In the winter, Shallow, his wife, and Hank
went to live in a log house with only one room,
about two hundred yards from a creek.

One chilly, rainy day in March,
Shallow and his wife's brother, Bob, were making boards
a few feet from the house.
Shallow went back to the house
and he and his wife began to quarrel:
he told her she could leave and take her bastard with her.

The boy ran out
and went down to the place where his uncle was;
Hank was bareheaded and his toes
sticking out of his shoes.
He began to shiver
and wanted to go back into the house
but his uncle must go with him.
After a while, he went alone
but soon came crying.
Shallow was standing in the doorway
looking at him angrily.

One morning in April, Shallow and the boy went down to the creek to
    fish.
There was an upper bank to the creek
with a steep descent to the sand below
before coming to the water.
Shallow came home on horseback at about twelve
without the boy
and found his brother-in-law's horse tied to the fence around the yard.
While they were waiting for the meal his wife was cooking,
Shallow and Bob went to the stable with their horses.

Bob was uneasy about his nephew
and kept looking towards the creek.
He asked Shallow where he had left Hank.
Shallow answered that he had left the boy down below fishing
and added, "He hangs on well for a little fellow,"
and then said they might go down and see what he was doing.

The weather was cold.
There was ice in the sloughs,
and the creek was muddy and swollen with the spring floods.
They found the boy's clothing on the ground—
pants, waist, worn-out shoes, stockings, and cap—
went down the creek another fifty yards or so,
and here they found his body:
a tree had fallen into the creek
and the naked body had been caught in the roots
so that it was near the surface.

Bob and Shallow went back to the house together.
As they entered the door Shallow fell back a little,
and Bob told his sister that Hank was drowned.
She cried out: "I knew it! I knew it!
My heart has been aching for two hours."
She caught sight of her husband. "Oh, Jeff!"
He took her in his arms
and told her to "hush and not take on."

Bob crossed the fields to two neighbors
who were mending a fence.
They helped him take the body from the water.
He carried it to the house
and placed it in his sister's lap.
There were tracks in the sand
from the place where the clothes were found
to the water's edge;
but these were the heavy imprint of a man's shoes.
There was the imprint of a boy's hand, too,
and the lines the fingers had drawn in the sand,
as though the boy had been pushed into the water
or had struggled to get out of the creek
and been pushed back.

§

Woods, a colored man, was a laborer
in a coal mine; a peaceable man
of a quiet disposition.
A colored orphan boy
about ten years old
lived with him.

The boy was in the habit of running away.
At times Woods punished him
with a switch; another way was to put him in a grain sack—
it had two or three holes—
and tie him in it.

Woods put him in the sack on a day in July.
Some of Woods' acquaintances came to the house
with a jug of whiskey
out of which they all drank;
and the boy was left in the sack for several hours.

When it was opened he was dead.

VI

PROPERTY

1

One of them saw the smoke rising
when they went for dinner;
the wind had been blowing
strongly from the west
but had increased greatly in force
when they reached the fire.

The fire had crossed the ditch:
there had been a dry spell
and there was no water in the ditch—
or neighborhood.
They had only shovels
to keep the fire from spreading;
and the soil was peat,
covered with moss and grass,
all dry and highly inflammable.

2

The grain elevator with almost a million bushels of wheat in its bins,
a hundred feet wide and three times as long,
resting upon a rubblestone wall almost two feet thick,
was on fire.

The wheat fell to the ground;
in some places it buried the wall.
Burning timbers were scattered through the wheat
and the wheat was burning briskly.

The fire had been burning eleven days,
although it had rained now and then,
and gangs of men were at work day and night
and much water had been poured upon the wheat—
when thirty feet of the wall

fell
on some of the men.

The stones were so hot
water had to be poured on them
before the bodies could be moved;
and the mortar,
because of the fire and water,
crumbled to dust in one's hand.

3

Blake put his paper money in his vest pocket
and his silver in his pants pocket,
and mounted his horse to cross the swamp.
Hazel and brier thickets were on both sides of the road.

A man crossing the swamp with a team that morning
heard the loud report of a shotgun,
and a quarter of a mile away
came upon Blake's horse, loose, with a saddle on,
and Blake, bleeding from his wounds,
lying in the road,
his pockets empty.

4

Tully had gone to Reilly's in the morning;
could not find him in the house or on the premises:
had stamped upon the porch and shouted,
but no answer;
looked through the kitchen window
and could see only the pans of milk on chairs.
The road to the house was frozen
so that it showed no tracks.

Reilly was found lying dead by the roadside,
gaping wounds upon his head,

his clothing stiff with frost;
the wounds were of two kinds:
those made by an instrument with a sharp cutting edge
and wounds by an instrument with a flat, nearly rectangular, surface—
the edge and poll of a hatchet.

Reilly had a wallet that he kept
in the top drawer of his bureau;
kept the drawer locked.
When the drawer was opened after his death,
no wallet was in it;
later, the wallet was found—empty—in a coal shed
on a rafter overhead
in a corner black with cobwebs.

5
Blunt and his wife lived on a farm
six or so miles from town.
The quarrel was over a note that was due:
he did not have the money to pay it
and asked her to sell her cows.

He asked her a couple of times,
and she said that if he asked again
she would hit him with the ax.
They were in the yard,
and he hit her with the water bucket.
He then went to the stable and watered the stock.
Coming back, he saw her lying near the well
and hit her again with the bucket.

The well was filled with snow—nearly to the top,
and there was blood in the snow.
The boys took a couple of shovels
and digging down
found clothing, shoes, and a pair of spectacles.
Then they saw the form of a foot,

and one of the boys reached down and felt of it:
that was Mrs. Blunt with her stockings on.

6

Perigo went to Hidiger's place
to take away a dog each claimed. Perigo caught it
and was going to tie a string about its neck,
when Hidiger approached, pitchfork in hand.
He had been loading straw—or manure—on a wagon.

Perigo drew a revolver
and, pointing it at Hidiger,
warned him not to come closer.
Hidiger stopped
and Perigo started away
taking the dog with him.

After Perigo had gone a few steps,
he turned to Hidiger and said
that he had scared him with an empty revolver—
there were no cartridges in it.
Hidiger with the pitchfork in his hand
kept following Perigo.

When they reached a fence
of two barbed wires and posts,
Perigo pressed the top wire down with his hand
and stepped one foot over it;
but his clothing caught in the barbs.

As he was standing astride the wire
Hidiger came upon him with the fork.
A blow struck by Hidiger
cut through Perigo's hat and gashed his scalp;
and Perigo fired two or three shots:
one broke Hidiger's right arm,
another lodged in his body.

7

Four of them were in the store
at one o'clock in the morning
waiting:
one had a sledge handle; another a gun; the other two, revolvers.
Quibble was not a policeman
but had been hired to find out
who had been guilty of a number of thefts.
He found Anderson in a saloon that evening,
after looking for him in several places,
and stuck to him,
getting him drunk
and urging him to come along and help break into a store.

One of Anderson's family was sick
and he wanted to go straight home,
but finally went along with Quibble.
They entered the building
by means of a ladder left standing
in the back yard
and reaching up to a window.
The window was usually held in place by a nail
but that night was left unfastened;
and the back door in the hall
was generally kept closed by a hook
but this was not in the staple.

Quibble went up the ladder first
and Anderson followed.
When Anderson walked into the store,
he was set upon,
badly beaten,
shot in the head,
and one of his eyes put out.

8

Meyer was partially paralyzed
so that he could not help himself,
but he had money
and used it as he pleased.
Trost and Trost's wife were his tenants and servants.
Good old Trost!
He liked Trost. They had been fellow soldiers.

Pete Segur came to visit him.
"Maggie," Meyer said to Mrs. Trost, "go and get my pocketbook—
under my pillow there—
and buy us some paper."

When she was gone, he said,
"Segur, what would you do?
I have sisters:
one sister here and one in the state of New York—
I don't know where.
Neither one comes here and asks me:
Gottlieb, do you want a drink of water?
or, how are you getting along?
or, do you get anything to eat?
Can we do anything for you?
and these people, Trost and his wife, do all for me what they can,
and see I get to eat and drink.
What would you do if you were going to make your will?"
Segur answered: "Leave it to them!"
and Gottlieb Meyer said "They shall have all that I own after I am
        dead."

9

She was lying in bed when the lawyer came in
and she made an effort to speak;
said something the lawyer could not understand.

He laid the will on a book
and gave her a pen to sign it.
She took hold of the pen
but her fingers were swollen and stiff,
and she could not move the pen.
The lawyer then said: "Make a cross and it will do."

She wanted to write her name:
made marks on the will with the pen
in the effort;
but finally made a cross instead.
Her hand had to be guided
even in this,
and she kept gasping for breath.

10

It got to be past ten o'clock at night.
Mr. Stokes read the papers over and over again.
Finally he said: "Don't you think I ought to take more time?"

Mr. Siren replied: "You are a businessman, Mr. Stokes,
and you understand this paper, don't you?"
"Yes."
"And you understand *this* paper, don't you?"
"Yes."
But Mr. Stokes sat there with the pen in his hand and kept hesitating.

Then Mr. Siren said: "Come, Stokes, if you understand it, sign it."
"I guess I had better take more time to look it over."
"If you put it off,
you will be no nearer tomorrow.
Come on and sign it.
Sign it. Sign it!"

11

The rest of the family did not like him.
Roy had been authorized to sell certain land in Vernon County—
for one of them—at nine dollars an acre,
and was to have a dollar an acre for making the sale;
he sold the land for twelve dollars an acre
and accounted for it at nine dollars an acre,
keeping the balance.

Roy was her cousin
but his attentions to Emily were so displeasing to her mother
that she refused to let him board with them any longer.
Emily then left her mother's house
and went to live with her uncle, his father.

Roy acted for Emily in transacting her business.
Her brother once met him in the street
and asked him
what Emily intended to do
about the division of the land in Nodaway County, out West,
that their father left to his children;
and Roy answered that he intended to let Emily do as she pleased,
for her mother had blamed him for meddling
and he would have nothing to do with it
and did not know what Emily intended to do.

When Roy was out West Emily wrote to him:
"Dearest cousin: do you think I had better start West
without having my dresses fixed?
If we are to be married,
you may meet me.
If not,
I would just as lief go alone.
And what shall I do with Nellie's squirrel
if I go?
I never got any cage.
Please answer me fully
everything I ask you."

She did go West
to look at the lands in Nodaway County
but, as she told Mrs. Smartwood—
one of the women at the hotel where she stopped—
she came to marry Roy.
Her folks did not like him
and she was worried.
Mrs. Smartwood said: "If I wanted to marry him,
I would."

Roy and Emily saw the lands together
and then went to the county fair,
but when they got back to her hotel
she was sick:
the doctor said she had typhoid—
and she never got any better
but worse and worse until she died.

She asked the doctor what her chances were.
He said they were against her.
"I reckon, then," she said, "that I must die.
If I have no chance, I want to marry Roy."
She turned to him and said:
"Are you going to keep your promise?"

He went out and got a license and sent for a minister.
Before the minister came
she spoke about her property:
wanted Roy to draw up a will
and said she would leave him two thousand dollars and the rest to her
     family
and asked: "Is that enough?"
He answered: "Oh, never mind me:
I have enough."

When the minister came,
Roy stood up and she held his hand.
By then it was almost midnight.

She was too weak
to repeat all it was customary for the bride to say,
but the minister asked her
if she understood what he was saying
and she said she did. After the ceremony,
she turned to the doctor and asked:
"Doctor, do you think I am really married?"
Someone in the room said: " *That* is the minister."
She then asked the minister the same question
and he answered: "Yes, you are really married";
and she seemed very happy.

Roy went to his room to write out her will
as she had told him to—
so he said.
But what he wrote was a deed
leaving all she had
to himself,
and she signed it.
The signature was hers
but she had been too weak
to read what he wrote.

12

Jane Dill's parents were poor:
her father was a boatman on the Morris Canal,
her mother kept a small cake and candy shop;
and she herself was a seamstress.
When a child,
her parents would send her to buy
at John Gray's store,
and there she met his father, Robin.

Old Robin Gray was a widower;
he had been a farmer but had sold his farm
and was now living with his son.
When Jane was sixteen and the elder Gray in his sixties

he began to court her:
visited her at her parents' home,
escorted her from church,
and took her to the village entertainments.
She did not encourage him:
at times even looked at him with aversion,
and at times made fun of him.

He spoke to her mother about marrying Jane
and her mother tried to dissuade him,
but he was so earnest and determined
that at last mother and daughter listened—
and consented:
after all, he was well-to-do,
had a house in a small town near the village where they lived,
and ten thousand dollars in a mortgage.

He would give Jane, he said, the house;
spend five hundred dollars furnishing it
for Jane and himself to live in;
and assign the mortgage to Jane—
a mortgage on the very house where her mother had the store;
however, he would keep the income during his life
for their living,
but Jane would have it all after his death.

He sent the deed to his house and the bond and mortgage
to a lawyer across the state line in Easton
and instructed him to have the deed to Jane
and the assignment of the mortgage
ready in time for the wedding;
paid promptly for the new furniture
and it was placed in the house.
Jane and her parents went to the office of the lawyer in Easton;
there, before a minister,
she stood by the side of her bridegroom;
Robin Gray told the lawyer to give her the deed to the house, the bond
        and mortgage and its assignment;

and so they were married.
The papers were left with the lawyer
to have them recorded and returned to Jane;
and, afterwards, she gave them to her mother to keep safely.
But, shortly before the marriage,
Robin Gray had deeded the house to someone else
and had assigned the mortgage to his son, John;
and this deed and assignment were promptly recorded.

A few months after the marriage,
Mr. Grubb, the landlord of the house where Jane's mother had her
    store,
pretending that he wanted to indorse a payment of interest on the
    mortgage bond—
a plain receipt would not do, he said—
asked Jane for the bond and mortgage;
took the document into the kitchen to write on it
and, when his back was turned,
slipped it into his pocket.
He pulled out for Jane an old canceled bond
that John Gray had given his father, Robin—
at a glance the papers looked alike—
and Grubb brought the bond and mortgage to the younger Gray.

Jane and her mother discovered the trick
and went to a local lawyer:
he discovered in the public records
that old Robin Gray had assigned the mortgage and conveyed his
    house
before his assignment and deed to Jane;
so that at the wedding
he had neither house nor mortgage to give.
When Jane came home
she found
that even the new furniture in the house was gone.

13

"I want to ask you
 a fair question:
 did he say
 that he killed the woman?"

"No.
 But if I say
 he said that he killed the woman,
 I am to get half the reward.
 He is just as well off
 to lay in jail
 as to get out and get mobbed;
 for if he gets out
 he will be mobbed."

"It is pretty hard
 to swear a man's life away
 for a little money."

"Yes,
 but this is pretty hard times,
 and I am pretty hard up."

VII
NEGROES

1

A Negro entered the restaurant
and sat down at one of the empty tables.
The waiter said to him:
"I can't wait on you here:
 it's against the rules of the house.
 Go to the other side."

The room was divided in two.
"The restaurant" side was furnished with tables
covered with tablecloths. Glasses were on the tables
with napkins in them,
and there was an electric fan overhead.
The tables on "the saloon" side were uncovered—
beer tables
such as are usually found in saloons.

2

Williams—a Negro—Davis, Sweeney, and Robb
were in a saloon together. Williams was talking to Davis
when Sweeney jerked off Williams' hat
tearing a piece out of the brim.
Sweeney and Williams were having words about this
when Robb stepped up and found fault with Williams
for wrangling with a white man.

The Negro said nothing to Robb
and was backing away
when Robb stabbed him twice with a dirk.

3

It was a Saturday night. The six had been drinking—
but only a couple of beers each.
They left the saloon at eleven.
As they walked along, two and two,
they saw a colored boy coming towards them,
and one of them said: "There's a coon!"

The last two tried to stop the colored boy
and he walked out into the gutter
to get past them;
but they jumped around in front of him
with their hands out,
and the others stopped to watch.

"Ginger" picked up a stone
and threw it at the boy,
but it struck the ground.
Then he threw another stone
and it struck the boy on the head.
He fell to the ground
and lay there
dying,
and the six walked quickly away.

VIII
PERSONS AND PLACES

1

She had a stand for the sale of fruit.
It was hot that day
and she seated herself in the shade of the building
upon the first step of the stairs
that led to a fish market in the basement.
A wagon, loaded with ice, stopped in front of the building.
The iceman took a cake of ice,
weighing about fifty or sixty pounds,
from the cool, dark inside of the wagon
full of cakes of ice,
and slung it over his shoulders
to carry it down to the fish market.

As he was going down the stairs,
the cake of ice slipped from his tongs
and fell upon her hand
resting on the step.

2

Ford was a doctor at White Pigeon
and Twiss had the only butcher shop in town.

After Ford left home on his rounds one day,
Mrs. Ford sent the hired man to Twiss for meat,
but Twiss would not give him any
because, Twiss said, he had an account against Ford of two years'
	standing.
The hired man paid for the meat with his own money.

Later, when Mrs. Ford sent the hired man for some apples,
he waited for Ford at a corner
and told him what Twiss had said.
Ford handed his medicine case to the hired man
and went straight to the butcher shop.

He found Twiss sitting on a box outside.
"Why in hell did you not let that nigger of mine have that meat?"
"Because I've let you have too much already."
"Have I ever bought anything of you that I have not paid for?"
"Yes."
"You are a damned liar!"

Twiss got up from the box and went towards Ford.
"Don't do that!"
and Ford pulled out a pistol and pushed it into the butcher's face.
"You damn son of a bitch, I will blow your brains out!"
Twiss stopped
and said his books would show the account,
and went into his shop
as if to show them.
Ford followed with the pistol in his hand.

Twiss turned to the safe where he kept the books
but raised the lid of the desk on top of the safe instead
and took out a heavy stock-whip by the small end of the handle.
Ford pointed his pistol at Twiss
and Twiss, dropping the whip, suddenly pushed Ford's arm down as far
	as he could.
The pistol went off
and Twiss was shot in the belly.

3

Ann Wood continued to run the farm
with the help of the farmhand.
Three years after the death of her husband
she gave birth to a daughter:
the farmhand was the father.
A few days after her daughter was born
she gave the child to his sister
at the urging of the farmhand and to hide her shame;
but she would see the child in her dreams.

The farmhand's sister was a married woman
with an infant of her own;
her husband was a common laborer—
a pauper.
They moved to Pittsburgh and then west to Iowa—
from place to place—
and somewhere in Iowa the farmhand's sister died.
Ann's child was passed from family to family
and finally put in an orphan asylum.

She would go to market with her farm produce.
On a Saturday, about five in the morning,
a woman came up to her
with a little girl about the age, Ann judged, of her own child.
The woman looked at Ann
as if the woman had something to say
but said nothing,
and went on to the end of the benches in the market house
and said to the little girl: "Wait here."

Then she walked back to Ann and asked:
"Are you Mrs. Wood?"
Ann said she was.

The woman was wearing a handsome silk shawl in gay colors—
a light ground and many red and blue flowers on it—
with a deep silk-fringe border;

the little girl was in furs,
although it was July—
a gray light fur like squirrel.
The woman put her hand up to her cheek
as if she had something on her mind—
and was silent.
Ann said:
"Have you anything to tell me?"
"Well, not now,"
and with that the woman walked away
and called to the little girl: "Come!"

Ann never saw the woman again nor the child.
Afterwards, she heard that her daughter had been taken from the
      asylum
by the rich woman;
and Ann was sure that the little girl she had seen
was her own, her very own, child.

4

For nearly a year, Hess, a young farmhand
had been making his home with Shwartz, a farmer;
he slept with Shwartz's son, John, about his own age,
in the same room
and in the same bed.

John was going to be married
and he knew that his father
was going to give him a tract of land
as a farm with which to start for himself.
But Hess was angry and unhappy:
he had hoped to marry Shwartz's daughter;
she liked him well enough,
and so did her parents;
but John thought another suitor the better man,
and Else said she would "mind" her brother.

About four o'clock one morning,
Shwartz,
awakened by a noise upstairs
in the room where his son and Hess slept,
stepped out of his bedroom
and met his son
at the foot of the stairs—
throat cut
and nightshirt dark with blood,
unable to speak.

Hess, in shirt and trousers,
with blood on both
and on his hands,
followed.

John went into the yard
and in a few minutes
was dead.
The pillow on which John slept
was soaked with blood;
and blood was on the floor.
So was a bloody razor.
It belonged to John
but both he and Hess used it.

When he awoke in the morning, Hess said,
John was sitting on the bed
with his feet on the floor and his hands on his knees.
It was still dark—
too early to get up, Hess thought,
and turned his face to the wall
to fall asleep again.
But could not;
got up and slipped around John,
still sitting on the edge of the bed—and silent.
Hess put on his trousers
and buttoned them with his left hand

reaching for the door with his right
when a push on his shoulder, Hess said,
sent him against the wall and sprawling on the floor.
He got up.
John was out of the room
and he followed
to find out what was the matter.

5

Market

The wagons of fruit and vegetables
were backed up to the sidewalk
on one side of the Common:

the hucksters on the sidewalk with their goods;
the noise of the stamping of horses' feet,
the rumbling of wagons, the rattling of chains and harness,
the shouting of men to their horses and to each other
and the sound of barrels and boxes
thrown from the wagons upon the sidewalk;
the hawking of goods,
and the hum and bustle of the crowd of purchasers:

the stench from the refuse
and from the smoke of the torches
used by the hucksters.

6

He was committed to prison in default of bail
and sent down in the van
with two other prisoners,
one drunk and spewing. In the prison,
he received two narrow blankets and a tin dish;
no knife or fork. Slept on the floor.
The room was filthy.

The stool had no cover;
the men made water in it at night,
and it ran over.

IX
RAILROADS

1

The bell did not ring nor was the whistle blown
and his view of the train was shut off
by the waiting shed—
until the train was right on him:
he hadn't time to snap his fingers.

2

The railroad crossed the highway nearly at right angles
in four tracks. The view towards the west
was obstructed by a high board-fence,
a two-story house, a coal trestle, and coal pockets.

It was snowing
and blowing hard from the west
as the teamster drove his horses hitched to a bobsleigh
at a slow trot.

He looked towards the west
but the snow was blown into his face
and almost blinded him.
He heard and saw nothing:
no bell was rung, no whistle blown.
He crossed the first, second, and third tracks;
had reached the fourth,
and was almost over it,
when the rear runner of his sleigh was struck
by the locomotive of a train from the west.

3

Rosenzweig had a thirty-day return ticket from Erie to Cleveland.
Between one and two o'clock in the morning
he took an express train [in] Cleveland to return to Erie,
stepped into a day coach, curled up, and went to sleep.
He was awakened by the conductor's call for tickets—
after the train had started—
and took his ticket from his pocket. The conductor reached for it
and said at once, "My orders are to put you off!"
grabbed the bell cord, thrust the ticket back, and added:
"Your ticket is no good!"

Rosenzweig tried to show the conductor that he was mistaken:
that the only limitation on the ticket was that it should be used within
      thirty days,
that he did not know it was not good on an express train,
and that he had used that kind of ticket before without any objection.
He offered to pay his fare but this was refused.
The conductor said: "My orders are to put you off. Come!"

The train had stopped in the midst of railway tracks and switches
on which cars and locomotives were standing and moving.
Rosenzweig begged not to be put off at that place in the middle of the
      night
and asked to be carried to the next station.
The conductor said: "My orders are to put you off and off you go!
I obey orders if I break the owners. Come!"

Rosenzweig followed the conductor out of the car.
On reaching the ground,
the conductor pointed to a light and said:
"Go that way:
it will take you to the depot."
Rosenzweig went towards the light,
and soon saw that it was on a locomotive coming towards him.
He tried to get off the tracks
and came against a freight train in motion,
turned to pass around the train,

and came to another train in back of it.
He then believed it safer to change his direction,
and as he did so
saw a light to his left on a train of cars backing,
and then a single car moving.
At the same time another engine passed him
and, as he crossed some tracks,
he was struck
from the rear.

4

The conductor asked her where she was going.
"Knoxville City."
He said: "You ought to have changed at Knoxville Junction."
"Why didn't you tell me when we were there?"
He told her to get off
but she wanted to stay on until the next station.

The train was stopped
and the conductor asked her if she was getting off.
He said if she didn't
he would kick her off
and that he was tired of "damn niggers."
He threw her bundle on the ground,
and put her baby beside it.
She followed and the train left her standing there.

5

As a freight train was passing through the town
he got upon it
climbing the iron ladder at the side of a boxcar;
but before he could climb on top
a brakeman saw him and ordered him off.
The train had gathered speed
and while he was pleading to remain
until the train stopped

or slackened its speed
the brakeman
stamped upon his hands and fingers
until he fell off—
and fell through the trestle the train was on.

6

Hinkelman was under arrest
for putting railroad ties
on the track of the Union Pacific;
and Stain, a detective,
was supposed to be under arrest
for this, too.
They were put in the same cell.

Stain had been in Hinkelman's company in town
and in saloons together
and Hinkelman thought he was a friend;
he let on he had seen a lawyer
and would very likely soon be free,
and told Hinkelman he had also spoken to the lawyer
about him.

The lawyer had told him, Stain said,
that it was no use lying
and that Hinkelman had better tell the truth:
it would do him as much good as anything else.
Hinkelman said he wanted to tell the truth
but how was he to go about it?

It was easy enough:
if he rattled the jailer,
the jailer would bring him some paper
and he could put it all down;
but he himself, Stain said, could not tell him what to write,
for he knew nothing about it.

"Yes," said Hinkelman, "I know you are innocent."
And he rattled the jailer
and the jailer came after a bit
and when he had brought the paper
Hinkelman put it up against the wall of the cell
and wrote:

"Regarding this wrecking affair
would say I had no intention to hurt human beings
or damage any property
but took especial pains to have the train notified
in time
to prevent all accidents
my object being to get into the good graces of the railroad company
and thereby get a job
which I was badly in need of
as I could find nothing else to do."
And he signed it.

Hinkelman then wanted to know
how he could get what he had written
to the judge,
and Stain said: "Rattle up the jailer again."
Hinkelman did and handed him the paper.

He was sentenced to ten years in prison.

X

MACHINE AGE

1

He left Lancaster with a load of furniture
on the afternoon of a bright September day
and went along a dirt road—
the "summer road."

Workers in a tobacco field saw him sitting under his umbrella,
the horses going at a walk.

One of those in the field
watched him on top of the wagon:
standing on the furniture
and trying to disengage the telephone wire
that had been stretched across the road—
now caught in the furniture
and taut.

She saw him fall—
falling towards the ground with his arms outstretched.
When she came up to him,
the team was standing still
and he was lying about twenty feet from the wagon,
unconscious:
the back of his head had struck a stone.
The telephone wire,
stretched across the road,
was still waving.

2

The steam planing-mill used the shavings and sawdust
to generate steam:

so great a noise of machinery
those in the house next door
could only carry on a conversation with difficulty;
the windows rattled in the casings;
dishes on the table or on shelves
shook and were jolted together;

a great deal of smoke and cinders
came into the yard—
and into the house whenever a door or window was opened;
clothes in the yard hung out to dry

were fouled so that they had to be washed again;
everything in the house was soiled—
floors and carpets, walls and windows and curtains;
even the table from which they ate—
plates were covered with soot;

and the sunlight darkened.

THE WEST

STAGECOACHES

1

The horse was young
and not broken to harness.
As the man at his head
tried to put him to a stagecoach with another horse,
he plunged,
struck the man down,
and trampled him.

2

Of the four horses attached to a stagecoach
one of the leaders was called "Bitter Root":
"Bitter Root" was bad about shying
and quick to start—
wild and tricky in starting
like a colt.
He was changed around often
and worked in different places,
and some of the drivers would not have him.

While the stagecoach was going along at a moderate speed,
they met a man on horseback
driving before him a pack animal
loaded with a camping outfit and a buffalo robe.
"Bitter Root" and the other horse in the lead
became frightened
but went on
and then stopped;
whirled around to the left—
breaking the tongue of the stagecoach—

and ran:
the passengers began jumping from the stage.

3
At a station
where the stagecoach had stopped at twilight
the driver saw that there were no lamps on it
and called for two lamps;
the superintendent brought them
and put them on,
but one was out of repair
and was not lighted.

The road ran through a canyon among the mountains—
level, with a gully on one side.
A rock was a foot or so outside the track of the roadway,
on the other side,
where there was no light from the stagecoach;
a wheel struck it,
and the stage was thrown over.

Fraser had been sitting at one end of a seat,
crowded close to the side of the stagecoach
by the other passengers on the same seat.
When the stage was turning over,
the other passengers were thrown upon him,
and his arm—
that had been resting on the railing—
was caught
under the stagecoach
and broken.

II

TOWN AND COUNTRY

1

The body had been buried face downwards.
Only the skeleton was left,
and it separated in handling
when dug up.
The coat was yellow ducking,
lined with a light-colored blanket;
overalls of yellow ducking, too,
and a patch on the knee:
a belt on the skeleton,
a knife in the pocket,
and a bullet hole
in the back of the skull.

2

As Hickey and a friend
walked along a narrow street
in Los Angeles,
Salazar was sitting in a chair
right in the middle of the sidewalk;
and, as Hickey and his friend passed,
one of them
brushed against Salazar—
struck him
with his foot on the leg
and knocked Salazar's hat off.

Salazar got up from the chair
and drew a knife
to strike at Hickey's friend,
and Hickey struck at Salazar
with his fist.

Salazar turned on Hickey
and chased him down the street
and kept stabbing him
until Hickey fell:
there were two wounds on the fingers of Hickey's right hand;
another near the left nipple of his breast;
and still another on the same side
just back of the shoulder joint;
and out of the wound in the groin
his guts were protruding.

3

Lee had told Peter Wells, for whom he worked:
"If I thought the man was hunting us
in the chaparral,
I'd take a rifle
and go down and get him.
If you would let me have a rifle,
I would put 'Uz' Waffle
in a prospector's hole";
and Wells had said: "No."

Wells asked Lee, one morning, to go with him to Oleta
and hunt for a horse
that had been tracked to a stable there.
Lee urged Wells not to go
because "Uz" Waffle would be in Oleta:
"it would be going into the enemy's camp."
Wells said: "I cannot help that.
I am going,"
and rode off with his son.

Wells and his son were at the stable four or five minutes
and then walked into Main Street.
"Uz" Waffle with a double-barreled shotgun
was sitting in front of a saloon
on the opposite side of the street.

He called out:
"Stop, you son of a bitch,
I've got you
where I wanted you!"
"Hold on," said the elder Wells,
"you are accusing me wrongfully."
Waffle raised his gun and cocked it.
The elder Wells stopped
and did not move at all,
his hands by his side.
"Hold now," he said, "you are too fast!
I don't want any of this!"
"I do," Waffle answered. "I've been hunting for it."
"Uz, put down your gun,
and come to me like a man,
and we'll settle it."
"You are a liar and a son of a bitch,"
and Waffle called to a woman across the street,
"Take the children out of the way
and get out of that window, woman!"
and then fired.

Wells fell backwards on the porch,
shot in the forehead;
and Waffle stepped into the saloon,
but stepped out again at once,
and started down the street, the gun in his hand.

4
Charlie Blue, acting as deputy sheriff,
arrested someone known about town as "Gunnysack Joe"
upon suspicion that he—with others—
had stolen a number of horses.
Blue said that "Gunnysack Joe" when arrested told him
that those having charge of the horses
were camped about four miles from town,
and Blue summoned a number of citizens as a posse

to help arrest them
and reclaim the horses.

"Gunnysack Joe" was put in a buggy to guide them to the camp
and Blue rode on ahead to find it.
He came back and said there was no camp
where "Gunnysack Joe" had said it was,
got a buggy whip
and dragged "Gunnysack Joe" from the buggy by the handcuffs
        he had on,
and began to whip him
to make him tell
where the camp was.

"Gunnysack Joe" appealed to the posse
to protect him,
and they protested against the whipping
and Blue stopped.
All went back to town,
and "Gunnysack Joe" was kept in the custody
of one person or another.

One night, not long afterwards,
he was in a saloon,
still in custody and handcuffed,
when Charlie Blue came in.
Blue took off "Gunnysack Joe's" handcuffs
and told him he was now a free man,
and asked him if he was glad of it.
"Gunnysack Joe" said he was.
Blue then asked if he would have a drink with him,
and "Gunnysack Joe" said he would.
Blue asked him if he was a friend of his
or an enemy,
and "Gunnysack Joe" answered:
"You have treated me in such a way
I cannot be a friend of yours."
Blue then asked what he was going to do about it,

and "Gunnysack Joe" answered
that he did not know that he was going to do anything.
Blue asked him again
if he was a friend or enemy,
and "Gunnysack Joe" answered
that he was not a friend.

Blue drew his pistol and pointing it at "Gunnysack Joe"
worked the hammer backwards and forwards
and repeated his question;
and "Gunnysack Joe" answered:
"I will have to be your friend now."
Blue told him that he was a coward
and lifting his pistol again
asked him again if he was a friend.
"Gunnysack Joe" said: "Do you want the truth?
Well, Charlie, I don't like you,"
and Blue shot him dead.

5
Fly's right hand was crippled
and, as he walked,
he held it—as almost always—
in his pocket.
Crossing Third Street,
when he got within fifteen feet or so of the sidewalk,
he looked up and saw "Sandy" Webber
standing at the water plug at the corner:
Webber's right hand—
in which he held a pistol—
was also in his pocket.

"Mr. Fly, I heard you have been around
looking for me,"
and Webber began shooting.
The first shot missed Fly—
who threw up his right hand

and started to go back—
the second struck him in the neck.
As he was falling headlong
with his arms out,
another bullet struck him.

His body was close to the curb and his face in the dust.
Webber walked up calmly
and stooping
shot him in the back of the head.
He walked around Fly's body once or twice
and said:
"Now, you son of a bitch,
I suppose you will go around looking for me!"
and, throwing back his coat,
put his pistol in his pocket.

He took out his handkerchief;
taking his hat off,
wiped his brow and the sweatband of his hat;
put on his hat
and walked down Third Street,
slowly at first
and then quickening his steps.

III
SOCIAL LIFE

Pride, the foreman,
and five others who worked under him at the ranch,
were on their way to a dance Christmas Eve,
riding in a small wagon on the highway.
All had been drinking.
Pride and two others were on the seat in front
and Green at the back,

his feet hanging over the rear end of the wagon.
Pride was driving.

Green shot at a dog
following a Mexican family
going in the opposite direction;
and Pride said to Green
that if he didn't behave
he would have to get off and walk.
After a while Green asked Graft,
sitting beside Pride,
for a drink:
there was a jug in the front of the wagon
in reach of Graft
and Pride told Graft not to let Green have it.
Green asked again
and when Graft again refused
Green jumped off the wagon and fired from the ground.

Five or more shots in all were fired:
Pride was shot in the back of the neck
and then in the face;
Graft halted the team and was wounded;
the shots at Green went through his hat and coat sleeve.
The man who had been sitting on the bottom of the wagon
leaning against Green
tried to get up when Green fired the first shot
and was killed.

IV
DOMESTIC SCENES

1

When they told her husband
that she had lovers
all he said was:

one of them
might have a cigar
and set the barn on fire.

2

Toller was a surveyor
and his business called him away from home
weeks at a time.
To help Wheat locate a claim upon the public lands
and give him a home until he did,
Toller asked Wheat to his ranch:
he was to help around the house.

Wheat began to tell Mrs. Toller about her husband:
how unfaithful he was to her.
After a month or two, Wheat and Mrs. Toller became more than
    friendly:
there was talk between them that she would get a divorce
and they slept together when they could.
During the hay-making season
Toller was on his ranch,
and the bitter feeling between husband and wife
flared up
because he had seen a whispered conversation
between his wife and Wheat.

Toller was drinking
for the first time during their married life;
his wife went down to the cellar
and brought up a bottle of home-made wine.
He finished it quickly and wanted more—
went down to the cellar himself and rolled a barrel out.
Mrs. Toller became afraid
and took her husband's pistol from where it was hanging
over the washstand in their bedroom,
and hid it under the head of the bed.

Wheat asked her for the pistol
and took it to his own room.

Just before dark Wheat went out of the house
to find Toller and bring him in to supper.
They came into the house together.
Toller was drunk.
Supper was on the table and both men sat down
but Mrs. Toller was standing.
Her husband asked her why she didn't sit down
and have her supper.
She said she didn't want any
and he replied that, since he paid for the "grub,"
he would eat.

He had a table knife in his hand
and began pounding the table with the point
until it was bent,
cursing and saying
he would "cut his heart out and hang it on a pole."
Wheat got up from the table
and went to his room for his pistol.

He was back in a few minutes;
stood at the door and asked Toller
if he meant him.
Toller sprang up
and they tussled in the next room.
Mrs. Toller heard one of them fall to the floor
and then a shot;
and heard her husband cry out:
"My God, Kate, I am shot!"

There were several shots after that
and Toller ran out of the house—
Wheat after him.
At the door Wheat stopped
and went back to his room for Toller's pistol

and then went out.
By this time it was dark.

She found her husband lying on the ground:
a bullet had entered his belly
and there were bloodstains from the house to the body;
he had also been shot through the top of his head
as he was sitting on the ground:
powder burns on both sides of his face
and the top of his head burnt to a crisp.

3
At the time of their marriage
Andrew was worth about fifty thousand dollars;
Polly had nothing.
"He has gone up to the mine,
and I wish to God he would fall down
and break his neck.
I just hate him.
I just shiver when he touches me."

"Andy, I am going to write a letter that may seem
hardhearted:
you know that I do not love you
as I should,
and I know that I never can.
Don't you think it best
to give me a divorce?
If you do,
I will not have to sell the house in Denver
that you gave me,
and I will give you back the ranch in Delta.
After we are divorced,
if you care for me and I care for you,
we will marry again. Polly."

Burglar's Tools

Those drills, in the right man's hands,
are called "safe drills," and used as such.
This might be used for a blowpipe—
for blowing gunpowder into a safe.
This is a whetstone and this a watch spring.
They would use the whetstone to sharpen a knife or a tool;
it would make a saw out of that spring.
This could be used for unlocking a lock—
a skeleton key for a padlock.
This for blowing open a safe,
and this for picking open a window sash.
This would open a handcuff, if in the right shape:
I don't know if you could use it for anything else.
This is an old key and would make a skeleton key,
and this is an ordinary skeleton key.

2

He entered the store with barley sacks upon his feet
and a barley sack over his head—
holes cut in front through which to look—
and carried a shotgun,
both barrels loaded with bird shot.

But the barley sack upon one of his feet
caught on something at the end of the counter;
the mask became displaced so that he could not see,
and the gun was jerked from his hand.

VI

A "squeeze" was going on in the Grass Creek Mine:
the partitions and columns left to support the roof were settling
into the floor,
and rock and coal were falling from the top and sides.
Bill was set to clearing up the debris
from the tracks and leveling the floor;
other workmen followed him,
timbering
to keep rock and coal from falling.
After a few days, Mr. Thomas had the timbering stopped
and told the workmen to help in clearing the tracks.
Coal and rock were still falling beyond the timbering,
and Bill said to Mr. Thomas:
"This is going to fall
if it isn't taken down."
"It won't fall yet," said Mr. Thomas;
"you have no idea how this will hang."
And he added: "I can't stop to take it down now.
Clear right up, boys!
Hurry now and clear up,
for I want to send coal out of here this evening."

Bill was set to load up some coal
which cumbered the tracks beyond the timbering,
and within a few minutes
a mass of coal fell upon him from the sides.

VII

The shovelers, unloading a ship lying at the wharf
with a cargo of coal,
had worked down to the "skin" or floor:
they had cleared a space of about three feet
under the hatch
and about twenty feet below the deck;

the coal around them
rising to a height of fifteen feet.

The two shovelers
filled the tub or bucket unusually high—higher than the edge.
"Frenchie" was one of the men to steady the tub
until it cleared the hatchway,
holding a line as the tub was hoisted.
The engineer was signaled;
the bucket cleared the hatchway but,
above the hatch,
it began to rock
and swing;
still hoisted,
the bucket swung against the mainstay,
thirty feet above the deck,
tilted over,
and three or four hundred pounds of coal
fell out—
back into the hold
and upon the head of "Frenchie."

VIII
CHINESE

1

"Joe Chinaman, do you know what God is?"
"I don't know what it is."
"Do you know anything about the obligations of an oath
  under the Christian religion?"
"I don't know what it is."
"Will you tell right
  if you talk to the jury now?"
"Yes, I talk some."

"What were you doing in Daisy Fiddletown's house
  when you worked for her in Albuquerque?"
"Cooking."
"What kind of house is it?"
"Whorehouse."
"Did she send you with her bankbook
  and one hundred and sixty dollars in gold and silver
  to the First National Bank,
  and did you go instead to the faro bank at Hope's Corner
  and gamble her money away?"

2

The Chinese woman in Cum Cook Alley lay dying.
"I don't know of any reason that Fong Ah Sing had for shooting me,"
she said in Chinese, "unless . . .
a few days ago I was bathing my feet
over a room in which Fong Ah Sing was sitting
and spilled a little water on the floor.
It leaked through and fell upon Fong Ah Sing.
He was very angry
and told the owner of the house
that I must apologize
and make him a present
to prevent bad luck coming upon the house.
The owner did make some little present to Fong Ah Sing,
and I thought the matter settled."

3

Johnny Cleek and Almira's husband
talked about burning Ladd's barn;
they were in the front room
and Almira in the kitchen:
only a board partition between the two rooms
and she could hear every word.

There was a stack of hay on the side of the barn
and they split the fuse so that it could be lit
and put the can of powder in the hay
and one of them touched a match to the fuse.
Almira could see the fire.
When her husband came into the house
he had his hat, coat, and shoes off
and had been running.

"What did you burn that barn for?"
"Keep quiet!
Ladd had no business
hiring Chinamen!"

IX
The Bastard

Miss Lavender had been living in Marysville
when she met Jed Wellington.
She came to San Francisco
when their child was about to be born,
and was placed by Jed
in the home of an old colored woman—
"a respectable Christian."

Jed visited Miss Lavender often
during her stay
and paid all the doctor's bills and expenses—
even her dentist's bill.
The child was his, he said to the dentist,
but he would not marry the girl;
would be just to her,
and pay all the expense of her care,
and take care of the child.

The old colored woman spoke to him about Miss Lavender:
"She is feeling very bad," the old woman said.
"Yes, I know," said Jed.
After the birth of her child
Miss Lavender left the city,
and Jed left the child with the old colored woman.
He did not want the mother to see the child again
because her parents might find out
about their affair.
In time, Miss Lavender married
and Jed Wellington was glad of that:
it got her out of the scrape—
and him, too.

He did not want the baby dressed in calico
but wanted him dressed in white always,
kept in white,
and whatever the expense
he would pay it.
If the child was awake when he came
he would take him up,
and play and talk to him;
if he was not awake,
he would wait until he woke.
As the boy grew older,
he was dressed in a handsome black suit
with a black cap
and wore his hair long.
Jed took the child out with him
often,
would take him and the boy's nurse—
the old colored woman's daughter—
down to North Beach,
for the little boy liked the birds and monkeys and wild animals
that were kept there;
and his father would bring him fruit and cakes.
"This is my son, Doctor.
Isn't he a nice-looking boy?

I think a great deal of that boy,
and I am going to raise him up and look after him
and educate him and make a man of him."

Jed called the boy Richard,
the name of Jed's brother, then dead,
who had left Jed all his money
and Jed said he hoped he might be able to raise the boy
to be like the boy's uncle.
When the old colored woman's daughter—
the child's nurse—
married and moved to Petaluma,
Richard was still very young;
he was taken to her home
and lived with her
and was brought up with her children
and went by their family name.

Richard was sent to a private school when he was ten;
Jed Wellington arranged for his board there and schooling;
but he was placed at school as a ward of his father—
not as a son.

The boy was not good at his studies.
When he was fifteen,
Wellington sent him to a ranch;
but Richard soon returned—
of his own accord—
to his former nurse's home in Petaluma:
it was the only home he knew.

He wrote to Jed Wellington for money once:
Richard knew him only as a guardian
taking care of him for a father and mother he did not know,
and Wellington sent it.
Afterwards Jed Wellington ignored his requests.
"Jed," Wellington's brother once asked,
"whatever became of that boy you were taking care of?"

"The boy?
  Oh, I tried to make something out of him,
  but he didn't amount to anything,
  and I let him go."

When Richard was twenty,
  he was a bootblack
  in a colored barbershop.

PART TWO   TESTIMONY

THE UNITED STATES (1891–1900)

RECITATIVE

THE SOUTH

I

SOCIAL LIFE

1

Old Mr. and Mrs. Ladendorf gave a birthday party
and invited the young people of the neighborhood.
One of the young men carried a jug of whiskey
and hid it in the yard; all of them were drinking from it
and Ashley Hunt became drunk.
Mrs. Ladendorf asked Pell to go into the yard
and invite Ashley into the house. But he refused to come
and became angry at something Pell said:
stabbed him and knocked him down.

Pell managed to get up and was holding Ashley
when Ashley's brother, John, ran out of the house
shouting, "Turn Ashley loose!" and struck Pell with his fist.
At that Blizzard, who had been sitting at the table,
ran out: "Part them! Don't let them fight!"
and caught hold of John Hunt, trying to pull him away from Pell.
John punched Blizzard, pulled him down and held him,
while Ashley stabbed him again and again
in the back and sides.

2

Belton and others were in a stable
to listen to a Negro playing the banjo.
While he was playing
Belton borrowed a knife from one of the listeners
to cut sticks
to be used in picking the banjo;
but when he reached the new wagon sheet
placed over the door

he cut it.
Bishop, who owned the stable, said,
"Bill, don't do that!
That's my new wagon sheet."
Belton replied, "Maybe you don't like what I am doing,"
and cut the sheet again.

Bishop got off the trough he had been sitting on
and walking over to Belton
the two began to curse each other
until they began fighting and clinching
and Bishop drew his pistol
and shot and killed Belton.

3
The stranger had come into town that day:
a man of forty or so with only one arm
and because he was lame
walking in a peculiar—and to some comical—way;
speaking with an Irish brogue.

Joyce and a companion were drinking in a barroom
and the stranger had a drink with each,
but, after a while,
Joyce began to tease and make fun of him
and then to scuffle with him:
snatched his cap
and kept slapping his face and head—
until one of the customers stopped Joyce
and told the stranger Joyce was really "a good boy"
and did not mean any harm.

When the barroom closed for the night
and the barkeeper and customers left,
Joyce and his companion caught hold of the stranger
and dragged him to the town lockup—
or "calaboose" as they called it—

pretending to arrest him;
and there Joyce pulled out his knife
and made believe he was about to cut the stranger's throat.
At that the stranger broke away
and ran to a drugstore nearby—
it was still open—
and asked the owner to protect him.
But the drugstore was closing, too,
and when the owner and stranger came out together
Joyce, wearing the stranger's cap,
was at the door,
sitting on the step.

Joyce stood up
holding a signboard, several feet long, in his raised hands
as if to strike the stranger,
and walked around in a circle,
brushing his feet on the ground as if to kick him
and making a mocking noise,
while Joyce's companion was sitting on a box laughing.

The owner of the store told them to get away
and not to raise a row
and then turned and went on.
But, in a little while, the stranger came running after him
and Joyce and his companion were throwing stones and bottles at the
        stranger—
until a stone thrown by Joyce
struck the stranger on the head
and broke his skull.

4
She was standing in a cotton patch
near a road
and he came out of some pines
about fifty yards away,
humming and whistling and talking to her.

He called to her three times
and asked who she was:
she was silent.

The fourth time, in a more threatening manner, he said,
"Who are you, madam?"
    And she answered, "Who are you?"
"My name is Jim Skinner," he said—
    that was not his name—
    and went on:
"Confound your soul, if you don't like what I said,
    I will take this to your head," raising a stick,
    and went towards her, adding,
"Don't give me any of your slack jaw!"

She was so frightened
she could not run at first
but then got to the road
and when she saw him coming
began to scream for help and ran.
As she ran she looked back:
he was only twenty-five steps away and gaining on her—
but then he turned and ran away.

5

In a town down in Texas
Andrews had been drinking all evening,
but still knew what he was talking about:
he took one of the men
out of the saloon with him
to a rock pile where he had hidden his clothing
and took off the rocks
and uncovered his clothing in a sack.
Then he got on his horse
and asked his companion to hand him the sack of clothes
and tied it on behind his saddle
and said he was going to leave the country,

but was going to kill some "damn son of a bitch"
before he left. He had his six-shooter in his hand
and struck his companion on the shoulder with it
but told him not to be afraid:
he was not going to shoot anybody right there.
His companion told him to put up his pistol:
he might hurt somebody;
and he replied that he knew how to handle a gun as well as any man,
and was not going to hurt anybody right there;
but added that he wanted to kill "some son of a bitch";
and did the man he was talking to ever feel that way?

6

Work was scarce and the weather bad.
Nash was sitting in a corner
and Dawson advising him to go home
and work with his father.
Nash said he would go home
if it were not for one or two things:
"If I go home," he said,
"there are two or three I will be bound to kill—
'Old Man Jackson' is one.
The damned old rascal ought to have been killed years ago;
he don't do anything but undermine people
and report them
for selling whiskey and toting weapons."
Nash's companion turned to Mrs. Dawson and said,
"Mrs. Dawson, did you ever know anybody to get rich by work?"
"No," she said,
"but I have known people to make a good living by work."
And he answered: "I am not able to make a living by work.
But there is a living here on earth for me,
and I am going to have it!"

DOMESTIC SCENES

1

Adams and his wife, Hester, and their three small children
were living on a farm about a mile from the James River.
Abingdon was the renter of the farm;
but he was a trapper—
had a number of traps along both sides of the river—
and had hired Adams and Casper Dill
to do the farm work for a share of the crops.
Abingdon was unmarried and lived in a room of the house
where Adams and his wife lived;
Dill lived with his old crippled mother—
who could not get about—
in a small house nearby.

One evening, Abingdon said he was planning a trip across the river
to "take" a bee tree.
They were in the house of Mrs. Dill,
the four of them, Abingdon, Adams, and the Dills;
Adams was unwilling to go with Abingdon
unless young Dill went along.
Both Adams and Dill said they could not swim—
everybody in the neighborhood knew that—
and Dill said he did not like water more than knee-deep,
and Adams nodded agreement.
Dill added he would rather plow than go,
but his mother said that since Mr. Abingdon was anxious for him to
        come
he had better do so.

The three men started in the morning
with everything needed: two large buckets for the honey,
two axes and a hatchet,
and a piece of netting to protect them from the bees.
The boat did not belong to Abingdon
but he had a key to unlock the boat from its fastening

to the bank. It was a small boat,
about ten feet long and two and a half feet wide;
Abingdon sat in the rear
with his face to the front; and Adams and Dill sat in front of him,
their faces also to the front and their backs to Abingdon.
They landed on the other side of the river
and went to the bee tree;
but when they reached it, Abingdon, so he said,
decided not to cut it down
because it was a large tree
and the hole small,
and the tree might not have any honey in it, after all.
On the way back, about fifty yards from the shore,
the boat suddenly filled with water,
and both Adams and young Dill were drowned.

When the boat was gotten out of the water,
three holes, freshly bored, each about an inch and a half in width,
were found under the seat where Abingdon had been sitting;
and fresh shavings, suiting the size of the holes and of the same wood
     the boat was made of,
had been thrown into the water
where the boat had been fastened
but the shavings had drifted ashore.
Here, too, were found corncobs cut to fit the holes in the boat.
The morning after the drownings, when they came to arrest Abingdon,
he was found in Hester Adams' room—and bed.

2

Jelly and Hill were brothers-in-law:
Hill, weak and sickly; Jelly, athletic and strong.
About ten years before, they had a falling-out
and since then Jelly had disliked Hill;
whenever they met had insulted him,
and had threatened to "whip" him and "kill" him.
Hill was afraid of Jelly
and tried to avoid him.

Now Jelly accused Hill of slandering the wife of one of Hill's neighbors
and the slander, as Jelly intended it should, reached the husband.
Hill heard of it, too,
and the very next Sunday evening went to see the man
and the angered husband told him he had better fix the matter up
    "damn quick,"
and gave him until the following night to prove his innocence.

Hill concluded that he must see Jelly,
but, before doing that, he thought it best to talk it over with a
    neighbor—
who lived on the road between Hill's house and Jelly's—
and try to get him to come along.
Monday morning, Hill mounted his horse
and, in case he might need his gun,
took it with him. When he was near the neighbor's house,
Hill saw him standing near the gate—
and Jelly beside him.
It seemed to Hill that the matter between Jelly and himself
might be settled then and there
and he dismounted, hitched the horse, and took his gun from the
    scabbard,
and, holding it down by his side,
went up to his neighbor and said that he would like to talk to him—
in the barn, some thirty steps away.
Neither Hill nor Jelly spoke to each other;
and Jelly glared at him with his malignant stare
and Hill kept an eye on Jelly.

When Hill and his neighbor had gone a few steps towards the barn,
Jelly followed them. He was getting closer
with his left hand stretched out
and his right near his hip;
Hill was afraid that Jelly was about to grab the gun with his left hand
and drawing a pistol shoot him with his right,
and called out to Jelly to "hold up."
But Jelly kept right on,
and Hill threw up his gun and fired.

Jelly fell at the second shot
and died in a few moments.
When his body was searched,
only a pocketknife was found on him,
and that was shut and in his pocket.

3

On Sunday morning Hazard left his house in Greenport
secretly
because he was afraid that he would be killed by Cora Fairbanks'
    brothers;
he had been away almost a month
and came back because his wife was sick;
had stayed in the house about a week
and did not leave it.
Now, early in the morning, he left the house in a closed hack
for Westerly
where he could catch a train that went to Chattanooga;
with him were his brother-in-law and a Negro servant.
All were armed.
They reached Westerly a little before eleven o'clock that morning
and the hack stopped between the town's hotel
and the passenger station of the railroad.
Hazard got out on the side next to the station
with his gun and baggage.
Just then a shot was fired at him
from behind the station platform,
followed by another shot from the same gun;
and then by other shots from another gun,
also fired from behind the platform;
and then shots from a pile of telegraph poles
a little way down the road along which the hack had come.
One or more of these shots struck Hazard in the legs
and he fell.

His brother-in-law was also wounded and ran away;
and the team that drew the hack ran away with the driver.

The Negro servant was not hit
but slumped to the ground,
rose at once and also ran away.
Hazard managed to get to a small oil-house,
a short distance beyond where the hack had stopped,
and here took shelter from those firing at him
and stood there, his gun in his hands,
looking towards the railway platform and the pile of telegraph poles.
But a man came up behind him
and shot him through the head
and he fell, twisting in the agony of death.

Soon after the Fairbanks brothers heard of Hazard's flight—
and they did almost at once—
as soon as they could get together, arm and mount,
they started after him.
They did not take any short cuts this time
in case Hazard would turn off the road
as he had when he fled from them before,
and they followed the wheel ruts of the hack—
and came in sight of it
as the hack was crossing a creek a mile from Westerly.
Those inside the closed hack did not see them.
They could have attacked Hazard here
and, indeed, one of the Fairbanks brothers said,
"Let's surround them
and make Hazard tell us where Cora is,"
but the others said that would bring on a fight,
and one of them might get hurt.
Instead, two of the brothers dismounted,
ran along the railroad track to town,
and took up positions behind the depot platform
almost as soon as the hack arrived and stopped.
The third brother and a cousin who was with them
rode on at a little distance behind the hack
into town. Here the third brother stopped at a pile of telegraph poles
before Hazard got out of the hack;

and the cousin somehow got beyond it and finally to a corner of the
    oil-house, behind Hazard,
and from there shot him through the head.

After the Fairbanks brothers left to follow Hazard,
their brother-in-law, the Judge, went to the railroad depot in Greenport
where the telegraph office was, and waited.
Hazard's flight and that the Fairbanks brothers were after him
became known in Greenport in no time,
and almost everybody in town talked about it that Sunday.
About nine in the morning, one of the doctors in town
saw the Judge at the telegraph office
and said to him that perhaps they had better send a hack and a doctor
    up the road
because Hazard or one of the Fairbanks party might get hurt;
the Judge replied that his folks could take care of themselves.
Perhaps, the doctor added, they ought to send a telegram to Westerly
and have them all arrested,
but to this the Judge made no reply.
He merely said that he was waiting for a telegram.

One of Hazard's cousins now came up to the telegraph operator—
just a young fellow and a stranger in town—
and walked with him down to the freight depot
where the telegraph office was. The Judge followed them into the office:
Hazard's cousin was seated at a table writing a telegram.
It was addressed to Hazard at Westerly and read:
"Four men on horseback with guns following. Look out."
A friend of the Judge was also in the telegraph office
and the Judge took him aside and said,
"What do you reckon that fellow would think," looking at the operator,
"if I told him I would put him out of the office
before he sent that message?" The Judge's friend said: "Judge, I
    wouldn't do that.
You might get into trouble and the young fellow might lose his job."
The Judge then said, "I am going to send a message myself,"
and wrote, "Do not let the party warned get away,"

addressing it to the telegraph operator at Westerly—an old
    acquaintance—
and handed this to the operator in Greenport.
Before the Judge left the office, he turned to him and said,
"Just add to that message, 'Say nothing,'"
and he also said, "This message has something to do with the one you
    have,"
meaning that both should be sent at the same time.
Then the Judge, his watch to prevent—if he could—a telegram of
    warning to Hazard over,
went home. Soon afterwards, a telegram from one of the Fairbanks
    brothers came to him:
"Hazard dead. None of us hurt."
The telegraph operator at Westerly did receive both messages at the
    same time
and went at once, without waiting to copy the message for Hazard,
to the hotel to look for him;
but Hazard had not reached Westerly as yet,
and the operator returned to the railroad depot.
Standing at the door, and thinking about the Judge's telegram,
he saw a hack coming from the direction of Greenport
and supposed—rightly—that Hazard was in it.
He wondered if he should go out into the road
along which the hack was being driven
and, if Hazard was inside,
then and there deliver the message.
But the Judge had asked him not to let Hazard get away
and he decided not to deliver the message just then
but to send for the town marshal;
he went away and went upstairs to the telegraph office:
his excuse would be that he went to copy the message.

If Hazard had been warned, before getting out of the hack,
the people of Greenport were telling each other afterwards,
he might have continued his flight;
or, when the first shots were fired,
since three men were firing at him when he tried to find shelter behind
    the oil-house,

as he stood facing them,
had he gotten the telegram
he would have known that there was a fourth man somewhere—
and kept a lookout for the man who killed him.

4
Hamilton and his wife were married
when she was pregnant.
He had been boarding at her mother's house
and they were living there when their child was born
soon after the marriage.
Her mother and sisters felt keenly
the disgrace of it
and her mother was particularly abusive.
All agreed that the birth should be kept secret,
and the doctor kept it a secret, too.

The child when born was feeble—
a seven-months child—
and Hamilton's wife too sick to nurse it.
Her mother and sisters tried to feed it
but it was too sick to take nourishment,
and two days after its birth
had spasms and lay gasping.
That evening, Hamilton was to take it away
at the urging of his wife's family
and bring the child to a neighboring town
where he knew of a woman who would take care of it
until his wife was well enough
to move from her mother's house
and take care of the child herself.

One of his wife's sisters came out on the porch
and gave him the child wrapped in a blanket—
ready for the trip.
As he held it in his arms
it made no sound and he felt no movement.

About three miles from town,
a wheel of his buggy ran over a stump
and the buggy was almost turned over.
He stopped the horse
and laid the child down on the seat,
and then examined the child.
It was dead and cold.

His wife's family must have known that it was dead
and got him to leave with it
to save themselves from a public funeral.
He made up his mind to bring the body back to town and leave it in
      the town's graveyard.
It was almost midnight when he got there.
He climbed a fence
and carried the body a little way inside
and put it under a cedar bush
where there was a good deal of high weeds,
and broke off a few twigs from the bush
and put them across the body.

Afterwards that night, thinking it over, he decided to have the child
      buried openly,
and early in the morning got into the buggy
and drove out to the graveyard
before someone should find the body.
As he drove up to where he had left it,
he was surprised to see that he had put it
in the yard of a man who lived across the street from the graveyard,
and the child's body was only thirty steps from the house.

He began to get out of the buggy
when he saw a woman standing near the edge of the gallery—
and drove on back to town.
The child's body was discovered three days later;
large red ants
all over it.

III
CHILDREN

1

The child, about six, thin and feeble
and sick of a disorder of its bowels,
was whipped by its father
for befouling its bed:
twenty or more "licks" with a switch
as thick as its father's finger,
and large "whelks" left on its body.
And then, on a cold and rainy December day,
sent to its grandfather's
in another county—
where it died in a few days.

2

Jessie was eleven years old, though some said fourteen,
and had the care of a child
just beginning to walk—
and suddenly
pulled off the child's diaper
and sat the child in some hot ashes
where they had been cooking ash cakes;
the child screamed
and she smacked it on the jaw.

3

Jimmie was about eight years old
when put to work in the factory:
given a stick and a piece of waste
and shown how to use it.
He was at work upon a machine,
cleaning out trash that had accumulated in the cogwheels,
when he was injured.

In a spirit of playfulness
he would manipulate the cogwheels;
although, as a judge was to say,
the boy had been repeatedly "advised"
by other employees—
and even by the assistant superintendent of the company—
as to the danger
of "a negligent attention to his business."

4

Before Fred was fourteen
he was hired by an oil company
to feed a "cake-crusher" in its mill.
The "cake-crusher" had cast rollers,
about a foot thick and a foot and a half long,
set close to each other;
and the rollers' teeth
when a cake of cotton seed came between them
broke it up.

The cakes were brought to Fred on a truck.
At first he stood on the floor
and threw the cakes into the hopper;
but he was still small
and a box, about a foot high, was placed for him on the greasy and slick
    floor
to stand on.

One evening, after he had been at work in the mill all day,
turning around
to pick up a cake on the truck,
the box slipped:
he threw out his arms
and one of his hands went into the hopper
and was caught by the rollers and crushed.

5

It was the rule in a well-regulated coal mine
with a single track
to have the space between the track and the side of the tunnel
about three feet wide.

For some time, the boy had been a driver in the mine
but never before in this tunnel;
he knew, well enough, that the wheels of the cars had to be "spragged,"
that is, blocked,
on a down grade
to keep the cars from running against, and perhaps over, the mule;
and it was the driver who had to get off the cars
and sprag the wheels.

When the boy was put to drive in the tunnel,
the man in charge of all the drivers
told him that in places spragging would be necessary
and he himself would go ahead
on the first trip
to show him where to begin spragging;
and the man did go ahead of him into the tunnel.

The boy saw him—by the light of the man's lamp—
beginning to sprag
and knew by the increased momentum of the cars
that a down grade had been reached;
he jumped off on the other side:
missed the wheels at first—
not uncommon—
and then ran alongside the cars
still trying to sprag
until he came to a narrow place
he did not know of,
where the track was only a foot or a foot and a half from the side of
        the tunnel
and not room enough for him between the cars and the wall—

and here he was jammed
and knocked under the cars.

6

The factory hours were the ordinary hours in the state—
eleven and a half to twelve hours a day.
He had been put to work at eight or nine years of age
and had now been working in the mill more than two years:
all day in the cotton mill
filled with machinery whirring at high speed.
His work was to carry spindles—
or "quills" as they were called—
from the "weaver room" to the "quiller room"
to be refilled;
and at this work had to go up an "alley,"
past a workbench in a corner of the room.

At the workbench just then
one of the help was cutting the wire for "pattern chains"
with a hammer and chisel—
he could not find the nippers usually used—
and as the boy was passing with a "turn of quills"
and looked up at a clock to see what time it was
a piece of wire flew into his eye—
and put it out.

7

Johnnie Cotton was a boy of fifteen or sixteen
but he was earning his own living as a laborer.
The engineer and fireman of the locomotive pulling a freight train out
     of San Antonio
invited Johnnie on board to ride to his home,
and he got on the tender.

While the train was in motion,
the fireman put the nozzle of a hose, connected with the boiler,

into Johnnie's hip pocket.
They were going to send a stream of cold water down his leg—
just for fun—

but the valve was turned to discharge steam and hot water,
and the engineer turning on the boiling water and steam
scalded Johnnie
from his hip to the heel of his foot.

8

Charlie was driving a wagon and two horses along the public road
on his way to get a load of wood,
and passed a gang of road hands at work—
among them "Buck." The boys knew each other
and "Buck" yelled an insult.
Charlie yelled another back
and "Buck" threw a stone at him as he drove away.

After getting his load,
Charlie came back along the same road.
"Buck" now had a sycamore switch with him
and when Charlie came up
"Buck" struck him a few "licks" on his bare legs
and went back to his work, laughing.

Charlie drove on, delivered his load,
and started back for another load of wood,
but this time took his gun with him,
loaded with squirrel shot.
He was not driving and, while a companion drove,
sat upon the wagon with his gun
across his knees. When he came again to the road hands at work,
"Buck" was in the ditch
and had just thrown out a shovel of dirt
and was getting ready to throw out another.
"Hello, Charlie," he cried, "what are you going to do with
        that gun?"

Charlie stood up in the wagon, cocked the gun,
and shot him.

9

His older brother was sick—
unable to deliver ice to his widowed mother's customers
and he asked his mother's permission
to take the ice from the factory
and deliver it.

Driving the horse and the small ice-cart
along the track of the electric cars,
the horse going at half trot,
the boy—all of fourteen—heard the gong of the car
coming up behind him.
He turned the horse off the track for the car to pass;
but, after the cart had cleared the track
and the car was still behind him,
he turned the horse again to the left
and the right end of the cart struck the side of the car:

the ice was thrown into the street,
the shaft of the cart broken—
and so was the boy's left arm.

10

Sobieski was about forty years old,
a strong, robust man,
living with his family about half a mile from the railroad depot,
and working at his trade of carpenter
about ten miles away.

When he was paid off, after his week's work,
he sometimes became drunk,
and his wife would send their two boys,
the elder twelve and the younger ten,

to meet him at the train
and help him home—if need be.

That night in December it was cold
and the two boys were at the depot in the waiting-room
where there was a fire.
They were not misbehaving
although one of them, it is true,
had been seen swinging on the steps of cars
and jumping off when the cars began to move.
The stationmaster asked them what they were there for
and the older boy replied that they were waiting for their father.
The stationmaster then said
they had been there before
and their father had not come—
and was not coming;
if they did not leave at once
and came around any more
he would have them arrested and put in jail;
and they were frightened.

The boys then waited outside the depot—
by this time it was nine or ten o'clock at night—
and a policeman told them to run on home
and come back when they heard the whistle of the train.
So they went home and fell asleep
and did not hear the whistle
and were not at the depot when their father came—
drunk.

He threw his bundle of working-clothes on the platform,
and then got out and leaned against the car.
A passenger took hold of him
and pulled him away
and he staggered from the depot
but turned back
and lay down between the track and the platform
in its shadow

and went to sleep.
He was found in the morning
run over by a freight train:
blood between the rail and the platform,
and his right arm mangled and so was his leg.

IV
NEGROES

1

Wisdom and his wife and three or four other Negroes
with tickets as passengers
got on the train for Vicksburg.
The conductor met them on the platform of the car shouting:
"God damn you niggers! Get back and around!"
Wisdom explained that all they wanted to do
was to get through
to the car for colored people.
By way of answer the conductor pushed him to the ground,
knocking his hat off,
and as soon as all the Negroes were off the car
signaled the engineer to go ahead;
and the train left them standing at the station.

2

The brakeman standing on the steps of the "ladies' coach"
told her to go into the coach for colored people instead;
but she insisted on taking a seat in the "ladies' coach."
And when the conductor came to her
and asked her to leave the coach or get off the train
she would do neither;
and so the conductor came back with two or three other men
who worked for the railroad,
and they took her by the arms
and shoved her from her seat and the "ladies' coach."

A railroad, said the court, has the right to set aside certain cars
for the colored;
in fact, has to under the laws of the state,
provided, of course, the accommodations are equal.
Not at all because colored people are inferior
but many, if not most, white persons
because of custom and tradition,
will not occupy a seat next to a colored person
or even travel in the same coach;
and it may be supposed that colored people, likewise,
prefer seats in coaches without white persons.

If the colored race should become the dominant power in the state
as has been the case, the court went on,
and should enact a similar law,
white persons would not assume that they are inferior
because they have to travel in separate coaches.
But, however this may be, it is better for colored persons to be
        separated;
for to ride in the same coach
might cause a disturbance,
disagreeable to both white and colored;
in fact, the seating complained of is more for the comfort and
        protection of colored passengers
than of white.

3

Greer Darlington ordered his supper
and Brown, the only waiter in the restaurant,
brought it. Something or other that Darlington had ordered
was not there, and he said to the waiter,
"This is not what I ordered,"
and Brown replied, "You are blamed hard to please."
Darlington got up at once and said,
"I take no insults from a damned nigger,"
and left. He complained to the owner of the restaurant as he did so
and the owner promised to send Darlington his supper

at the hotel where he was staying;
but, busy with other customers,
neglected to do so. Fifteen or twenty minutes afterwards,
Darlington returned to the restaurant and said,
"I am going in back to see about my supper."

The owner lifted his hands and said:
"Greer, for God's sake, don't make any trouble in my place!
I have had trouble enough."
But Darlington went through the dining-room into the pantry,
and through the pantry into the kitchen;
there he met Brown, the waiter, and cursing him said,
"You have insulted me!"
Brown replied, "I beg your pardon."
The owner of the restaurant had hold of Darlington's arm
and stood between him and the waiter:
"Greer," he was saying, "he has begged your pardon.
Now, come on and let's go out."
But Darlington drew his pistol
and sent two bullets into Brown's body.

4
Several white men went at night to the Negro's house,
shot into it,
and set fire to his cotton on the gallery;
his wife and children ran under the bed
and, as the firing from guns and pistols went on
and the cotton blazed up,
ran through a side door into the woods.
The Negro himself, badly wounded, fled to the house of a neighbor—
a white man—
and got inside.
He was followed,
and one of those who ran after him
put a shotgun against the white man's door
and shot a hole through it.
Justice, however, was not to be thwarted,

for five of the men who did this to the Negro
were tried:
for "unlawfully and maliciously
injuring and disfiguring"—
the white man's property.

5

The Negro was living at a dugout on his own land
when a notice was posted in his neighborhood:
it had a rude drawing of a man hanging from a tree and a coffin
and read: "We don't allow a nigger on Hog Creek.
We give you warning in time;
so if you don't want to look up a tree
you had better leave. The White Caps."

Franklin and three or four others
were riding up to the Negro's dugout,
and Franklin was saying to the man riding beside him:
"I don't want to have anything to do with it;
I don't want to have any trouble with the Negroes.
All right, go ahead and buy the place
but I'll have nothing to do with it now,
and after you have made the trade
I'll come in."
But the Negro shot at them
and killed Franklin and another in the party.

6

The colored tenants on the Judge's plantation
were giving an entertainment on a Saturday night
to raise funds for the building of a church;
but, while the entertainment was going on,
a number of white men, young and old,
with a party of friends who lived in Mississippi—
the plantation was near the state line—
appeared:

drunk, singing and swearing and cursing around.
The colored people scattered,
returning to their homes;
and some were followed by white men
who tried to get hold of the torchlights they carried:
"Blow the lights out! Or we'll shoot them out!"
The women heard their voices down the road a piece
and ran.
When a few took shelter in the cabin of a Negro
and closed the door behind them,
white men surrounded the cabin
and called upon those inside the cabin to come out
and threatened to shoot into the cabin.

The next day, one of the older men
called on the Negro
in whose cabin the others took shelter
and apologized
for his conduct and that of his friends.
But it was a common report in the neighborhood
that some of the colored people
intended to report the matter
to the local authorities.

"The clock had just struck three
that night
when they rode up:
there were eight at the door with guns
and about nine or ten behind them in the road.
They called for me three times
and my wife answered.
They asked if I was at home;
yes, I said, and opened the door,
and they asked me to come out on the gallery.
But I would not
and told them I could hear all they had to say where I stood.
'We would like to talk with you for a few moments,' their leader said;
'no harm—no danger whatever.

We came to see about that little disturbance
the boys had here on Saturday night.
If this is reported
and those young men are put to trouble,
we are going to burn the last house there is on this place
and swing the last nigger's neck from a limb;
yours, too!
You can go tomorrow and report it,
but you had better make your coffin
before you leave home.' At this one of them spoke up,
'If you can't make it, you had better hire me:
I am a good carpenter.'

"The man who spoke first went on:
'It is in your power to keep out of the courthouse.
Tell your surrounding friends what I had to say.
You understood it, didn't you?'
'Yes, sir,' I answered. 'every word.'
'Do you know who I am? A free white man
from the free state of Mississippi;
twenty years of age and with a white heart.
Good night!'
And all the while the others kept shooting off their guns and pistols."

"My wife was scared and left home with the children.
Everybody on the place left,
except myself, my grandfather and my grandmother.
I was sitting out in the thicket
because I was afraid to stay in the house;
and about half-past ten o'clock I heard the fire of two guns.
I went back in my house at half-past eleven,
and between midnight and day
I heard another gun."

"I was scared to stay at my house.
I carried everything I had to the woods before I left.
When I left home I shut up my doors;
when I returned, they were open.

And there were horse tracks all around—everywhere;
a pile of cotton was in the house
and my dog was lying on it dead—
shot."

"All the hands had scattered into the woods
and went to another plantation a while—
and some never came back—
left their crops in the field ungathered
and turned the working animals loose.
Pretty much all the hands were gone
four or five days;
and after that would come back and work in the day,
and go away for the night.
The stock ate up a good deal of our crop
and the cattle destroyed as much as they wanted to
because everybody was scared to go for them:
my corn was damaged about twenty-five barrels
and my cotton about a bale."

7

Mrs. West was at her father's house in the evening
talking with a neighbor in the back room
when someone at the back door called: "Miss Mary!"
He called three times
and she got up and went to the back porch
and saw the Negro standing in the back yard.
He looked as if he was drunk.

She knew him: he had been living nearby a long time
with his wife and children;
and she said, "Will, you scared me."
"Well, Miss Mary, if I scared you,
I will leave." "No," she said,
"if you have anything to say to me, say it."
If he were to say what he had to say, he answered

the white people and the black people would be after him with
    shotguns;
and she said, "If you say anything you ought not to say to me,
I will shoot you myself,"
and started to go into the house.
"Oh, Mary, don't go!"
"You call me 'Mary'? Get out of this yard!"
"Excuse me, Miss Mary; I did not mean to say it."
But he added, "I will get out when I please;
I will go out as I came in: I will walk out." And he did.

8

Mrs. Holtz, fifty years of age and a widow,
worked in the kitchen of the Madison House
as an assistant cook. Williams, a young colored man,
had just been hired as assistant meat-cook
in the same kitchen.
A day or two after he had been hired,
sitting down and facing each other at their work,
he said to her: "I like your looks—
mightly well.
Let's you and me live together: be as one."
Mrs. Holtz replied that she had not as yet got low enough
to live that way with a white man—
let alone a Negro.

Saturday night, after her work,
she went to her room in a house in the same yard as the kitchen,
and about two o'clock that night
was awakened
by a man putting his hand upon her leg.
When she opened her eyes
there was Williams
in the light of the electric lamp shining through the window.

9

The Negro had spent the afternoon in Selma
distributing gifts
from the Christmas tree
at the Sunday school where he was the superintendent.
There had been trouble in Selma that evening
between white men and Negroes:
a white man had beaten a Negro with a stick
and another had shot a Negro.
A month before there had been trouble between white men and
    Negroes in Wilmington, too,
and the Negro had been reading about it
and brooding over it;
and now there was trouble in Selma.

Three white men, wearing masks, were still celebrating Christmas:
wearing women's skirts, singing, shouting and laughing,
and firing off Roman candles.
One of them had pistols which he was shooting off now and then.
They had been drinking
and still had a pint of whiskey with them.
They, too, had been in Selma
but their celebration had been stopped by the sheriff's men or the
    city's police
and they were going out into the country
where they could be free to shoot off fireworks and pistols,
and sing and shoot if they felt like it.

The man with the pistols fired one not far from the Negro's house—
a small frame house on the public road near Selma—
and one of his companions, the three still masked,
fired a Roman candle into a tree in the Negro's yard,
and the Negro's dog began to bark.
At the sight of masked men at his gate
he had taken a butcher's knife
and now rushed at the three with his knife:
killed one, wounded another—
and frightened the third into running away.

10

Jasper White, a colored man, had rented about twenty acres
from two tenants of Tom Fulton and his brother,
and was working the land with "Wash," Jasper's son:
the rent to be paid was half the crop
and the Fultons were to furnish supplies.
But the tenants of the Fultons who had rented the land to White
had not paid their rent,
nor had the supply bill been paid by Jasper White.
Now "Wash" swore out an attachment against the property of his
      father
for the money due him for his work;
and the attachment was served on Jasper White's cotton and corn.
He agreed at once to a sale of the property attached.

Early in the morning, a day or two afterwards,
Tom Fulton took his gun and bird dog
and with his brother—also with a gun—went hunting.
They stopped to tell their tenants who had sublet to White
to take the wagon
and haul the cotton from White's field to the gin.
After hunting through field and wood,
the Fultons were going towards the house of the Whites
when along came the wagon:
one of their tenants driving and the other
walking alongside.
They saw no cotton in the field and went on to the house.

One of the tenants had heard something or other about the
      attachment,
but Tom Fulton said:
"What in the world would he attach his own cotton for?
That is only some talk among you colored people."
The cotton had been hauled from the field
to the house of the Whites
by the order of the attaching officers. The wagon was stopped a couple
      of hundred feet from the house
and Tom Fulton and his brother walked into the yard.

Jasper White and another colored man,
who had been placed by the officers in charge of the cotton,
were standing on the porch talking to each other.

The shoelace of Tom Fulton's brother had become unfastened
and to tie it he put his foot on one of the blocks used as steps to the
        porch,
his gun lying across his arm
and the muzzle pointing sideways—away from the house.
"Good morning," said Tom Fulton. "We thought, White, we would
        come down
and get everything straight. Where is the cotton that has been picked?"

Jasper White pointed to one of the two rooms.
Just then "Wash" White looked through a doorway
and said, "Is you come to haul it?"
He poked his shotgun, loaded with buckshot, through the doorway
and "pulled down" on Tom Fulton—
shot him dead through the forehead.
And in a flash emptied the other barrel—through the window—at
        Tom Fulton's brother,
who was tying his shoelace,
breaking his jawbone, putting out an eye, and wounding him badly
        about the throat.

11

One of Cary's clerks—who roomed and boarded at his house—
was going from the store to supper
when he heard a "fuss" between another of Cary's employees
who worked at the cotton gin
and a Negro who had brought a load of cotton
for a customer;
but the clerk said nothing.
However, one of Cary's daughters
came to tell her father about the "fuss
between some persons" at the cotton gin, and Cary went out on the
        piazza,

stopped a moment,
and then started towards the gin.
As he went up the steps of the platform,
the Negro jumped off into a wagon
and from there to the ground.
Cary asked his employee what the fuss was about
and the employee said the Negro had called him "a son of a bitch,"
and that was more than he would take from any "nigger."
But Cary told the man to shut his mouth and go back to his work,
and then turned and went down the steps,
around the wagon and to the Negro
now standing near a tree.
"Are you the man who has been fussing here?" Cary asked.
The Negro did not answer;
and Cary repeated his question—
his voice still gentle—and, as he spoke,
put his left hand on the Negro's arm
and asked him to come around to the light
for it was dark under the tree;
he just wanted to find out, Cary said, what all the fuss was about.

For answer, the Negro stabbed him,
the blade going into his belly,
and jumping back
cried, "Hands off!"
and ran away.

12

The sheriff and his posse were about to remove a Negro prisoner
from the county jail
and take him to Savannah,
when, at the ringing of a church bell,
a crowd of about seventy-five—
though others said as many as two hundred and fifty—
left whatever they were doing or working at
and gathered quickly.
The members of the crowd ran about

shouting and cursing,
and some showed the weapons they had with them:
one was shouting that, if they were going to take the prisoner away,
he would "see about it,"
and a woman said she would be the first
"to throw a couple of shots among the white sons of bitches,"
and still another
that they ought to "kill out all the white people in town."

13

Philip and Crystal, both colored, were engaged to be married.
She was eighteen and of good standing in the county;
taught in a Sunday school
and had a class of little girls.
During their engagement, Philip got her with child
and, at his urging, she went to Pine Bluff on a visit;
he was to meet her
and they were to be married there.

She came back when he did not come when she thought he would
to learn that he was to marry another woman in a few days;
and she would not eat or sleep:
would start to do one thing
and do another;
start to say one thing
and say another.

She went to bed Sunday night
but quickly arose
and kept walking backward and forward,
or would just squat down
and put her hands on her breast.
That night Philip and the other woman were married
and next morning Philip and his wife
walked past the house where Crystal lived with her parents.

She saw them pass,
took a pistol and followed.
"Philip, you have fooled me long enough;
now you must die!"
And she shot and killed him.

14

There was a fair—a "festival," as they called it—
about a mile and a half from Tallahassee,
but Small did not go
and went "up to town" instead
to pay Mandy some money on a razor he had bought from her.
When he got to town, he found that she was in the city lockup
for being drunk on the street;
and he went to see about getting her out—
and did get her out
and went home with her. After dark, when he was about to leave,
he heard "the boys" coming up the road,
back from the festival; chewing cane and talking loudly
and blowing their harmonicas.
Small decided to stay a while
and see whether they were going to stop at Mandy's.
He had been trying for some time to get her into the house
but she would not go.

"The boys" did stop and when Charlie Dade came up
Small was sitting by the side of Mandy on the steps to the porch.
Dade told her he wanted to see her
but she said: "Go away! I am not in any seeing condition now."
He said he only wanted to speak a few words to her;
and Small got up and went into the yard
and stood by the gate outside.

Just as he got outside of the gate
Mandy started towards her room
and Dade was right behind her.

She told him to go back
but he would not go,
and she turned around and grabbed a scrub of a broom
and hit him over the head with it three or four times.
He was standing near the door with his right side pushing against it
when she was striking him,
and he jumped towards her with a razor in his hand
and threw the razor around her throat.
Then he jumped off the porch and started to run.

Mandy ran out into the yard,
picked a picket from the ground,
and looked around for Charlie Dade—
but he was gone.
Small saw the blood streaming from her throat
so that by the light of the lamp burning brightly in the house
she seemed to be wearing a red waist.

15

Amanda, a Negro woman, came to Florida from Georgia
with Joe, a Negro. He was jealous
and would "jump on" her
if he saw a man around or his tracks.
Joe's job was getting out ties
for the Orange Belt Railroad and Joe and Amanda and others were
        camping
about a mile and a half from town
among the pines and oak bushes.
After a while, she brought her daughter, going on seventeen,
        from Georgia.

Willie Lamb, who had also come from Georgia with Joe and Amanda,
came to their tent
and asked her to keep his coat there.
He had a pistol in his coat pocket
but she did not know that
and told him to put his coat in the tent.

When it was dark enough to build a fire outside for the light,
she sent for Joe to come to supper.
He came, after a while, and said, "Amanda, where is that whiskey I told
        you to get for me?"
She told him to look in her box inside the tent
and then was sorry—
because she had one of those fifty-cent baking-powder cans
full of silver dollars in her box.
Joe came back cursing and said,
"God damn it, if I am not going to kill two niggers tonight,"
and kicked her in the side as hard as he could.
She could not straighten out at first
and then screamed;
her daughter came running up to her and said,
"What is the matter?"
Amanda did not answer but turning to Joe said,
"What in the name of the Lord did you kick me for?"
And Nancy, her daughter, said: "I told you to come away from him!
The first thing you know Joe will kill you."
And she and Joe got to quarreling.

Nancy said, "You are mad at me
because you haven't me and my mother both!"
"If you don't hush," he said,
"I will blow your brains out."
She turned around to go away and when she had gone about ten steps
he stood on a railroad tie and shot at her with Willie Lamb's pistol;
Amanda was in the tent when she heard the shots
and came out. Joe turned on her.
She broke into a run
and he chased her;
shot at her, too, and hit her right in the small of the back.

16

The body was found in a swamp at the edge of town
forty or fifty yards from the wagon road
at the side of the swamp:

a leg was sticking out of the mud.
The dead body was that of a Negro—
a girl or woman by the clothes:
the dress made out of homespun
and the buttons white
(homespun goods and white buttons
were common among the Negroes there).
One of the men got a pitchfork
and picked up the bones with it,
put them in a box
and brought the box to the courthouse.
Hill had a daughter of fourteen or fifteen,
missing ever since July;
and some of the coroner's jury went to his house about sundown
and told him about the clothing
and asked him to go down to the courthouse
and see if he could identify the body.
He seemed unwilling to go
and had to be asked two or three times;
and when he did go
said there was nothing to prove to him
that it was his daughter;
and his wife, the girl's stepmother, agreed.

A large black oilcloth, about seven feet long and five wide,
had been found in the swamp, too,
about twenty-five or thirty yards from the body:
in size and color it looked like the one Hill had used to cover his wagon
(he would carry passengers in his wagon
out to mills and stills).

Among those who testified at the trial of Hill for murder
was a Negro woman who lived near the swamp
and on a night, about the beginning of August,
heard a girl screaming in the swamp;
and a Negro who had been in jail
for having a "fuss" with a preacher.
When the Negro was coming out on bail,

Hill who was then in jail said to him—
so the witness said—
"We colored people ought to stand by each other.
If you will," said Hill, "I will see that you don't regret it."
Then he said, "Go up to Georgia
and write a letter to me as my daughter,
and sign my daughter's name to the letter:
it will do me a lot of good in my case."
And another witness said: "I am a fortuneteller
and I tells a little something in the cards.
I was at Hill's restaurant"
(in which his daughter had worked as a waitress)
"and he said to me: 'Come into my room:
I want you to do a little something for me.'
I told him: 'You see that card? You are in trouble.
Tell me your trouble.'
And Hill said: 'I killed my daughter.
I got to fooling with her
and bigged her.
I told her not to tell anyone,
and when the time came I would send her off,
but she told it around to white and black.
My son held her hands
and I cut her throat with my razor.'"

17

Steve, a young Negro "black as a crow," seventeen years of age,
industrious and well-behaved,
left behind him a matured cotton crop
and some clothing
he never called for.
He had said nothing about leaving the county,
had made no preparations to leave,
and there was no reason why he should have left.
Three weeks after his disappearance,
the headless body of a Negro
was found in a creek

several miles from where Steve was last seen:
the body and the arms
in a sack
tied together by a piece of rope;
and the legs tied up in another sack;
in each sack
a heavy rock.
The head was never found.

On the body
was part of a plain, hand-sewed shirt,
with a sleeve
hemmed back at the wrist.
Steve's mother knew the shirt as her son's,
for she had made it with "my own fingers"
and knew her sewing,
and had turned back the wristband and hemmed it
because it was too long.
Steve had put it on Sunday when he left her house
late in the forenoon of the day when last seen alive.

Tifton was "very partial" to his sister-in-law—
she was living with his wife and children—
and Steve was attentive to her;
but Tifton told Steve to let her alone
and said of her, "She is mine."
Some two weeks before Steve's disappearance
he went to a party at Tifton's house
and danced with her.
In the evening, when Tifton had become drunk,
he tried to shoot Steve
while Steve was sitting with her outside the house,
and would have shot him
if Tifton's father-in-law had not stopped him.
"He will hear from this," Tifton said,
showing his pistol
and pointing "the bitter end of it" at Steve.

Somebody met Steve a mile or so from Tifton's house
going towards it between sundown and dark
on the Sunday he disappeared,
and Steve said he would probably "come to meeting" after a while—
services were held in the neighborhood—
but never came.
Monday morning, a man met Tifton and his son:
Tifton was riding on a horse with a sack in front of him,
and his son on another horse with another sack;
the sacks were full
and blood was dripping from under the sack in front of the boy
down the shoulder of the horse.

v

Arlington, a wealthy merchant of Richmond, had never married
but had lived with a woman who was half white,
formerly his slave, and Alice was their daughter.
He had always recognized her as his child
and she called him father. After the War,
he bought a small farm outside the city
as a home for himself and Alice
and there they lived for more than twenty years,
sitting and eating at the same table:
a father who loved his daughter "passing well"
and a devoted and dutiful daughter.

He was a man simple and frugal in his habits,
honest and just in business,
but, living as he did, he had only business friends
and as for relatives—other than Alice—he had only cousins:
strangers who never visited him
and whom he knew only by their letters.
And of these he complained: "Here is a begging letter,"
or "another begging letter";
he never answered them
and shoved them into the wastebasket.

Alice once said, "Don't be so hard on them,"
and he answered: "I had to look out for myself since I was very young,
and others might do the same.
I am not going to give them a cent."
But he had the not uncommon dislike about making a will,
and did not make one.

As he lay on his deathbed, he called his daughter to his bed and said:
"Alice, I am a mighty sick man
and do not know what might happen.
Look into my pants' pocket
and bring me my keys and my two purses;
and look in the inside of my vest pocket,
and bring me the package of papers tied with a red string."
She brought them to his bed and he said,
"Alice, I am going to give you all these as yours";
and he took up the package of papers and said:
"In this you will also find my bankbook,
showing how much I have in the bank;
and whatever it calls for you can have.
Take these papers
and put them in your trunk
between your clothes for safekeeping;
for, Alice, you will have to take care of these things now:
your very life hangs on them
and the bread that you eat."

The judges said that he did not need a will
to give all that he had to Alice,
except for his money in the bank:
that went to his cousins—
at least what was left of it
after the administrator of the estate and the lawyers took their fees,
for the cause was argued at great length several times.

VI
PROPERTY

1

Bristol was the treasurer of a company
for which West had made some barrels.
When West went into the company's storeroom
to get paid, asking the usual five and a half cents each,
Bristol told him that the company was now paying only five cents
for six-hoop barrels
and West replied, loudly and angrily,
that he should have been told,
and still wanted five and a half cents a barrel.

Bristol explained that the difference was only fifteen cents—
too small a matter to get mad about,
but West kept on swearing and getting louder than ever
until Bristol lost patience and said, "Damn fool!"
At that West picked up a chair
and went for Bristol but—
after a moment's hesitation—
set it down again
and Bristol, remembering how West, much the stronger,
had once slapped him through a window,
hurried into his office
and picked up a paperweight
and opened his knife.

He came out, stopping at an opening in the counter,
and told West to leave;
but instead West started for Bristol again
and Bristol was about to raise the paperweight
when, before he could get it up to strike,
West grabbed his arm. In another moment
they were scuffling on the floor.
Bristol stabbed West in the hip
and, on his knees first,
stabbed West again in the shoulder.

2

Jim Forester went to Bates, a sharecropper on the land of Jim's father,
and got his own plow back
and told Bates he would need it himself for a few days.
Returning to his field early the next day,
Jim found that his plow had been taken away
and thought from the tracks he saw
that Bates must have taken it again.

Jim went back to his father's house
and told him that Bates had taken the plow
and asked his father to get the plow back
reminding him that he was to furnish Bates with team and tools.
His father asked Benton, a son-in-law, to get the plow
saying that Bates was friendly to Benton.
Benton, on a visit with his wife and child
and about to start for home,
said that he would not go if there was to be any trouble;
but Jim assured him there would be no trouble—
on his part;
and both went to the field where Bates was plowing.

Benton, followed by Jim, went up to Bates
as he came to the end of a cotton row
in which he was plowing with Jim's plow.
"Good morning," said Benton, and added,
"you are plowing her out,"
to which Bates merely said, "Yes."
Benton then said that Mr. Forester sent him over
to get the plow
and that Mr. Forester would get him another.
Bates replied that he would not let the plow go
until he got another.

"My name is Benton," Benton went on. "Don't you know me?"
And he stooped to unhitch the horse from the plow.
Bates picked up a stick "of heart pine and good weight"
and, as Benton started off with the plow,

stepped towards him.

Jim then spoke up and told Bates if he did not put the stick down,

he would arrest him (Jim was constable of the township and carried a
    pistol).

Bates said, "You will have to call in some of your neighbors to help
    you";

and Jim shot him:

at the second shot Bates was falling

and was upon the ground dying

when the last shot was fired.

3

Clinton found Dick Parson's cow in his cornfield

and drove her down the road to Parson's place.

He stopped near Parson's house

and called out several times

but, getting no answer, drove the cow to his own place.

Dick Parson's wife heard him

and saw him in the road with the cow

and told her husband.

He started out at once after his cow

but his wife and mother went after him

and persuaded him to come back.

The women, however, followed Clinton:

when they reached his place,

he had put the cow in his barn

and gone on into his house.

Clinton saw them and invited them into the house

at his friendliest

saying that he wanted to see Dick's new wife;

but they said they were not dressed for calling

and would not come in,

though Clinton sent his wife and daughter out to urge them to.

The meeting between the women was cordial,

and Clinton's wife and the elder Mrs. Parsons kissed each other.

By this time, Parsons who had followed his wife and mother

had come up and Clinton, who had come out to the road

to join his wife and mother, invited him also into the house;
but Parsons said he did not have the time.

The elder Mrs. Parsons then turned to Clinton and said,
"We want to get our cow," and he replied, friendly enough, "You can
        have the cow
but keep her out of my corn,"
and crossed the road to the barn to turn the cow out.
He had hold of the latch of the barnyard gate
when the elder Mrs. Parsons remarked,
"I don't think our cow has eaten any more of your corn
than your mules ate of ours."
At this Clinton said brusquely: "I don't want any foolishness!
If you want a fuss you can have it."
Parsons had been standing a short distance away,
eyeing Clinton,
with his right hand in his pocket;
and now Clinton heard a click in Parson's pocket
like the cocking of a pistol.

Clinton turned suddenly and went back across the road into his
        house—
and came out with a shotgun. He walked outside of the yard
and said to Parsons, his voice mild again,
"Take your hand out of your pocket,"
but Parsons remained standing with his left hand on the fence
and his right hand in his pocket.
Clinton said to Parsons again, "Take your hand out of your pocket,"
but this time his voice was loud and angry.
Parsons, an angry look on his face, still said nothing
and remained standing where he was—motionless.
Clinton repeated his command a third time,
waited a moment or two,
and then raised his gun to his shoulder and fired.
Parsons staggered off a few steps,
tried two or three times
to draw his pistol out of his pocket,
and then fell to his knees and died.

4

Park was Black's tenant and was to pay his rent in baled cotton.
In October, after a wagon had been loaded with cotton,
they began to argue as to where it should be ginned:
Black wanted it ginned at one gin and Park at another, four miles away,
but where, he claimed, it would be ginned at fifty cents less,
and fifty cents was as much in his pocket
as it was in Black's.
But the wagon was driven by Black
to the gin he wanted,
and Park followed.

Black got down from the wagon and was on his way towards the platform
but turned back when he saw Park at the gate,
and they began to fight with their fists.
Park was forced against the gate and out of it,
and Black started back to the wagon.
He saw Park coming
holding a knife,
seized a piece of fence rail,
five or six feet long,
and, holding it with both hands,
struck Park with it once and again.
Park dodged under the rail
and began using his knife;
Black fell, face up,
his head striking the ground,
and then stood up, walked a few steps
only to lie down and die.

VII
RAILROADS

1

When the headlight is beaming, the earth between the railroad ties
shows up white;

but the spaces between the railroad ties on a bridge
are dark.

The railroad had been fenced off but the fence was down in places
and the jack came on the track at night
and was now on the bridge,
its feet down between the ties.
Lying there, the jack
was not easily seen
and, struck by a train,
was carried more than a hundred yards
dead on the cowcatcher.

2

Whipple lived about ten miles from the railroad
and drove his daughter, going away to school,
to the depot. When the train came,
he went with her into the cars
looking for a seat
and carried her valise, for it was large and heavy.
His team and wagon were waiting.
Before they could find a seat
and say good-by
the train was moving.

He got on the steps of the car
but it looked like a dangerous place to jump off:
there was a ditch there
and the ends of the cross-ties were sticking out.
Whipple waited—
the train did not seem to be going fast—
and jumped where the ground looked level;
the moving train gave him "a send"
so as to throw his whole weight on one foot:
his leg was broken
and he rolled over and over down the embankment.

3

The draw of the railroad bridge over the river
had been taken out for repair
and false works had been built upon piles
so that the trains could cross.
But drift wood lodged against the false works
and the pier of the bridge. To save it
fifteen or twenty workingmen were ordered upon the drift.

Ropes were fastened to the drift
and carried to pulleys upon the bridge
and then fastened to locomotives at each end
to dislodge the drift by their power.
On the third day, it suddenly broke in two:
one portion floating down the river,
and the false works above tumbled down.

The workingmen upon this portion of the drift
escaped to the other—
except one man struck by a falling timber;
but the rest of the drift seemed about to break loose, too,
and the false works above it were cracking:
the workingmen, it seemed likely, would be in danger
from the falling irons and timbers—
but the false works didn't fall
and those who jumped into the river were drowned.

4

A young man about nineteen, eyesight and hearing good,
had been in North Danville a couple of days
looking for work; and now, a little after six in the morning,
left the place where he was staying
and went along the railroad track
to the neighboring mills and factories.

Upon one side of the railroad
was a fence, eight feet high,

put up by one of the cotton mills;
and, upon the other side, an embankment,
from fifteen to twenty feet in height;
but, upon both sides of the track,
was a space, wide on one side and just enough on the other,
for people to walk,
and largely used by those who worked in the cotton mills in North
    Danville
and in the mills and factories on the other side of the river.

He had just passed the largest building of one of the cotton mills
when a train going south, an hour behind schedule,
came from behind a sharp curve
and along the track on which he was walking.
The engineer saw him as soon as the engine
came off the sharp curve
but it was too late to stop the train
before it struck him.
The engineer did blow his whistle,
and the young man might have heard the train coming
and the squeal of the whistle,
if it were not for the noise of the machinery in the mills he was
    passing
and the roar of the waters over the falls nearby—
besides, he was thinking of the work he might find and do and was lost
    in thought.

VIII

DEATH OF A SALESMAN

On an afternoon in December, a traveling salesman, about sixty years
    of age,
left a small town in Alabama
in a buggy he had hired at a livery stable
for another place about nine miles away.
As he went along the state road

the driver, a colored man,
was about to turn off
to drive along a byway through the plantations,
and this was three or four miles longer.
But, he explained, a boy driving some mules a couple of days before
could not cross at the public ford
and had to use the byway;
he himself was not afraid to cross the ford
but it was cold and he did not want to get wet.
The salesman stopped him
and told him to drive on to the ford:
the water might be high at one time
and easily fordable in a few hours.

When they reached the ford,
they saw the road dipping into the water
and it was thirty or thirty-five feet to the opposite slope;
but there was no current
and the water was still.
"There's no water here to stop us," said the salesman.
"Go ahead!"

The driver took the salesman's valise from the floor of the buggy
and put it on the seat, and they started across.
After a few steps the horses were swimming
and the water striking the salesman and the driver in the face.
The salesman grasped at the lines
to turn the buggy around
and pulled the horses off the road;
and the driver caught hold of the lines
to get back on the road
but the buggy struck a stake driven into the ground
and hung there.

"What do we do now?" the salesman asked.
"I am going to cut the horses loose," the driver said.
"Let them alone! I will pay for them!
It's not the first pair I have paid for.

Save me and yourself!
  Can you swim? I can't swim a lick."
"Yes," said the driver.
"Then swim," said the salesman, "and take me on your back!
  Don't think hard of me
  but do all you can to get me out of here!"

"I cannot swim with you on my back."
"Well, what in the world am I going to do?
  I am freezing!"
"You are not freezing," said the driver.
"You are just a little cold.

  You have better clothes on than I have and I lack a heap from freezing."
  The salesman took hold of the driver. "You must not leave me here!"
"But how am I to get you out?" the driver said.
"I can't swim with you on my back.
  What are we going to do? Just stay here and drown—
  unless I go off and get a boat?"
"Go ahead!" said the salesman and turned him loose.

  But the driver could not get a boat,
  and when help reached the ford
  the salesman was found out of the buggy—drowned.

IX
THE BURIAL

  Juan came to Francisco's house one morning
  and asked him to come along to the ranch
  where Juan lived with his father and brother.
  Francisco mounted his horse and went with him.
  On the way, they met Juan's brother
  on foot, coming from the ranch,
  and he asked Juan, "Have you got him?"
"Yes," said Juan. Juan's brother mounted behind him,

and Juan said, "Come on, let's go!"
"Where?" asked Francisco,
and Juan answered, "Somewhere."

But Francisco wanted to know where they were going,
and finally Juan said, "To bury Pedro";
and they went on together
until they turned off the road and along a path:
the woods became too thick for the horses to pass
and they dismounted, tied the horses,
and went on
until they came to an opening in the thick brush.

Here a body was lying,
head and shoulders covered with a coarse cloth
that had been white
and was now bloody.
Francisco knew the sandals and pantaloons as Pedro's.

Beside the body was a spade and an iron bar.
Juan pointed to the tools and told Francisco to dig the grave;
and Francisco loosened the earth with the bar
while Juan's brother threw out the dirt with the spade.
They dug a hole about a foot deep
and Juan and his brother lifted the body
and placed it in the hole.
Francisco then covered the body with earth,
filling the grave;
and the three returned to where they had left the horses.

As they rode away, they met the father of the brothers on horseback,
wearing a pistol,
and he said to Juan, "Have you finished the job?"
"Yes," said Juan. Then Juan's father turned to Francisco
and placing a hand upon his pistol said:
"Be very careful about this.
If anything of this becomes known,
I or my boys will hurt you."

X

The weather had been the coldest in years;
it snowed during the day
and the ground was covered with ice and snow.
The town prison was only a small room
and several panes in the three windows were broken.
There was a stove next to a window
and an officer put in a little coal at nine that evening
but the fire went out.

He was put in the cell at twilight.
The floor was zinc and because of a leak in a water-pipe
had been covered with water and this had frozen.
The cell had a bunk for sleeping
and a dirty shuck mattress;
there was only one blanket
and that wet and dirty.

XI
SOUNDS AND SMELLS

1

For about fifteen years Mr. Bishop had lived with his family in a house
      on half an acre of ground—
a cottage with seven rooms,
trees in the yard and shrubbery.
When his neighbor began to build near Mr. Bishop's front door
he had a talk with Mr. Balch:
Mrs. Bishop was uneasy about what Mr. Balch was building
and Mr. Bishop asked him not to build a barn
so near the front of his house,
and Mr. Balch assured him he would not;
he would not treat a neighbor like that.

When Mr. Balch actually began to build a barn,
Mr. Bishop spoke to him again,

and Mr. Balch assured him that he was only building a small barn
for the use of his own family.
But when the barn was built, barn and lot covered about a fourth
of an acre
and Mr. Balch kept quite a number of cattle there,
as well as two or three horses—a stud horse—some hogs, a bull and
a boar, and a number of dogs;
and the stench!

Mr. Bishop went to him again and asked him to remove his cattle
and Mr. Balch said he would shortly:

he was only keeping the cattle there for a while
to please his wife to whom they belonged.
But he did not remove the cattle—
eighteen to twenty-five head of Jersey cows—
and younger cattle, and a Jersey bull, a stallion, some hogs and the boar;
and sold milk and butter all over town;
and people were bringing their cows, mares, and sows
and breeding them to the bull, stallion or boar;
the stallion squealed, the bull roared, and the dogs kept barking all
night.

2

The ice company owned a lot next to his home
and built a stable and wagon shed
for the wagons and horses.
He could not raise his windows at all
in hot weather or when the weather was damp
because of the stench from the stable;
at night the horses would run around the lot
and get into the feed house—
it had a wooden flooring—
and when chased out by the stable boys
made a lot of noise;
and the stable boys, too, when feeding the horses
hallooed at them.

The wagons in hot weather would begin to leave at three in the
     morning
and the drivers would be cursing and swearing
and singing "vulgar" songs.

THE NORTH

1

The road ran beside the river
and, because the ground was low and flat,
at times it was flooded.
For several days the weather had been warm—
raining at times
until the water was running over the road.
That morning it began to freeze.

When the driver reached this piece of ground
ice, two or three inches thick, was on it.
As the horses went on,
they would break through the ice;
and, after going several wagon lengths,
the water was up to their knees;
just before reaching the washout
the team hesitated and stopped.
The driver whipped them on
and they stepped into the hole, two or three feet deep,
reared upon the ice with their fore feet—
the ice held for a moment—
then one of the horses slipped,
fell and was drowned.

2

The ice company was cutting and removing into its ice-houses
the ice on the lake; they had hired an extra span of horses
and the driver drove them upon the ice
to use in scraping away the snow.
As he was hitching them to a scraper
they were frightened—
perhaps by the noise of the other scrapers:

became frantic
and tried to run away.
The driver was at their heads
trying to hold them
but they reared and plunged

and, after moving away a hundred or two hundred feet,
reached a place where the ice was thin:
here it had been cut and removed
and two or three inches of ice had formed again
but the fall of snow had covered the lake,
and the line between thin ice and thick was no longer to be seen;
and the horses broke through the thin ice
into deep water
and were drowned.

3

He was driving a bunch of horses and mules
along the highway; shortly before he reached the railroad crossing
he "slacked up"
and walked the horse he was riding
to see if any train was coming;
looked two or three times each way
and could not see or hear any.
Before crossing the highway,

the railroad ran for some distance through a deep cut
and a train, while in the cut, could not be seen
from the highway;
and the noise made by the trotting horses and mules
kept him from hearing it.

The head horse was just about to step upon the track
and the others—horses and mules—were strung out behind her,
when for the first time he heard
the engine's whistle

and the train was coming down on the horses and mules—
but no man on earth could have stopped them then.

4

While the services were going on,
some boys were talking about buying "hot drops"
and putting them on a dog waiting at the door
but they did not have the money;
and Mr. Crouch suggested that they go to a little store nearby
and have the purchase charged to him.

The dog darted into the church,
barking and yelping and scraping himself on the floor;
some of the women and children were so frightened
they got up on the benches
to keep out of his way.

Mr. Crouch explained to the judge afterwards
that he did not intend to disturb the congregation,
but the judge held that though the dog was expected to remain during
    the services
he could hardly be expected, under the circumstances,
to wait until after the benediction.

II
SOCIAL LIFE

1

They were coming back from a "church sociable"—
Mary, Jessie, and young Butler. The young man was driving.
They had had a very good time,
and now it was almost midnight.
When the buggy came to the bridge—
only a single span of wooden planking over a small stream,

without any guard rails—
as the horse stepped on it,
Jessie, the younger sister, dropped her hat from the buggy.
At the end of the bridge was a high bank
with projecting rocks,
covered with bushes and briers;
and a spring ran over the rocks
in a waterfall.

Young Butler prudently drove over the bridge
and stopped about fifteen feet beyond the planking,
and then gave the lines to Mary,
who had some experience in driving,
and got down from the buggy and went back for the hat.
Just then the horse was frightened—
perhaps at the fluttering of birds in the briers
or at the noise of the waterfall in the night—
and backed the buggy to the bridge.
Mary tried to get him to go forward
and Butler ran up
and caught the horse by the head,
but they could not stop him from backing—
until the buggy went over the side of the bridge;
the girls fell backward,
the buggy on top of them,
and the horse partly on the buggy.

2

Scot, who worked on a farm near Rockville,
came into the waiting-room of the railway depot in the evening,
shortly after eight o'clock,
and was waiting for his employer's son to bring him some money.
There was a festival at a church not far from the depot
and Scot was dressed for it.

At first, he was the only person in the room
but soon three or four others entered—

some of the young people who lived in Rockville
would gather at the railway station in the evening—
and Scot, talking of someone they all knew,
said that the fellow told lies "on him,"
and that he could whip him and all his friends.

Hall, among those listening,
spoke up and said that their acquaintance had done nothing of the
    kind,
and, some further words passing between the two,
one of the group took Scot by the arm
and led him out of the door to the platform.

But Hall followed and, as he came out of the door,
said to Scot, "Now, if you want anything, you can get it right here."
The platform lamp hung between the window of the waiting-room and
    the door.
They began scuffling, Hall facing the depot building
and Scot with his back towards the window,
when a shot was fired
and the bullet entered the back of Scot's head.
His body fell forward on the rail of the track.

They carried the body into the waiting-room,
Scot's overcoat still buttoned up,
kid gloves on his hands,
and a flower in the buttonhole of his coat collar.

3
Lottie and a man who called himself Belton—
although that was not his name—
were living together in Sedalia.
Early one night, a young unmarried farmer who lived about ten miles
    from the city
and his cousin were walking along
when Lottie and another woman with her winked at them;
and the young men followed the women down the street.

They came to the house where Lottie lived
and she invited them in
but, as they were about to follow her,
Belton stepped in front of them
and said, "Stay away from my house or I'll fill you with lead!"
The farmer's cousin, who had been drinking too much, said:
"What have you got to do with it?"
and was about to go inside,
but the young farmer hesitated
and told his cousin they had better let the women alone.

But they did go in
and the farmer's cousin seated himself near a table in the center of the
        room,
and the young farmer sat on a trunk near a window.
Belton came in, soon afterwards,
and asked Lottie for his pistol.
She went to the trunk, got it, and handed it to him,
and saw that the farmer's cousin had his feet on the table.
She asked him to take them off
but he would not at first
and, when he finally did, stood up and looked at Lottie as if about to
        strike her.
Belton stepped between them
and struck him across the face with his pistol.

They began to fight
and the young farmer went to his cousin's side,
trying to get him to leave the house.
Belton fired two shots at them.
One struck the young farmer
and he ran a short distance from the house
and fell unconscious on the sidewalk.

4
She was about nineteen; had no settled home,
and most of the time worked for others as a servant.

When not at work she stayed with her stepmother.
Ned's father also made his home there
and he got her to say she would go to Ned's home—
about twenty miles out in the country—
to help in the house
while Ned's wife—any day now—would be in childbed.

Ned drove her to his house. He brought along a bottle of whiskey
and had given her a drink,
and she got to feeling pretty good.
When about two miles from the house
it had become dark
and he began to urge her to get out of the buggy with him
but she would not. "No, sir, I am not that kind!"
He answered that he was that kind who, when he went after anything,
was going to get it;
pulled her out of the buggy,
threw her on the ground,
and held her down so that she could not get up.
She fought pretty hard,
slapped him and bit him,
but, struggle all she could,
it did not help her.

She went on with him to his house—
what else could she do?—
and stayed about eleven days
and then told his wife's mother.

She could hardly expect help or any sympathy
at her stepmother's.

5
Emily, a little over sixteen years of age
and still wearing short dresses,
left home to visit relatives in another state.
In the evening, she changed trains in St. Louis

but the conductor of the train she had taken
told her it did not stop at the station she wanted
and that she would have to get off at the next stop
and take another train.

Weatherford went up to her while she was still on the train,
asked her where she was from and where she was going;
she told him, and then he told her that he lived where she would have
    to get off
and that he would see her to a hotel—
a good place to stop at for he took his breakfast and dinner there daily.

When she came to the hotel her eyes were red
as if she had been crying,
and she seemed nervous and excited.
The hotelkeeper showed her to a room
but she could not sleep
and went down to breakfast about seven o'clock.
She then asked the wife of the hotelkeeper to come to her room
because she wanted to talk to her,
and, in a short time, the hotelkeeper's wife, followed by the
    hotelkeeper,
went to her room.
They found her walking the floor,
crying and wringing her hands.

She told them that when she and Weatherford got off the train
he took her to the saloon where he was the bartender—
she thought at first it was a hotel—
but he locked the door, lit the lamp and turned it down.
She begged him to take her to a hotel,
cried out and hallooed;
but he took hold of her and told her she had better not make any noise,
stripped her and himself of their clothes, except their undergarments,
and forced her on to a blanket or quilt on the floor.
She struggled all she could, or all she dared,
but he had his way.
And he kept her in the saloon until about five in the morning;

then he took her part of the way to the hotel,
pointed it out and left her.
She let the hotelkeeper's wife look at her underclothing
and the hotelkeeper's wife saw a splotch of blood on the chemise
larger than her own hand.

Weatherford admitted that he got into conversation with the girl on
    the train
and she asked him where he lived and what business he was in.
He told her that he lived at the very place she was to change trains
and that he worked in a saloon.
She asked if there was a hotel in town
and he answered that there was one near the depot—
a good place to stop at for he himself boarded there.
She then told him that she had a toothache
and asked if he could get her some whiskey for it
when they reached the station. And he said he would.
They got off together
and he pointed out the hotel
and then she asked if he was not going to get the whiskey for her
and was it far to the saloon where he worked.
They went there and he lit the lamp,
and she walked right behind the counter
and set out a bottle and glasses just like a man.
She kept putting the whiskey in her mouth and spitting it out
and then stood at the counter a half hour and more talking to him
and told him she was a dressmaker, a cutter and fitter of dresses,
and asked him about the chance of getting work in town
and he gave her the name of a woman to whom she might apply
and she wanted him to write her if he found any place for her
and asked him to write down his name on a piece of paper
and he did—or he gave her his name and she wrote it down.

She then asked him when the train she was waiting for would be
    along,
and he told her in an hour or two;
and she said she would rather stay in the saloon than go to a hotel
and asked him to lock the door and turn down the lamp

for somebody, seeing the light, might want to come in.
He got her a chair and then sat down in another to get a little sleep,
but she set the basket she had with her in the chair he had brought her,
and sat down in his lap.
After about twenty minutes, he suggested there might be a better way
        to spend the time
and she agreed:

she took off some of her clothing
and he took off some of his
and they lay down together on a rug that was there.
Afterwards, she asked him if he could not get her a room
with a lock
so that he could sleep with her—if she did get work in town.
And, as they went towards the hotel,
she suggested that, since he would be recognized
and the landlord might "catch on and put her out,"
he had better go back. So he did.

6

John and Joe were boarders in the same boarding-house:
both about twenty-seven, Joe a powerful man
weighing more than two hundred pounds,
and John frail,
weighing about half as much.

On a cold Sunday in January, John was in the sitting-room of the
        boarding-house
waiting for dinner and reading,
when Joe came in from work. He greeted John good-naturedly with
        "Hello, Birdie!"
and John replied, just as good-naturedly it seemed, with "Hello, Fatty!"
As Joe passed John, he poked his cold fingers down the back of John's
        neck
and John, jumping up, punched Joe on the chest—
a feeble blow.

Joe took off his overcoat,
dropped it on the floor,
and taking John by the throat
backed him up against the wall of the room
and held him there a few seconds at arm's length,
and then left. But he came back
to pick up his overcoat and went out into the hallway again—
this led to the stairway and the floor above—
and left the door of the sitting-room open.

John, who had taken his seat,
jumped up and slammed the door shut.
Joe opened the door and said he wanted it open
to see his way, for the hall was dark
and the only light came from the sitting-room.
John answered, "I am not going to get cold for you,"
and slammed the door shut again.
Joe opened it again, and the two clinched
and struggled about the room,
Joe striking John in the face three or four times
with the back of his hand
until John's nose began to bleed.
One of the other boarders now spoke to them
and they separated, John went upstairs,
took his loaded revolver out of his dresser,
looked into Joe's room through the open door as he passed
and found Joe—his back towards John—in the little washroom off the
    kitchen
at the washbowl in the corner. "You boys have gone far enough,"
a woman boarder said to John in the kitchen,

"Don't go near him! Your face is all bloody!"
But John drew his revolver from his hip pocket
and fired shot after shot at Joe
until Joe staggered into the dining-room to die there.

7

Hyde and his family of six lived in a shanty
in the woods, half a mile from the highway;
the shanty had only one room,
and in this the family lived, ate, and slept
upon two or three straw ticks on the floor.

Sherry was living with the Hydes.
A farm laborer, he worked in the neighborhood
but had spent the day helping Hyde
in putting up a woodshed next to the house.
He was usually quiet and peaceable;
a syphilitic, however, and lots of times sick.
But Mike, the Indian, was strong and healthy;
from time to time he went about
in the business of bottoming chairs;
he was a visitor at Hyde's shanty.

Mike had spent the night there but was away all day
and had come back at dusk
and brought with him sausage and beef,
and Mrs. Hyde cooked some of it for his supper.
He invited Sherry to eat with him
and Sherry did; but he could never eat much, anyway.
After a while, Sherry suggested that since they had a visitor
they ought to have some beer,
and Hyde went to the neighboring village for it
and brought back two jugs of beer and two pints of whiskey.
In the meantime, Mike took a pint of alcohol
which he had brought with him
and mixing it with water, half and half,
put it into two pint bottles
and passed it around. When Hyde came back,
the beer was also passed around,
and then one of the pint bottles of whiskey;
all the grown-ups had some. Hyde played on his violin
and the others danced and jigged.

Mike danced a good deal with Gussie,
who was next to the oldest of the Hyde girls
and all of sixteen, and Sherry with Mrs. Hyde
and now and then with Gussie.
It was past ten when they were through dancing,
and Sherry in his shirt sleeves sat next to Mrs. Hyde
and watched Gussie on the other side of the room
and Mike at her side talking to her;
watched them and kept muttering to Mrs. Hyde
about "that black, damned Indian."
Suddenly he jumped up and crossing the room
to Mike, "What do you talk to her for?"
Mike answered, "Ain't I a right to talk to this little girl?"
"No, you ain't, you son of a bitch!"
And he struck at Mike with his fist.
Mike pushed him against the wall
and Sherry sprang at him again,
striking him several times about the body,
and then ran out of doors.

Mike staggered to a chair and sat down
but soon fell upon the floor.
Hyde tried to pick him up
and then saw that he was covered with blood:
Sherry had stabbed him six or seven times.

8

Klump, a German, in a saloon in St. Louis
called "The Tunnel House," frequented mostly by Negroes,
was playing pool
when Tompkins, a young Negro, came in
and Klump challenged him to play.
Tompkins said he had no money
but another Negro, who was watching,
"staked" Tompkins;
and Klump and Tompkins played several games,
Tompkins winning every one—

until the amount at stake was four dollars—
and the stakeholder paid it over to Tompkins.

Tompkins started to Leave. Klump went up to him
and, without a word,
slapped him
and knocked his hat off
and then Klump drew a pistol from his hip pocket.
Tompkins ran out of the rear door
into the alley,
and there asked a colored woman to go into the saloon
and get his hat.
Klump was kicking it over the floor.
He left the saloon and, turning a corner,
reached the alley
and there was Tompkins waiting for his hat.
Klump went towards him
and Tompkins ran past a small house
into a vacant lot
and back to the street.

A Negro woman had a room in the house
right on the alley;
she heard the noise of running feet
and went to the door.
Just then Klump came up to her and shouted, "Let me in!"
And she said, "What do you want?"
"I want that nigger!"
"There is no nigger here!"
He tried to push his way in
and she picked up a seashell from her bureau
and said, "I'll knock you in the head!"
Klump stepped back
and she quickly closed the door
but he drew his pistol, fired twice through the door,
and then, forcing the door open,
fired at her
and she fell, shot through the heart.

III

DOMESTIC SCENES

1

For the first seven or eight years of their married life
they were reasonably happy:
he kept a saloon and also served food—
his wife was in charge of this—
and the business prospered.
So much so that he gave it up
and went into selling liquor wholesale,
and this business, too, prospered.
But then he began to go with other women, loose women,
and even caught a disease one of them had;
and at home was always fault-finding,
dissatisfied with whatever his wife did—or cooked.
They always had wine or beer on the table, of course,
and now she took to drinking;
and they quarrelled more than ever.

One morning she went out marketing
and, on the way back, stepped into the store:
he was talking to a friend about a clerk he had sent away
and went on to say that early one morning,
while he was still in bed asleep,
his wife had been in the parlor with the clerk.
"It's a lie!" she cried. He struck her in the face with his newspaper,
and then with his straw hat;
and she struck back with a fish she had just bought
and then with the pocketbook she still held in her hand.
The steel clasp scratched his face and it began to bleed.

As she left the store,
he shouted after her that she should not come back
and his house was closed to her forever!
He went upstairs to the rooms where they lived
and gathered up all her clothing he could find
and cut and slashed it with knife and scissors.

2

She and Templeton had been engaged to be married.
She had been with child before by Templeton:
that had ended in a miscarriage.
Now she was with child again.
In the morning he called at the house
to bring back whatever he had belonging to her.
She met him at the front door
and asked him upstairs
and when he entered her room she asked him to sit down.
"No," he said, "anything you want to say to me
say it now."
She had a ring in her hand and said,
"Won't you take some little thing to remember me by?"
"No," he said.

She went to the drawer of her bureau
after "some little thing," he supposed,
and took out the revolver:
he had left it lying on the table some time before
and had forgotten to take it away.
She held it in both hands so that he could not see it
and put it against his belly and fired.
The next shot struck him in the back
just as he turned to leave the room,
and the third when he was standing at the foot of the stairs
trying to unfasten the front door.

3

Fredericks was a young man in his early twenties—a student in a
        medical school in St. Louis—
at the time of his marriage,
and his wife a schoolgirl about sixteen.
They lived with her sister
and his parents sent them money from time to time
to pay their board
but finally stopped;

and his brother-in-law, depending on wages for a living,
said that though he was willing to support his wife's sister and her
    child
he could not support him, too:
Fredericks had stopped being a student long before
and had never worked at a job.

One evening at supper time,
packing his valise to go to Chicago
to work there,
when his brother-in-law had gone upstairs with the newspaper,
Fredericks suddenly threw the valise into the yard,
struck his wife several times
until he knocked her down
and then kicked her in the head
so that blood spurted from the wound
spattering the wall and his wife's clothing
and left a scar she carried to her grave.

His wife found employment as a saleswoman in a department store
and began suit for a divorce.
After a while Fredericks was back in St. Louis.
He called at the store where his wife worked and asked her to drop the
    suit
and come and live with him again,
but she asked him where he wanted her to go
for he did not have—and never had—
a place for her and their child to live at
except at her sister's.

A couple of weeks later, he was in the store again.
She saw him coming
and asked a saleswoman working near her
where she could hide.

The saleswoman pointed to some curtains
and her husband—who did not see her—went down on the elevator.
But the saleswoman who had told her where to hide

was called away,
and Mrs. Fredericks who thought her husband had gone from the store
came from behind the curtains
and back to work.
In a few minutes her husband was on the floor again;
seeing his wife, he smiled, raised his hat and bowed,
and then walked up to where she stood behind the counter.
She asked him what he wanted
and they walked down to the end of the counter
talking quietly to each other—
she behind the counter and he on the other side.

When they reached the end
he drew a revolver and fired at her.
The bullet struck her,
she staggered and reeled;
he caught her by the shoulder and fired again.
Now she fell behind the counter
and he stepped around; leaning over her body
he fired three more bullets into her.
He then turned and walking up to the floor manager
told him calmly he had just killed his wife
and handed him the revolver.

4

Mrs. Faust, a widow, was living on a farm
a few miles from town; on a January night her house was in flames,
and the neighbors gathered quickly.
It was a small frame house of pine
and so quickly did it burn
one of the sides was soon gone and the inside of the house seen:
she was kneeling by the side of a bed—
or partly lying on it—
her hair burned away showing her head split open;
and the body of one of her little girls
was lying across the bed
with her head split open like her mother's.

Then the flooring gave way
and fell into the cellar.

It snowed that night, a heavy, clinging snow,
and the ground was covered to the depth of three or four inches;
then the sky cleared up
and the moon was shining.
Those who had gathered saw fresh tracks in the snow
where someone had gone from the house
to the hay piled up against the end of the barn.
The top of the pile was covered with snow
but had been turned back
and an armful of dry hay taken;
here and there straws of hay
showed that whoever it was had gone to the house with an armful
and under what had been the floor—
against the wall of the cellar—
hay was still burning.

The tracks also led from the farm over a fence
and four young men in the crowd
started at once to follow them:
through the underbrush of a wood pasture
and then through several farms
until they came to a road;
and across another farm and down to a creek
and then back to the road
and down the road until it turned
but, instead of turning with the road,
the trail led to the middle of the railroad track
and along the track
to the railroad yard in town.

Here two of the young men hurried to get the town marshal
and the other two followed the trail
as it ran alongside a line of freight cars standing in the yard;
and they saw a man running through the yard
among the freight cars.

Men working in the yard saw the young man climb a fence
into a lumberyard
and then leave the yard and go up the main street
into a hotel. When the town marshal went into his room
the young man had undressed
but was not yet in bed; his pants were wet above the knees
and so was the lower part of his overcoat
and the snow on his cap had not yet melted.
The marshal asked him to dress
and he asked, "What does all this mean?"
The marshal answered that a house with a woman and four
        children in it
had been burned,
and the young man said, "But I haven't been in the country tonight";
and the marshal said, "I didn't say the house was in the country."

The young man was Mrs. Faust's cousin
and had come into the neighborhood
and kept his trunk and clothing at her house;
at first he worked as a farm hand
but now was teaching in a country school.
Some time before the fire,
he and a friend were walking to Mrs. Faust's for dinner
and he told his friend that Mrs. Faust was "in the family way"
and that he was the father of the child.
She had been taking medicine
to cause an abortion
but it had failed to do so;
and, if she did not get rid of "the damned thing,"
he would:
he did not intend to have his reputation ruined.
After dinner, the young man and Mrs. Faust
went into another room
but his friend could hear them talking about the child she was with
and the young man angry and abusive.

5

A DIVORCE

He was a colored man, now twenty-nine years of age,
and his wife somewhat younger—
a hard-working laundress.
He had been apprenticed to learn the trade of a painter
but went north
before he had completed his term of service;
he was then about eighteen.
Both were born in Virginia
and had known each other from childhood.
For a year or so after they were married
they lived happily together;
but, after a while, he left her for the company of other women,
particularly a white woman known as "Dutch Maggie."
He was at Dutch Maggie's rooms often,
ate there and slept there,
and passed as her husband.
But he still lived largely upon his wife's earnings.

When his wife left for Virginia
for her sister's funeral
he was at his wife's seat in the railroad car
and asked her how she expected him to live while she was gone.
"I see that you don't care anything about me," he said,
"and I have a good mind to cut your throat
and send you to hell where your sister is."
On her return in about ten days,
he beat her with his fists,
blackened her eyes and bruised her face
so that she wore a veil to hide it,
and she left him to live with another sister in the city.

He stored his furniture
but had no money for the expressman
and handed his revolver—a six-shooter—
to a friend

and asked him to pawn it.
About a month later, he pawned his overcoat, too,
redeemed the revolver and bought some cartridges for it,
and went to the house where his wife was living.
"She's out at work," her sister said.
He answered that he would be back
and his wife would be sorry for everything she had done to him;
and in a few days he was back. When her sister came home,
she found the outer door shut
but not locked
and the rooms full of smoke from gunpowder.
His wife lay dead on the floor,
the body still warm and bleeding from bullet wounds;
at her side, the broken frame
in which she had kept her marriage certificate hanging on the wall
but the certificate itself was gone.

6

That Sunday, as always, he had come home from his store
about nine o'clock at night. His wife was not at home;
probably at her sister's with the children, he thought,
as he went into his wife's bedroom.
And, there upon a stand, he saw her pocketbook
partially opened. He could see a letter—
and read it. He had recognized the handwriting:
that of his bookkeeper, a neighbor and close friend
and a frequent guest at his home.

John was ten years younger, still unmarried,
and he had hired him when John lost his job as the village postmaster
because of politics.
The letter had no date. It began:
"My own precious darling, you ask if I miss you.
Yes, indeed, I do miss your sweet, smiling face.
I would like to have you with me just now
and your dear, sweet lips pressed to mine
for, well, just about an hour . . ."

7

A colored man and a white woman
were living as man and wife
in a room on the west side of New York.
He had been out of work for several months
but she was working as a waitress in a restaurant.
One morning, she told him that she was going to the theater that
      evening;
and in the evening he went down to the neighborhood of the
      restaurant
and waited on the other side of the street
until she came out. She went to a house nearby
and he followed her. In the vestibule
a white man was waiting
and the two hugged each other and went inside the house.

The colored man waited behind a lamp-post
the opposite side of the street
until, in about an hour and a half,
she came out of the house
and went to the avenue where she took a streetcar
going towards their home.
But he had no money for carfare
and walked home. When he got there,
he found her sitting in the kitchen with the landlady
waiting for him, for he had the key to their room.

In their room he said to her,
"I thought you were going to the theater."
"Well," she said, "I intended to go
  but I had so many people to wait on
  it kept me until after seven,
  and I could not go."
"You are a stinking liar!" he said.
"Is that what you are doing
  going around meeting men?"
"It is none of your damned business!" she cried.
"Stop this swearing in here," he said.

"It is bad enough for you to do wrong—
   leave me do the swearing."
   She went on: "I will go where I please,
   and meet whom I please!"
"You ought to be ashamed of yourself," he said.
"It is bad enough for us to be living together
   without being married." At that she struck at him
   and he choked her,
   put his hand around her throat and kept choking her for three
      or four minutes.
   Afterwards, he put a clean handkerchief in his pocket
   and came to the door of the kitchen
   where the landlady was now chatting with another tenant,
   and said that he wished to speak to her at the front door.
"What do you want to make me go downstairs for?" she asked,
   but she went down with him and he gave her the key to the room
      and said:
"I am sorry I am giving you the key this way.
   You have always treated me like a lady—
   and I appreciate you as such—
   but I am giving up my room:
   I think I have killed Kate and I am going to the station-house,"
   and with that he went out of the front door and was gone.

The woman the landlady had been chatting with
ran for a policeman. When he came,
he took a lamp and the key and went into the room:
sure enough, Kate was lying on the bed, dead,
dressed in her black skirt with a purple waist,
and a lavender ribbon around her neck.
The skirt was neatly spread out
and her clothing evenly arranged.
The pocket of her dress, however,
was wrong side out, and upon the floor was a penny.
Blood had trickled from the eardrums
and froth had come from her nose,
and her face was blue.

8

Jones had been blind for about a year.
He was a member of an association of locomotive engineers
that would pay three thousand dollars,
after one year,
for the total loss of a member's eyesight.
A year before, when alone in his bedroom with his wife,
a bullet fired from the outside
had passed through his head,
just back of his eyes,
and had blinded him.

His wife was much taken with one of her roomers
and spent much of her time with him
by day and at night:
gave him clothing—
and even the money with which to open a saloon
out of her husband's savings;
and, talking about the money to be paid her husband because of his blindness,
said that when she received it
she would leave him for the roomer.

Now she put some pills into a piece of lemon pie
which she served her husband
and when he complained that the pie was bitter and would not finish it
she fed it to him,
and then left the house with the roomer
to spend the evening.

Her husband became sick
and when his wife and the roomer were back, both drunk,
about midnight,
she filled a capsule from a box labeled "Rough on Rats"—
mostly arsenic—
and gave it to her husband.
When he felt much worse—he was dead by morning—
it was the roomer who went for a doctor,
but she followed him, overtook him, and got him to come back.

9

She had been his housekeeper for a few months
when he married her. His daughter was then fourteen
and she and the housekeeper had been getting along together
pleasantly enough,
but about a year after the marriage
they had become unfriendly to each other
and their quarrels frequent.
Once, when he came back unexpectedly
after leaving for his place of business,
he found his wife chasing his daughter from room to room,
and, when reproached, his wife said,
"You had better keep her out of my way
or I will do her up."
And, for a while, he boarded his daughter away from home.

On a Saturday morning, when his wife asked for her monthly
        allowance,
he would not give it to her; the next day she asked for it again
and again he refused.
On Monday she said to him: "I want my money! I am going
        downtown."
He kissed his daughter good-by and said good-by to his wife also
but did not kiss her. After he left, his wife went into the back parlor
where his daughter was sitting,
and his daughter said
that she was going away and this time would not return.
Her stepmother asked her if her father gave her any money that
        morning,
and she answered, "None of your business!"
Her stepmother then said, "When he gives you money,
he won't give me any,"
and her stepdaughter, picking up a cigarette box,
threw it at her and went upstairs.

A few minutes later, their servant in the backyard
heard a scream
and could not recognize the voice

except that it was a woman's.
She went into the kitchen,
then into the hall,
and opened the door to the stairway
and heard a door locked
and someone screaming on the third floor.
But the screaming stopped while she was listening
and she went back to her work
for there was the washing and the ironing to do.

Later that morning, her mistress called her
and told her that she was going to leave her husband
and would give up the house;
she paid the servant her wages, and five dollars besides,
because the servant had been given no notice;
and she asked the servant to mail a letter for her
and to leave the house that day, before her husband came home,
because she did not want him to ask the servant any questions.
In the letter to a neighbor and friend she had written:
"I make you a present of my rubber plant and bicycle."

Her husband came home after six
and as he was hanging up his hat and coat in the hallway
and was about to go into the back parlor
he heard a noise at the head of the stairs
and saw his wife coming down.
As he stood there, she struck him on the head with a hatchet she held
    in her hand
and struck him again on the side of his head.
He tried to reach the front door
and received a third blow on his hand:
But he did reach the door
and was helped to a neighbor's house
and from there to a hospital.

Those who entered the house, afterwards,
found his daughter in her room on the third floor
dead upon her bed.

Blood-stained mucus was oozing from the girl's mouth
and a little was upon the pillow:
she had been smothered.
Her eyes were partially open but discolored and flattened:
the pupils a darkish blue and the white of her eyes darkened
as if burnt.
Her stepmother had taken some acid in a white powder
and putting it in a glass of water
had gone to the door of her stepdaughter's room
and, after asking her why she was making so much trouble,
had thrown the acid into her face and eyes
blinding her.

The stepmother was found in the front room
lying upon the floor
and gas escaping into the room
from two burners she had torn down—
but she was alive.

10

Frieda was a milliner working in a store in town
and lived at the house of Dr. Douglas:
Mrs. Douglas and she were very friendly.

Dr. Douglas had a bottle of strychnine in a cabinet;
the cabinet was generally unlocked
but the bottle had a poison label on it,
and "strychnine" was printed on the label.
One day, Dr. Douglas took the bottle out of the cabinet
and, as Frieda and his ten-year-old son watched,
mixed strychnine and some cheese
to poison mice and rats in the house.

At the beginning of the year, Mrs. Douglas gave birth to a child
and was not in the best of health for some time—
and suddenly died in convulsions.

Frieda had been taking care of her before her death
and had given her medicine Dr. Douglas had prescribed.

Frieda would not go into the room where the corpse lay,
when the others did,
and said no money could get her to do it,
for the sight of a corpse made her deathly sick.
On the day of the funeral, she went to the church
but it was crowded
and she and others went into the parsonage until after the services.
When those who had come to the funeral
went up the aisle to look at the corpse
Frieda began to go with them
but was, indeed, taken sick and had to be helped out of the church.

After the funeral, Frieda continued to live in Dr. Douglas's house;
and now there was an old woman to take care of the baby.
Frieda told a friend that Mrs. Douglas had said
should she die, the Doctor would be paying attention to Frieda in two
        months
and would marry her in six.
But, after a while, Dr. Douglas began taking a girl called Gracie for buggy
        rides.
Gracie, a bookkeeper in a store, was in her early twenties;
in the best of health and always cheerful.
The Doctor and Gracie spent a lot of time together:
just then they were preparing the music for Christmas entertainments
at the Methodist and Baptist churches;
and, in the gossip of the town, it was said he would probably marry her.

Frieda got up a party at Dr. Douglas's for several young women
and invited Gracie and her sister;
bought oysters and oranges for the party—
and five cents worth of chocolate creams.
After the young women sat down to supper,
Frieda suddenly said she was sick and excused herself.
After a while, one of the young women went upstairs to see how Frieda
        was feeling

and as she stepped into the hall that led to Frieda's room
saw that the room was dark
but, by the light in the hall,
Frieda was walking about in her room;
and, when the young woman came near the door,
Frieda threw herself on the bed.
But the bed showed that she had not been lying down at all.
After a while, when most of the young women were gone,
Frieda came downstairs:
she found Gracie's sister in the kitchen helping the hired girl wash the
    dishes,
and Gracie and Dr. Douglas's little son in the parlor playing the organ
    and singing.
Gracie's sister asked Frieda how she was feeling
and Frieda said she was better,
but it was strange how many persons just then were having
    convulsions and dying—
persons who appeared to be perfectly well:
whatever it was, "the air was actually filled with it."

When Gracie and her sister left, Frieda helped them into their wraps,
and then took some chocolate creams
and, pouring the candy into her hand,
gave some to Gracie's sister,
and then poured out more of the chocolate creams
and gave these to Gracie.
After the girls left, Frieda went upstairs,
came down with a small package in her hand,
went to the stove and, lifting the lid,
dropped whatever she held into the fire;
then sat down at the table and had a hearty supper.

As Gracie and her sister were leaving the house,
Gracie ate one of the candies
and then another. It was bitter, she said.
In a few minutes, her legs were beginning to feel strange—
they had never felt like that before—
and then her arms, too, were feeling strange.

She could walk no farther
and fell down in the snow;
before long she had spasms and went into convulsions.

11

He had lived with his parents until he was forty
and, after he was old enough to work,
had worked for them in their business of market gardening
on their small tract of land;
he had no wages—
nothing but board and clothing for his work.
Two or three years before his father's death
he married
and brought his wife home to live with him,
but his mother and sister disliked her
and after that there was always wrangling in the house
until he and his wife left.

His parents had only two children
and his father would say
he would divide all that he had between his son and daughter
      equally—
just as he would cut an apple in half
and give a half to each.
Now his father was old and weak
and even childish and wandering in his conversation
and, his working days over,
would sit by the fire
or lie on the lounge.
Mother and son had a quarrel
that began about some boards he had taken for kindling
and, in the end, she went up to him,
shaking her finger in his face,
and saying: "I will fix you!
I will cut you off without a cent!
Just wait!
I will fix you!"

To her husband she said,
"The lawyer is coming tonight and the witnesses
and makes the will,
and you have to shut Mike out
and not give him a cent—
or I shut you out of the house
like I shut out Mike and his wife."
And he answered: "God damn it! Take it all—
but leave me rest!"
And that was the kind of a will he signed
a few days before his death:
all to his wife
and, if she died before he did,
all to his daughter—
and nothing to his son.

12

Perry was the city treasurer
and had just been elected auditor;
it was then discovered
that he had pocketed almost eight thousand dollars
of the city's money,
and his bondsmen were notified.
They were officers in three of the city's largest banks
and were willing to keep the matter secret,
provided, of course, they were not out of pocket.

His mother-in-law, a widow of seventy, had been left a farm by her
    husband—
it was worth, perhaps, five thousand dollars—
and it was all she had.
She had moved from the farm to the city
to be near her daughter; and now Perry came to see her
and begged her to mortgage the farm
to help him raise the money
or he would surely lose his job as auditor
and might, very likely, be sent to jail.

She was flustered
but told him stoutly
that she would not mortgage the farm:
it was all she had.

Perry's bondsmen were willing enough to get their banks
to take his notes
and lend him the money—
if secured by a deed of trust of the farm;
and he had the deed ready, drawn up and the notary waiting,
and came to her home again in the morning
to beg her to sign the deed.
He went into the sitting-room and waited
until she had cleared away the breakfast dishes;
and she could hear him walking up and down,
groaning.
When she came in, he fell on his knees before her
and took her hand
and begged her to save him from jail
and his family—and hers—from disgrace
by signing the deed of trust;
if not, he would cut his throat
and she would have to care for his wife and child.
"Harry," she said, "I cannot do it."

While they were still talking,
her daughter came in, excited and weeping,
and their little boy went up to his grandmother and said,
"Grandma, what will become of us?"
And she signed the deed.

13

They had a farm of almost two hundred acres:
a house with a cellar and tool-shed,
garden and fruit trees,
a horse, three cows and three sheep, and the chickens;
but neither was any longer able to take care of the farm.

Lear was seventy-three and his wife sixty-eight;
and he had sick spells
when he had to lie down on his hands and knees
until the spell passed,
and it left him weak.
So they gave the farm and all that went with it
by deed
to their son who was living with them
and he was to give them whatever they needed for the rest of their
        lives:
food and clothing and medical care,
plenty of firewood and water ready for use,
good flour, beef and pork, potatoes and oats and corn,
good coffee and granulated sugar—and at death a decent burial.
There was some talk of baking their bread, fixing the meals,
washing the clothes and scrubbing the floors;
but his mother said no: she would do it herself as long as she could.

Their son left them to care for themselves as best they might;
even when his mother was bedridden for weeks,
he never came into the room where she was sick,
although he was living in the same house;
never offered to do anything for her
or had anyone in to help her;
as far as she knew, never asked how she was.
And then in the spring of the year he married
and went to live on another farm.
They did not know that he was leaving
until they saw their son and daughter-in-law going away;
and since then there was no one in the house
but Lear and his wife.

O yes, their son gave them what they were to live on,
gave it regularly;
but when the pump at the well broke down and was taken away
they had to draw water themselves
with a rope and chain;
and he took away the firewood. There was quite a lot of it—

thirty wagon-boxes in the woodshed
and a large pile outside—
and some of it his father had cut himself.
Sometimes their son took it himself and sometimes sent his hired man
    for it,
and when his father asked, "What am I to have in the winter?"
he left about half a box—
as much as his father thought would last about a week.

14

The young man had been at work during the day
clearing land about their home:
it was a small, one-story log house
reached by a bypath from the road,
among some small jack pine and scrub oak brush.
The house was lighted by two small windows:
one on the north and one to the east.

His wife—a young woman of sixteen
who had been engaged to be married to a neighbor,
a man of sixty,
before she married Peter—
lighted the lamp
and spread a light meal on the table—
bread and milk. The meal over,
Peter took his accordion from the shelf
and sitting right opposite the window to the east
played "Home, Sweet Home."
He had just finished playing it
when a shot was fired from the outside.
Several buckshot pierced his head
and death was so sudden
he still sat upright in his chair
with the accordion in his hands.

15

Addison was a man of some importance in the city:
fifty-four years of age, a man of family and property,
and for years in the insurance and real estate business.
Annette was a married woman and a recent immigrant—
about thirty-five years old;
she had kept a saloon in the city she came from
next to a whore-house.

The first time Addison saw her she was at the house of one of her
    neighbors,
sitting on the steps of the porch, peeling apples,
and she greeted him warmly as if she knew him.
He sat down beside her. When he did, he brushed her thigh lightly
    with his hand without meaning to,
and she smiled and shook her head.

On a Monday he came to her house to get her husband—
who had asked him for work—
to help in digging a well.
She and her husband were in the kitchen
but she motioned her husband into the sitting-room
where he was eating his dinner, and she said to Addison
in her broken English,
"You come tomorrow."

Next morning Addison was at the house again.
He asked if her husband was at work and she said yes
but asked him in
and sat down in the rocking-chair in the kitchen
and went on mending stockings.
There was a low kitchen-chair in front of her
on which her foot rested,
and she motioned to Addison to take that chair.
He did—
and put his hand under her clothes upon her thigh.

She just sat there
and looked at him
and he took his hand away and sat back.
She then raised both her hands and began to scratch his face
and motioned for him to leave.
She followed him and picked up a stick of kindling wood
as he was getting into his buggy
as if to throw the stick at him;
and that day went before a justice and swore out a warrant for his
    arrest—
for assault with intent to commit rape.

In the evening he came to her house with a countryman of hers
to see if the matter could not be settled:
her husband wanted fifty dollars
but his wife said they would take twenty-five
and, finally, her husband agreed "to let it go for twenty."
Addison left the money on the trunk in the room
and she took it.

16

When his wife would get the house cleaned
and the floor freshly mopped,
he would go scuffling through the house
with dirty shoes; and once he emptied the teapot
upon the freshly-cleaned kitchen floor.
After he washed his hands and face,
he would wipe them upon the window curtains,
and more than once upon the freshly-washed white dress of his wife
as it hung to dry.

IV
CHILDREN

1

When Willie, Jenny's bastard, was about two years of age she married;
but Jenny and her husband were hopelessly poor
and, after a few years, parted.
She went to live in the house of a woman in Weybridge
and took the child to a home for destitute children in Burlington;
Willie was then eight.
After a few months, an officer of the home
had the child brought to the woman's house in Weybridge,
but she would not let Willie in
and he stayed on the doorstep for about two hours.

Then the woman brought the child—
across the bridge—
to the overseer of the poor in Middlebury.
By then it was three o'clock in the afternoon.
The overseer explained that the child was not for him to take care of,
but he would take it until the next day;
however, she did not return
and the overseer took Willie back to the woman's house—
and left him there.

2

The young man and his wife were separated
but they had a child—a daughter,
and the mother kept the child with her.
She found it hard to maintain the child and herself
and kept demanding that the father help in its support.
He was taken to court at last
and agreed to pay a small sum weekly,
and did for about ten weeks—
and then stopped.

His wife left the child with him
against his protests
at the livery stable where he worked;
and he took the little girl—then about four—
to his mother;
but she said she could not take care of her
because she herself was sick and too poor;
however, she added, he might leave the child for a while
until he found a place for it.

At the end of a month, his mother sent the child back to him at the
     livery stable
and with the child a small basket of her clothing.
The little girl remained at the livery stable all that day,
and the father tried to get someone to take her—
and could not.
He had no home other than the stable,
and here he slept
and got his meals where he could:
his work irregular and his wages uncertain.

He borrowed a horse and buggy from his employer,
for the purpose, he said, of taking the child home,
and drove away with the child
into the gathering darkness,
but he left the basket of clothes at the stable.
In less than an hour he was back—alone.

The next morning the child's hat was found on the bank of the river
about a mile from town,
on a path which led down to the bank
where there was an open space clear of underbrush.
The water here formed an eddy or pool
and was about ten feet deep;
and here, in the river, the child's body was also found.

3

The street ran beside the railroad tracks; a hundred trains and more
would pass the house daily.
The house itself was about a dozen feet back from the street,
with a high fence along the street and a gate
which she kept closed and fastened with a string.
Between the bottom of the gate and the ground
was a space—six to eight inches in width.

That day, after feeding her child, about a year and a half of age,
it was sleepy
and she left it on the floor,
put a chair across the door to the street
to keep the child from getting out,
and went into another room
to arrange the cradle and put the room somewhat to rights.

She took her time, since the child was quiet,
and came back in about ten minutes
to find the child gone.
She ran into the garden in back of the house
to look for the child:
here were weeds as high as the child
and she could not see him. Then she ran
to see if he had fallen into the cistern.
At that moment she heard the whistle of a locomotive
blown sharply twice—
looking up she saw a train coming up the street
and her baby crawling on the tracks.

4

The boy was only four years old
and his mother left him on the front doorstep
with his little sister; told them to stay there
and went into the house to do her washing.
The house was about two hundred feet from the railroad track

and the boy and his sister climbed the embankment
and the boy went upon the track.

A freight train had just broken apart
and the forward part of the train had gone by
leaving about thirty feet between the forward part
and the rear cars that followed.
The boy took off his hat and waved good-by
to the part of the train that had passed.
His sister called to him to come back
and he replied,
"Why the train has gone by!"

But he was run over by the cars that followed.

5

The railroad company was building a side track
beside its main track, and drawing sand and gravel to it.
In the morning the gravel train stopped in front of the house,
and the foreman took Tommy, all of seven,
to where the men were working;
and at noon Tommy went home with some of the men who boarded at
    his father's house.

The foreman told him to come back in the afternoon
and he would give him a ride.
He did go back and carried water for the men.
At three or four o'clock, as the foreman and Tommy were sitting on
    some ties
watching the men at work,
they saw a freight train coming down the main track.
Tommy said that he was hungry and wanted to go home.
The foreman said: "Here comes a freight train.
You can get on that.
It will go slow by the house and you can jump off."

When the train came alongside,
the foreman said to Tommy, "Get on the back car—the caboose."
He was then about ten feet from it.
He went over to the moving train
and got upon the gravel
which had just been thrown off from the gravel train
and was piled two feet high.
When the caboose came along,
he reached up to catch hold of it
but, reaching out,
the gravel slipped from under him
and he slid down
between the moving wheels.

6

She was married to a Chinese laundryman.
As she and her husband were ironing—
her husband on one side of the store
and she on the other—
Joey looked in;
and she came to the door, holding her hands behind her,
shouting, "You will look in here, will you!"
And dashed the contents of a bowl into the boy's face.
The child began to scream with pain
and was led home by a passer-by,
wailing.

Both his eyes were burned,
and so was the skin of his face and lips;
his clothing discolored
and smelling of lye.
His mother came to the laundry
and shouted, "Why did you do that to my poor little boy?"
And the wife of the laundryman answered: "Yes, I done it,
and will do it again if I have a chance.
I will make them keep away from my door!"

The boy's eyes ulcerated,
burst and sloughed away,
and the lids grew together on what was left of the eyeballs.

7

He was thirteen years old and at work in a sawmill:
they gave him a pike six feet long with a hook on it
and stationed him near the chute that led from the floor above
to keep the slabs of wood from clogging,
but he had trouble reaching them;
so they built him a platform
four feet above the floor
and put him on it.

Now he was near the revolving shaft
that turned about a hundred times and more a minute,
and, sometimes, to amuse himself,
he would throw a string at it
to see the string winding quickly around the shaft.
But the foreman caught him
and told him angrily to keep away from the shaft,
for if his clothes were caught on it
it would wind him up.

Sure enough, one day, when the angling slabs were badly clogged in
        the chute,
he stuck his pole into them to clear it,
and a slab coming down
pushed the end of the pole against his chest
and would have shoved him backwards off the platform;
to save himself he clutched at the whirling shaft—
and in no time his arm was wrapped around it
and he was flung into the air,
and then his body was lying on the floor
with his arm torn off
and still wrapped around the whirling shaft.

8

Jews were living nearby
and their children passed her house
on their way to and from school.
She had a large dog
and her son of seventeen
would set the dog upon the little "sheenies."
Some of the children
went to another neighbor—not a Jew—
to complain.

He told them to go along on the other side of the road
and mind their own business
and he would see to it that they got through safely.
As they came near her house
the dog ran out barking;
and the man picked up the branch of a tree,
broke it over his knee,
and ran to protect the children.
He tried to reach the dog before it reached the house
and then went right into the house without knocking,
stick in hand,
to protest this treatment of the children.
But the woman of the house pushed him out
and let him know her mind plainly,
calling him a "sheeny" too.

V

NEGROES

1

Benton bought two tickets for seats in the orchestra of a theater in
     Kansas City
and he and his companion, a colored woman, went to the orchestra
     floor,
where he gave the stubs to an usher,

and the three started towards the seats.
On the way, the usher was met by another usher
and the two talked in whispers—
Benton overheard the word "nigger"—
and then one of the ushers told him he could not have the seats called
     for by the tickets:
there had been a mistake.

The usher was going to seat Benton and his companion in the balcony
but Benton refused to follow him,
and went to the box-office instead
where he showed the stubs to the man who had sold him the tickets
and asked why he could not have the seats.
The man said angrily, "Of course, you can!"
and then looked at Benton again
and must have discovered, to use Benton's words,
"that drop of African blood" in him
and said: "It is a mistake. Those seats are occupied."
He offered to give him seats in the balcony instead
but Benton refused them
and with his companion left the theater.

The court held that Benton had no right to sit in the orchestra:
why, white persons at a place of amusement
especially for the colored
might very well be required to occupy separate seats!

2

About six months before, Fan had a room at the house of Rose's
     mother;
now she was working and living at Mrs. Cobb's.
Rose came there about six in the morning
and called to Fan. She was asleep
but woke up and looked out of the window
and Rose asked her to come out.
She put on her clothes, slipped on her shoes, and did so,

closing the door behind her.
The door locked as it closed.

Rose asked her to walk with her,
for she didn't want the white folks to hear
what she had to say.
They went about half a block and then Rose said:
"I heard you said I stole a trunk full of fine clothes from you.
You exposed my name!"
Fan answered that she had no fine clothes
but did have a trunk of good clothes, and added:
"You know they were mine!
But there's no use to fuss about them."

They sat down at the door of one of the houses on the block
and went on talking.
Rose then said she heard that Fan had said
a bracelet Rose's sister was wearing
was Fan's,
and that Fan was going to take it off.
"I am going to wear the bracelet to the Indian show tonight,"
Rose added. "Come and get it!"
Fan replied, "If you wear it,
I'll come and get it."

Nothing more was said by either,
and Fan sat there with her hand on her jaw.
Suddenly Rose cut her in the face with a razor.
Fan threw up her hand and Rose cut one of her fingers off,
and began cutting her on her shoulders and arms
and in the face.

3

Amy and Ella, Negro women, were both in love with Seth,
a young Negro who worked as a porter in a saloon.
On a night in May, Seth and Ella had been to a Negro dance
and, on their way to Ella's home,

were met by Amy.
She went up to Seth and wanted to know where he had been.
Ella spoke up and said, "Is you and Seth married?"
And Amy struck her.
She ran across the street and into an alley
and Seth caught hold of Amy
and held her—
until he thought Ella had been gone long enough
to be out of danger.
Then he turned Amy loose
and went towards the saloon where he was working—
and heard Ella screaming,
"Seth she is cutting me!"
He ran into the alley and found Amy on top of Ella,
knife in hand and stabbing her again and again,
saying, "I got you now for going with my Seth!"

4

Molly, a Negro woman, about thirty-five years of age,
made her living by taking in washing.
Steve, a Negro, wanted her to marry him
but she would not because he was quarrelsome;
and, to get rid of him,
made up her mind to leave the state and go back to her mother.
All day Saturday and most of Sunday they had been quarreling
and late Sunday afternoon, just before dusk,
she left to bring the clothing of a woman for whom she did washing.
She took the bundle of clothes and started on her way home
but her dead body was found near the old baseball grounds,
and a man who lived near there
had heard a woman screaming
and, after a while, groans.
Near the body was the bundle of clothing Molly had taken;
near her also a bloody brick,
and a pipe and a pocketknife—now bloody—which belonged to Steve.
One side of her head had been beaten in,
and there were sign of a scuffle where the brick was found.

Steve had now and then gone with her for the washing
and knew the way she usually took.
Bloody water was found in the bucket in their room
and blood was spattered over the shoes he had worn Sunday night
and on the edges of his undershirt.
In a stove in the room were the burnt remains of a bloody towel,
and in the trunk the pants he had on Sunday night,
and on the pants blood marks that looked as if they had been rubbed
      with a wet cloth.

When arrested, he said he had been staying up with a sick woman
      Sunday night praying
and to another policeman he said he had been to a prayer meeting at
      church,
and to explain the blood on his clothes
said part of a house had fallen on a man and a horse and he had tried to
      help them.
But nobody had seen him at church or at the place where the house
      had fallen.

5

In the evening, a large crowd, mostly Negroes,
gathered in front of a saloon in St. Louis,
blocking the sidewalk,
to witness the sparring
between Jeff Trenton, who kept a barbershop next to the saloon,
and another Negro barber. A policeman
pushed his way through the crowd
and ordered them to move on,
and those who were sparring to stop.
He said to Jeff, "Go where you work!"
But the barber turned to the policeman,
fists lifted.

The policeman repeated what he had said
and added, "If you don't, I'll have to take you away!"
At this the crowd began closing in on them

and the policeman put his hand on the barber's arm;
Jeff's brother, Jimmy, struck the policeman a blow in the eye
and the two brothers, helped by others, set upon him.
There were cries in the crowd of "Let's kill the son of a bitch!"
The policeman was hustled through the crowd,
struck and kicked again and again;
finally, his club was twisted from him
and the two brothers took turns beating him over the head with it
until he was left lying in the gutter.

The policeman came to, took out his pistol
and fired twice in the air
to get the help of other policemen on the same beat;
and Jeff Trenton ran into the saloon.
The policeman followed but, still weak,
was unable to open the door. Someone did that for him
and he went in.
Jeff was in the billiard-room in back:
this was six or seven feet higher than the bar-room floor
and reached by two short stairways on either side.
The policeman, his pistol in his hand
pointing it at Jeff, went up the stairs nearest the barber
and said "I want you!" The barber started to go with him
but when they had nearly reached the stairway
they heard a cry, "Don't shoot!"
The policeman turning his head at the cry
was struck on the head by a billiard cue
with such force that it knocked his hat off
and sent him reeling, bleeding from a gash over his eye—
and the barber was gone.

The blow was struck by Jeff's brother, Jimmy,
whom the policeman had not seen on the platform.
Now Jimmy sprang forward
and twisting the pistol out of the policeman's hand
ran across the platform
and down the other flight of stairs.
Just then, two policemen who had heard the shots

came into the saloon
and saw the first policeman staggering down the stairs,
his hat off
and blood streaming from his forehead down his face.

The owner of the saloon, also a Negro, standing near Jimmy,
pointed him out and cried, "Here is the man who did it!"

At that, while one of the two policemen who had just come in
was trying to keep Jimmy from darting behind the saloon's counter,
the other policeman hurried across the saloon and called out,
"Throw up your hands! You are my prisoner!"
Jimmy Trenton replied, "Yes?"
And fired a shot at the policeman coming towards him
and another at the policeman trying to head him off.
Neither policeman had drawn his pistol
and Jimmy managed to run behind the heavy counter
and crouch beneath it.

Both policemen now went up to the counter,
pistols drawn. Jimmy sprang up
and shot at them,
and crouched again behind the counter.
A fourth policeman was now in the saloon.
He went towards the counter; leaning over
he fired a shot at Jimmy—
only his legs and feet were to be seen.
Jimmy sprang up again and shot him
and the policeman fell over—dead.
At the same time, both the other policemen who had come in to help
    the first
fired at Jimmy,
wounding him slightly in the side,
and he dropped behind the counter again.

While the two policemen were looking after the dead man,
one of them saw Jimmy trying to slip around the counter,

pistol in hand. The policeman covered him at once with his own pistol
        and said:
"Make a move with that gun and I'll kill you!
 Stop where you are!"
Jimmy Trenton threw the pistol, all its chambers now empty,
 behind the counter and let the police arrest him.

VI
PROPERTY

1

Mrs. Boon was more than ninety years old
and lay dying:
the doctors had given her up and were giving her opium
to ease her pain.
She owned two buildings in Bridgeton—
one a double house—
and her estate would be worth at least a couple of thousand dollars,
perhaps as much as five thousand.

Her husband—her second husband—was almost eighty
and her next of kin was an only brother, about her husband's age.
This brother had a son, Ethan, who was now forty.
He was an only child. Mrs. Boon had taken him into her home
treating him as though he were her own child,
but when he was sixteen or seventeen they quarreled
and afterwards met seldom.
Her brother who had moved into her house and helped the neighbors
        nurse her
would talk to her—when he had the chance—about her property and
        to whom she should leave it,
urging his own claim. Her husband once became so angry at him
they came to blows in the bedroom of the sick woman.

She had made several wills but now she sent for her lawyer
and told him she had been bothered a good deal about how to leave her
       property—
now one side at her, now the other—
and she wanted to make a will that would satisfy everybody,
and have the thing over with:
she wanted to leave her husband and brother everything
in shares as nearly equal as possible;
her husband had been a good husband to her,
and yet her brother was poor and old and ought to be taken care of.
Her nephew, Ethan, should get nothing,
because when his father died he would get his father's share;
and all she cared for with regard to Ethan was that he should be well
but she would leave him nothing.

Ethan lived in Philadelphia and, a few days before his aunt died,
came to Bridgeton. A neighbor was taking care of Mrs. Boon that
       evening
and told her that her nephew had come to visit her;
she replied drowsily—for now she was almost always under the
       influence of opium—
that she would like to see him
but was too sleepy to talk . . .
Would the neighbor give him a cup of coffee
and make him a bed on the sofa
so that she could talk to him later?

About three in the morning—in the stillness of the night—
she was awake and sent for him.
She asked him to sit by her bed and, taking his hand,
asked him why he had not been to see her before this.
He answered that he thought it was better for him to stay away and
       not worry her.
She said that she was glad he had come
and she wanted him to see about her burial:
she wanted to be buried in the old Presbyterian graveyard
beside her brother, Joseph;

she had been to the graveyard and there was room for her grave beside
    Joseph's.
And then she and Ethan spoke about the undertaker she wanted and
    her tombstone.
But, Ethan said, he could do nothing unless he had "something to
    show" that he had a right to,
and she told him to draw up whatever was necessary and she would
    sign it:
"I may not be able to sit up but I can make my mark."

Later, that very day, Ethan found a lawyer
to draw up a will for his aunt—so he said—
by which she left him everything,
except twenty-five dollars each for her husband and brother,
and with two men as witnesses
Ethan came into her room that evening.
Her husband and brother had gone to bed
and only a neighbor was with her.
Mrs. Boon was roused and exclaimed,
"What does this mean?" And Ethan answered,
"Here are the papers to sign,"
and began to talk to her about burial by a big tree in the graveyard.
She said, "If I am going to sign any papers, I want to do it now,"
and a pen was held for her as she lay upon the bed.
She could hardly make her mark
and then sank back drowsily. In a few days she was dead.

2

Duncan was a native of Scotland; a stonecutter by trade
and by religion a Protestant.
Years before his death, he had warned his niece, Mary,
that if she ever married a Catholic
he would not leave her any of his money.
She did not listen to him and was heard to say,
"I would not give up my Catholic husband
for all my uncle's boodle."

The very month Duncan made his will and died,
his nephew, Mary's brother, wrote him:
"I write a few words to let you know that Mother
is very sick: she had a stroke and has not been conscious yet.
And what do you think? Mary wanted to bring a priest in,
but I soon let her know no Catholic need apply."

His uncle answered: "I heard of your mother's sickness
and I hope that whatever is best for her
God in his goodness will give her.
Mary and her wooden gods don't count for much.
If you will be a steady man
and not give your hard work to the taverns,
I will try to make your labor lighter.
I hope no Peter pence
shall ever come out of my labors.
Johnny, I am a very sick man
and can scarcely walk across the floor of my room,
but the doctor says he thinks I will get better."

In a few days, his nephew wrote him again:
"Mother died at 7:30 Sunday morning.
She never did come to herself.
She tried very hard to say something,
but it was too late.
It looks at her house like an Irish wake;
all is needed are pipes and toddy.
I am very sorry to know you are so sick.
I wish you were better,
and if you ever need me I would come."

That John's sister wanted to bring a priest to her dying mother
was untrue: Mary had sent for a Protestant minister—
and John was not even present;
and there was nothing like an "Irish wake" after his mother's death:
whatever liquor was drunk
was by John himself and a man who had been a boarder in the house.
His uncle's will left half his money to John

but made no mention of Mary,
and when the scrivener called his attention to his niece,
Duncan merely said,
"She has a husband who will look out for her."

3

Kelly, by trade a steam-and-gas fitter,
worked as a common laborer in St. Louis,
saving from his earnings
until he was able to send for his wife and children;
and now they were on their way north on a steamboat.
He was living in a cheap lodging-house
where he paid a dollar a week for his room;
and he had forty-one dollars—
a new ten-dollar bill, five five-dollar bills, and six dollar bills—
which he carried about with him in a small tobacco pouch
in his inside vest pocket.
Casey, Powers, and the two O'Neills—
laughing and drinking together—
lodged in the same house on the floor above,
and each paid ten cents a night for his lodging.

On a Sunday afternoon, Kelly went to the water-closet on the second floor
and while there took out the pouch and was counting his money.
The door was slightly ajar
and he looked up to see Casey watching him.
"Quite a nice roll you have," Casey said.
The evening before, because Kelly did not want to break a bill,
he had been asking two or three of the lodgers
for the loan of a quarter
to get his wash from the laundry.
Surprised and somewhat alarmed, Kelly replied,
"Only a few pennies I have been saving,"
and put the money back at once into his pouch and pocket.

Afterwards, as Kelly was going to his room,
the two O'Neills grabbed him around the neck and shoulders,

Powers caught him by the legs,
and Casey was striking him on the head with a loose banister
	or bed-slat.
Kelly, dazed and bleeding, was thrown down,
and in the scrimmage
Casey ran his hand into Kelly's vest-pocket
and took the money.

4
It had been drizzling all afternoon
but by eight o'clock it was clear:
the streets, however, were still wet and muddy.
At the entrance to the driveway
leading to a stable in back of a house
was a swinging electric light,
and there was another electric light in the street—
strong and brilliant.
Baldwin, a live-stock commission merchant—
somewhat too fat—was on his way home.
He had two hundred dollars or so with him,
and in his vest-pocket
a gold watch with the likeness of his little dead son.

Three Negro women were also going home
along the street:
two of them servants who lived with the families for whom they
	worked,
and now returning from church together,
and Flo walking home alone.
The women saw three men come up to Baldwin,
heard something or other said,
and then saw the four of them tussling:
the three men getting Baldwin against the hitching-post near the
	entrance to the driveway,
hitting and kicking him, jerking him around,
and one of them grabbing him by the throat and choking him

until Baldwin was gurgling; and then they pulled him into the
    driveway
and he fell to the pavement.

The tallest of the three got on Baldwin with his knees
and was going through Baldwin's pockets;
and one of the other two went to the sidewalk and, looking around,
saw the colored women watching: "Get away from here!
What do you damned nigger bitches want, raising an excitement?
It's only a friend of ours,
and we are trying to get him away from the collars."
"It's no such thing," said Flo,
"that man there knocked him down!"
The second man rushed his hand into Baldwin's vest-pocket,
pulled out the watch and said, "Come on, let's go!
The collars will have us in a minute.
Let's go!"
The last to leave was the man who had been kneeling on Baldwin
and before he left gave him a farewell kick in the belly:
to one of the women it sounded like the slosh of water
in a slop-barrel on a wagon going down the street.
And the three men ran around a cable-car that was coming down.

Flo ran up to a man walking along the street calmly
and cried, "Those three men were beating this man to death!"
Baldwin tried to get up
but he was so weak he could hardly get his hand up.
"Oh," the man heard him say,
"they have my watch with my dead boy's picture in it."

5
Gladstone was not married
and lived by himself on a small farm
about a quarter of a mile from where Jim Parsons lived.
Hazel was Ray's sister-in-law
and Ray and his bride—they had been married five days—and his
    sister-in-law

were at Jim Parson's house that evening.
Another visitor
saw in Parson's house—
on the mantelpiece beside the clock—
a revolver.

As the family and their guests—
except Ray and his sister-in-law, Hazel—
were eating supper in the kitchen,
Hazel came to the door
and asked Ray's wife for her cloak, adding,
"You know what I mean."
The rest kept on eating
until they heard a shot and after that screams
which the young man who had seen the revolver on the mantelpiece
took to be an owl hooting in the woods.
"No," said another at the table, "someone's shot,"
and at that all jumped up.

The young man grabbed his rifle
which he had left on the bed
and said to someone, "Get that revolver!"
But the young man he spoke to said, "It isn't there."
When they got out,
the yelling and hallooing had stopped
and the night was quiet.

They went towards where the sound of the shot had come from
and met Hazel coming towards them.
There were others in the neighborhood
and they had also heard the shot and cries.
Webb, who lived nearest Gladstone's house,
went out
and stood at the gate,
and heard someone running and hallooing, "Webb, help me!"
It was Gladstone.
"He has killed me!" Gladstone said, out of breath.
"Ray Dexter shot me!"

Gladstone fell to the ground
and Webb helped him up
and brought him into his own house.
Gladstone sank to the floor
and Webb helped him on the bed.

"I was coming with a load of corn," said Gladstone,
"when the horses looked south:
 they had seen something in the brush
 and were kind of scared like.
 Ray stepped out of the bushes
 in front of the wagon
 and spoke to me. I knew his voice
 but I kept the horses moving along.
 And Ray said, 'Stop, Nat!
 You don't want to go home now.'
 'Yes,' I said, 'I must go on;
 I'm in a hurry.'
 Ray kept moving along with the horses and said,
 'Jim Parsons and the boys and Hazel is down there;
 they are going to rob you and kill you for your money.'
 I spoke to the horses and they stopped after maybe a step or two.
 'Why,' I says, 'you are joking;
 me and Jim Parsons has always been good friends.'
 'Well,' says Ray, 'they are going to kill you.
 Come here in the brush
 and I'll tell you something.'
 'Ray,' I says, 'I have been a good friend of yours,
 and loaned you money and let you have my team;
 loan me your revolver.'
 'I haven't got no revolver with me,' he says,
 and then jerked it out.
 He pointed it up—shoved it in my face—and I saw it glitter.
 I grabbed at it, held on to the muzzle,
 and pushed it down.
 Ray said, 'It's your money I want, damn you!'
 And I said, 'I haven't got none, Ray.'
 'Yes, you have,' he said, 'damn you!'

I held on to the revolver
but Ray was stronger
and pulled me off the wagon.
When I struck the ground
I fell on my knees
and I got up running;
but when I got about ten steps
the bullet struck me in the back.
He ran after me
and tried to shoot me again,
and I kept on running.
Then he turned away
and I ran towards my house.
And there was Hazel standing close to the hen house.
She asked me where I was going
and what was the matter
and said, 'Come here!'
But I feared she would hold me until Ray came
and he would kill me;
so I run on past to your house."

Webb said, "Nat,
I think you are scared worse than hurt."
"No," said Gladstone, "he has killed me.
Ray Dexter killed me!"
And he lingered a day or two—
and died.

6

Earl was about twenty-one;
his left hand had been caught in a cotton gin:
three fingers and the thumb were gone,
and only a stub of the forefinger remained;
the rest of the hand was mangled and useless.
With two other young men he left his home in Arkansas
to canvass in southwest Missouri
for a family photograph-album issued in Chicago.

Each had his own outfit—a horse, a cart, and samples.
The young men met with indifferent success.
The other two went to work on farms
but Earl, unable to do farm work,
kept on canvassing
but still with little success.
He decided at last to make his way home.

Jerry was about the same age as Earl,
taller and with a swarthy complexion.
He had worked in mines in Kansas and had left Ft. Scott afoot,
explaining to an acquaintance at whose house he stopped
that he had had a "difficulty" with some "niggers" in Ft. Scott
and was now getting over into Missouri.
Earl and Jerry met somewhere and went on together,
Jerry riding in the cart with Earl,
a borrowed pistol sticking out of his pocket.

They drove into the town of Arcadia together.
Earl went into a bakery and told the baker
where he was going,
showed his crippled hand and said he was out of money
and asked for some bread.
The baker gave it to him.
Jerry went into another store at the same time
and asked for crackers;
gave a false name
and said his father living nearby would pay for the crackers in the
    morning
and explained that he had been in Ft. Scott
and had been on a "spree" and was "strapped."
The storekeeper did not know his "father"
but gave him some crackers, anyway, in a paper sack.

Some time after dark, Earl and Jerry left Arcadia together in the cart.
Later, they were seen trying to read a signboard by lighted matches
and a man came up with a lantern
and held it up for them to read by.

They asked their way of him
and he told them there were two roads—
one the main-traveled road and another,
a little nearer but rough
leading through a creek bottom and not much traveled.

About sunrise, next morning,
some teamsters driving along the road that led through the creek
    bottom
found Earl's dead body by the roadside
"just as if he had been asleep."
His head was lying on a bunch of hay,
a bullet wound in his right temple,
and the hair and skin powder-burnt,
showing that the bullet had been fired at close range.
There was no sign of a struggle
but his companion and his horse, his cart and valise were gone.

7

Ann was a widow, about seventy or eighty years of age,
with a passion for gold coin
which she kept in a wardrobe and would not spend
or deposit in a bank.
One morning in December, she was found dead,
hands lifted, the mark of a blow on her face,
her throat cut
and her money gone.
Blake lived in a room next to Ann's sitting-room,
separated from it by a partition
with a glass door. Ann had covered the door with wrapping-paper
but a corner had been torn off,
and it left an opening through which it was possible
for Blake in his room
to see what Ann was doing in hers.
Blake could not pay his rent
and his things were put into the hall in a bag:

a small amount of clothing,
a plate, a dish, a cup and saucer, and a knife.

The door to Ann's sitting-room, leading from the hall,
was broken open and stood partly ajar.
On the washstand was Blake's knife
with a steel blade—stained with blood—about eight inches long
and a wooden handle,
on which was the word "Bread" in raised letters.

8

The Lodger

She was a widow in her fifties
and lived in two rooms with her son—
no longer a boy but not yet a man.
August was an immigrant
who had been a gardener in the old country
but was now drifting about the city
without steady work
and often without means.
He rented the back room from her
and was to pay her a dollar a week for it
and she was to serve him breakfast, too,
for which he would pay eight cents a meal.

On a Friday evening in summer, while the widow, her son, and the
    lodger
were in the front room, she took her pocketbook from the closet
and left to buy bread for supper,
and when she came back
put the pocketbook—it had only a few pennies in it—
back in the closet
and left the closet door unlocked.
Her son—who slept on a cot near the open window—
woke at midnight at his mother's scream

and, by the light of the streetlamp, saw the lodger standing beside his
　　mother's bed,
a knife in his hand;
the door of the closet open.
The son jumped out of bed
to get at the lodger,
and the lodger turned upon him, knife lifted;
and he ran in terror to the open window
and climbing out of it
climbed upon the cornice of the building
shouting for the police.
Some of the neighbors saw the lodger running out of an alley
at the side of the house,
in his shirt and trousers but without his shoes,
and found the woman lying senseless on the floor
bleeding from a wound in her neck.

9

Ford, part owner of a stock of goods in a store—
in a small wooden building—
was insolvent.
His life was insured
and most of the money would go to his wife on his death,
but until then
there were the premiums to pay.
He had been robbed, too—
the safe blown open—
and he was sure the thieves would come again;
so he set a trap for them:
mixed morphine with whiskey,
not enough to kill
but enough to leave the drinker unconscious,
and put the bottle
when he closed the store for the night
on a shelf behind the counter.

On a cold afternoon in February
a young Irishman came to town in his wagon
and dropped into the store
and stayed on:
no better place to go, perhaps,
or because "the boys" had borrowed the wagon for a ride
and he was waiting for it.
Later, Ford asked him out for a drink
in a neighboring saloon
and he was still in the store
when Ford went down into the cellar
to bank the fire in the furnace
before closing the store for the night.

When Ford came up,
he found the young man drowsy
and, looking at the whiskey bottle on the shelf,
saw that he had taken a long drink from it.
The young man kept getting drowsier
and, finally, Ford helped him to a cot on the upper floor
where he himself sometimes slept.
In no time, the young man was sound asleep
and Ford, looking at him, saw his own troubles ended.
He slipped the metal identification tag that he always carried
into the young man's pocket,
and going downstairs
set the building afire
and stole away from the flames and the billowing smoke
into the silent street—
and out of town.
The body was found in the morning
under a heap of ashes and debris,
burnt beyond recognition.
By the tag, it was thought at first to be Ford's.
On the body, however, there was also "the cord of St. Joseph,"
given to the young man a few years before
as the member of a Catholic society—

and Ford was not a Catholic.
He was finally tracked to the Klondike and arrested for murder.
The "cord of St. Joseph" may not have protected the young man
but it avenged him.

10

A stranger with a carpetbag called at the office of the stockbroker
and asked to see him about some bonds
and said he had a letter of introduction from Mr. Rockefeller.
He was asked to send it in
and said he preferred to present it in person
and that he only wanted to say two or three words.
The stockbroker, accordingly, came out of his private office
into the anteroom,
and went to the window in the partition and looked into the lobby:
there he saw the stranger sitting upon a settee.

In the lobby was another man whom the stockbroker knew
and who went up to the window when he saw the stockbroker
and said he had a message from one of the stockbroker's customers.
The stockbroker turned the knob of the door
to let him into the anteroom,
and then spoke to the man with the carpetbag.
The man stood up at once, took the carpetbag in his hand, and walking
        up to the window,
handed the stockbroker the letter supposed to be from Mr. Rockefeller.
The stockbroker opened it and read:
"The bag I hold in my hand has ten pounds of dynamite.
If I drop it on the floor,
the dynamite will explode
and leave this building in ruins
and kill every human being in it.
I want a million dollars or I'll drop the bag.
Will you give it? Yes or no?"

The stockbroker read the letter twice,
folded it and handed it back;

and said that he had another engagement
and would the man with the carpetbag come back later in the day?
After a second or two the man said,
"Then, do I understand that you refuse?"
"Oh, no!" the stockbroker answered,
"but I have an appointment
and I think I can get through with it in a few minutes,
and then will see you."

Upon coming into the anteroom,
the man with the message from the stockbroker's customer
had gone to the table near the center of the room
and stood waiting for the stockbroker.
The stockbroker stepped backwards into the anteroom
and then, resting a thigh on the corner of the table,
put his right hand on the messenger's left shoulder
and his left hand on the messenger's left arm,
and—so the messenger afterwards said—
holding the messenger's left hand in both his own,
the stockbroker moved the messenger gently
until he stood between the stockbroker and the man with the carpetbag
        in the lobby;
and the stockbroker said, over the messenger's shoulder,
"If I trust you, why can't you trust me?"
The man with the carpetbag answered,
"I infer from your answer that you refuse";
and he also walked backwards, holding the carpetbag at the end of his
        fingers,
looking at the stockbroker through the window in the partition—
and a flash!

The man with the carpetbag was blown to bits
and the clerk beside the stock-ticker at the window in the anteroom
hurled through the window to the street and killed;
and everybody else in the office injured.
The plaster was down from the walls and the floor torn up,
the partitions, desks, tables and chairs wrecked,
the window sashes and window frames blown out,

and even the large steel safe in the private office of the stockbroker
was blown open
and its contents scattered about the floor.

As for the messenger, even if the stockbroker did use him as a shield,
as the messenger said,
was he worse off in the whirlwind of the explosion—
so the judges were to ask—
because he was standing in front of the stockbroker
than if he were anywhere else in the office?

11

The coal had dropped along the railroad track
while being shoveled from a railroad car
into a wagon, and Annie and Fannie were picking it up when arrested.
Of course, you shall not steal, said their lawyer;
but how about the passage in Leviticus:
"You shall not wholly reap the corners of your field,
nor gather every grape of your vineyard:
you shall leave them for the poor and the stranger"?

12

The savings bank failed; almost all of its deposits
were by servant girls, washerwomen, sewing women, and
    workingmen,
and it had been kept open
every Saturday,
and Monday night until eight o'clock,
to receive their earnings and savings.

The money of a minister
who had been saving in the bank for years
was lost,
although, when the minister was about to draw out his money,
the cashier took him into a private room
and assured him that the bank was "as sound as the Bank of England

and the very place for an old man to leave his money";
and the money of the small tradesman
who had just sold his business for two thousand dollars
and had deposited the money
after the cashier had assured him
that the bank was safer than any national bank,
for it loaned money only on first mortgages and gilt-edged securities,
and did not take commercial paper like a national bank;
and the money of the servant
who had saved for many years
until she had six hundred dollars—
after she had worked "the best years" of her life
and was saving to pay off the mortgage on her home,
and was assured by the cashier
that her money was as safe
"as if she had it in her own pocket."

And the money of the old widow who sewed for a living;
and the money of a family of five brothers and sisters
who had been saving their money together for years;
and the savings of the man who had more than three thousand dollars
        on deposit,
the savings of over twenty years
as a "street laborer"—
all was lost.

13
Sharp and shrewd, he had come to the city—
it was then a village—
and had bought for a few thousand dollars
farms in the neighborhood that had become lots in town—
land now worth half a million and more;
besides, he had bank stock and railroad stock
and railroad bonds and stock in other corporations.

He was now an old man
walking with a cane;

he did not recognize at times persons he had known for thirty or forty
     years;
his eyes were often staring at nothing
and his mouth was often open
but saying nothing;
and he would bring home empty tin cans he had found and rusty nails,
barrel hoops and old shoes that had been thrown away,
and once the piece of an old stove.

VII
MACHINE AGE

1

A boy of fourteen was one of several helpers in the spinning-room:
his work was to sweep the floor,
pick up waste, change bobbins,
mend broken threads,
and, now and then, oil and clean parts of the machinery.
The shaft from which the belt was hanging
was about fifteen feet above the floor
and revolving three hundred times a minute.
The second hand in the spinning-room
was mending the belt,
and the boy
was standing near the top of the stepladder
holding the belt from the shaft
to keep it from crawling
There was nothing by which the boy could steady himself
but the ladder.

On first going up the ladder
the boy became frightened
and, returning to the foot of it,
told the second hand
he did not want to stay up on the ladder
for fear he would be hurt;

but the second hand, clapping his hands together,
told him with an oath to go back
or take his hat and go home.
And so the boy went up the ladder again—
to be caught by the belt and drawn over the shaft,
his arm wrapped around it.

2

All revolving shafts are dangerous
but a vertical shaft,
neither boxed nor guarded against,
most dangerous.

The girl's work for the company was changed
to sweeping the floors:
among other places the floor of a room
where the shaft in a passageway—
between the wall and a machine—
ran from the floor to the ceiling.
In sweeping around it one morning
her apron was caught
and drawn about the shaft
and she was whirled around
striking the wall and machinery.

3
Part of the machine consisted of a round table
on a revolving disk;
and in the table were eight pair of molds.
These were brought, as the table revolved, under a spout;
and from this the clay
dropped into the molds. About a foot from the spout
was an upright frame of iron
and within it a heavy iron beam, "the plunger," driven by steam,
sliding up
and coming down with great force

pressing the clay into bricks.
The table's motion was intermittent:
stationary during the feeding of clay and the pressing,
and then it revolved to bring the next pair of molds
to be filled and pressed.

The boy had to oil and insert a piece of metal, called a "gib"—
to give an ornamental shape to the bricks—
into the empty mold before it reached the spout;
and then to step into the narrow space between spout and plunger,
and, within ten or fifteen seconds,
while the mold with the gib in it was passing from spout to plunger,
take off about two handfuls of clay from the mold
and press what was left evenly into the corners.

But this machine had a jerky motion
so that it might suddenly pull the mold—
and the hand upon it—
under the frame.
A "pressman," to be sure, had charge of the machine
but just then he was going to dinner
and after he had turned his back on the machine
and taken only two or three steps
and the machine had pressed four or six bricks,
the boy's hand was drawn under the frame
and crushed under the plunger.

4

The stone-cutting machines of the marble company
were driven by compressed air
brought into the quarry through an iron pipe;
underneath this pipe was a ledge or jog in the rock,
extending ten or twelve inches from the almost perpendicular wall;
and at each point where a pipe led from the main pipe to a machine
was a valve
so that the air could be cut off;
water was dripping from the valves upon the ledge,

and in cold weather
the ledge was more or less covered with ice.

He was not quite sixteen,
but for quite a while had been working
as a helper at a stone-cutting machine.
The weather had now been cold for several days
and the ledge slippery.

The valve at the pipe to the machine at which he worked
was fifteen or twenty feet above the floor of the quarry,
and to reach it
one could go along the ledge
or could climb the stairs, at the other end of the quarry,
and go down the ledge to the valve.
The air for some reason had been shut off
and, about thirty minutes before quitting time,
the man in charge of the machine sent him to turn on the air.
By this time it was quite dark
upon the floor of the quarry and along the ledge.

The foreman saw him again
lying at the foot of the stairs
with a pool of blood near his head.

5

No longer a boy, in fact almost eighteen,
he had a job in a steam saw-mill
handing up the wood to be sawed into kindling.
Sawing a stick of wood was simple:
the wood was pressed against the revolving saw by hand—
a hand on each side of the saw—
and this was done again and again
until the stick was cut into pieces.

When he was given a chance to work at the saw—
the sawyer was away taking care of the boiler—

the saw was dull and two teeth had been broken off.
The man handing him the wood hallooed to him that he was sawing
    too fast—
to look out and take his time;
but he sawed on in his own way.
Just as he was sawing the last piece
and shoving it hard against the saw because it was dull,
when the saw came to where the two teeth were out,
it jumped,
and three fingers of his left hand were cut off.

6

The sawmill, run by steam, was lit by electric lights at night
but for two or three hours after midnight
the lights would grow dim.
Was it lack of power
because of the failure to keep up sufficient steam in the boilers?
Whatever it was,
there was not enough light to inspect the logs he was sawing:
find a stone stuck to them
or a piece of embedded iron.

That night a piece of iron,
more than two feet long and four inches wide,
had been driven—
maliciously perhaps—
into a split in the butt end of the log he was sawing;
when the saw struck the iron
the teeth broke off
and one of the teeth flew into his right eye
and blinded it.

7

The man who had oiled the machine that day
did not adjust the cylinders properly,

and when the immigrant—not long in the country—fed the two pieces
    of rubber into the machine
with his hands,
as the foreman had taught him,
the rubber fell through almost at once.
He had been told that the machine was dangerous,
and now that the cylinders had not been adjusted properly—
too far apart—
it was more dangerous than ever.
But he was new at the work
and his knowledge of English, to say the least,
imperfect;
so he looked at the foreman for advice
and the foreman, who was watching him,
merely laughed.

He thought that a direction to go on
and did,
feeding the same pieces to the machine again;
and his fingers were caught, cut and broken.

8

The boys had just been brought to this country
by their parents
and neither boy spoke nor understood any English.
The elder, thirteen years of age,
was working as a "back boy" in the mule spinning-room
and he got his little brother of eight
into the room
to learn the work of a "back boy";
other boys were taking their brothers in to learn
and he understood from their motions what they were doing.

The younger boy went to work cheerfully enough
picking up bobbins
and putting waste into a box—

and if the man in charge ordered him out
he did not understand him.
But he had not been at work a day and a half
before his hand was caught in a gearing—
which the other boys had been told to stay clear of.

9

The pile of iron ore, about seventy-five feet long and as high
was packed solid
and dynamite was used to loosen it at the bottom;
but much of it was still in large lumps
which had to be broken by picks
before the ore could be put into the "buggies"
and wheeled to the furnaces.

The Pole was one of those who loaded the loosened ore
into the "buggies,"
and when the lumps were too large
broke them with a pick. His work—at night—was by light of torches;
but that night it was dark and snowing heavily
and the place poorly lighted:
he went to look for the foreman
to ask for another torch and more light.

The foreman replied, "Get back to work, you Goddamn son of a bitch!"
and walking ahead of him to the place where he was stationed—
the side of the steep pile,
straight up for three to ten feet before it sloped back—
took up the pick
and struck the pile of ore
a number of times,
and then threw down the pick
and still swearing at the Pole
ordered him to get to work.

He did, and a short time after the foreman left,
a large piece of ore,

about eight feet long and three feet thick,
weighing several tons
fell from the straight side of the pile above him
upon his foot and crushed it.

10

The company making sugar and syrup
had, on one side of its building,
a trough through which ran an endless chain,
and this carried the canes of sorghum into the building.
As the sorghum cane was hauled in from the farms
it was thrown off in a long pile
a few feet from the chain. A few feet from a side door
was a small uncovered cistern
into which was discharged
the waste water from the boilers in the building.

He had been hired to carry the cane
from the long pile outside
and place them on the carrier.
About four o'clock in the morning of an October day
it became very cold,
and he asked the foreman's permission
to go into the factory a while and warm himself;
but going towards the side door in the darkness
he fell into the cistern filled with boiling water.

11

The iron in the foundry was melted in large cupolas
in which were tap-holes with spouts
about five feet above the floor. The cupola-tender
would draw off the melted iron when needed
and when enough had been drawn
would stop the flow by a "bot-stick"—
a round iron bar with a wooden handle
and a flat disk at the end. (A piece of damp clay was put on the disk

and molded by hand into a cone
and this stick with the conical clay stopper at the end
was driven through the stream of metal
into the tap-hole
and by a quick turn of the hand and arm
withdrawn
leaving the stopper in the hole.)
But the cupola-tender that day was unfit for the job:
he had been burnt twice by the hot iron
and was afraid of it;
wanted to get away from it as fast as he could
and not the man to leave the stopper always fast and fixed.

Joe Murray had been working for years as a cupola-tender
—a very good hand at it, too—
but now his work was charging the cupola with metal
so that a supply would be ready;
his post on a platform
twenty feet above the ground and reached by a stairway.
The flow of melted iron had not been properly stopped
and was leaking through:
at any moment the melted iron might press out through the spout.
A number of men were working in front of it
along a common gangway
and if the hot iron oozing out would burst through the stopper
and fall upon the hard floor
it would fly up
and come down in a shower on top of the men—
every man within twenty feet would get it.

A workingman saw the metal oozing out and shouted,
"Joe—oh, Murray—this is leaking!"
Joe Murray was in no danger himself.
He sprang down the stairs,
grabbed a bot-stick and a piece of clay
and put it on the bot-stick;
but just as he was about to use it in stopping up the tap-hole
the hot metal burst over the stopper then in the hole

and struck him on the body and face
splashing into his eyes—and blinding him.

VIII

The gas main had been put down several years before
and there was a leak at the sleeve
(the earth around it was afterwards found to be blackened by gas).
There had been common talk in the neighborhood
of the smell of gas: so strong at times
the passers-by would walk on the other side of the street
to get away from it; and after a heavy rain the gas was seen to bubble
    up
through the water.

But she had not been bothered by the smell of gas
because she had lost all sense of smell years before.
The ground was now frozen above the pipe
and the gas was flowing from the leak in the sleeve
through the loose gravel and sand
in which the pipe was lying
until it reached the foundations of her house
eighty or ninety yards away, across the street;
and came out between the bricks
and from the ground along the bottom of the walls.

That evening she lit the lamp
and went into the cellar to get a crock of milk.
She had opened the cellar door
and set the lamp on a bench nearby
to light the way into the cellar.
As she went down, the light, it seemed to her, grew dimmer
and as she came back, when halfway up the stairs,
she looked up at the lamp on the bench
and it seemed to her that the light had grown small and was blue.
And immediately afterwards, before she reached the top of the stairs,
she saw the lamp blaze up—

and remembered no more until she found herself in the ruins of the
     house
and what was left of the house on fire.
The gas continued to burn
in jets from two to eight inches long
around the inside of the foundation walls.

IX
RAILROADS

1

Many years before the railroad was built
the highway they were on was fully sixty feet wide,
and it was much used day and night;
but when the railroad constructed its crossing
the highway was narrowed at that point
by the railroad's embankment, ditch and fence
until it was only about ten feet wide;
and at that there had been a washout,
so that part of the highway had been washed into the ditch
and was even narrower.

The horse was gentle and well-broken
and the man and his wife in the buggy
drove on at a "jog trot."
The railroad as it neared the crossing
ran through a deep cut,
and the embankment on either side,
bushes and trees, and the board fence of the railroad,
hid the train
until it was about to go over the crossing.
Then the man and his wife in the buggy
heard the whistle of the locomotive
and saw the train coming at them in a rush
as they were about to cross the track.

The horse saw the train, too,
and lunged forward.

If there had been space enough, the man—who was driving—
might have jerked the horse around
and turned,
but in the space that was left of the highway
he would have upset the buggy;
and he just held back on the lines.
But he could not hold the frightened horse:
it rushed on and—in a flash—
the train struck the horse and buggy, man and wife.

2

The old man, quite deaf,
on his way home from work
had to pass over a canal bridge and the grade-crossing near it;
but a gang of boys
loafing near the crossing
would hoot at him
and pull at his coat-tails for the fun of it.

Now there were only two boys
and they, too, were shouting at him
and pulling at his coat;
for a locomotive was coming down the track he was about to cross.
The old man thought that they were just having the usual fun
and turned, lifting his stick as if to strike them,
and pulling himself free
stepped upon the track just in front of the speeding train.

3

After the train left the station
a man, almost seventy,
left his seat,

and went to the rear door of the railway car
in which a pane of glass
would let him view the country and its farms
where he had once lived and worked.
He stood at the rear door
looking out;
his right shoulder against it
and his left hand—
to steady himself against the train's rocking—
upon the door of the water-closet
in the corner:
his left hand against the casing
and the little finger over the place
where the edge of the door—
on which were its hinges—
met the casing.
The conductor, taking up tickets,
came into the car
walking silently down the carpeted aisle,
and when he came to the water-closet
opened and shut the door quickly
to see if any passenger was inside.
The old man's little finger
slipped into the crack between the casing and the door
when it was opened
and was crushed by the door when it was shut.

X
SHIPPING

1

He was at work with others between decks
when the fire broke out and hurried to get his maul and coat.
The others ran up a ladder
to the main deck. As the last two or three came through the hatchway,
it was nearly covered with a tarpaulin,

and shortly afterwards completely covered.
One of the men who stood near the officer who had ordered the
    hatches covered
said, "There's a man down there!"
and the officer answered, "Cover the hatches!"

The firemen heard knocking in the compartment where he was
a long time after the hatches were covered
and, after the fire was out,
he was found dead
near the foot of the ladder
with his coat wrapped about his head.

2

On the voyage from the West Indies to the United States
the seaman, suffering from chills and fever,
was ordered by the mate to "turn to,"
but he said he was sick and unable to go on deck.
The captain came into the forecastle
and ordered him to go on deck.
He said again that he was sick
and the captain struck him several times
as he was lying in his bunk
and pulled him out of it
and said, "Will you go on deck now?"
But he answered, "I feel sick."
The captain hit him several times with his fist
and, when he caught hold of the captain's arm,
the captain kicked his leg,
breaking the bone beneath the knee.

3

The steamboat was lying at a wharf in Cincinnati
and, just before it was due to start out,
the deck hands were ordered to help turn the wheel:

it had to be turned part of a revolution
to adjust the "wrist."

When the men got to the wheel
they were ordered by the mate to get on it
and to do so had to walk along a poplar plank
sixteen feet long but only eleven inches wide
and a little more than three inches thick.
It reached from the floor of the boat to the wheel
and over the water.

Some of the men hung back
but were ordered by the mate, with an oath,
to hurry.
An ash-hauler on the boat was watching
and said, "Look out!
That plank is cracked!"
But the mate kept shouting at the men to hurry.

When a number of men had gotten on the wheel,
and some were still on the plank,
the wheel turned
and, as it turned,
several of the men on the wheel got off
and back on the plank—
it broke in two
and some of them fell into the river and were drowned.

4
The brig had left Maine with a cargo of ice;
the weather was fair at the time
but, after a while,
a storm began on Friday
with high winds and rain and a light snow
and continued through Saturday and Sunday,
and finally the captain hove to
to ride out the gale.

During the storm the captain had but little rest:
had not gone to his berth
and had eaten little,
and for forty-eight hours
had been constantly on deck;
it was not until early Monday morning
that the captain went below.

When the captain turned the vessel over to the mate
the storm had abated,
but there was a heavy roll of the sea
and the captain—after telling the mate to keep the vessel by the wind
until he made the Cape Cod light—
lay down upon the lounge in his cabin.
Before doing so,
the captain took a heavy dose of quinine;
for he felt sick
and was afraid he would have an attack of malaria.

At about eleven o'clock in the morning,
the second mate, to whom the vessel had been turned over,
called the mate
saying that the vessel was not acting well.
The mate went upon the deck
and in about half an hour the steward called the captain.
He was still lying fully dressed upon the lounge
and did not get up at the first call
and the steward had to pull him off.
He then got up
but within a few minutes was again found lying upon the lounge.
The steward finally got him up on the deck.

While he was there,
a tug came up on the weather quarter
and the captain was told that the rudderpost of the brig was split
and asked if he did not want a tow.
The captain said no:
that he guessed "we are all right."

But the brig began to go off and come to
and would not mind the helm,
and the sea kept edging her towards the beach.

The mate looked over the stern
and could see nothing;
then he got into a rope with a noose in it around his waist
and was let down over the stern
to look at the rudderpost:
sure enough it was split.

But the captain said he didn't think it was
and added, "I can't see it and I don't think you can."
The captain did not seem to be himself.
He told the mate to square the yards
and see if the vessel would not go off;
and the vessel did go off
but came right back.
The mate then lowered the main trysail
and hove the helm up again,
but this time the vessel did not go off
and went sideways onto the beach
and struck—
to become a total wreck.

XI
MINING

1

His work was to shovel and load coal;
and one day he was told to go to a part of the mine
where he had never been,
and bring a car, loaded with dirt, then in the entry near one
        of the rooms,
to an empty room;
but he did not know of the steep grade in the entry.

He found the car and began to push it along
but, for some reason, it would not move;
he went to the front of the car
and, sure enough, there was some dirt in front of the wheels.
He cleared it away
and pulled at the car to see if it was free;
and it began to go forward down the steep grade
gaining speed as it went.
He tried to stop it as it started
so that he might get behind it
but could not and, in trying to stop the car,
the light on his cap went out,
and he was left in total darkness—
and the speeding car struck him.

2

A brick mason by trade, he had never worked in a mine
and went into the mine on a Saturday
and was shown to his work—
the place where he worked was some distance from the shaft.
On Monday morning, he went back to his work,
and was lowered through the shaft,
as he had been on Saturday. But his "boss" was not at the surface when
    he got there,
nor did he see him below in the mine.
He thought he could find his place of work without a guide;
but there were no lights in the mine,
except those used by the miners on their caps
and such light as shone down the shaft.

After going some distance, almost a fourth of a mile,
he asked for the "boss,"
and was told that he worked on the other side of the mine.
He made his way back to the shaft.
When he reached it, several men were standing near it—
on the opposite side—
with lighted lamps upon their caps:

these were the "cagers" who worked at the bottom of the shaft,
loading the coal to be lifted into the cages.
There was a passageway, high and wide enough to enable him to go
        around the shaft,
but he began to walk directly across the bottom.
The "cagers" might have called out and warned him of the danger
but did not;
and one of the cages that was being lowered
came down upon him.

XII

He was a cutter in the clothing-trade—
a first-class cutter, "filled the bill exactly"—
and was hired. The job was steady;
but, soon after he was hired, the local branch of the Knights of Labor
complained of his employment in a letter to the firm
because he did not belong to their union.
He was willing enough to become a member
and asked a friend of his to present his application;
but the union would not act on his application just then:
there were too many union men out of work
and they had passed a resolution to take in no more members.

Later, the firm received a formal notice
that if they kept him in their employ
the union would notify all labor organizations in the city
that the firm was non-union;
and the man who had hired him told him they would have to let
        him go.
If they did not, the man who had hired him explained,
the name of the firm would be dropped from the list in the union's
        newspaper
of those friendly to labor;
all their union cutters would be ordered out—
and not only those who cut the goods

but those who sewed it—
and the firm would lose heavily because they had many contracts to fill.

No such threats had been made by speech or letter, of course,
and, indeed, by the by-laws of the Knights of Labor and its branches,
they could not call on their members to strike because of the
        employment of non-union help.
But they would.

XIII
THE GOOD NEIGHBOR

Beach's house—a small box house—was a few hundred feet from the
        railroad;
the grade at this point was about ten feet high
and the railroad fence was the yard fence.
His mother, feeble and nearly blind, lived with him
and so did his daughter, about fourteen years of age,
and his son, almost seven; his wife was dead.
Huston and his wife pitched their tent near Beach's house
and not long afterwards Huston's stepfather and Huston's mother
came in a covered wagon
and stopped beside the tent.
His stepfather and mother lived and slept in the wagon
and cooked their meals on Huston's stove
and ate at his table. But, finally, Huston and his wife fell out with his
        mother
and would not let her into the tent.

Huston's mother was taken sick in the wagon
but neither Huston's wife nor Huston would do anything for her
and they pulled the wagon
away from the tent and into a slough.
The neighbors came to help her
and Beach—at their suggestion—
took the old sick woman into his house,

gave her a room and bed,
and his old mother took care of her.
But Huston and his wife never came to see her.

One day, Beach's little boy and a little cousin
were playing near Huston's tent
and he got them to fighting each other,
and Beach's daughter came to take the children home.
Huston cursed her and called her names.
The next day as Beach, taking his horses to water,
was passing along the public road
he saw Huston and his wife near their tent
and asked him why he had treated the children so;
and Huston and Beach got to quarreling.
Beach told him he did not want to have anything to do with him
and never to come to his house.

Huston now told a neighbor
he was going to Beach's house
and would not go alone
for he would take his pistol along—
his British bulldog revolver,
every chamber loaded—
and Huston and his wife, the pistol in his hand,
did go to Beach's house.
But he was not at home,
for he was working on the public road.
No one told Huston and his wife to be gone
or said they could not stay;
but they did not stay five minutes
or even sit down
and went off, saying they would be back that evening.

When it was nearly six, Huston's wife said to him:
"Come on, honey!
We'll see fun before the sun goes down";
and they walked along the railroad track to Beach's house.
Beach had come home from work

and was sitting on his doorstep resting,
for it had been a hot August day.
He saw them start down the railroad grade
and told them not to come into his yard
but they kept on coming.
Huston had his pistol in his hand
and his wife had a heavy piece of iron
she had picked up as she crossed the railroad fence.
Beach's mother, hearing her son's voice,
had also come into the yard,
a dishcloth in one hand and a table knife in the other,
for she was just putting supper on the table.

Huston's wife struck Beach on the head
with the piece of iron
and he returned the blow with his hand.
Then Huston fired. The first shot struck Beach's mother
and she fell with a bullet hole in her head,
her brains running out on the ground.
Huston fired again,
and this time the ball struck Beach in the belly.
Then Huston and his wife turned and went up the railroad grade
and Beach followed,
but on top of the grade his strength was gone
and he fell down on the track.

XIV
THE PATRIOT

The Doctor was a member of a secret society
organized to assist their native land—
by arms, if need be—
to free itself of those who for a thousand years had ruled and
    misruled it.
The executive committee of the society
was at first composed of a member from each "camp,"

as the branches of the society were called;
but this committee was thought too large to be effective
and years before it had been reduced to five members;
of these five, three had taken control
and were known among members of the society as "The Triangle."
But the policy of "The Triangle" in disposing of the society's money
was disapproved of by many of the members,
and one of their leaders was the Doctor.
He was called, accordingly, a traitor and a spy.
A member of the society—the owner of an ice-house—contracted with
      the Doctor
for his services
in case an employee should be injured;
and someone rented a cottage near the ice-house,
and moved furniture and a trunk into the cottage
but did not move into it himself.
One evening, a man in a hired rig came to the Doctor's office
and asked him to come at once,
for "one of the ice-dealer's men has been badly hurt."
The Doctor gathered up his instruments, bandages, and some cotton
      batting,
and got into the rig,
and was driven quickly towards the ice-house.
About three weeks later his body was found in the catch-basin of a
      sewer miles away.

At about eight o'clock of the night the Doctor had been called from his
      office,
a woman passing the cottage
heard the sound of blows and a cry, "O God! Jesus!"
Later, others passing the cottage heard the sound of nails
hammered into wood,
and at midnight two men were seen driving away
in a rig with a trunk in it.
That night, the horse and rig were returned to the livery stable,
the horse bespattered with mud;
and next morning, a trunk, broken open and blood-stained, with some
      cotton batting in it,

252]

was found in another part of the city.
Stains were also found on the steps of the cottage
and on the sidewalk in front of it;
and the floor of the cottage had just been repainted.

XV

It was a cold starlit night in February
and Nodaway, a peddler of spectacles,
eighty or so years of age
and crippled, was hobbling along the road
leaning on his crutch. He had a cane to help him
but now held it over his shoulder
and on it was the satchel with his stock in trade.
He had just asked for shelter for the night
at a house down the road and been refused.

He was overtaken by two young men,
Smith and another, riding in a buggy,
and Smith to tease him said:
"Howdy, old man! What are you doing?"
"None of your business."
"You want a night's lodging?"
"Yes."
"You can't get it."
"Do you live around here? Can't you keep me for the night?"
"No!
And what are you going to do about it?"
"None of your business."

At that Smith got out of the buggy
and struck Nodaway in the face,
knocking him down,
and, wearing a pair of heavy boots,
kicked him in the side.
Two or three other men had come up, and Nodaway was raising his
    head

when Smith shouted, "Don't raise your head,
or I'll stomp the liver out of you!"
But Nodaway reached out
to help himself up
and Smith said: "God damn you!
You can't stick your hands in my pocket,"
and struck Nodaway again.
One of the other men said by way of a joke:
"The old man is getting into his satchel.
Look out! He's getting his gun!" Smith shouted: "God damn you! You
    can't draw no gun on me,"
and jumped on Nodaway with both feet
and began kicking him in the head.

XVI

He had tried to jump on the engine of a train
and slipped; his left foot was caught under the tender.
Penniless, he was taken to the city's almshouse,
and there one of the city's doctors employed to care for the destitute
treated him. About ten days afterwards,
the doctor amputated his leg above the ankle
and, six or seven days after that,
because gangrene had set in, amputated the leg at the knee.

However, the doctor did not save flap enough to cover the end or the
    bone:
the stump became a running sore
and the bone of the leg stuck out three or four inches.

XVII

Stone had been quarried there
but now it was nearly filled with water.
In the summer there was green scum on top of the water;
now and then the dead body of a dog could be seen floating in it—

dead dogs and dead cats
and dead fish at the edges;
and once a dead baby was pulled out of it.

In the spring of the year
as soon as the ice was off and the weather became warm
eel grass was growing from the bottom,
and the pool was full of toads and bullfrogs:
those who lived near it could hear the bullfrogs at night
and smell the stink of stagnant water.

A Note on the Texts of Parts One and Two

Apart from minor regularizing of punctuation and typography to achieve a consistent book style, I have followed the texts of the published editions, with the following emendations.

In *Testimony (1885–1890)*, "The North," IX ("Railroads"), 3, line 3, I have substituted "[in]" for the first "to" as found in the book and MS—

> he took an express train to Cleveland to return to Erie,

—judging that the sense required it. At the end of the last poem of "The North" a production error in the New Directions volume has caused the disappearance of a portion of the text. I have supplied the missing five lines from Reznikoff's corrected proofs now in the library of the University of California, San Diego. (My thanks to Kathryn Shevelow of the Mandeville Department of Special Collections.)

In *Testimony (1891–1900)* I have corrected a dozen or so obvious typographical errors, such as two versions of a proper name in the same poem (Belton and Benton, Fran and Fan, for example). I have not used square brackets for such changes, nor for supplying an obvious missing word or two on MS authority. I have also taken the liberty of changing "forty-six" to "forty-one" (p. 215) and "two handsful of clay" to "two handfuls of clay" (p. 232) as the context seemed to me to require.

SEAMUS COONEY (1978)

PART THREE

TESTIMONY

THE UNITED STATES (1891–1900)

RECITATIVE

THE WEST

I
SOCIAL LIFE

1

Before daybreak, Clay, a professional gambler,
went to a colored prostitute's tent
in the outskirts of town. About fifteen minutes after he got there,
sitting on the bed and taking off his shoes,
Ross, who "kept" her and whose mistress she was,
knocked on the screen door.
She called out that she had company
but Ross was drunk:
he jerked the screen door open
(it was only fastened by a hook over a nail),
kicked open the wooden door, closed but unlocked,
and came in.

The light in the tent was dim
but the two men knew each other:
Ross was also a gambler by profession
and had once gone to Clay's gaming-table
and punched a pistol in Clay's money
throwing it around.

Clay jumped up from the bed where he was sitting
and, pistol in hand,
asked Ross why he "broke in" on him.
Ross answered he didn't break in:
the door was "already open."
He had one hand at his mouth, holding a cigarette,
and asked Clay for a match.
Clay said he had no match,
but Cora got up from bed to get one
and Ross lit his cigarette.

Clay asked Ross if he had a "gun"
and Ross said no
and added that Clay was welcome to search him.
Clay did, Ross smiling during the search,
and Clay did not find a gun. He then caught Ross by the lapel of his
    coat
and told him, with a curse, that the best thing he could do was to go
    back to town,
and turned him loose.
The two men stood there facing each other for a few moments
and then Ross said that Clay had the best of him
but was acting like "a damn son of a bitch"—
and Clay shot him.

Cora ran out of the tent, screaming,
and heard three more shots.
When all was quiet in the tent again,
she came back.
The smoke blinded her for a minute or two
and then she saw Clay sitting astride Ross's body—
Ross was dead—
and striking the face a good "lick" with the handle of the pistol.
She begged Clay not to strike Ross again
and went down on the floor
and began talking to the dead man,
screaming, "Oh, my darling! Oh, my darling!"
And Clay put on his coat and left.

2

Late that night while they were upon the public highway,
he told her she could scream all she chose to
because there was nobody within three miles;
and then he stopped the buggy and got out
and took the lines and whip with him
and went around in front of the horse
and fastened the lines to the bridge railing.

Then he came back and asked her if she would get out without any
     trouble
and she said, "No!"

He said he would pull her out
and she told him he would not;
and he caught hold of her
and she caught hold of the buggy,
and he pulled her hands loose
and pulled her out of the buggy.

II
DOMESTIC SCENES

1

She saw her father in the morning
as he came through the gate and up the steps.
She and her mother were in the kitchen
cooking breakfast;
and her father came in through the side door.
She had opened the door for him;
"Good morning, Pa," she said
and he had answered, pleasantly enough it seemed,
"Good morning."

Her mother was lifting the mush from the stove
and both were about to sit down at the small table in the kitchen
and have their breakfast.
Her father sat down. She took away his hat
and hung it on a nail in back of him,
and asked him to take off his overcoat
for it was warm in the room;
he did
and put it on a chair
and sat down again.

Then he asked his wife if she thought of coming back to him
and she answered that she had not been thinking anything of the kind
   just yet;
and his daughter spoke up and said,
as pleasantly as she could:
since they were both happier apart,
she thought they had best live apart and be friends—
it would be better for both of them.
At this her father jumped up
and she thought he was going to slap her
and ran out of the back door:
the door had a spring screen
and it slammed shut.

She turned to look at her father:
he was pulling a pistol from his pocket
and she heard her mother say, "Oh, George, don't shoot!"
But he did and shot her mother.
Then he went towards the back door and fired at his daughter—
she was out on the back porch looking in,
fixed to the spot.
He fired through the screen door
and the bullet struck his daughter through the left breast.

2

For several years Daffodil had been living with an Indian woman
and earning his living as a fisherman; living in a shack built upon a scow
moored to the shore of a river.
On the afternoon before Christmas,
they went in a rowboat to the home of her sister
who, with her husband, was also living in a shack
about five or six miles away.

They stayed until about eight o'clock Christmas night—
the company drinking much beer and some whiskey—
and while there Daffodil, jealous because of something the woman he
   was living with said,

struck her with his fists.
They left to go home:
he carried her
and threw her into the bottom of his boat.

Later that night, he was in a saloon near the waterfront,
only about a mile from the shack where they had been visiting,
and bought a dollar's worth of whiskey,
and went back to his boat.
They went on to their home
but, about midnight,
were still out on the bay
quite a distance from shore;
and he was seen striking the woman
who was seated near the stern
with something he held in his hand,
and those who watched
could hear the sound of the blows
and the woman screaming.

In a few days her body was found
in about eight feet of water
tied by a rope to the end of the scow
and held under water by a sack containing lead.

3
Ned did not like his brother-in-law
because of a claim for money Ned said was due him
and among his threats were
he would "maul Jackson" and "stamp his guts out."

Stopping at Jackson's house one day
Ned told his sister that he had heard at a rodeo
someone charging Jackson with stealing hogs
and even stealing the salt to salt them with.
Ned went on
to spend the night with a friend camping a short distance away.

When Ned's friend broke camp next morning
and, as he had arranged with Jackson,
brought the camping utensils to Jackson for storage,
Ned went along.
Jackson and his wife had kept breakfast waiting for them
and now invited them to the meal.
The young men, however, had eaten their breakfast
before breaking camp
and so sat down on the threshold to the front room of the house
while Jackson and his wife went to their breakfast in the kitchen.
The door of the kitchen was open
and they could talk to each other.

Jackson asked Ned's friend if he had been at the rodeo, too,
and had heard him charged with the theft of hogs.
Ned's friend answered that he had been at the rodeo but had not heard
     the charge
and either Jackson—or his wife—then asked Ned who besides himself
     had heard it.
He gave them two or three names
and then wanted to know if his word was doubted
and not good enough for Jackson.
Jackson replied that of course his word was good enough
but he wanted to have someone else's word, too,
so that when he went for the man who had made the charge,
should the man deny making it,
the matter would not rest simply on the man's word against Ned's.
But Ned was angry
saying that Jackson was not big enough to question his word
and wanted him to come outside and settle their quarrel—
Ned younger and stronger.

Jackson said that he would not come out
and Ned said he would make him;
Jackson then said he wanted no trouble
and Ned replied he was going to have it.
Jackson rose from the breakfast table
and went into the front room; as he did so

Ned stepped out of the front door
and picked up an iron-bound singletree.
Jackson stopped at the open door
and told Ned to leave the ranch
and said again that he wanted no trouble.
Ned answered that he would not leave
and could not be put off,
and again challenged Jackson to come out.
Jackson asked him what he meant to do with the singletree
and Ned replied that he would show him.
Then Jackson picked up Ned's rifle
standing inside the door—
Ned had placed it near the threshold when he sat down—
and saying, "Damn you, I'll learn you to fight me!"
fired,
and Ned, standing eight or ten feet away,
fell to the ground.

Jackson left the house
and his wife went to find him,
leaving her little boy to take care of his uncle.
While she was gone,
Ned with his pocketknife
cut his own throat:
the bullet passing through his intestines
lodged in the hip bone
and he was in agonizing pain.

4

Mrs. Bell owned a quarter-section of land
and had used water from a ditch for irrigating;
but, some years before, a new ditch had been dug
and now the water of the old ditch was flowing through it.
Her brother had helped in the digging—
the new ditch passed through his land
next to that of his sister.

She claimed the right to use the water
but her brother said she could have none of it
until he was paid for his work;
and he built a dam on his own land
to stop the flow of water to hers.
And now the alfalfa upon the Bell place,
as well as the trees,
were suffering for lack of water.

Her husband said he would have the water
and her brother—
the stronger
and, overbearing and quarrelsome, he had beaten up Bell more than
      once—
said that if Bell interfered with the dam
he would put him in the ditch
and make a dam out of his body.

Bell went to the ditch and removed the dam
but later found that it had been replaced.
His brother-in-law had also fastened a rifle to a post
as a spring-gun,
running a cord from the trigger across the second dam
so that interference with it
would discharge the rifle and sound an alarm.
But the rifle was set not to cause any injury—
the muzzle pointed directly downward
about six inches from the ground.

After supper, on a night that was clear and still,
Bell and his wife drove to the dam in a buggy;
they carried a shovel
and under the seat Bell had placed his shotgun—
loaded.
Her brother and his wife had gone to bed,
but he heard the sound of the buggy,
dressed himself and went down to the dam.

His wife put out the light the better to see
and sat up in bed looking out of the window.

She saw a man in the buggy
and by his way of whistling
knew it was Bell.
She heard her husband and his sister talking
and Bell, too, but not what they were saying—
and suddenly there was a flash
and she heard the report of a gun.
She was sure it came from the buggy
and heard her husband crying out in pain,
"Oh, oh!"
Right afterwards, before she could get out of bed,
she heard a second shot;
and ran out of the house in her night clothes
towards her husband.
She could hear her sister-in-law saying,
"Go on, Papa; go on!"
and found her husband's body
near the post to which the spring-gun had been attached.

He had fallen across a barbed-wire fence
and was hanging over the wires;
still alive but gasping for breath.
And then he stopped breathing,
and she began to scream.
The string of the spring-gun
was under the body—
drawn and taut
and the rifle discharged.
So much for her story.

And this was Bell's story and that of his wife.
Neither knew about the spring-gun;
when they reached the dam,
she took the shovel and began to use it
because the land to be watered was hers.

When her brother came he took hold of her,
and pulled her towards the bank of the ditch;
there was a scuffle between them
and she fell on her knees.
Just then a shot was fired.
The horse hitched to the buggy
lunged to the left,
and her husband shouted, "Whoa, whoa!" two or three times.
He believed that his wife was shot
and that he himself would be shot next;
holding the lines with his left hand,
he reached down with his right for the shotgun—
did not take the time to draw the gun to his shoulder—
and fired.
Her brother relaxed his hold on her arm
and fell limp in front of her:
just sank down.
She called to her sister-in-law
and when she came, her sister-in-law screamed
and then said: "You had better both go home!"

Did the first shot come from the spring-gun
set off by Mrs. Bell and her brother
scuffling on the bank of the ditch?
Or did Bell himself fire the first shot and was the second set off by his
    brother-in-law
as he fell dying?
Anyway, this is what the jury believed.

5

Watson was a mechanic, a hard-working man
earning from sixty to eighty dollars a month,
and, because of his work,
away from home much of the time.
His wife had died about ten years before
and there were three children—
twin girls of fifteen or sixteen and a boy of twelve.

Watson had to go to San Francisco
and stay there at work
several months. His daughters drew his wages—
and spent much of it for clothes
and theater tickets. When he came back
and found this out
he whipped his daughters with a leather strap he had;
and the next morning whipped them again
because breakfast was not ready.
They then decided to run away
and for three days hid in the basement of the house.

Later, he missed his silver watch
and asked his daughters about it;
at their answers
he charged them with lying
and beat them with a cane and a poker;
took one of them by the throat
and knocked her to the floor
and then kicked her in the side.
The next morning they ran away again
and lived for three weeks under the stairs
leading to an empty house.

6
The Mother-in-Law

His mother was much displeased by the marriage:
Jill was a country girl, the daughter of a farmer;
about twenty-six, and Jack a year younger.
Before the two left for the West,
Jack's mother got him to transfer his stocks and bonds to her.

Jack and his wife settled in Denver and, in two or three months,
Jack's mother came to Denver
to board and lodge in the same boarding-house.
For a while, she and Jill got along very well.

Jill hired a horse and buggy and drove her around;
and they went to church together.
Everything was pleasant enough
until, one evening, Jack wanted to go to a friend's house to play cards
and Jill objected: "Mrs. Tompkins is coming here tonight.
Can't you put your visit over until tomorrow?"
His mother heard them and said:
"If you want to go out, John, go out;
if you want to go to the theater
or to play cards with your friends,
do so.
She has no right to interfere with your pleasures!"

The next day, Jack's mother told Jill
that, from the letters she had been getting from Jack,
she didn't see how Jill and Jack could live together;
they would be better apart—
a good deal better for him and for her.
Her mother-in-law went on to tell her
there was no law in the land
that could compel a man to live with a woman
if he did not wish to—
as long as he paid her board.
She herself would pay Jill's way back to Brooklyn
or to her father's—
either way.
Jill said she would not go to her father's.
Then, her mother-in-law said, we will pay your way back to Brooklyn,
and offered Jill a hundred dollars
if she would give Jack a separation,
thinking that Jill might ask for two or three thousand
and she would pay it
and have done with Jill right away.

But Jill didn't say she would accept anything.
"Well, I am not going back," said her mother-in-law,
"and leave you two together;
I have all of Jack's money

and will leave him here without a cent—
without a red cent.
You should get a lawyer
and I will get my lawyer,
and they will draw up papers for a separation.
You have friends to advise you whom to go to."
Jill answered that she had no friends in Denver.
"You have friends in the boarding-house,"
and her mother-in-law added
that she had heard that Jill had been hanging around Jack
and that was why he had married her.

Jill began to cry—
as her mother-in-law explained afterwards,
"Of course, she did!
She could do that at any time"—
and got very angry.
"We are living happily together
and I don't see why we should separate!"
But her mother-in-law said coldly:
"I will give you three dollars a week to live on
for a separation,
and you must take that and live in Denver;
otherwise, I will leave you in Denver
without money or friends;
but you must not come back to New York.
You can go either to your sister's in Nevada or remain here,
but I don't want to lay eyes on you again!"

III
CHILDREN

1

The mining camp was near the top of a range of mountains;
no wagon road nearer than eight miles
and the rest of the way by trail

on foot or on the back of a horse or mule.
The community was under the rule of one man
whom they called their "Moses"—their teacher,
the teacher of all of them, parents and children.
The little boy was six years old
when he took a piece of a stove
and dropped it in the bushes,
and then said he had not taken it.
The "teacher" took the child
and ducked him in a pond
before six or more of the community
and the child's mother:
picked the boy up
and with one foot on the bank of the pond
and the other on a rock projecting above the water
dipped the boy into the pond
where it was shallow;
the child screamed in fright,
struggled
and held close to the man who was ducking him
and clutched at everything in sight;
when he was brought up
he had the mud and gravel at the bottom of the pond
clutched in his hands.

2

Nancy, all of twelve, living with her mother on the south side of the
        river,
was sent on an errand to her grandmother
who lived north of the railroad bridge;
and her brother, nine years of age, was sent with her.
When she reached the bridge, she stopped
to look and listen for a train,
for she knew trains were passing over the bridge
all hours of the day and night;
but she did not hear or see any
and with her brother started across.

When about halfway—
the bridge had no railing or planking
nothing except the ties to walk on—
she saw a train coming from the north
rounding the curve to the bridge.
The children were frightened
and began to run back,
but the little boy caught his foot in the ties
and fell.
His sister stopped, got him up,
and they ran a few steps farther.
Then she stopped again,
placed him on the end of a beam projecting from the bridge,
outside the rails for safety,
and kept on running
away from the train.

But when she was almost at the end of the bridge
she was struck by the engine
and, face up, pushed along the track about thirty feet
until the train stopped.

3
There were four machines for making horseshoes in the shop
and the boy—he was fifteen—
was put to work at one of them as "press boy."
The machines were worked by belts
running over a revolving shaft
and to reach the shaft—about twenty feet from the floor—
one had to go up a ladder.
The belt which ran the machine the boy was working at
was old. It broke twice
and the machinist went up and fixed it.
It broke again in the afternoon
and the machinist told the boy to go up and hold the belt
while he tried again to fix it.
The boy took the belt, weighing about forty or forty-five pounds,

on his shoulders
and started up the ladder;
when he got to the top he stepped off upon a plank
resting on a stringer of the building and on one of the uprights of the
    ladder
and walked along to the revolving shaft
where he was to hold the belt.

The shaft was running at full speed
as he put the ends of the belt over it
and dropped them down
and he was starting back when the machinist called up,
"Go back and hold that belt!"
He did and was holding the belt up from the shaft in a loop
for about ten minutes
when the machinist called up again,
"Wait! I am going to get some lacing."
The boy became tired and moving his feet a little
the plank turned—
and he fell on the shaft:
his right arm was caught between the belt and the shaft
and torn off at the elbow.

IV
PROPERTY

1

The Miles boy tore down Shelby's fence
so that the cattle got into the crop
and Shelby whipped him, "whipped him right":
fetched the boy up to the ranch,
said he wanted him to help put the fence up;
the boy stayed there that night
and the next morning was sitting in the kitchen,
peeling potatoes, when Shelby came in and put a gun at his head;
made him walk down to the barn, lie down on his belly,

tied a rope to him,
and tied him up to the "reach log" of the barn;
and when he was swinging there
took a blacksnake whip and whipped him a while;
then sat down on the sill of the barn,
rolled a cigarette and took a little rest,
and said, "As soon as I rest, I will whip you some more,"
and whipped him again;
and then let him down
and ordered him off the place.

The boy brought a damage suit against Shelby—
placed it in the hands of a lawyer—
and an information charging him with the crime of assault,
and Shelby had to give a bond for whipping him.

Hamilton was a young colored man, about twenty-two,
and had worked for Shelby. They met in a saloon in town
and had a drink together,
and Shelby said, "I want to see you in the wine-room a minute,"
and in the wine-room said to Hamilton:
"That Miles boy is in town
and he has had three or four indictments served on me.
Do you know anybody I could trust?"
"What for?" Hamilton asked.
"To get him out of the way—kill him."
"I don't," said Hamilton.
"My arm is hurt," said Shelby.
"I am just getting so I can ride
or I would have killed him long ago;
and rolled him up in a canvas
and thrown him into a burning coal bank."
Later, Hamilton heard Shelby say to a friend,
"If I could get that Miles boy in the hills
I would put his foot in a stirrup
and let the horse drag him to death."
And another time heard Shelby say, "I intended to get him to running

and rope him
and turn the other way and drag him to death."

Shelby was away in Chicago
and Mrs. Shelby had written Hamilton a letter to come up to the ranch.
The Miles boy and his brother were returning in a wagon with a four-
      horse team
along the main wagon road
to their home on a ranch, some fifty miles from town,
and on their way passed the Shelby ranch.
Mrs. Shelby was ironing in the kitchen
and saw them through her field-glasses.
"There comes the Miles boy!" she said to Hamilton,
and added that she did not want the boy to get back to town
and get on the witness stand
to swear against her husband.
"There's fifty dollars or more in it for you," she said to Hamilton,
"or anybody else that will do away with the Miles boy."
Hamilton said that he could not do it.
"Why not?" she said. "Aren't you going to do that for Mr. Shelby?
Go on and kill him!"
So she said, according to Hamilton.

He went to the dining-room and got the Winchester
from its case in a closet
and six cartridges right on the shelf above the gun,
and got on his horse;
put a black silk handkerchief over his face
into which he had cut holes with his pocketknife
and rode up behind the wagon
pointing his gun at the Miles boy,
and shot him through the body.
The Miles boy fell out of the wagon,
and Hamilton galloped around a big butte
and rode off to the hills.

When he got back to the ranch, he said, "Mrs. Shelby, I done it."
And she said: "I'm not a damn bit sorry.

He put us to a lot of trouble."
But Hamilton said, "I done something I am sorry for,"
and she said, "I am not,"
and took the black silk handkerchief, so he said,
and burnt it up in the kitchen stove.
But all this was not enough to find Shelby himself
guilty of the boy's death—so the judges held.

2

Their bodies were found about a mile apart:
young Mrs. Thorsen's under the refuse of a hogpen
upon the farm of Jeremiah Saxon;
the body of her young husband in a trail made by cattle
close to some large logs,
in the hollow made by the cattle
jumping over the logs where the ground was swampy,
and covered by a little earth and some sods—
just enough to hide it.
Both had been shot through the head.

About a month before their death
they had made their home on government land,
next to Saxon's farm,
and were living in a boat-house floated up on some logs at high water.
The land had been occupied by several claimants
who had all abandoned it,
and Thorsen intended to clear the record of former filings
in the land-office; but the land was almost worthless
for any purpose.
The Saxon farm, however, over a hundred acres,
had a house on it, outbuildings, and an orchard;
it had been a farm for many years
and was used by Saxon as a place to keep cattle and poultry
and for raising supplies for his hotel in Bayview.
The country around the farm, however, was wild and uncultivated,
and the only means of travel by boat.
Jeremiah Saxon himself was now a man of seventy

and had lived in or near Bayview for many years;
about forty people were regular boarders at his hotel
and he was well-known to everybody in the neighborhood.

The school in Bayview closed at the end of January
and the school-mistress, before she left for her home in Oregon,
gave a dancing-party. She had been boarding at Saxon's hotel
and his son, Jim, now all of eighteen,
went about the stores in Bayview, Thursday afternoon, to get ham for
    the party
and, after supper that night, he and another young man and the
    school-mistress
were in the kitchen of the hotel until late
making cakes. Jim spent most of Friday
clearing out of a new building the debris left by the carpenters
to get the floor ready for dancing, and that afternoon
he went to the exhibition with which the school closed.
On Sunday, he took the school-mistress in his boat
to the village from which she left for home,
and after that, feeling blue, he stayed around the village,
in and out of the saloons, and was "pretty full of liquor."
About four or five in the afternoon,
he bought a pint of whiskey—which he could not pay for just then—
took the whiskey and his gun and left in his boat for his father's farm.
On the way to the farm he made up his mind to kill Thorsen.
He slept at the farm,
got up in the morning with his head feeling pretty bad,
finished the whiskey he had brought with him,
took his shotgun and went to Thorsen's house.
He told him that a calf had got its legs between two logs
and that he could not get the logs apart alone
and would Thorsen help him get the calf out?
Jim went ahead and Thorsen followed along the cattle trail.
When Jim got over the log where Thorsen's body was found,
he turned: Thorsen was just getting up on the log
and Jim said, "Look here, Thorsen!"
Jim had his gun ready and as Thorsen looked up
Jim fired. The charge struck Thorsen just below the eye

and he dropped dead.
Jim took whatever money Thorsen had in his pocket:
it was a little more than fifty-nine dollars.
Out of that money
he would buy several chances in the seal-skin lottery.
His father might ask him where he got that much money
and he would answer that the Land Company owed it
for work he had done in the fall and had just paid it.
As he started for the farm
Jim thought he had better do some more shooting
to make people think he was out hunting;
and so he shot away the rest of the cartridges he had with him.

He waited about the farm for an hour or so,
and then concluded he would have to kill Mrs. Thorsen, too,
because she had seen him going away with her husband,
and when Thorsen didn't come back there would be trouble.
He took the rifle kept in the house to kill cattle
and put a cartridge in it
and went down to the Thorsen house and told Mrs. Thorsen her
    husband had broken his leg
and he could not get him home
and that Mr. Thorsen wanted her to come right up to the house.
She put on her rubber boots and started along with Jim.
When they were near the hogpen, Jim held the rifle close to her temple
and fired.
He waited in the house until it was almost dark
and buried her under the manure pile at the hogpen;
next morning he went to Thorsen's body
and buried it just where it was lying.
In Thorsen's house, he found a pistol and more money on a shelf;
and then went back to Bayview and told those whom he happened to
    meet
that he had seen the Thorsens leave in a dinghy;
that, shortly after they left,
a squall came up and, after the squall was over,
he could see nothing more of the dinghy,
and thought it had been swamped and the Thorsens drowned.

Thorsen's pistol had a leather handle
and Jim cut the leather off
and also Thorsen's initials on the wood beneath the leather.
He kept the pistol under his bed and his mother found it.
When his father asked him where he got the pistol,
he answered that he had bought it from a man in Bayview.

The people of Bayview, now and then, went searching for the bodies of
      Thorsen and his wife—
they might have been washed ashore if not eaten by the seals—
and someone came upon Thorsen's body late in February.
Jim himself then pointed out where Mrs. Thorsen's body lay
and wanted to help the men digging it up.

The sheriff arrested Jim in the presence of his father
and the old man, naturally, was much agitated.
When the sheriff was taking his prisoner to the boat for the county-
      seat,
Saxon stepped up to his son and said:
"Now, Jim, don't you talk to anyone until you come up before the
      court,
and then tell the truth:
tell the court about seeing Thorsen and his wife go out in their boat,
and about the storm coming up and that you thought they were
      drowned."
And then Jim's father told those near them that Jim had wounded a
      wild goose near the farm
and had tied a string to its leg
so that it would draw other wild geese by its cries,
and Jim had managed to kill thirteen geese by the trick:
"I didn't know but what people would think it strange
that there was so much shooting going on up there,
and I thought I would tell you what it was
so that if anything was said about it you would know."
And he sent a young man along with his son to help protect him—
Gibbs had come to the neighborhood only three weeks before
where his work was slashing timber
and he boarded at Saxon's hotel—

for there was angry talk in the villages along the bay.
But when it was suggested that he go himself
he said he dared not: threats had been made against his own life, too,
for he would not help in the search for the Thorsens.

"My father," Jim told those who questioned him,
"wanted this land that Thorsen took.
He wanted Jones"—the young man his father had hired
to take care of the cattle at the farm—
"and Gibbs—one of the meanest men that ever came into this
        country—
to take the land
and pay out on it and then deed it over to him;
and Gibbs and Jones and my father
made it up how they would kill the Thorsens.
My father came to me and said
he wanted me to go down with him to the farm next day
to look after some cattle. Gibbs stood near him
and said he would like to go down with us,
and so, next morning, we three went down to the farm,
and when we got there Father says to Jones,
'You better go up and get Thorsen to help bring the cattle down.'
As we walked along the bluff,
there was a hawk set up on a tree,
and Gibbs says to me,
'Give me your gun and I'll see if I can kill that hawk.'
I let him have the gun
and, after he shot the hawk, he kept the gun,
saying he might see some geese to shoot at.
We walked on until we got down by the cow trail,
and Gibbs walked ahead and Thorsen behind.
I heard Gibbs say to Thorsen, 'Look here, Thorsen!'
and just then he shot him, and I turned around and said,
'That's a pretty way to use a man
after calling him to drive the cattle up,'
and Gibbs says,
'That's the kind of cattle we came after.'

"After Gibbs shot Thorsen, Jones walked into the brush
and got a spade out,
and began to look around for a place to bury him—
it was in the cow trail—
and Father says, "That's a good enough place right here.'
Jones went to work and dug the grave,
and I went off ten or fifteen feet
and never looked up at them until they had the grave ready,
and called me to help lay Thorsen in the grave.
They had his gum boots off and his gum coat,
and laid them down where he had dropped;
and I helped put him in the grave
and throwed over what loose dirt there was,
and then they pulled some grass sod up,
and put it on top of him,
and after that Father picked up Thorsen's gum coat and boots,
and threwed them down in the slough
where the tide flows in and out.

"As we walked along the beach to the house, Father said,
'Better hurry up and get Mrs. Thorsen down:
she may suspect something.'
And Jones said to me, 'Give me your shotgun.'
I told him I would not,
and Father commenced cursing and swearing at me
because I would not let Jones have it;
and Jones said: 'I will get the rifle.
Don't make any fuss about it.'
They was gone after Mrs. Thorsen about twenty minutes,
and I heard someone scream
and I went out and looked,
and saw her coming along the fence:
Father had hold of one arm
and Jones had hold of the other;
and just as they got inside the gate
Jones picked up the rifle. When they got inside,
Mrs. Thorsen asked what they had done with her husband.
Jones says, 'We shot him.'

And she says: 'Then kill me, too! I don't want to live any longer.'
Jones raised the rifle to her temple—
she never moved a muscle—
and shot her.

"They buried her right there behind the pigpen
and, after the grave was dug,
Father called me to help put her in the grave,
and we covered her up, and threw some sods on top of her,
so people would not see the loose dirt.
And Father and Jones went back to Thorsen's house
and when they came back Gibbs carried the pistol.
Father called me out to the front of the house,
and he had fifty dollars and gave it to me,
and said if he ever found out that I told this on him
I would be dead first;
and, what's more, if I went down to the farm next week,
and it came up stormy,
and anybody asked me what became of the Thorsens,
I was to say that I saw them go out on the day of the storm.
Before we left that evening,
Gibbs gave me the pistol.
I told him I did not want it
but he gave it to me and I kept it.
Jones was to take Thorsen's boat out that night
and sink it—swamp it."

This is what Jim also told in court
when his father and Jones were tried for the murders—
and the jury believed him.

3
Clark had a cabin a few miles from town:
a small building of boards,
battened with shingles. The lock on the door fitted loosely
and it could be pushed open
without unlocking it.

In December, Clark went into the mountains
for a hunting trip
to be gone most of the winter.
The morning he left he placed a loaded spring-gun
inside the cabin: the muzzle aimed at the door
so that someone standing in front of it
and putting his hand on the knob
would, upon pushing the door open a few inches,
get the charge in his body.
Clark then nailed up the door
and put a sign with the word "Danger"
over it. The best of what was in the cabin
had been taken to the house of a neighbor
and what was left was of little value.

Swenson and a companion had been several times to a construction
        camp,
looking for work. That morning they started for the camp again
and thought it best not to carry their blankets all the way
and left them in the stump of a tree near the cabin.
When they reached the camp, they found that they would have to
        go back to town
to find the man they had to see;
they found him and were to go to work the next day.

After that, Swenson and his companion bought a loaf of bread
and some sausage for supper
and began to walk back to camp.
By that time it was dark and raining and the road muddy.
When they came near the cabin,
Swenson said he did not think anybody had lived in it for a long time
and he would try to get in;
if they could, they had better get their blankets and sleep there,
instead of going on to the camp that night.
Pushing at the door—
the spring-gun was discharged
and the full charge

went through the door
and killed him.

4

Dr. Yard was a physician in Rhode Island,
and for some time had the management of Mrs. Lancaster's estate:
this amounted to more than a hundred thousand dollars,
most of it in stocks and bonds
all in the name of Dr. Yard;
for she had absolute confidence in his integrity and business sagacity.
For years she had suffered from a partial paralysis
of one side of her body
and he had been her physician.
When at home, in Providence, she would visit his family—
his wife and aged mother—
and while traveling would write him often upon business and other
    matters:
her letters were always respectful and showed her esteem.
She had also left him a legacy of twenty-five thousand dollars
in the wills she had made,
and he was to be her sole executor—without bond.

His letters to her were of like character,
showing respect and esteem—
except two:
she was thinking of selling some of her stocks and bonds
and buying property in the Adirondacks,
near a place she used to go to—"The Ramble,"
under the management of friends.
He wrote her then that the executors of her late husband's estate
were much displeased with the plan
and would take steps to have a guardian appointed for her
if she persisted.

She had been traveling in California and, on the way home,
was stopping with the Craigs, her friends in Denver.

Shortly before her arrival, a package came for her by mail:
a bottle holding about half a pint of a dark liquid.
Some of those present when the package was opened
took it to be blackberry wine;
but, although it had been mailed at the end of March
and was not received until some time in April,
the bottle had the following inscription:
"Wish you a happy New Year!
Please accept this fine old whiskey
from your friends at The Ramble."

Before leaving Denver,
she spent a day in the country with Mrs. Craig
and came back to the house, very tired.
She took the bottle from her trunk to make "a couple of toddies,"
using no more than two spoonfuls of the contents for each;
and Mrs. Lancaster drank one and Mrs. Craig the other.
Soon after, both became sick
and their symptoms were those of arsenic poisoning;
in fact, when the fluid left in the bottle was examined,
it showed a strong solution of arsenic.
The next morning, Mrs. Craig's daughter sat down by Mrs. Lancaster's
    bedside:
Mrs. Lancaster seemed somewhat better and even inclined to talk:
yes, she knew that she had been poisoned.
The young woman asked if she supposed that her friends at The
    Ramble could have sent it.
"No," she said. "Oh, no!"
"Have you any enemies that would do such a thing?"
"I don't know of an enemy in the world!"

She thought for a moment and then said,
"The last maid I had was angry at me:
she was not a lady and I did not care to keep her."
"How did you happen to employ her?"
"Dr. Yard employed her for me.
He was anxious that I should spend the winter in Cuba
with her as my companion, and I didn't want to go."

"Can you think of anyone who knows that they will benefit by your
        death?"
"I left Dr. Yard twenty-five thousand dollars in my will."
 She went on to say that she didn't have as much confidence in Dr. Yard
        as she used to have:
the medicine he had sent her lately
didn't seem to do her the good it used to;
 and she didn't like the way she had been treated while in California:
 she didn't get money when she wanted it,
 and at one time she and her maid had only fifty cents between them.
"As soon as I am able to travel, I'll go East
 and put this matter in the hands of a good detective."

But next day it was hard for her to breathe
and, after lingering several days in agony, she died.

5

She sold the twenty acres she had in Michigan
and this was the money she brought along to Portland—
seven hundred dollars in a draft of deposit on a bank
safe in her bosom.
She arrived in Portland with her three children
at seven in the morning, worn out by the long journey
and sick.
Her husband was at the depot to meet her
and brought her and the children to a lodging-house
run by a Mr. Flugel.
She had never seen the man before
but her husband told her he was a member of his family.

After breakfast, she went back to the room they had taken
to rest, and her husband told her Mr. Flugel had a place to sell—
a tract of ten acres near Portland—
and urged her to buy it. All his own own money was gone.
That evening, Flugel invited her into his room
and he, too, talked about the place he had for sale:
only eight miles from Portland along the road usually traveled,

and worth not less than fifteen hundred dollars in the market.
He would let her have it for fourteen hundred and fifty,
and take in part payment the draft of deposit she had with her,
and in the morning would take her out to see the place.
She said she didn't want to see it;
besides, she hadn't enough money,
and went back to her room.

But he came there that very night,
and she said she didn't want to see him—
she didn't want to buy the land.
At six in the morning, bright and early, he was back again
and said he was ready to take her out to see the place,
and had a team ready.
Before he left the room,
he said he would have a paper made out
by which he would let her have the place
for fourteen hundred and fifty dollars—
a good deal!
She became very nervous at that:
not sure that she understood him
or that he understood what she was saying—
a native of Germany, she was as yet uncertain about her English—
and sent the two eldest of her children after him
to tell him that she didn't want any paper drawn up.
The children caught up with him in the street
and told him: "Mother wants no paper, no writing today.
She is going crazy."
But he came back with the paper, anyway,
and brought along pen and ink.
She signed a contract to buy the land, finally—
she thought she was getting a deed—
and indorsed the draft in part payment.
But the tract of land was not worth even the part payment; and,
    besides, it was mortgaged.

6

A Letter

Friend: has a young man in Ohio got a little nerve to come out to
        Montana?
There is a man here has got some scrub horses he thinks is fast—
range horses without any mark;
him and his friends will bet their money
as he is a man without any knowledge of horse racing.
Has been in the country a long time
and done business in the early days with the half-breed Indians;
now a saloonkeeper.

I want a man to come out and bring a good horse with him,
a pace or a trotter,
and we will match this man with a dead mortal cinch.
We can win several thousand dollars—
like finding it.
The way I would want to bring the horses in the country would be
        to sneak them in the town;
put a hair brand on them so they would appear range stock:
it is meat for someone.
The main object is to make it appear that the horses are undeveloped;
to give them a sure thing in the way of thinking.
It is a big snap for someone to match a horse race.
This is no josh: we have got the biggest sucker here in the state
and has got plenty of money.
Please don't send us your envelopes with your advertisements as a horseman,
or anything with your name on it.
Don't want these people to get on to anything that would throw us off.
Whatever business I have to do with you,
expect to be honorable and upright:
that is the only way for a person to transact business.

7

Jacobs and a partner had a large store
but business was bad and the firm losing money.

One day, Jacobs left the store for lunch
and went to a restaurant in the neighborhood
with two companions—one a friend of many years.
They had just seated themselves at the table
when Jacobs got up and said he wanted to let his partner know where
     he was:
there was a telephone in the room
and he came back pale and excited
and wanted to leave at once.

On the way out, they stopped at the cigar-stand
and Jacobs bought cigars for himself and his companions
and managed to tell his friend
that he wanted to get rid of their companion
for the two of them to talk about a business matter;
and when their companion left them
the two went on towards Jacobs' place of business.

Jacobs became more excited than ever and said:
"They've got me!
The sheriff is in possession of the store right now
with an attachment!" And turning to his friend he said,
"I want you to promise me one thing:
be as good a friend to my wife as you have been to me."

His friend made up his mind to stay with Jacobs until he had calmed
     down
and, when they reached the store, Jacobs went inside
and his friend remained at the entrance.
It might be a good thing, his friend thought then, to see someone he
     had to see—who had an office nearby—
and be back in a few minutes.
When he was back, Jacobs had left the store.

There was a hotel nearby and Jacobs' friend, in his search for him,
went in and saw Jacobs' name on the register
and the number of the room he had been given.

His friend went up to the room at once
but found the door locked.

He finally got a boy who worked at the hotel
to go through the transom
and when the door was opened from the inside
they saw Jacobs lying on the bed,
flat on his back, dead:
he had taken off his shoes and coat, his vest was unbuttoned,
his necktie untied and the collar loosened;
and his head was thrown back,
mouth and eyes partly open.

There were brownish stains on his lips and chin.
On the dresser was a tumbler
with a little of a brownish liquid still in it—
about half a teaspoonful—
and it had a peculiar, unpleasant smell.

V

RAILROADS

1

The company was constructing a railroad
through mountainous country. It was the fall of the year
and it had been raining for days.
Several hundred laborers had been at work at the end of the track—
handling the ties and bedding them and laying track.
That morning it was raining again
and a number of the workmen
did not want to leave their boarding-camp.
But the head track-layer ordered them to leave:
they could go to work
or "get their time" and be discharged;
he wanted no "dudes" on the job
and he was "going to be in hell or in Aspen by Christmas!"

The construction train consisted of an engine and a tender,
a flatcar carrying two large water-tanks,
and another flatcar loaded with curved steel rails.
Forty or fifty men were on the engine, tender, and tank car
and two hundred or so crowded as close as they could stand
upon the car with steel rails.
The train was running about eight miles an hour down grade
when it reached a curve in the roadbed—now water-soaked and soft—
on an embankment that had been built along a gulch.
The tank car lurched to one side;
and when the flat car with its heavy load of rails
came upon the embankment, the track slid
from the ties and the ends of the ties sank in the mud;
the front trucks of the car slipped into the gulch
and the steel rails began to slide from the car.

The men on the edges had a chance to jump
but those in the center were hemmed in and could not move;
Ryan was among those caught under the rails.
His body and hands were free
but his legs were caught fast and crushed:
blood was all over his overalls
and the raw flesh showed where they had been torn.
His legs had to be amputated
a few inches below the knee-joints;
and he was unable to straighten out the stumps
and use artificial legs.
Now his only way of getting about
was to drag himself along on his knees.

2

The boy was fourteen years of age and had been hired to carry water
to the men building and grading
the roadbed of the railroad.
The powder used for blasting often became frozen in the mountains,
even in May,
and it was the duty of the "gang boss" to thaw it.

The "gang boss" would thaw the powder
before an open fire. One day,
when he had to use a lot of it,
he laid about seventy-five sticks of the blasting-powder
against a log in front of the fire
and, as the powder became warm on one side,
turned the sticks to thaw them evenly;
and when they became sufficiently warm
laid them in a pile near the fire.

The water-boy came along with some tools from the blacksmith shop,
and stopped at the fire to warm himself;
and the "gang boss" picked up about forty sticks of the powder
and carried them in his arms to the boulder he was about to blast
leaving four or five sticks behind
for the boy to carry. When they reached the boulder,
the "boss" began putting the sticks of powder
in the hole drilled for it. He had put seven or eight sticks in the
     boulder
when someone called out, "The powder's on fire!"

A pile of logs and brush was between the fire and the "boss"
but he could see by the peculiar blaze
that some of the powder left at the fire was burning.
"Billy," he said to the boy, "run!"
Throw the burning stick away!"
The boy jumped up and ran towards the fire.

When the smoke of the explosion cleared up
the boy's body was found
a few feet from where the fire had been.

3
The Favor

At midnight, when the freight train was about to start from Pueblo
a young man—a cripple with an artificial leg—

came up to the conductor in charge
and asked if he showed favors to crippled railroad men:
he wanted to go to his brother
who lived near the line between Pueblo and Denver
in order to make his living on a farm.
The conductor answered that he sometimes did a fellow railroad man a
      favor—
it depended—
and the young man showed him a letter:
he had been a brakeman on another road for ten or eleven months.
The conductor asked why he did not apply to the Brakemen's
      Brotherhood for aid,
and he answered that he had not been a brakeman long enough to get
      into the Brotherhood.
The conductor then said: no, he would not let him ride on the train;
besides, the letter was too old.

The conductor went up along the train
to take down the numbers of the cars
and did not come back to the caboose at the rear end
until the train had left Pueblo and was well under way.
He found the young man in the caboose
with two or three men traveling with live-stock on the train—
and left him there.

The train went on to Colorado Springs
where another railroad crossed the roadbed
and the train stopped at the crossing
to do some switching in the railroad yard.
The last six cars with the caboose were cut off
and left on the track.
Here the grade went downward
to a station they had passed;
two of the cars had air-brakes
and the conductor set these,
and ordered the rear brakeman to set the brakes on the other cars.
The brakeman noticed that the air-brakes were not holding
and set the hand-brakes on three, perhaps four, of the cars;

and the stockmen and the train crew left.
But the young man stayed in the caboose.

The brakes became loosened
and the cars started down the track:
they ran as far as the next station
and here crashed into the engine of another train.
The cars immediately in front of the caboose
were loaded with explosives—
these went off at the collision;
and the mangled body of the young man was found
by the side of the track.

4

At a stop, she left her seat in the "immigrant car" to stand near the
    stove
and get warm. When the train started with a jerk
she put out her hand to steady herself
and caught hold of a post beside the berths.
It might have been the newsboy going through the cars
or a friendly brakeman who had raised the upper berth
but had not pushed it up far enough
for the fastenings to catch,
and it came down—
and caught two of her fingers
and crushed them.

5

As the train approached the station,
the family got up and stood at the door of the car
to be able to step off without delay.
As soon as the train stopped
they began to leave,
but the stop was so short
only some of the family were able to get off,
and the train moved away

with the father still on it—
and his little girl and the baby on his arm.

The conductor of the train was on the platform of the car
and said: "Go to the next station.
It's only a short distance
and you can walk back."
At the next station
the man left the train;
he looked about and saw no way to get back
other than the roadbed of the railroad;
and, in fact, there was no other way:
on one side the water of the bay,
and on the other swamp.
There were two tracks, and he supposed that if a train would come
      along
it would be on the east track,
for the train he had just left was on the other;
and began to walk along the west track,
carrying the baby on one arm
and holding the little girl, a child of six, by the hand.

He had gone several hundred feet
when he heard the noise of a train behind him
and looked back
but, because of a curve in the road,
could not see on what track the train was running.
He looked again
and saw that the train was on the track on which he was walking

and crossed to the other track,
all the time holding the little girl by the hand.
But, frightened by the swift approach of the train,
she broke away
and ran back to the track they had been on—
right in front of the engine—
and was struck by it.

VI

That morning when the stevedores came to work
they were told by the foreman
to go down into the hold of the vessel
and help stow away a cargo of coal
from the vessel alongside. The stevedores had to go forward
down to the steerage deck
and then along this deck to a stairway
leading to the orlop deck, and along the orlop deck
to the hatchway
where there was a ladder leading into the hold.

The foot of the stairway to the orlop deck
was about ten feet from the coaming of the hatchway
and the deck was pitch dark.
When the hatchway of the main deck was open
the light from above lit up the orlop deck, too,
so that the hatchway and the ladder to the hold
could be seen; it was also usual
when the men were stowing coal in the hold
to have a lighted lamp hung near the hatchway—
but this morning the hatchway on the main deck was closed
and the lamp had not been lit.

The men went down the narrow stairway to the orlop deck
in single file
and, as each man reached the foot of the stairs,
he had to go on
to make room for the others behind him.
They had just commenced to light the lamp
but, before it was lit,
O'Brien was going along the orlop deck in the darkness—
the others behind him coming down from the steerage deck
pressing him forward—
and down he went into the hatchway
falling twenty feet into the hold.

VII
MINING

1

The miner was working in a shaft sunk to a depth of about ninety feet
from a tunnel in a silver mine;
there were no ladders for going up or down the shaft
and he had to use the cracks between the timbering—
green bark, wet and slippery.

He had placed a cartridge in the hole
drilled by him at the bottom of the shaft
and had fired the fuse, and then climbed up the timbering
to wait for the explosion.
When there had been time and enough for it,
he made his way down the shaft
to see if water had reached the drill-hole,
and stopped about ten feet above the bottom—
high enough to be safe should the cartridge explode.
Turning to look down,
he held on to the timbering with one hand:
the fuse was alight.

But, as he turned to go up the shaft again,
his foot slipped—
the timbering was close at this point—
and he fell.
At the bottom of the shaft, he reached at once for the fuse
to pull it out before the cartridge exploded;
but, before he could get his fingers on it,
the explosion—
rock now feeling like sand—
struck his face and arms
blinding him forever.

2

Vic had been mining coal since he was fourteen;
now, all of seventeen,
he was working with John in the same room;
and Vic, the elder and more experienced,
did the talking.
John was looking at the rock overhead
and testing it with a pick—
pounding it with the head of the pick
for the purpose of sounding it
to tell if the rock was loose;
and John called Vic's attention
to a crack—or slip—in the rock.
Vic didn't think there was any danger
but they started to put a prop under it.
They had a prop that had been cut the day before
but this was too short
and they threw it away.
Vic told John to get a prop where the props were kept
but there were no props around;
and Vic went out himself to get some props that had been left
at a prospect hole along the creek,
but these, too, were gone.
Then he decided to wait
until he had loaded the car with coal—
after all, the roof was all a little cracked.

They had nearly finished work for the day
when Vic heard a crack
and jumped back—
he supposed that the coal was about to fall
from the face of the room;
but it was a rock that fell from the roof
and his right arm was caught under it and crushed.

The rock that fell was about fifteen feet long
and four feet wide at the widest part
and was near the center of the room.

If there had been a prop or two under it
and the rock was going to fall,
Vic would have had some warning:
the prop would have bent or broken—
and the rock might not have fallen at all.

3
Graham was working in the "silver room,"
where the silver was separated from lead and gold.
Although usually only three sets of tanks were used at the same time,
on that day all four sets in the room were being used
and the waste acid from all four was to be poured into the "waste tank"
        at the same time.
But there were only three hoses in the silver room
through which to pump it,
and the foreman fixed up a fourth hose
by connecting two pieces of short hose that had been lying about—
old hose, worn and eaten by the acid in which they had been used—
slipping one end of each piece of hose over a piece of lead pipe
so that the two ends met near the middle;
he did not tie them to the pipe by wire or twine
and they were held only by what elastic force was left in them.

Graham began using this improvised hose
but in about ten or fifteen minutes
it parted:
one of the pieces slipped from the lead pipe
and the scalding hot acid was emptied upon his shoulder and back.

VIII
LABOR TROUBLES

Oaks, his son, and another man working for Oaks
were lathers at work in a building;

in the morning, two men came to the building and told Oaks to quit
        working.
He would not. "Why not?" they asked and he answered:
"We are not members of the Union and are not going to stick it out.
We stuck it out a week,
and are not going to stick it out any longer."

One of the two asked him if he was willing to pay his help three
        dollars a day—
that was what the Union journeymen were striking for:
three dollars a day for eighteen bunches of laths,
eighteen hundred laths for a day's work;
and Oaks said he was willing.
Then, said the man, if he would come down and join the Union,
he would get all the Union men he wanted.
But Oaks said he would not.

They came back about three or four in the afternoon
with forty men—fully forty.
Oaks and his son were at work on a stage in a bedroom
and the party of forty came up the narrow stairway.
The lower part of the walls was not yet lathed
and was open between the studding;
one of the crowd stuck his head through the partition
where it was open at the bottom
and said, "Don't you think you fellows have done enough today?"
And another in the crowd said, "Yes, we don't want no scab work!"

The elder Oaks turned around and said he was not a scab
and was not doing scab work;
but the first of the crowd to speak now spoke up and said, "You said
        enough!"
The younger Oaks asked his father to say no more—not to provoke
        them,
and the strikers told father and son to come off the stage,
three or four shouting, "Come down!"
And they did.

As they were making their way through the crowd to the stairs,
one of the men said to the younger Oaks:
"Get your father out of here!
They nearly killed a man on Post Street."
The younger Oaks turned to his father
and saw one of the strikers punch his father on the back of the head
and another man striking at his father's face;
the younger Oaks tried to make the man who held him
break his hold
to get where his father was,
but a couple of men caught him around the neck
and he went down on the floor.

The crowd left, all of them,
in a rush down the stairway,
and the younger Oaks went to his father:
the elder Oaks was much excited
and showed his son a mark on his nose
where he had been hit.
His son told him to come home right away
and they would see what they could do,
and they went down the stairway together.
The younger man was in a pretty "banged up" condition himself
and his father was pale, very pale,
and had a lump on the back of his head.

That night the elder Oaks complained of a headache
and could not eat his dinner,
and about twelve that night
got to breathing hard
and was soon unconscious.
In a few days he died.
His death, the doctors said, was caused by a broken artery:
it might have been caused by a blow on the side of his head
or just the excitement—or both.

IX

Klein, a peddler of spectacles,
rode to the next station on the railroad:
the country was desert with houses few and far between.
There was a platform from the station to the section-house
and he went towards it to sell his spectacles
but before he reached it the section foreman,
calling him "a spotter" and spy for the railroad,
began to beat him with a shovel.

The foreman followed Klein
and gave him five minutes to get away
or he would "kill him";
and Klein started to walk along the track.
Two men who had been "hanging around" the station
followed him
and a quarter of a mile away
took his satchel of spectacles and his pocketbook
and whatever money he had.

Klein went back to the railroad station
and the two men followed
but stopped near the pump-house.
He wanted the ticket-agent to send a telegram to Green River
telling of the holdup
but the section foreman told the ticket-agent not to,
and went across the track to where the two men were standing
and the three came into the waiting-room
and began beating up Klein.
He called for help
but none of the spectators helped him
and all the ticket agent did
was to order the four of them out of the waiting room.

MEXICANS

1

Brown and Jackson, cowboys on neighboring ranches near the Mexican
    border,
had their saddles stolen,
and started on the trail of four Mexicans
who had camped close to one of the ranches
the night before.
The Mexicans left behind two old saddles.

On the road Brown and Jackson passed the Mexicans:
they had stopped to cook dinner
and the cowboys saw their own saddles on horses two of the Mexicans
    were riding.
Jackson left Brown to watch them
and rode back to hurry along
those who had promised to help make the arrest;
but he could not find them
and he and Brown followed on after the Mexicans.

Later in the afternoon,
the Mexicans who had gone into ambush near the road
rushed upon them.
Jackson and Brown fled—
galloping off in different directions
as the Mexicans kept firing;
two of the Mexicans went after Jackson
and the other two after Brown.
Jackson got away
and rode on back in search of help.

Those who had gathered to help him and Brown
found Brown's horse without its bridle
and not far off his hat.
There was a pool of blood on the road
and from it the trail of a body that had been dragged away.

They followed the drag
and came upon Brown's body
with two knife wounds in his breast:
the Mexicans must have overtaken
and lassoed him,
jerking him from his horse,
and then plunged their knives into his breast;
and with their lassoes
dragged the body off the road into the brush and grass.

2

Campbell was over six feet tall and unusually strong,
Zapota small and slender.
He and his wife were milking in the cowpen
when Campbell came up
and ordered him to get the horses and go to work.
Zapota said that it was too cold—and raining.

Standing outside the fence, within a few feet of Zapota,
Campbell asked him again if he was going to go to work.
The Mexican stood up where he was milking,
in his hand only a milk can,
and refused.
Campbell aimed his Winchester at him
and Zapota's wife caught the gun
but Campbell jerked it away and struck her on the head with it,
knocking her down;
then turned and shot Zapota through the breast.

Zapota's wife carried her husband to their home nearby
and laid him on some cotton
and covered him with a quilt and blanket;
they had no bed—no furniture at all.
There was no fireplace and it was freezing.
A neighbor, when Campbell asked him to, called at the Mexican's
        house,
and found him sitting on the floor,

wrapped in the blanket,
and his wife squatting by a little fire under the shed
her head gashed and bleeding from the blow.

The neighbor told Campbell the Mexican was doing badly.
Campbell's house was fifty yards or so away
but neither Campbell nor his wife
sent food, medicine, or clothing to the Zapotas.
The day after the shooting
Campbell did ask a doctor to visit the wounded man
but the doctor never went;
and Campbell insisted that Zapota leave the place
and was so insistent
a try was made to move the dying man.
However, in an hour or two he died.

XI
INDIANS

Early in the spring it was nice weather
and the trees just budding;
the other Indians on the reservation were plowing
and had been plowing for several days
when an Indian on horseback with a carbine
came to the tepee
and asked the Indian who lived there
to come along with him—
out riding or roaming around.

The other Indian got a sorrel horse belonging to his wife—
also a gun;
and both had belts with cartridges,
the kind soldiers use.
They went to still another Indian's tepee
and he, too, saddled up a horse and got his gun and some cartridges,
and the three of them started.

By this time it was the middle of the forenoon.
They followed the road along the river
until they came to a road that ran off into the hills
and took it, but did not find anything to shoot at
until they saw a bunch of five cows,
and one of them shot and killed a cow.
Then they all got off their horses and started to skin it,
cutting down the legs and getting ready to take the hide off;
their guns laid on the ground
and their horses held by ropes.
But a white man who must have heard the shot
came up close;
did not say anything
and went away.

Then the Indians said to each other:
this man has seen us
and will know us.
He will go and tell on us.
So they took their guns and got on their horses
and followed him—
keeping off quite a way—
until he got back to the sheep he was herding.
Then all three charged and shot at him.
He fell
but started to get up
and one of the Indians shot him again.

A little dog was running around
and they said to each other:
this dog will go down to the ranch
and they will search for the man.
And one of the Indians shot it,
and put it beside the body.
In four or five days some of the sheep strayed back to the ranch,
two or so miles away,
and the owner and his hands went in search of the herder.

Nothing was left of his body but the bones
with some flesh on the hands
and the hair of his head.
The bone of his left arm was broken
and his woolen shirt was burned where the bullet had entered his
    breast.

PART FOUR

TESTIMONY

THE UNITED STATES (1901–1910)

RECITATIVE

THE SOUTH

I

SOCIAL LIFE

1

Al and Jim's brother were calling on the same girl:
she lived with her parents in a dugout, partly covered with white
    ducking,
and called by some in the neighborhood, "the White House."
One of the young men in the neighborhood
said something or other to Jim's brother about "the White House"
and Jim's brother, thinking that he was talking about the President of
    the United States entertaining Booker T. Washington,
answered that he did not think much of the White House since
    "niggers" were eating there;
and Al when he heard of this thought that Jim's brother had called him
    a "nigger"
and called Jim's brother "a son of a bitch."

They met after church—Al and Jim's brother—
and Jim's brother told Al he ought to apologize
and Al answered, "Apologize? Hell, I never carry that around,"
and wheeling his horse got down.
"If nothing else but a fight will do you," he said,
"God damn you, I can give you that!"
and added, "Shut your knife and get ready;"
for Jim's brother was standing among some of their neighbors
    whittling.

Jim's brother closed his knife, put it in his back pocket,
laid his coat down, and said, "A fair fight!"
And Al hit him;
first on one cheek and then on the nose
and the blood ran over Jim's brother.
Just then Jim rode up,

saw his brother and Al fighting
and his brother covered with blood
and thought he had been stabbed. Jumping off his horse,
he ran around the crowd
and fired at Al and killed him.

2

A Christmas Party

The trouble began in a bawdyhouse on Gas House Alley.
The woman who kept the house was in the kitchen making eggnog—
it was Christmas—
and Joe and Ed met.
Joe said that he had it in for Ed a long time
and struck him on the head.
Ed's head was bandaged
because of a wound he had gotten in a fight with another man—
and he said, "You see I can't fight now."
But Joe struck him again
and Ed said that if he wanted to fight,
he should put his pistol away
and they would go into the alley
and he would fight him a fair fight.

Joe threw his pistol on the bed
and said he would go with Ed anywhere
and struck him again.
They started out of the room for the alley
but, before they left, Joe knocked Ed over a washstand
and, as he stood over Ed with a knife,
Ed in knocking away his hand
thrust the knife into Joe's neck.

The woman who kept the house
now opened the door to the alley—
Joe was a favorite of hers—
and told Ed to leave.

He ran down the alley
and Joe, picking up the pistol,
ran after him.
Ed, meeting an acquaintance,
begged him for his pistol
but the man did not have it with him
and as they were still talking
Joe came towards them pistol in hand.

Ed jumped behind the man he was talking to
and held him between himself and Joe,
pushing the man this way and that
as a shield
and the man kept asking Joe not to shoot
not to be shot.

As Joe got near enough to reach around the man's body to shoot Ed,
the man Ed was holding
broke away
and Ed ran towards a saloon,
Joe after him,
snapping his pistol to shoot Ed
before he could get away;
and then followed him into the saloon
and, as Ed crouched behind the counter,
shot him and killed him.

3

There was a dance at a house in town, and one of those at the dance
walked out of the house at midnight, sat down on the steps,
and lit a cigarette. Another Negro, standing near him,
said, "Give me a draw off your cigarette."
The man smoking said, "What do you mean?"
And the other man replied, "Give me a draw off your cigarette, if you
    want to;
if not, go to hell!"

The man smoking said, "I won't give you a draw
and I won't go to hell either."

They were having some more words, when another Negro who had
    been at the dance,
walked out and said to the man smoking,
"What are you doing here? Let's go!"
And the man who had asked for "a draw" turned to him and said,
"What in hell have you got to do with it?"
The other man answered quietly, "I haven't anything to do with it, my
    friend,
but I am not speaking to you,"
and added, "I am going home";
and he and the man who was smoking walked off together.

The man who had asked for "a draw" shouted at the smoker's
    companion,
"I don't care nothing for a nigger like you!"
And the man shouted at answered, "I don't care nothing for you,
    either."
Someone in the crowd that had gathered shouted at the man who had
    asked for "a draw,"
"Get him, Archie!"
But others were saying, "Don't have a fuss, boys."
Archie grabbed at the smoker's companion with his left hand
and made a pass at him with his right
in which he held a knife.
The man broke loose;
Archie struck at him again
and cut him on the hand;
and the man ran, Archie right after him.
He ran about fifteen yards and fell
and Archie got on him
and stabbed him twice.
Others were shouting, "Don't, Archie!"
And someone was pulling at Archie's coat
and the man who had been smoking was kicking him.
Archie got up—

the knife in his hand and blood on the blade—
and was gone.

By the time the doctor came the man who was stabbed was dead;
and the police found Archie in the house of a girl friend,
between the mattress and the slats of the bed.

II

NEIGHBORS

1

George and Joe, brothers, had hauled up from the fields
corn belonging to George and John;
the wagon was John's,
and the brothers asked if they could use it
to haul away George's corn a mile or so.
John, at first, would not let them have it
but, after a few words, said they could
if they would pay him for the use of it,
adding, "It costs something to keep a team."
At this George said, "It doesn't cost anything to be a damn rascal."

Both brothers were still sitting on the wagon
and a fence was between them and John,
but John got over the fence and, with a plank about two feet long and
    an inch thick in his right hand,
went towards the wagon saying, "Take that back!"
George got down from the wagon but John, who was left-handed,
caught hold of George by the collar;
and Joe took the brake stick, weighing about ten pounds,
and jumping off the wagon,
using both hands
hit John on the back of the head.

A farm hand lifted John up
and asked him if he was hurt much

and John answered he thought not;
but his skull was fractured
and he died from the blow.

2

A few years before
Roy and the elder of two brothers
had a fight at a party
and from that time on
there was ill feeling between them.
But Roy and the younger brother were still friendly.

On the day of the killings
Roy had been to town
and getting back rode past the home of the brothers
just as they were harnessing a team to their father's buggy
and about to go to their father's "lower farm."
Reaching the gate that led to it down the road,
they had to make a semicircle with the buggy
to go through the gate
and the rear of the buggy was across the road
within a few feet of a tree.

The younger brother got out of the buggy to open the gate
and just then Roy—
whom they had passed on the road—
went around the buggy
although he had to duck his head to go under the limbs of the tree.
But, even at that, his leg scraped a hind wheel.
The elder brother caught him by the coat
and pulled him off the horse.
Roy's coat was buttoned
and a button was torn from the coat
and left hanging by a strip of cloth.
Then the elder brother—in the buggy—drove into the field
and Roy, shouting in anger, asked him "what in hell" he meant by
        doing what he did

and, receiving no reply, cursed him.
At this, the elder brother called Roy a "God damn son of a bitch"
and reached for his target rifle

Roy began shooting
and fired three times
and one of the horses drawing the buggy
jumped and threw the elder brother from his seat.
Now the younger brother came running towards Roy
to take away his pistol
and Roy fired two or three shots at him, too.
The elder brother reached again for his rifle at the bottom of the buggy
and Roy fired six more shots.
Both brothers were wounded
and both died of their wounds.

3

Hunch had left his home to go hunting; when he was near John's
    house
John hallooed to him to come in.
It had become dark.
Hunch set his shotgun down by the door
and went in: a lighted lamp was on the table
and John was seated near the fireplace,
his legs crossed;
and Hunch sat down in a corner.

Hunch was afraid of him: thought him somewhat of a conjuror;
and Hunch had seen him run up and take hold of Hunch's wife
with both hands
and hug her
when she was at John's house at Christmas.

John and Hunch got to arguing about the Scriptures
and John said something Hunch did not like:
he jumped up and stepped out of doors
and came back with his gun:

the shot went into John's throat
and he was left sitting in his chair,
legs crossed, his head fallen to one side, and his hands hanging down.

4

The two men were neighbors and lived on opposite sides of a creek.
They had differences about religion
and about the trustees and the teacher of the local school,
and one of the two set about putting up posts and nailing a board
    across them
where the path from the house of his neighbor
crossed the ford of the creek
and ran across his own land to the public road.

While he was nailing up the board,
his neighbor came down to the creek and said,
"I see, Tom, you are nailing me in."
"No," he answered, "I am nailing you out."
And his neighbor said, "You run around and pretend to preach and
    pray,
and ask the good Lord to have mercy on you;
but they kick better men than you out of hell every day."
And he added, "I will put you out of the way
as soon as I go to the house and get my ax."

Tom finished nailing up the board
and went to his house and got his shotgun
and went back to where the board was nailed up,
set the gun down by the fence
and went to pulling weeds.
Looking across the creek, he saw his neighbor coming on a mule with a
    double-bitted ax on his shoulder,
and said, "Stop there!
Don't you come on me with that ax or I'll shoot."
But his neighbor kept coming until he was within a few feet
and then rose in his saddle and said,
"Shoot and be damned!"

And he did shoot.
His neighbor was hit, and the mule he was riding
whirled and ran back;
but his neighbor was found dead
lying in the bed of the creek.

5

Now and then something from his farm was missing—
a clevis, a singletree, and now a sweep and a hammer.
He went into the pasture of the farm next door with his gun
to look around: they might be hidden in the high weeds.
He looked around a good while and did not find anything
and came to his neighbor's tank,
and then saw his neighbor coming on a horse.

He did not want to be seen
and squatted down in the brush
and saw his neighbor leave the horse drinking at the tank
and go into the brush
and pick up the missing sweep and hammer
and throw them into the tank.
At that he stood up, gun raised, and said, "I caught you!"

His neighbor, by way of reply, said, "God damn you, I told you to keep
     out of my pasture!"
The first shot hit his neighbor in the breast.
His neighbor sank down on his knees
and then he shot a second time and killed him.

6

He worked at night in and around a mine
and came home about six in the morning
to breakfast and bed.
His wife came into the room
and lay down on another bed
and, thinking him asleep, began to cry.

But he was not asleep and asked her what was the matter
and she told him that his friend
had come to see her that night
and after they had been drinking together
threw her on the bed
on her back
and in spite of all she could do and say
did what he wanted to.

At that her husband jumped out of bed
and began to shout,
"I want my pistol! My pistol!"
She had hidden it
but he struck her
when she would not give it to him;
and when she ran to her sister's house
and then to her father's
he followed
demanding his pistol
and at last she told him where it was.

He entered his friend's house
and found him in bed asleep,
shot twice at the ceiling to wake him
and then shot him four times.

7

On a Sunday, the woman who kept a lodging-house across the street
came to see her;
she had never been to her house before nor had spoken to her.
And she said, "I hear that your little boy is missing
and you think maybe he has drowned;
but I hear that bad people have him
and, if they have, you will hear from them.
They will want money
and you had better give it
or you will never get the boy back."

Next morning, the postman did bring a letter
asking for six thousand dollars.
No sooner had the postman delivered it
than the woman who lived across the street
came over and said, "You see, you have got a letter!
Is it from the bad people who have taken away your son?
If so, pay what they want
or they will kill the boy."
The letter told where the money should be delivered
and threatened all the family with death
should they fail to pay—
or call in the police.

But the child's father did call in the police.
And next morning he received another letter which read:
"We know everything that is going on in your home
because good friends of yours keep us on the lookout:
if you want your child back
the same as he went out of your house
bring the money—
without any detective."

On Saturday afternoon, their little boy—
all of eight years old—
had been playing in the street in front of his home
when a man came along and showed him a nickel and led him away a
        couple of blocks
and then put him in a wagon
that had been waiting.
Early next morning, the wagon arrived at a farmhouse in another
        parish
and the little boy was set down in the yard
and he ran across it at once screaming, "Mamma, Mamma!"
The man who lived in the farmhouse and had come out to meet the
        wagon and the two men who brought the boy
caught him
and put his hand over the boy's mouth

and the three put the boy in one of the outhouses.
That evening he was heard calling, "Oh, Mamma!"

A younger brother of the two sons of the woman who kept the
    lodging-house
and who were in the gang that had kidnapped the boy
"gave the whole thing away," according to one of the two;
for, chatting with a fellow workingman,
he told him how his two brothers and their companions
had gathered in his mother's house the evening before the kidnapping
and one of his brothers had promptly put him out of the room;
and, after the kidnapping,
he asked his fellow workingman what he thought of it
and added, "It was a slick trick."

But whether or not he had given the whole thing away,
in a couple of weeks the police searching for the boy
came to the farmhouse to which the child had been brought
and the man of the house led them to a swamp
and there, in the mud and mire,
half hidden under the limb of the tree under which it was lying,
was the child's body, badly decomposed,
and the head, cut off, beside it.

III
DOMESTIC DIFFICULTIES

1

He had failed in business and his wife went to live with her sister—
both thought it was better for her;
and he went to another town,
for he had been told it was a good place in which to make money.
They wrote letters to each other
with the usual words of affection;
but his wife told her sister

she would live in a hollow tree
before she would live with her husband again.

He went to see his wife
and asked her to leave the house for a ride
in the buggy in which he came;
but her sister said she wanted his wife to help
at something or other they were doing
and his wife said she would go with him another time.
Later, that evening, as he was having supper with his wife and her
     sister,
her sister said things could not go on as they were:
he was not trying to provide for his wife.
When he left, his wife went out on the porch with him
but her sister called her in,
slammed the door and locked it.

2

His wife was living at the house of another woman
but he and his wife were still on good terms,
and he would visit her every week or so
to stay the night.
That night, as he rode up at ten o'clock
and hitched his horse,
he saw another horse hitched to the fence.
Walking up to the house
he heard his wife and a man talking in the back room—
dark without a light.

He tried the back door that opened into the room
but it was latched,
and then he pushed the front door open
and went into the front room
where the woman of the house and her husband were asleep,
the dim light of a lamp burning at the foot of their bed.
He called his wife's name
and, getting no answer,

stepped through the partition door into the back room
and saw his wife and a man in bed.
They sprang up as he came in
and his wife rushed past him
blowing out the lamp
just as he fired.

He had fired at the man,
but when the lamp was lit again
the man was gone through the back door
and there was his wife—
lying dead in her night clothes.

3

Alicia had left her husband and gone back to her parents.
On a Sunday in April as they were going to spend the day in the
        country—
Alicia, her parents, and her younger sister—
soon after they had left their home and were on their way to the
        railroad depot
they met her husband
carrying a shotgun and a Winchester.
He asked them where they were going
and they told him. He then said to his wife,
"Alicia, get your clothes
and let's go home!"
But she would not and, after some words between the two,
his father-in-law said, "You were here yesterday drawing your knife
and making your threats,
and if you do it again today I'll have you arrested."

He did not answer but said to his wife,
"You are not going to live with me anymore?"
And she said, "No."
At that he threw up his shotgun and fired at her
and then shot his father-in-law.
His wife and her young sister ran up the railroad track.

He followed and his wife, seeing that she could not outrun him,
came towards him with her hands lifted.
He shot her through the breast with his Winchester
and, when she fell,
fired another bullet through her head
and killed her.

4

Her daughter had given birth to twins
and she helped take care of them,
but her daughter was sick
and grew steadily worse.
Her son-in-law went to his mother and asked her to take care of one of
    the twins,
but his mother said, "I raised my children—
and you raise yours."

The day the daughter died,
she called her mother and husband to the bed
and said to her husband,
"Promise me this:
you will never take my babies from my mother as long as she lives,"
and he said he never would.
And she went on to say, "If I know anything after I am dead,
and know any other person has my babies,
I could not rest in my grave,"
and her husband said, tears rolling down his cheeks,
"I will never bother your mother as long as I live."
And, even as her mother was looking at her,
she stopped breathing.

Her mother took both children
and took care of them as best she could,
but when they were four years old
her son-in-law wanted them back.

5

At noon, he and his wife came home for dinner
from the cotton patch
and the baby was crying.
"What is the matter with the baby?" he asked.
"Well, you know it has been sick," his wife said.
He then said, "I'll be damned if I don't stop its crying,"
took off the leather belt he wore—
three fingers wide—
and hit the baby two or three "licks" with it.

The baby was in the arms of their little girl
and she ran with the baby from the kitchen to the bedroom.
He followed and told her to put the baby on the bed.
He then struck the baby with his hand on the side of its head,
knocking it over,
and its head hit the footboard.
While the baby was lying on its back,
he struck it on its belly just as hard as he could
with the belt doubled three or four times.

The baby stopped crying
and began to tremble and quiver.
After a while it came to
and never cried any more
or ate anything—
the belly was badly swollen
and his wife put some cotton leaves on it—
but it died.

6

Jones lost an eye a short time before
and was sitting around the house.
At noon, when he went into dinner,
his sixteen-year-old daughter
who usually sat beside him at the table

was not there
and the family did not know where she was.

After dinner he went to the home of a neighbor
and asked for her
and was told she had not been there
and he said, "Looks like the children want to slip off."
He then went home, got his pistol and put it in his pocket,
and searched the neighborhood.
Near an old abandoned house in a field, he saw a boy
who told him he had seen a girl and a boy run out of the house
and across the field
but he did not know who they were.

It then struck him that maybe she had run off and married his
    neighbor's son
and he went to the ordinary's office
but no such license had been issued
and he found no one who had seen them.
When he came home, his daughter was there
and he asked her where she had been
and she answered, "Nowhere."
"You are a liar," he said and then said he would whip her
if she did not tell him where she had been,
and he did,
but she would tell him nothing.

Next morning he took his children
and went into the woods to chop wood.
He had cut down a tree and was sawing it
when his daughter came up to him and said,
"I will saw for you. I just want to."
He left the woods
and went to the home of his neighbor again
and asked for him and his eldest son
and was told they went rabbit hunting.

One of the younger children told him he thought they had gone to the
      branch
and as he went towards it
he heard the dogs running
and went on until he came upon the hunting party.
A young man and Jim, his neighbor's son, were sitting on a stump
and his neighbor and a younger son were fifty or sixty yards away.
The young man who was sitting with his neighbor's son
asked Jones why he did not have a gun
and he told him he could not see a rabbit as far away as some briers at
      which he pointed.
Then he called to his neighbor, "Come this way a minute."

When his neighbor came up to him,
Jones said, "I want to ask your son a few questions,
and I want you to hear what I ask him."
He then turned to Jim and said, "I want to know where you were from
      eleven o'clock until four o'clock yesterday."
Jim answered, "If you want to know the truth, come along and I'll tell
      you."
Jones and his neighbor and Jim moved away about twenty steps
out of the hearing of the young man who had been sitting beside Jim,
and Jim said, "Now, what do you want to know?"
And Jones repeated his question: "Where were you from eleven until
      four o'clock yesterday?"
Jim replied, "In half a dozen places."
Jones said: "I don't care anything about that.
I want to know if you were in that old house with my daughter."
Jim answered, "Yes, I was.
And I ain't afraid or ashamed to own it."
Jones jerked out his pistol and said, "You won't be there any more,"
and as Jim turned to run Jones fired.
Jim's father had his gun on his shoulder
and jerked it down
pointing it at Jones, and Jones fired at him twice and killed him.

7

A married woman, thirty-one or so, living in the home of her father,
had a lover—a sergeant in the county chain gang.
On a night in August he left the camp, about fourteen miles away,
to visit her in her bedroom;
hitched his mule in the woods near the house
and went to the open window of the bedroom
and there was a knot in the curtain—
the signal agreed upon.
He came into the room through the window,
placed his hat and trousers on the floor
and his pistol on top of his clothes.

The room of the woman's father was just across the hall.
He heard them, got up,
and set a lighted lamp in the hall
on a table almost opposite the door of her room
and opened it slightly.
She nudged her lover in the side and whispered,
"There's a light!"

He got out of bed and started towards the door
but her father had pushed it open
and stood between him and the light—
the best target her lover had ever shot at—
and he shot her father through the heart.
He left the room without his clothes
and went to where his mule was hitched,
but she brought his clothes to him
and they rode away together.

8

He was in "show business"—
a horseman showing his skill in handling horses—
and his little son was with him,
not quite six but also skilled in riding
and part of the show.

At eight o'clock that night
he was standing in front of his tent—
one of the tents during a carnival in the city—
announcing that his show would soon begin
and asking the passers-by to come in,
when two policemen came up
and two women leading a little girl—the daughter of one of the
        women
followed by a crowd of about fifty.
And one of the women said, "There he is!"

The policeman asked him if he knew the little girl
and he said he had seen her playing around the tent.
Had he given her a dime? Yes. What for? To buy ice cream.
At that one of the women began shouting at him: "We know all
        about it.
You ought to be killed!"
And the other woman, the mother of the little girl, began to cry.
The little girl had told "bad stories" about him when she came home
and her mother wanted him arrested.
He said he had never wronged the child in any way
but one of the policemen touched him on the arm
and said, "Come with us to the police station."

"I want to get my coat," he said
and they went with him into the tent;
the crowd tried to follow
but the policemen stopped them.
He could hear one of the men shouting, "If I had a rope I would hang
        him!"
And others shouting, "Lynch him!"
Inside the tent, he unlocked the box in which he kept his coat
and one of the policemen noticed that his mind was not on what he
        was doing
and thought he was going to try to run away.
But he called to his little son who was in the tent
and when the child did not answer
said, "I guess he's asleep. I want to undress him."

The child was asleep under a cot
and one of the policemen said,
"Isn't there anybody to take care of your little boy
but yourself
when you are gone?"
"No," he answered, "I am alone."
Then the policeman said, "Very well, undress him."
As he did so, pulling off the child's shoes and stockings
and opening the collar of his waist,
he thought: a mob would not believe him
and would lynch him.
People listened more to a woman than to a man
when such a charge was made.
And his little boy would be left helpless and alone—disgraced.

"Hurry up!" one of the policemen said.
"We can't stay here long."
And he came out from under the cot and said,
"Now you can have me,"
and tried to cut his throat with his pocketknife.
One of the policemen struck him and stunned him
and the other knocked the knife out of his hand.
But under the cot his little son was lying
dying, with his throat cut.

9
Dr. Warren was a stern father.
When his son was fourteen
the boy ran away to New Orleans
and worked in a restaurant.
After he came home, his father said,
"Go back to school—
or get out!"
But when the boy was not quite sixteen
he quit school again
and left—without his parents' consent—
to stay with an elder brother in Los Angeles;

and this time was away
almost a year. When he was seventeen,
his father whipped him with a pair of bridle reins
because he had taken his father's team
to carry some boys to a baseball game.
The day before his father was murdered,
his father had gone to a neighboring town
to borrow money to send his son to school again.

The night was cloudy and it was raining a little.
Dr. Warren was going to a Masonic meeting in town
and had asked his son to come along
but his son said he would rather go to bed.
A man sitting in his backyard
stirring a kettle of lard he was rendering
heard a shot;
and, after the first shot, a man shouting for help.
And another man, also living close to the road,
had heard a buggy going past
and then a horse in a lope going pretty fast
in the same direction.
After three shots were fired,
he heard the same horse loping back;
and the hoofbeats of the horse were like those of Dr. Warren's big
        mare.

About ten o'clock that night a man saw beside the road
a horse and buggy in a hollow:
the buggy overturned and the horse entangled in the harness.
He went at once to some neighbors
and soon they were searching about the place with lanterns.
But it was not until daylight that one of them saw far off in a field
what looked at first like the stump of a tree
and proved to be Dr. Warren's body.
A gunshot wound in his abdomen
and another just below his heart;
the back of his head crushed in

and likewise one of the cheek bones—
he had been clubbed as well as shot.

Dr. Warren had been running to where his body was found—
the ground was soft because of the rain—
and next to his track, parallel to it,
another track, that of his pursuer;
and both tracks met
where the ground was trampled.
An empty shell to fit a shotgun
was also found near the hollow beside the road
and nearby another empty shell:
both of a size to fit Dr. Warren's shotgun.

Those who were searching for the body
had recognized the buggy and horse as belonging to Dr. Warren
and had gone to his house to see if he was there.
They had come back with his wife and son.
His son did not have much to say
and did not even seem particularly bothered
when his father's body was found:
looked at it almost casually
and did not shed a tear.

And some of those who had been helping in the search
saw that the son's shoes were making the same impression in the soft
        ground—
the left shoe run down on the inside—
as those in the track beside that of the dead man.
And when they were searching for Dr. Warren's shotgun—
he had not taken it with him—
one of the men had gone to the dead man's barn
and saw Dr. Warren's son glaring at him.
The shotgun was afterwards found hidden in a hole in the barn,
the barrel bent
and hair and blood on it.

10

Four colored coalminers were rooming in a shanty together.
Two of them were now playing checkers until bedtime
and one of the two asked the other for a piece of bread;
the other answered, "Cook your own bread," and then went out,
    saying,
"I am feeding the bread to the hogs."
The man who had asked for it said, "I don't want none of your
    damned bread!"
And the man who would not give it to him answered, "Don't you
    cuss me!"

He had loosened his suspenders for the night
and waited until his companions were asleep,
and then sat down at the table
and wrote a letter to his mother
and another letter to one of the men with whom he had not quarreled,
and left it on the floor near the man's bed.
"Charlie," it read, "I will ask to draw my money
and send it to my mother"—
she lived in a small town in Virginia.
"I hate to leave you. But I will not take Pete's cursing."
He then shot Pete through the heart
and, satchel in hand, fled into the night
leaving the door of the shanty wide-open.

11

The Negroes slept in a log cabin—
only one room and no window;
a stick to close the door: one end propped against it
and the other end on the floor.

IV

MACHINE AGE

1

The company had brought the boiler to the town by rail
and crib work had been built
to support the boiler from the platform on which it had been unloaded
to its place inside the boiler-house.
The space—only a few feet wide—between the crib work and a side wall
was left empty.

A young Negro, known as "Beebee," whose parents were in what was
       politely known as "lowly circumstances,"
was working with five or six other Negroes at putting the boiler in place.
It had been brought to the unfinished front wall
and inside the building was being pushed on sills along round wooden
       sticks—
when it rolled from the cribbing
and crushed Beebee's skull against the side wall.

The company as "an act of charity"—
with the understanding that the parents of the young man were not to
       make any claim—
donated the funeral expenses:
bought the coffin and what else was needed
to give the young man "a decent burial."

2

He was working for an iron and coal company—
running at night the blowing-engine and nearby pumps—
and had to go from engine to pumps
across a plank laid over a large and deep cistern.
The plank had become slippery with oil
and the electric light to light it
would become dim at times
and even die out
leaving the grounds in darkness.

Going to a pump across the plank
at such a time
he fell into the cistern—just then full of hot water—
and was drowned.

3
The young man's parents lived in the country
and grew rice for their living
but he had a job in a slaughterhouse
that rendered the fat of the animals killed into tallow
and their feet and shinbones into neat's-foot oil.
He was not quite twenty-one,
active and eager to work,
and gave six dollars of the nine he earned weekly
to his parents and grandparents.

He had been at work in the slaughterhouse
three or four months
skimming tallow from the vats—
standing on the stationary platforms alongside.
But one day he was asked to skim the neat's-foot oil
from a tank on another floor of the building
where the water in the tank was heated to 180 degrees or more
and the tank had no stationary platform
on which the man who did the skimming of the oil
as it floated to the surface
could stand—
but only a movable bench.

As the young man leaned over the edge of the vat
standing on the bench
it tilted
and one end slid away—only six inches or so
but enough to send him into the boiling water.

4

Betty was about eleven. She had no regular work at the mill
but did one thing and then another
and sometimes would take shirts to a table
attached to a mangle.

That morning the machine had not been started
and when she had placed the shirts on the table
[she] rested her fingers on the rollers;
and another little girl who also worked in the mill
started the machine:
it caught Betty's arm and crushed it.

5

His father brought him to the foreman
to work in the mine—
the two to work beside each other—
and the foreman asked the boy's age.
"Not quite fourteen."
The foreman shook his head
and smiling said, "Too young."

When his father, soon afterwards, was hurt at work,
the son said to his father,
"You are mashed up and can't work;
our house rent is to be paid and we've got to live,"
and the boy went to the foreman again—
alone.

Then the foreman said, "Son, you have to work now, do you,
since your father got hurt?"
And the boy said, "Yes, sir," and went on into the mine.
The foreman came around where the boy was at work
and showed him how to shovel and how to "run under" the coal,
and the coal the boy got was weighed by the man who weighed the
      coal for the other miners,
and the company kept the money for the rent of the house in which
      the boy's family lived.

Later that month as the miners were leaving the mine,
riding a train of six or seven cars—a "shot" was to be fired—
the boy, riding a rear car,
saw a friend on a car in front,
and making his way to him
over the cars loaded with coal
fell
between the third and fourth car
and was run over and killed.

V

STREETCARS AND RAILROADS

1

One afternoon in March, a colored woman and her daughter of
        thirteen with two other colored girls
left her home in Richmond
to look at the high water in the river.
On their way home, boys kept throwing stones at them
and they went off into the countryside
and were lost.

When it was growing dark
they saw a man with a lamp,
and called to him for the way to Richmond
and were told to follow the road they were on—
to go straight ahead:
"that will put you to Richmond."

The road turned to cross a stream
but the track of the electric streetline that ran along the road
went straight on,
crossing upon a trestle,
sixty feet high and more than four hundred feet long.
The trestle had no way for walkers
except to step from joist to joist—

about a foot and a half apart—
with nothing between them
and no room on either side of the track
to stand on
while a car was passing.

The woman and the girls
followed the track,
and when they reached the trestle
tried to cross it by crawling on hands and knees
from joist to joist.
By this time the night had become pitch-dark
and the rails slick with drizzle.

One of the electric cars came along:
the woman's daughter was swinging under the trestle,
one of the other girls was knocked off—
the other had jumped down—
and the car struck the woman and killed her.

2

A widow with her child was living in a small house,
forty or fifty feet from a railroad track that ran through the city
and took up most of the street with embankment and roadbed.
She was scrubbing a floor that morning
and her child was with her in the house
playing around
but then quietly left
without his mother noting,
crossed the yard and went through the old broken-down fence
which the railroad company had built,
and got upon the railroad track.
A train was speeding at thirty or forty miles an hour
towards the depot
and the engineer as the engine went around a curve
saw what he took to be a dog—or a goat—on the track.
It was not until the child who had been lying on the ties or stooping

raised his head
that the engineer tried to stop the train—
too late.

3

The boy was fourteen and worked in a large cotton mill.
The railroad had a track for freight from the mill to the main line
and the boy would hitch a ride
although his mother told him not to.
She even complained to men working for the railroad
but all one of them said was:
"Let him break his neck for all we care."
On a curve of the track there was a slant—
so great a loaded car would tilt
and the load apt to fall on those who happened to be in the car.
One day, when the car had a load of heavy cross-ties,
they did tumble over
and fell on the boy.

4

The railroad company had a Fourth of July excursion
to the picnic grounds for colored people—
a one-day excursion going out in the morning and coming back at
     night.
Going out the train was crowded, even the platforms.
Towards evening, a drizzling rain set in
and neither the grounds at the lake nor the railroad station
had any shelter
for the eight or nine hundred people waiting in the rain
on both sides of the track.

It had become so dark
one could not recognize his "elbow neighbor"
except by his voice;
and when the train came it was without a single light
except the headlight of the locomotive.

There was a scramble to get aboard
even before the train stopped;
and a colored girl, who had been on the excursion with another girl,
scrambled with the rest
and thought herself lucky
to get on the platform of one of the two coaches,
her feet standing at the very edge
and her back pressed against the railing of the other coach.

The track was slippery and the train moved slowly—
people riding even on top of the box car and on the locomotive—
and had gone only about three miles an hour
when a bridge beneath it gave way.
The platform on which the young woman was standing
slipped down
and stopped at a steep angle among the wreckage of the bridge,
and she found herself up to her waist in wreckage,
both of her legs caught under the platform behind her
and one of her feet crushed against the piling.

There was not even a lantern to see by
and three hours before an ax could be found
to chop away the piling,
and only the voice of the young woman crying out in her agony
to guide those who would help her.

5

A driver with a team of mules
hitched three abreast to a grainbinder
was coming along a road—
beside a railroad—
that led to the field where he was to cut the wheat;
and a locomotive was backing slowly down the track
to a water tank.

The engineer of the locomotive
when nearly opposite the driver and his mules

suddenly increased its speed:
opened the cylinder cocks
adding a shrill hissing to the quiet
and sending a dense cloud of smoke and sparks from the smokestack
together with steam from the cylinders
about the driver and his mules.
Frightened, they reared,
the reins the driver held broke,
and the mules ran away.

VI
SHIPPING

The river was at a high stage with a rapid current
during the early part of the night—
a few clouds and afterwards moonlight;
but, about two in the morning, fog.
The captain of a steamboat towing ten barges loaded with coal
ordered all men to their places
and lines to be ready for a landing;
but many rafts of logs were tied to the river's banks on both sides
and he thought it best to run below the bridge
before the fog became too thick.

The order was given to "gong the boat"—
that is, put on full steam;
but, before the boat had gone half the distance to the bridge,
the fog had become so thick
it was impossible from the pilothouse
to see the lights on the bridge
or even on the banks of the river.
The engines were then reversed
and the wheels set to revolving backwards
to slacken the forward movement of the steamboat
as with its tow it floated down the river
whistling in the fog.

The front end of the tow struck the pier of the bridge
and the steamboat swung toward the river bank;
some of the crew jumped on shore and made her fast
while others cut the cables and let the barges go.
The wharf boat, moored to the bank, about two hundred feet below the
    bridge,
was struck by one of the barges
and the barge crushed a hole in it,
tore the boat from its moorings and set it adrift on the river.
But the men of the steamboat did not know what had been struck—
or even where they were.

VII

WHITES AND BLACKS

1

The Negro went to his hogpen on a Sunday
bringing the hogs slops;
and just below the hogpen were two white men.
After the Negro had fed the hogs and started towards his house,
one of the men called to him:
he wanted a match.
The Negro told him he was in a hurry to get back home
to dress
and go to preaching,
but the man who had called him said,
"Come here, you!"
And the Negro answered, "I'll come."
The white man said, "You are too damned slow.
Why can't you come when I call you?"
The Negro answered, "I did."
At that the white man snatched the Negro's hat off
and said, "Take your hat off!
Like a damned nigger ought to when I talk to him,"
and taking a knife out of a coat pocket
put the blade against the Negro's throat,

and then tapped him on the head with the handle of the knife
and told him he could go home.

2

The collector for the store—a white man—went to the house
to collect money due for furniture
sold on the installment plan. He drove up in front of the house,
got out of his wagon, went to the door,
and was invited into the house
by the buyer's wife—an old colored woman.
She asked him politely to have a seat
and he sat down in the rocking-chair she handed him;
his Negro helper sat on the porch.

She asked him what the money was due for and he said a bedstead,
and she said she did not have the money to pay for whatever was due
but asked him to wait until her husband came. At that he jumped up
     from the chair
and said he was not going to wait: he would have the money then and
     there
or take the bedstead away—or go to hell trying!
And he went to the bedstead
to see if it was scratched;
took a tablecloth lying on the bed
and threw it on the floor,
and an underskirt also lying on the bed—
the old woman had been washing and ironing
and had just placed them there—
and threw that also on the floor.
At this she said, "Let my things alone!"
but he began to throw back the covering of the bed
and the mattress—
and she hit him on the back of the head with her son's baseball bat.

3

A traveling-salesman went to the depot of the railroad company
to take a train to another city; he had never taken that train before.
At the depot he bought a ticket and, handing his baggage and overcoat
    to a boy,
went towards the train. It had two coaches:
half of the first coach for baggage and half for a "smoker,"
and half of the rear coach for colored passengers.

The boy tried to get aboard the rear coach at the forward end
and the colored porter standing in front of it
would not let him pass. The salesman, a few feet behind,
did not hear what the porter said
but thought the boy could not board the train because he was without
    a ticket
and the salesman showing his ticket to the porter said,
"Well, I guess I can get in; I have a ticket,"
and tried to get on the steps of the car.
But the porter answered gruffly, "No, you can't get on here!"
and jumping up on the car placed his arms across the steps,
catching the iron railing at each side,
and raised his foot as if to kick the white man in the face.

A flagman who heard that something or other was going on
now came to the front of the car
and asked what the trouble was. The porter explained:
the salesman was trying to board the car at the front door.
The flagman said, "Why not?" but the porter said,
"You are the flagman and I am the porter—
attend to your business and I'll attend to mine."
And the salesman insisting on boarding the train,
the porter locked the front door of the car and walked away.
The salesman then went to the rear end of the car,
where the flagman was standing, and boarded the train.
Going into the rear compartment, he saw a sign on the wall:
"For colored passengers only."
The sign was not taken down until after the train had started, heading
    south,

and the front half of the coach was now for colored passengers and the
    rear half for whites—not the usual way.

4

The white man in the waiting-room of the railroad station had been
    drinking,
talking and cursing, and was now asleep
on a bench where the partition between the seats had been torn out.
The door slammed and woke him:
a young Negro had come in
and was at the stove
warming himself.

The white man tried to fall asleep again
but felt chilled and called to the Negro,
"Put some coal in the stove!"
The Negro answered, "I am not working here."
The white man shouted, "Damn you, do it!"
And the Negro answered, "No,
I have nothing to do with it,"
and turned his back on the white man.

The white man jumped up
and caught the Negro by the collar
and shoved him from the stove;
dropped a pistol, picked it up,
and shot the Negro between the eyes.
Then he pushed the door of the waiting-room open
and went out.

5

The two policemen on duty at the Union Depot began to talk about
    two Negroes:
one a boarding-house keeper and the other a drummer for a saloon—
both met trains at the station.
The conversation was friendly at first:

one of the policemen saying that the Negroes were troublesome to the
    passengers
and he would arrest them every chance he got,
and the other that they were doing no harm
and he would "run them in" or drive them away
only if they blocked the walk.
But before long one policeman was calling the other a "God damn
    fool,"
and they were catching each other by the coat collar;
the policeman who found the Negroes troublesome
had his club out of his hip pocket
and was holding it in his left hand,
and the other was pulling his pistol from the holster.
He fired:
the policeman he had been arguing with
dropped to his knees
shot,
and then fell on his back—dead.

6

The old Negro, two or three hoe-handles on his shoulder,
and his brother
went into the Syrian's store;
and one of them asked the price of cabbage—
"Too dear!"—
and the other took a strawberry and put it in his mouth.
"Mr. Nigger," said the Syrian to him,
"when you come into a white man's store,
  look
  but never touch."

"Well, we are in the wrong place," the old Negro said.
"Yes," said the Syrian, "get out and never come back."

The two Negroes went into the street
and stopped in front of the screen door
and stood there talking to another Negro.

The Syrian went out
and told them to clear the doorway
and let him do his business;
but the old Negro said, "We are in the public road."
At that the Syrian said to him,
"Mr. Nigger, I don't want any trouble
but you had better go and don't bother anybody,"
and, placing his hands on the Negro, said,
"Go on, Nigger, out of my way!"
The Negro said, "Don't shove me, White Man,"
and lifted the hoe-handles he had on his shoulder
as if to strike him
and the Syrian struck him in the face with his fist;
and the scrimmage began.

7
About ten o'clock at night, four or five Negroes were shooting craps in
         a tent
and a white man came in, picked up the dice,
and challenged any of the Negroes to bet him twenty-five cents
on a throw of the dice.
They were silent.
And then one of them threw the money on the table;
the white man rolled the dice and won.

He then challenged the Negro who had lost to bet him fifty cents;
and the Negro put down twenty-five cents.
The white man won again,
picked up the money,
and said he had won twenty-five cents more
and wanted payment.
With that he drew a pistol from his pocket and placed it on the table.

The Negro grabbed the pistol by the handle
and the white man grabbed it by the barrel;
and, after a struggle,
the Negro wrenched the pistol from the white man's hand,

struck him in the face with it
and quickly shot him three times.

8

The players shooting craps in the basement of a white man's saloon
were at two tables: white men at one and Negroes at the other.
But the Negroes were making a great deal of fuss
and the man in charge tried to quiet them. As he was going away
one of the Negroes said it was the Negroes' night
and cursed him.
The man turned
and the Negro rising from his seat
drew his pistol and fired
once and again.

That night the Negro heard that the man he had shot was dead.
Sitting alone in his room
in the dark, he heard men gathering outside the house
and was frightened.

9

Unlucky Gambler

He and the Negro had been gambling
and he won all the Negro's money.
Then the Negro insisted on staking his shoes
and he won them, too;
then the Negro put up his hat
and he won it.
At that the Negro shouted, "If you wear that hat you will wear it in hell!"
grabbed him and threw him down
and the Negro put his hand in his pocket for a knife.
But he stood up
and the Negro began to chase him around the room.
He seized an ax near the hearth
and struck the Negro across the face and jaw—
and killed him.

10

The Negro had been at a gin-house all day
and when it was closed for the night
went off along the public road.
He saw a wagon coming towards him
and behind it Shelley riding on a mule.
Shelley rode around the wagon and came towards him.
Within a few feet from the Negro, Shelley stopped
and pointing a pistol in the Negro's face
said, "Halt, you son of a bitch!"
The Negro halted and Shelley added, "I am going to kill you,
you damn black son of a bitch!"

The Negro said, "I have done nothing for you to kill me, Mr. Shelley,"
but Shelley answered, "Yes, you have, damn you!"
and snapped the pistol in the Negro's face
three times.

When Shelley saw that his pistol would not fire,
he rode off at a gallop.
The Negro had a shotgun, loaded with buckshot, in his left hand,
hanging down by his side;
and now he fired at Shelley,
who was leaning forward in his saddle,
the pistol still in his hand.

11

About seven o'clock on a morning in July
a white man of some importance in his county
ordered a Negro working for him
to vacate the house in which the Negro was living;
and in the quarrel that followed
shot the Negro in the breast, the bullet lodging in his back,
and the Negro shot and killed the white man—and fled.

The sheriff of the county arrived about ten o'clock. By this time
several parties of white men, armed with guns,

were hunting for the Negro.
His father, fearful that his son would be killed if found,
agreed to take the sheriff to where his son was hiding
if the sheriff would protect him,
and the sheriff took his son to the jail at the county seat.

But the jailer was afraid that a mob would gather
and took the Negro out of jail at dusk
and brought him to a graveyard in the neighborhood
and left him in charge of another man;
and, sure enough, not long after the jailer had come back to the jail
a mob was there. The jailer told them he did not know where the
    Negro was
but the mob searched the jail;
and, when the night train stopped at the station,
they went through the train looking for the Negro.

Next morning the Negro was placed on a train and taken to the jail in
    a neighboring city
and from there to the jail in the largest city in the state.
In the meantime, four Negroes, two of whom might become witnesses
    for the Negro who did the shooting
and two who were merely members of his lodge,
were arrested on some charge or other
and put in the local jail. Later, at night, a mob gathered;
the jailer did nothing—or at least thought he could do nothing—
to stop them and they took the four men out
and hanged all four.

12

Four or five young Negroes working about the town
were arrested
and charged with breaking into stores and robbing them:
of meat, a sack of flour, some lard, and a pair of pants.
A day or two after they were arrested,
a constable, the jailer, and the sheriff of the county
took them out of jail about dusk.

A handkerchief was tied over the face of one of the young Negroes
and he was tied, hand and foot,
his pants pulled down
and he was whipped,
and then thrown into a pile of brush
and the brush set afire near where he was lying.
As for another, he was taken to the courtroom—
dark now except for the light of a candle
held by the jailer—
and a slick rope, perhaps to leave no mark,
put about the young Negro's neck
and he was pulled up until he was hanging
and was asked, "Where are those things?"
"I don't know," he said when they had lowered him.
He had almost lost his breath
and had to blow for it "mighty hard."
They had seen that the knot placed behind his neck was not hurting
    him
and turned it around until it was at his throat
and told him they would hang him until his tongue stuck out
unless he told them where the stolen goods were.
"You know where they are!" and he said again, "I don't."
and they pulled him up again.

13

Three young white men were on their way from a prayer meeting in a
    church,
riding at night along a road which passed the house of a Negro
where a "festival" was going on.
They stopped to see it.
Two or three hundred Negroes were at the festival
and the owner of the house was selling refreshments
and had another Negro to help him.

The three young men went in
and bought something or other—
the owner of the house showed no displeasure at their presence—

and then two of them went out. They said nothing as they left
but were followed at once by the owner of the house with a shotgun
and the Negro who had been helping him with a pistol.
As the two young white men were walking to where their horses were
    hitched
one of them looked back and saw the two Negroes following them.
Both Negroes fired at him at once
and killed him.
The third young man had started to follow his companions
but when he reached the door of the house
he found it shut
and guarded by a Negro with a shotgun.
He turned to go out of the back door
and found that also guarded by a Negro with a shotgun;
and the Negro said, "Take your hand off the door!"
He did but put his hand back again and the Negro said again,
"Take your hand off that door!"
The owner of the house who had followed the young man's
    companions
was back and the young man heard the owner say,
"I have killed one damn white son of a bitch
and will kill the other one."
At that the young man grabbed the door,
pulled it open and jumped out—
and got away.

14

The pike Miss Lucy was riding on
had trees on both sides, a few houses, and was rather lonely.
She had left her father's house
about two or three o'clock in the afternoon
and went riding with a friend
and then started home alone.

She saw a Negro under a tree
and he got on his horse and came facing her
pulling into the middle of the road.

She pulled off to one side
and as she pulled off he pulled towards her;
and she kept pulling off
until she was off the road;
and still he pressed towards her.

She was riding slowly,
afraid to go fast for fear he would get in front of her
and stop her.
When she got even with him—
he was close enough to touch her
but did not—
he said something or other she did not understand;
and when she got past him
he wheeled his horse
and followed.

She then started her horse in a lope
but he was gaining on her fast
and she screamed.
By this time they were in sight of her father's house—
and he wheeled his horse and left.

15

A white girl, about fourteen years of age, was walking along the
    railroad track
with her little brother
when she saw a young colored man, about nineteen or twenty years of
    age,
walking on the railroad track ahead of her
and going in the same direction.
He slowed his gait and she slowed hers;
he would stop and look back
and fold his arms in front of him—
as if hugging her—
and open them again;
and once shook his hat at her.

She would change from the railroad track to the dirt road alongside,
and he would likewise change but keep in front of her;
she kept changing
and he kept changing,
until she was about thirty feet behind him—
when he turned back.

She became frightened at that and ran up a side way towards her
    cousin's house
holding her little brother by the hand—
the house could not be seen at this point
because of the corn standing in the field—
and the young colored man ran after her about sixty feet
but within fifteen feet of her—
perhaps because he saw the house—
stopped.
He did not speak nor did she;
and when she got to the porch of the house,
she looked back
and saw him walking along the railroad track again.

16

She arrived in the city late at night
and asked a hackman at the railroad station
to take her to a cheap hotel.
They drove to a building in which she could see neither lights nor
    windows
and he said, "This is the place."

He jumped down from his seat,
came to the hack door and opened it a little,
and said, "Lady, you wanted a cheap place.
Get out here and accommodate me
and I will take you to a place where it won't cost you anything."
"I am not in that kind of business," she said, adding,
"and you are a colored man!"

He kept begging her
and she tried to get out of the hack
but he caught her by the arm and pushed her back
and she was frightened—
afraid even to halloo
for fear he would choke her.
But she did jerk the door open
and began to cry
thinking I have no money and no friends and look what is happening
       to me.

He began to beg her again and again she said, "No, no!"
And then he said, "Get back in the hack
and I will take you to the hotel."
She did not know what to do
and in her confusion
got back in the hack.

He drove on
and they came to a still darker place
near a ditch
and he stopped.
As soon as he did
and before he could "hit" the ground
she jumped out.
She saw no lights anywhere
and said, "This is no hotel!"
"No," he said and began asking her again.
"Give me my grip," she said.
He reached up to his seat and gave her the grip
and said, "Pay me what you owe me."
"How much?" she asked.
"Fifty cents."
But this time she said, "I will not pay you anything,"
and he grabbed the grip out of her hand,
and she began to run as fast as she could
looking for a street where the lamps were still lit.
As she turned the corner

he overtook her and said, "Here, lady, here's your grip!
Here it is!"
And she grabbed it and ran.

17

The guard of the Negro chain-gang had a shed built out of tin,
just outside of the car in which they slept,
and he let them build a fire there
so that they could warm themselves, smoke and talk,
and sit there until time to go into the car—
for there was no heat in the car—
and when they had gone in he would lock them up.

That night it was dark and foggy
and ten or twelve of the convicts were on the chain
all sitting around the fire, singing and joking,
when the guard heard them begin to quarrel,
and he hallooed to them
and asked what the trouble was.
One of the Negroes answered,
"Blindy is cutting up"—
one of them was called "Blindy" by the others
because he was blind in one eye.
As the guard went towards them, strap in hand,
another of the convicts met him and said,
"You had better watch out. He's got a knife."

The guard saw Blindy at the end of the chain—
by himself.
He was sitting on a bench quietly
with the knife between his legs
whittling,
and the others were standing away from him.
The guard said, "What are you doing with that knife?"
And Blindy said, "I just got it."
Then the guard said, "What is the trouble?"
and Blindy answered, "These boys are trying to run over me."

At this the guard said, "You have been cutting up some
and I will have to correct you;
I told you about it several times."
Blindy answered, "No, sir, you won't."
"I reckon I will," said the guard. "You are not running this business."
"I know that," said Blindy, "but you ain't going to whip me.
No, sir, you and no other man don't whip me."
And the guard said again, "I reckon I will.
Throw that knife away and get down on the bench."
"No, sir," said Blindy. "I ain't going to give that knife to nobody."
He stood up, took off his coat, and laid it on the bench,
looked at the guard and stepped back a step or two
and looked at the chain that held him to the others.

At that the guard called one of the trustees, a big Negro, called
    "Big Boy,"
and he went towards Blindy,
but Blindy pointed the knife at him
and Big Boy moved back.
The other convicts on the chain pulled away
and the chain tightened up.
Blindy then turned towards the guard
and the guard struck him the the face with his strap
but Blindy could not get to the guard,
for the tightened chain stopped him.

The other convicts, frightened, kept tightening the chain;
pulled back and pulled Blindy along.
Blindy wheeled
and made a spring at the convict nearest him
and stabbed him in the breast.
The guard raised his strap and shouted,
"Stop! Don't cut that boy!"
The convict Blindy had stabbed
was now on all fours
and Blindy stabbed him in the back.

Another guard got a fence rail
and struck Blindy on the head
knocking him down,
and one of the other convicts grabbed Blindy's hand—
the hand that held the knife—
and wrenched the blade out of the handle.

VIII
THEFTS—AND THIEVES

1

The owner of the place in leaving home
told Johnson, who was working for him,
"I want you to watch what I have on the place—
particularly the melon patch.
They are stealing my watermelons;
and if anyone comes to steal them,
shoot him."
That night, between eight and nine, a neighbor of the owner came and
      said,
"Old man Johnson?" And he said, "Yes, sir."
"There are some fellows hanging around the melon patch.
They are going to steal the watermelons."

When Johnson got down there with a double-barreled shotgun, loaded
      with buckshot,
two middle-aged men and a young fellow of seventeen were in the
      patch;
and Johnson said, "What are you doing in here?"
One of the men answered, "What is that to you?"
And Johnson said, "If you don't get out,
I'll make you."
And the man said, "If you don't get out,
we'll make you!" And all three started towards him;
but the young fellow stopped to pick up a watermelon
and Johnson shot and killed him.

2

They had been stealing his corn
and one evening two of his neighbors told him
they had seen a young man near his barn;
and he told his wife he would sleep that night
in his barn, and took a cotton mattress and his gun along.

A young man who was a clerk in a town a few miles away
had been visiting his father-in-law
and riding back—
the road led through a gate in a fence not far from the barn—
the young man got down from his horse to open the gate.
The farmer saw him and fired.

When the farmer came up to the man he had fired at
he found him dead.
The horse at the shot had wheeled and run off.
The young man did not look—nor was he dressed—like one who
      would be stealing corn
and there was no sign of silk or shucks of corn on his clothing.

3

Early one night in December, Wash went to the store of the plantation,
about a mile from his cabin,
and arranged with the storekeeper and the plantation manager
to make a crop for another year,
and the storekeeper gave him twenty-five dollars in silver.
A man was peering through the window.

The man—who had followed Wash—
saw his companion strike Wash in the face with an ax
and helped carry the body into the cabin
and place it on the bed,
face down, beside Wash's dead wife—
killed by the same ax.
They left the ax on the floor
and set fire to the cabin

and went off with Wash's fortune—
all of fifty-five dollars and twenty-five cents.

4

He went into the Chinese restaurant
and ordered a bowl of soup
and left without paying the nickel he owed for it.
The man who kept the restaurant
followed him:
he had reached the sidewalk and was walking away
and waved his hand.

The Chinese who kept the restaurant thought the man had left the nickel
and stepped inside,
but came back at once saying, "Me no see money. Give me my money!"
The man who had had the soup
turned
and threw at him some crackers he had taken;
then, drawing a pistol,
said, "Here's your money," and fired.
The Chinese fell to the sidewalk
and died within the hour.

5

At about nine o'clock at night
a white man and a Negro came into Sol's store
and the white man asked for a pack of tobacco
and Sol went to the counter
to give him the pack,
and while he was standing there
the two men drew pistols
and both said, "Hold up!"

Sol said, "I have no money in my pockets:
I have nothing on me.
All my money is in the drawer under the counter:

it is easily opened.
Just take it—
anything you want.
The drawer is easily opened:
it ain't fastened."

But his wife who had been sitting in the store
had run back to their bedroom to get a pistol
and when she came out
fired at the Negro.
In her excitement she did not hit him,
and when she had fired
the white fellow shot her husband.

Her husband took the pistol from her with his left hand
but the pistol dropped on the floor at his side,
and he said to his wife, "Fannie, I am dying";
and he did die soon afterwards.
The cash drawer had been taken from under the counter
and was left on the floor—empty.

6

A white man came to San Antonio from Cincinnati with his wife and
      baby
for his wife's health; he looked for work
but could not find any. In San Antonio he became acquainted with a
      Negro
who had a horse and wagon
and the two agreed to go into the country
to sell oranges and buy chickens and eggs.

They left on a Tuesday morning
and the white man had fifty dollars in his pocket.
On Thursday the Negro was back alone;
they had not gone far along a street in the city, he said,
when they met a man with a horse and wagon
which his companion liked better than his and left him.

Early that morning, a man going on horseback along a road that led
       from San Antonio
had seen the Negro standing beside a fire three feet high in a ditch
       near the road
and standing nearby a horse hitched to an express wagon.
Saturday morning, passing along the same road with his team,
the man saw a dog eating at what looked like a bone
where he had seen the Negro at the fire.
His team became frightened
and he stopped to see what had frightened the horses
and found what was left of the body of a man:
the right foot and leg sticking out of the ashes and earth.
Tracks near the body
showed where someone had been carrying wood from a tree near the
       road
and raking dirt together to put on the body.
There were two wounds on the man's head
as if made by a hatchet or ax
and the skull was fractured.

The Negro who had been with him, when arrested, was wearing the
       white man's hat:
a soft black hat
and inside the sweatband were folds of a Cincinnati newspaper.
And he had—for him—plenty of money:
when he had left San Antonio
he did not have any
or at most very little.

7
The body of a young Negro was found in a gully
about two miles from town,
in a thicket about thirty steps from the road;
wounds on his head made by a billy
and each wound enough to kill him.
The body had been there several days:
the shoes taken from the feet

and a piece of a watch chain hanging from the vest;
in a pocket his miner's time-card.
And his pocketbook was also found—empty.

Three or four days before
the young Negro had been in a Negro saloon in town
and about midnight had gone up to the barkeeper
with three twenty-dollar bills in his hand
and had asked the barkeeper to change them.

A man who had gotten drunk and had gone across the street to lie
     down
was awakened by a cry
and saw a group of Negroes around the young man later found dead
and heard him crying out,
"Oh, Lordy, don't hit me any more"
And later a one-horse wagon drove up
and three or four men threw a body into the wagon and drove off.

The dead man had on a pair of patent-leather shoes
the night he was killed
and one of the men who had also been in the saloon
was seen wearing them afterwards;
and another had a watch from which part of the watch chain had been
     torn;
and still another had plenty of money—for him—
and had been saying he did not have to work for it.

8

The boy, about eleven or twelve—
a bright boy—
had been working for him four or five years
at the house and in the store
and even acting as clerk.
But he caught him stealing—
just a petty theft—
and he stripped the boy naked

and whipped him for it about an hour
with a leather strap that had a knot at the end
until more than a hundred welts were raised on the boy's body
and the boy was blistered all over.
But still he whipped him
until the blisters burst
and kept on whipping him.

He was interrupted once
by a visitor
and then went back to whipping the boy,
although the boy kept begging him to stop,
until he was interrupted again—
by the boy's death.

9

Samaritan

Smith was about fifty or sixty years old
and for about ten or twelve years
had lived beside a river as a fisherman
about ten miles from the nearest town.
He had been doing pretty well:
had built himself a houseboat
and had bought a gasoline boat
and had almost five hundred dollars
which he carried about in his pocketbook.

In town he met Davis, out of work
and down to his last dollar,
and invited Davis to live with him in the houseboat
and join him in the fishing business.
Smith and Davis lived in the houseboat about a month
and then Smith was no longer seen.
Davis told the neighbors that Smith had met a man
who had asked Smith to help him build a boat
and Smith had gone away to do so—

to one neighbor Davis said that Smith had gone to a town forty or fifty
     miles away
and to another all the way to Memphis—
and to both that he himself had bought all that Smith had left behind
for a couple of hundred dollars.

Parts of a human body—parts of both legs
as well as both elbows—
caught in the drift
were found a few hundred yards below the houseboat.
A log was then found near the houseboat
with human hair and hacked places on it
and pieces of flesh and bones,
and nearby the foot of a man
with a knob on the instep
just like Smith's foot
ever since he had broken his instep when a boy
so that he always walked crippled.

And in the houseboat were all of Smith's clothes
and his shoes, too, and his spectacles.
In the ashes of the stove
were charred bones and human teeth;
and on the floor, though it had been scrubbed,
were deep stains as of blood;
and splotches of dried blood on the bedstead.
Davis had Smith's watch and a thick roll of paper money.

IX

EPISODE IN THE LIFE OF A LAUNDRESS

His wife kept her jewelry in a little chamois bag
fastened to her chemise—
and now bag and jewelry were missing.
She had given the chemise to be washed

and when the woman who did the washing
came to work early next morning
he went for a policeman.

She knew nothing about the missing jewelry,
the woman who did the washing said,
but she was willing to help look for it
and did
but the jewelry was not found.
The policeman then told her than unless she confessed the theft
she would end up in jail;
and by this time the other servant, a Negress who did the cooking,
had come. She, too, said she knew nothing about the missing jewelry.

The policeman took them both to the police station;
but, before doing so, he told the husband of the woman who found her
    jewelry missing,
that sometimes those accused of a crime
confessed on the way to the station;
and so the policeman and the cook walked about fifteen feet in front of
    the husband and the woman who did the laundry
to give him a chance to talk to her
and he urged her to think of her children
and give the jewelry back
or she would end up in jail.

And she did. For when the four reached the police station
the laundress and the cook were both booked as "dangerous"
and each put in a separate cell.
However, in half an hour or so,
the jewelry was found by the woman who thought it had been stolen:
she had put it somewhere or other
before giving her chemise to be washed—
and had forgotten.

X

EPISODE IN THE LIFE OF A SCHOOLTEACHER

The Negro schoolmistress gave birth to a child—
her parents did not know and she did not want them to—
gave birth in the school's water-closet
and left the child under the water-closet on the ground.
Three Negro girls who went to the school
at recess saw the baby under a hole in the seat.
One of the girls had jumped up and said,
"Oh, there is a baby!"
It was raising its hands and kicking its feet
but its eyes were shut
and its mouth full of sand.

XI

EPISODES AT A TRIAL

At the trial, the woman he was accused of raping
suddenly began to scream at him from the witness stand,
"You know you are guilty!"
And her husband stood up and took hold of his chair
as if to strike the accused.
At this, those who had come to hear the trial
stood up, too;
and some got upon the benches and others crowded forward.
The judge also stood up
and, two or three times,
ordered them to sit down and told the sheriff to keep order;
after a while, they did sit down
and the trial went on.

But that night, as the jury were in their room
considering the case—an officer outside the door—
a large noisy crowd gathered in the courthouse yard
and an angry voice was heard:

"Why is the jury taking so long?
 We will give them until ten o'clock to convict him,
 and, if they don't,
 let's take him out of jail and hang him!"
 And other voices shouted,
"Hang him! Hang him!"

THE NORTH

MACHINE AGE

1

The Noise of Civilization

The hum of machinery, the noise of wagons on the public highways—
and the crowd watching a baseball game on a Sunday afternoon,
perhaps as many as two or three thousand,
shouting and stamping on the steps of the grandstand,
cheering and shouting
and heard half a mile and more away.

2

Life in Town

In the summer when the windows were open
the noise of the iron works—
of the air drills, hammers, riveting machines,
of the air drills, power hammers, power chippers, and riveting
    machines.

3

Life in the Country

There were about a hundred dead horses and cows—with maggots
    and flies—
lying about the rendering factory
to be turned into fertilizer;
and when the wind was from the east blowing across the fields
the stench
would make the women sick

and they would have to close the windows
to eat or sleep.

4

The rendering plant making fat into tallow
had a narrow covered passageway
between its factory and engine-house,
and in the passageway were four tanks for the hot fat.
One of the tanks, five by four feet and three feet deep,
was right at the door of one end of the passageway
but with a wooden cover on hinges.

The man who skimmed the fat in the tank
had opened the cover
and left it open;
and Dixon bringing a message to a fireman in the engine-house
from the fireman's brother
left the stable to go into the engine-house through the passageway.
A workman at the stable
saw him but did not trouble to warn him about the tank;
and neither did the engineer standing on a platform
within a few feet of Dixon
as he was about to enter the passageway.
The door had no latch but swung outward
as Dixon opened it,
and he did not see the tank-cover leaning against the wall—
the color of the hot fat almost that of the greasy cement floor—
and at his first step into the passageway
he plunged into the open tank,
its fat heated to a temperature of about two hundred degrees,
and was scalded to death.

5

An immigrant working at a cotton-picker in a mill
had only been there a few weeks
and had never worked at such a machine before;

and that morning the fluted feed-rolls—through which the cotton was
    drawn—
became clogged and stopped.

The foreman seeing this lost his temper,
shook his fist at the immigrant
and told him to start up his machine at once and keep it running.
Now the immigrant had never been shown how to free the feed-rolls
    if clogged
or, if told, did not understand what was said;
and the foreman, without offering to help him, left.

The immigrant had to act quickly
for the other three machines in his charge
were running.
He tried at first to free the feed-rolls of the machine that had stopped
by pulling the cotton back from the side where it had entered,
but that did not help;
then he raised the cover of the "beater"—
to which the cotton passed through the feed-rolls—
and saw some cotton between the rolls.
Within the beater
were knives
moving so rapidly
one could see nothing of them but a blur;
and he reached down into the beater to remove the cotton.

6

The company that ran the worsted mill began doing its own mending
    of the belts.
A belt manufacturer would unite the joints by hydraulic pressure,
but the worsted company trimmed the ends
and put them together with cement.
The air in the spinning-room was kept moist
so that the machines might spin the better,
but the moisture was apt to loosen a cemented joint.
Whatever the reason, while a carpenter was on his knees

fixing the floor of the spinning-room,
a belt
more than seventy feet in length
and on a pulley revolving ever so many feet a minute
parted
at a joint the company had mended.
One end struck the carpenter:
broke the glasses he was wearing
and drove the glass into his eyes,
blinding one eye
and injuring the sight of the other.
So that he could not see beyond a few inches
and would soon lose whatever sight he had.

7

The electric-light company had an extension ladder for attaching its
    wires to buildings
and a line-man for the company was sent up the ladder by his foreman
to put brackets into the corner of a house at a point thirty feet from
    the ground
and attach wires. When he was ready to go down,
his work completed, he held the top round of the ladder with his right
    hand
and put his left foot upon the roof of a bay window
to reach for a handline; got hold of it in his left hand
and began to pull himself back to an upright position on the ladder
    with his right hand
when the round of the ladder he had hold of—dozy on the outside and
    rotten inside—
broke
and he fell over backwards towards the sidewalk.

8

The storm came up suddenly
and lightning
struck a telephone pole, splitting it

and sending electricity along the wires.
A quarter of a mile away
a doctor was sitting in his house
quietly reading a book under his telephone—
and was found in his chair
dead, his hair on fire
and red lines along his neck, chest and side.

II
CHILDREN AT WORK

1

Cutting corn with an ensilage cutter and filling a silo
he had a boy of nine or ten helping him:
the boy to poke the corn with a stick
from the cutter to the carrier. Safe enough—
as long as the knives and cogwheels
were covered with an iron cap.

But a nut that held the cap came off
and the boy was told to hold the cap in place with one hand
and poke the corn with the other,
and he did: crossing his hands,
his left hand on the cap and poking corn with his right.
But after a few minutes
the mitten on his left hand was caught in the wheels
and his hand drawn into the cogs.

2

He was fourteen or fifteen years old
and worked on a machine in the mill.
He started to go to the water-closet
and had reached the stairs
but returned to tell the man in the room
whom he was required to notify

of his absence.
Going back in the darkness between the machines—
for the gas had not yet been lit—
he slipped on some oil on the floor,
threw out his hand,
and it was caught and crushed in the gears of a machine.

3

Jimmie, all of thirteen, was a "doffer" in a mill:
taking off the full bobbins,
putting them aside,
and putting empty ones in their place;
and, while the machines were in motion,
sitting and waiting on a bench.
He had been at work for about two weeks
when one morning, at about six—
after he had been at work for almost twelve hours that night—
the foreman came up to him as he was waiting for another doffing and
    said,
"Hey there, boy, take that cotton out of the cog, quick!"
He jumped up from the bench,
turned,
and saw that a draught from the window had blown threads into the
    cog wheels,
and took hold of the ends of the threads
giving them a twist to break them off;
but they were twisted into a thread
too strong to break
and his fingers were drawn into the cog wheels
and crushed.

4

When Lea was twelve she became a "doffer" in a spinning-company's
    mill:
removing the full bobbins from the machines they called "twisters"
and putting them back empty.

The twisters stood in a row on both sides of a narrow aisle,
three feet or so wide,
and the floor was always slippery because of oil
dripping from the machines.
The bobbins were at times too tight for her—
stuck—
and she was told by the foreman if stuck to kick the bobbin
until it was loosened.

In kicking a bobbin she slipped
and fell against one of the twisters;
her hair, caught in the rollers,
was torn off—
hair,
scalp,
an ear,
and part of her face.

5

When Susan was about eleven, she worked in a cotton mill:
at first sweeping the floor and afterwards "doffing" bobbins.
There were five girls, about Susan's age, to do the "doffing"
and when they were through in the spinning-room
they had to go out on the platform, or "shanty" as it was called,
and wait until they were called back by a bell.
If they were standing around the spinning-room
in the alleys between the machines,
the foreman would say, "What are you doing here?
Go out on the shanty!"
Nor were they allowed to sit in the hallways on the winding stairs
nor stand at the windows.

The "shanty" was about nine feet long
and on one side it overhung the ground.
This side had a railing—
two iron pipes the length of the platform,

fastened to the wall of the building at either end
and a single horizontal iron pipe in the center—
the lower pipe about a foot and a half from the floor of the platform.
There were no seats or benches.

One day when Susan was seated on the floor,
her back to the railing,
another girl tried to slap her in play
and, dodging,
Susan went over the edge of the platform
and fell—
thirty or forty feet to the ground.

6

He had just been hired to feed a machine tearing up the waste in
    making cotton and woolen goods.
A belt ran from a wheel near the bottom of the machine
to the wheels on the hub of a large cylinder at the middle;
and the belt was tightened or slackened
to quicken or lessen the speed of the machine
by placing the belt on a larger or smaller wheel.

The foreman showed him how to feed the machine
but the very first day the boy was at work
the belt came off one of the wheels
and the foreman's helper replaced it.
The next day the belt came off again
but this time the foreman himself replaced it
and told the boy he would have to learn how to put the belt on
    himself;
and when, on the morning of the boy's fourth day at work, the belt
    came off,
the foreman replacing it scolded him and kept cursing.
That very afternoon, when the belt came off again,
the boy tried to replace it
and his hand was caught between the belt and wheel.

7

He was only thirteen when hired by the steel company—
he had said he was fourteen to get the job
and his mother had signed an affidavit that he was fourteen—
and he went to work in the company's rolling mill:
twelve hours each day, six days a week,
from five in the afternoon until four in the morning,
his work to open and hold open the doors of furnaces
in which iron was placed every half hour;
and he was told to wait between opening the doors
just where he worked.

It was chilly that night and he was tired and sleepy—
for more than a week they had made him work fourteen hours a day—
and he sat down under an iron door just to rest
after iron had been placed in the furnaces.
As a rule no cars were run over the track
after one o'clock at night
until the iron in the furnaces had been taken away
and he would have nothing to do for about twenty minutes
until they were going to feed ore into the furnaces again.

He fell asleep.
As he slept he heard the cars coming
but he could not get up.
When he sat down his legs were doubled up under him
and now in his sleep he stretched out one of them
until it crossed a rail
and a car crushed his leg—muscles and bones.

8

When Ben was all of thirteen
he got a job in a factory making chain belts
and was set to work at a machine
reaming out holes in the curved links of the belts.
The machine was on a table
and above it a vertical revolving shaft

with the drill at the lower end
and Ben was to keep pulling it down
with his left hand on the lever.
On the table was a jig
to hold the links rigid
so that the drill would strike and make the holes
where it should;
and he was given an oil can to be filled with water
to squirt on the drill
and keep drill and link from heating.

But the jig on the table had become worn
so that it no longer held the links tightly
and Ben had to help hold them;
nor did the oil can work well
and the links became too hot to be handled with comfort;
the drill itself was worn
and it no longer reached the second hole to be made in each link
if Ben did not turn the link over.
He complained
and asked to be put at other work
but was told to go back to the machine—
or go home.

He went back but at noon made a clever device—so he thought—
of a piece of wire:
bent one end into a hook
to pull the links away from the jig without touching them,
and to lose no time
by putting the hook down and picking it up
bent the other end of the wire
into a loop
and put it around the two middle fingers of his right hand.

The wire
hanging from his hand
as he kept turning each link
and putting it in place on the jig,

after about half an hour or so,
was caught
on the revolving shaft of the drill
and winding rapidly
Ben's fingers were pulled—
and torn off.

9

The factory was in a building three stories high:
on the ground floor a blacksmith shop
and a tank which held benzine and gloss oil.
The top story had a door which opened on the flat roof of the second
        story—
here the workers on the top story would lounge at the noon hour—
and a ladder led from the roof of the second story to the flat roof of the
        first story,
and from this roof to the ground was not more than seven feet.
There were about twenty-five men and boys at work on each floor
when the fire was first seen in the tank on the ground floor;
the fire was then no larger than the light of a lamp
but the building quickly filled with thick black smoke.
Johnny, not quite fourteen, worked on the top floor
and when the whistle sounded the alarm
he went from the room in which he was at work
to see what it was all about
and heard someone shouting, "Fire! Get out! Get out!"
He ran back to get his coat—
there was neither fire nor smoke on the third floor as yet—
and tried to go down by the stairway at the end of the building
but was driven back by the smoke.
He then went to the stairway at the other end
and reached the second floor
but the door at the foot of that stairway
was opened just then
and the smoke drove him away,
and he ran back to the third floor.

He did not run to the door that led to the roof of the second story—
where he had been time and again—
and then to the ladder that led to the first story;
but in his panic dropped from one of the windows of the third floor to
    the sidewalk—
nearly forty feet below.

10

A girl, about fifteen, working for the telephone company,
stopped work at ten that night.
A few minutes afterwards she left the office
with two other girls, and the three went into a candy store
where they spent five or six minutes.
Then she went to the street corner—alone—
where she usually took a street car home
but the car had gone.

She had walked about four or five blocks to her home
when she saw a man cross the street;
he walked beside her
and spoke to her
but she did not answer—
except to walk a little faster.

Suddenly he took hold of her,
forced a handkerchief into her mouth as a gag
and dragged her into an alley;
and then dragged her to an empty sleigh
halfway in the alley;
tore nearly all her clothing off
and, as soon as he was through with her,
ran away.

As soon as she could gather about her what was left of her clothing,
she went to the back door of the nearest house
and, disheveled, bruised and bleeding,

sobbing and trembling,
asked to be let in.
There were three women in the house
and she told them what had happened
and, as nearly as she could,
what the man looked like.

The police arrested a man about midnight
wearing a long black overcoat, light trousers, a black derby hat and a
       black muffler—
he had no collar—
and the girl had no doubt that he was the man:
by the way he looked and was dressed
and the sound of his voice.
The man arrested was a porter or janitor
who took care of a bank and offices
about six blocks from the alley.
The police had taken his shoes off
after he was arrested
and his shoes fit the footprints in the snow—
a light snow had fallen that night.
At each place where the man and girl had scuffled in the alley
the snow was beaten down
and the man's tracks showed the heel of the shoe for the right foot
mended and a piece set in
just as in the shoe the police had taken from his foot.

III
STREETCARS AND RAILROADS

1

On Labor Day a boy of sixteen had gone from the city to a park
where the labor organizations were having a picnic;
after nine o'clock that night, as the last streetcar was about to leave,
the conductor stood at the entrance to the park
calling out, "Crowd on!

This is the last car for the city!"
When the car left the park,
all the seats were taken
and the aisle and platforms crowded.

The boy was on the steps of the front platform
and two other boys were seated on the step
on which he was standing;
he paid his fare and asked for a transfer.
The motorman, meanwhile, had turned on all the power the motor had
and, as the car was speeding along,
the conductor crowded his way onto the front platform,
calling out, "Transfers?"

The boy had been holding on to the handle of the car
with both hands
and now held one hand out.
At that moment the car lurched and threw other passengers,
who were also standing on the crowded platform,
against him
and they pushed him from the car.
His left foot went under the car
and the wheel of the car crushed it.

2

The railroad was running an excursion on a Sunday in July
from the city
and a group of eight or ten young men from a town near the city
went along. On the way back at night—
they had been drinking and had cut sticks from the branches of trees
to use as canes and clubs—
they kept going up and down the aisles of the cars
troubling the other passengers with what they said and did
and having "a good time."
When they left at their station,
they threw cinders, sand, gravel and stones at the train
and at the passengers through the open windows.

A young woman and the young man, her companion,
were sitting together—she next to a window—
and one of the young men who had just left the train
thrust his stick through the open window
and punched her with it in the breast.
The young man with her promptly closed the window
and, just as the train started,
an iron bolt came crashing through the glass
and struck her in an eye.
The young man she was with
caught her in his arms
and, as he did, the fluid of her eye
ran out upon his hand.

3

The newsboy was selling his newspapers out in the street
when a passenger on one of the streetcars signaled him:
it was an open summer car with a running-board
used by the passengers to enter and leave the car
and by the conductor in collecting fares.
The newsboy jumped on the running-board
looking for the passenger who had signaled him
when the conductor ordered him off
and went towards him; the newsboy turning
to jump off—
his feet slipped from the running board
and his right leg went under the wheels of the speeding car.

4

Along the avenue came a young man
driving a one-horse coal cart loaded with a ton of coal;
a row of box cars just then was standing on one of the railroad tracks.
The safety-gates were down
but the gateman raised them after a few minutes
and signaled the driver to cross.
He jumped from the cart and, holding his horse by the head,

started to cross the tracks
just as an engine was coming
without sounding its whistle or bell—
but because of the row of box cars could not be seen.
The horse began to lunge;
a trace snapped and the horse was out of harness.
The bell of the safety-gates began to ring,
and the safety-gates the driver was facing were coming down.

The gateman called to the driver to back up—
and the engine came from behind the row of box cars
and struck the cart, shoving it six or seven feet;
and the cart loaded with coal was pushed over upon the driver.

5

The brakeman of a freight train for many years
at his post on top of the fourth car from the engine,
as the train left a town at eight or nine o'clock in the evening—
a moonlit night and freezing—
had the low bridge they were approaching
well in mind
and as always lay face downward
flat upon the car.
But suddenly, choking in a cloud of smoke and steam from the engine
so dense
as to cut off his view of everything about him,
he lifted his head to catch his breath
and was struck by the bridge—
or perhaps by the ice hanging from it.

6

The seamstress, a woman of sixty and deaf, had been working for a
    family in the village that day
and was now hurrying home
on her way to the station to take the train that stopped there every
    evening.

The sky was clear and the moon shining brightly
but there had been a heavy fall of snow
and the day was cold and windy.

She and another woman went along the path beside the railroad track:
a path the villagers had been taking for years to reach the station
in spite of a warning the railroad had posted,
but the notice was old and the cloth on which it was printed
had been cut from corner to corner—
to read it
one would have to hold the pieces together.

As the seamstress walked along with her companion
the women saw a train coming from the north—
a mile or two away—
and both thought it was the train the seamstress was to take
and she said to her companion, "The train is coming."
But her companion soon realized from the speed of the train
that it would not stop at the station
and, in fact, it was the Montreal Express, almost two hours late and
        going fifty miles or more an hour.
The seamstress's companion shouted a warning and stopped
but the seamstress did not hear her and hurried on.

Near the station, railroad ties had been piled along the path
almost to the station
and snow shoveled between the ties and the path
so that a person walking along it had to stay on the path
because of the snow heaped beside it.
The body of the seamstress was found near the station:
drawn under the speeding train by its suction.

7
The railroad company was raising the tracks
and building a flight of stone steps to the new station.
An arc light across the street was now shining brightly
but there was no cross-walk or flagging across the street to the steps

from the paved walk on the other side.
A girl of sixteen, quite excited
because she was going to the theater in the city
with her sister, her sister's husband, and another young man,
thought they were late
and—never in the neighborhood before—
ran up the flight of steps
ahead of the others—
and fell to the ground from the top.

8

It was early in the morning,
drizzling,
and because of the fog
still dark.
The old woman began to cross the railroad tracks
slowly.
No sound of whistle or bell
or glow of headlight—
and the speeding engine struck her.

9

The first thing he knew the light of the train's engine was on him
and it was "zip"—
and all over.

IV
SHIPPING

1

Ten days out the wind came from the northwest and blew a blizzard.
Early in the morning the captain of the three-masted schooner, laden
    with coal, anchored at a good harbor for a west wind

but no harbor at all for a wind from the east.
It was very cold and the wind still blowing a gale.

But an east wind was coming
and the vessel had to get under way and farther off shore.
It was short-handed: the frozen sails reefed and iced up;
two anchors down, each weighing about three thousand pounds
with fifty or so fathoms of chain.
Hard work to get them up without steam.

V

DOMESTIC DIFFICULTIES

1

Cora and Will ran away and were married;
she was seventeen and he twenty.
For a while they stayed with his parents in Kansas City
but she was called back to her former home in a small town in Kansas
because her father was sick. After her father's funeral
she returned to Kansas City
but soon went home again to her mother
and her husband went with her, stayed a while,
and then went back to his work as a machinist in Kansas City.
But he soon became worried and anxious:
someone had told him that his wife went skating on a Sunday
    afternoon
with some young men
and one of them had walked with her part of the way home;
and her letters worried him—
was she thinking of a divorce?

They began to live together again
with her mother: his mother-in-law
was kind and cheerful, although after two months
he had been unable to find work that he liked
in the small town where they lived.

One day his wife brought his revolver to her mother and said,
"Keep it. You don't know what an awful temper he has."

On a morning in April, he asked his wife to drive out with him
to plant a rosebush on her father's grave,
but she would not go and said to her mother
that he merely wanted to take her out to quarrel with her.
Later that morning, the two came into the house together
and went upstairs. He went to their room
and she to her mother's room
and sat down beside her mother on the bed
and told her Will was going back to Kansas City
on a train that left in the evening.
As she sat there, she heard him call her
and said to her mother, "I am afraid"
but her mother told her there was nothing to afraid of
and she arose, looking at her mother,
and went into the adjoining room where her husband was waiting.

Her mother heard pistol shots
and rushed into the room:
Cora was lying dead on the floor with a bullet in her brain;
and Will upon his face, wounded on the side of his head but alive,
with his revolver near his right hand.

2

She was nineteen when they were married
and he forty-four: crippled in one arm and hand
and in both legs—
impotent.
Later that year, they both went to a lawyer's office
and there he signed a will giving her on his death
all he had,
and this was read aloud to her.

She had known a young man of the neighborhood
before her marriage

and when she left home to work in a railroad camp where he had
      worked
he drove her to the station;
now they met in the doorway of his father's barn at noon.
She began to cry and said,
"Oh, I can't live with him any longer!"
But he said nothing and did not even take her by the hand to comfort
      her.

One evening, that fall, she and her husband
went for a drive to a neighboring town.
In town, her husband walked to a saloon he knew
and bought a dozen bottles of beer, well corked and wired;
placed these in the back of the buggy
and they started for home.
But then her husband said he wanted some sausage
and turned his horse
and went back to get it.
They shared the sausage
and both drank from the bottle of beer
which her husband took from the back of the buggy.
Later he reached down
and got a second bottle of beer
and drank about half of it.
The first bottle had foamed when he opened it—
this did not.
He handed the bottle to her and said,
"Taste how bitter this is;"
she drank a little and said, yes, it was bitter
and handed the bottle back to her husband
and he finished it.
Later, he was in great pain.
At night, when they reached the village where they lived,
they stopped at a neighbor's
and called him to the roadside.
As the neighbor left his house, she cried out,
"Quick! My husband is dying!"
and when he came to the buggy, her husband said,

"She poisoned me! She did it; yes, she did!"
They asked him to drive to a doctor
and the neighbor did, standing in the buggy,
driving with one hand and holding her husband with the other.
When they finally found a doctor
at the third stop,
the doctor saw no use in doing anything—
by this time her husband was unconscious—
and said he should be taken home:
he was carried from the buggy into his house
and in a few minutes was dead.
Then she was charged with murder.

3

She had seen her husband hugging and kissing Essie—
yes, had even caught them in the water-closet together
and upstairs on the floor—
oh, lots of times.
Now, when she had put her dinner pot on the cookstove
and the meat into it
and had picked up some glass fruit-jars and empty catsup bottles
and had taken them to the garret,
just as she was stooping to put down the bottles
the door opened and Essie came in.
She asked Essie what she wanted
and Essie grumbled something or other
and suddenly she found herself hitting Essie with a catsup bottle:
the first time just above the ear,
and when Essie turned around
she hit her again on the top of her head.
Essie went down on her knees
and then Mary remembered the knife she had in her pocket—
she had put it there to rip some of her sewing—
and she caught Essie by the shoulder.
She could not remember how many times she struck Essie with it:
there was a cut just above the girl's forehead in the edge of her hair
and cuts on her hands and arms

as Essie tried to keep her from cutting her throat—
and could not.

Then Mary went downstairs
and looked at herself in the mirror:
her hair was all down
and her hairpins gone,
and her apron bloody.
She burned it in the cookstove;
there was blood on her dress, too,
and she took a little wet rag and wiped it off.

4

The young colored woman said: "My husband Tom and me was in
        town on Saturday night
and we started home in a wagon.
Tom and me got out of the wagon
but Tom run and caught up to the wagon
and rode home. I walked.

"I went into my house and the light, sitting on the mantel,
was burning. I looked around for Tom
and could not find him,
and so come over to his father's house
and asked if Tom was there.

They answered, 'No, ain't he over home?'
I then come on back to the house
and went in and pulled the bed out of the stairway—
we used the winding stairway in a corner of our room
to store our bed and mattress—
and I heard someone stomping around on the steps.

"So I goes up and Tom was up there
with his feet on the steps.
'Tom,' I called, 'ain't this you?'

He didn't say nothing.
So I called again, 'Tom, ain't this you?'
And he answered, 'Yes.'
And I said, 'What you doing up there?'
And he said, 'What in the hell is it to you?'
I said, 'If I was you I would come down:
this is the way you been doing all the time.'
A young woman not living with her husband
was living in the room above
and the stairway led up there.
And I said, 'If this is the way you going to be doing all the time,
I going to leave,' and I grabbed my hat off the table
and started out of the door. He grabbed his gun.
He was standing on the third step of the stairs
and pulled back the trigger. The gun said click.
He pointed the gun at me
and I shoved it
and the barrel of the gun went up
and fired,
and he said, 'O Lord!'
I ran to his father's house and cried,
"Tom is dead! Tom is dead!'"

They found him
with his head and part of his body resting upon the winding stairs
and his feet on the floor.
A hole was shot straight through the top of his head
and part of the head was shot away,
brain and blood scattered in back of him
up the stairway and against the wall.

The gun was resting under the mantel
and his father turned to her and said,
"If he shot himself through the head
how come the gun is sitting under the mantel?"

5

John had slept with the wife of the man at whose home he boarded
for over a year and told her that if she were a widow
he would marry her and that he had it in mind
to kill her husband.
She told him to do as he pleased.
John and the woman's husband were in the habit of drinking together,
and John told the barkeeper of the saloon at which they drank at times
that he had bet five dollars he could drink more than the other man;
and when he called for gin
to put plenty of water in it.
On a Sunday afternoon both of them came into the saloon
and stayed there drinking until about ten in the evening
and by that time the man at whose home John boarded was so drunk
he fell off his chair to the floor;
and John said to the barkeeper,
"This is the man at whose home I board—
I will take him home."

John lifted him and took him to the embankment
along which the railroad ran
and after John had managed to climb it
with the other man in his arms
John struck him twice on the back of his head
with the lead mallet John used at his work in the factory
and which he had carried with him in an inside pocket.
The other man was dead to the world,
dead drunk and his skull badly fractured,
and John left him lying across the railroad track
to be run over and crushed by the next train.

6

Joe was Karl's hired man, helping him on the farm;
and, on an afternoon in June, Joe went with him
to the "Old Settlers" picnic.
They came home about midnight;
Joe went at once to his room

but Karl's wife helped him with the horse,
for he told her he was not feeling well,
and then he had coffee and more whiskey.
She helped him take off his shoes and shirt
and they went to bed;
his wife had undressed
but he was lying on the bed with his trousers on.

She awoke shortly before it was day
and found her husband gone;
looked for him in the house
and then in the barn;
and there he was hanging in front of the horses
from a joist above
with a rope about his neck.

She ran into the house for a knife
and cut the rope
and then ran to his brother's home nearby
and came back with his brother and his brother's wife.
They found Karl's body on the barn floor
where it had fallen when the rope was cut:
his face calm as if he were asleep,
eyes and mouth closed
and hands open.

The rope had left a bluish-red mark about his neck
just below the "Adam's apple";
but on his throat, each side of the windpipe near the jaw,
were marks, not as dark as the mark made by the rope,
looking like fingerprints.
He had his undershirt on, his trousers and stockings;
but the stockings were clean,
though the barn was a hundred feet from the house
and there was only bare ground between: not soiled
if he had walked from the house to the barn.
He had been dragged or carried.

The hands of a man who has died by hanging
are clenched;
face distorted,
the eyelids partly open, eyeballs protruding and bloodshot;
froth about the mouth,
and the tongue, too, protruding and somewhat swollen.
The knot of the rope about Karl's neck
was under the right ear,
though he was right-handed;
and if knotted by himself
the rope would likely have been tied on the other side
and drawn close to the head.

A person chloroformed
would offer little or no resistance
to a man strangling him;
nor would a man who had been "doped."
In the evening of the day of the picnic
Karl and Joe had entered a saloon
and Joe had called the saloonkeeper aside
and had asked for a bottle of "doped" whiskey
and said he would pay well for it;
and a druggist sold Joe four ounces of chloroform,
but Joe would not sign his name as the purchaser—so the law
        required—
and the druggist had signed the false name Joe had given.

A brother of the dead man had been at his house
the forenoon of the day of the picnic;
and, as he waited for his brother—
out in the field ploughing—
Joe came down from upstairs,
and his brother's wife came down shortly afterwards.
There was only one room, a bedroom in the second story.
And Joe had said to another brother,
although the brother had said nothing that called for what Joe said:
"You think there is something wrong
between me and Karl's wife, don't you?"

7

The two families lived next to each other in a town near Kansas City
and the children became friends. After they were grown up
the daughter of one family lived in Kansas City after her marriage
and Don's elder sisters would visit her
and stay with her two or three weeks at a time
and now and then she would visit them, too.

When Don was twenty, he went to Kansas City to find a job
and stayed at her home almost a month;
her husband, a printer, worked nights
and she and Don would go to the theater together and to dances.
On her last visit to the town where both grew up—
Don did not find a job in Kansas City and had gone back—
she and Don would go buggy riding;
too often his family thought,
for the two had clearly become fond of each other.

One evening when they were out riding
they began to talk of running away together—
they had talked about it before—
and now she said she could not do that while she was married.
"But we can get rid of him," she said of her husband. "We can kill him."
Don said, "Oh, I don't want to do that!"
"That's the only way. It won't do just to run away:
my husband will follow us."
They talked it over for some time and she said,
"The best way is to hit him with a club."
In the end, they planned that she should go back to Kansas City
and that he would follow in a few days.

Don's grandfather had a billiard cue which he used as a cane
and Don cut a part of it off
and took the heavy end with him.
She had been home a week when he came to Kansas City
and she met him at the railroad depot and they stayed together two or
     three hours
and she arranged to meet him at the depot the next morning.

Next morning they went over to Kansas City, Kansas,
to a rooming-house
and again stayed together two or three hours.
She said she expected her husband home that night
and told Don to come to the back door of her cottage
a little after one o'clock
and she would be there to let him in.

Don went through an alley to the back door
and she had the door open and was waiting for him
but said in a whisper, "He's awake," and added, "wait a while."
Don waited in the kitchen
and then she came back and said, "He's asleep,"
and both went to the room where her husband was.
As Don came in, he sat up and said, "Here you are again!"
And Don hit him on the head with the heavy end of the billiard cue.
He clinched with Don and both kept falling on the bed
until the slats under them broke;
and then they got out of bed and kept on scuffling.
As they were scuffling her husband kept shouting,
"Help! Murder! Let me alone!"
and turning to his wife cried, "Honey, help me!"
Don managed to get the husband's hands down and held them at
        his side
and his wife came up with a razor in her hand
and cut his throat. He began to weaken at once
and Don let him down on the floor,
face down,
and she kept stabbing him in the back
with a pair of sharp-pointed scissors.
Afterwards, blood was found in the handle of the razor
and in the hinge of the scissors.

When he was dead, she brought a pan of water into the room
for Don to wash his hands.
One of his cuffs had come off during the struggle,
and now Don took the other off—
there was blood on it—

took the cuff buttons out and threw the cuffs on the floor.
He had gone into the house with his hat on,
and in the struggle it was knocked off;
now it had blood on it, too, and he left it where it fell.

She gave Don one of her husband's hats
and ten dollars for his fare—
it was all she had just then, she said.
As she let him out the back door, she said she would say "niggers"
        had broken into the house to rob
and had killed her husband;
and, after the matter had quieted, she would come to Don.

8

Dominick, a large, well-built, powerful man
accused his boarder, Pietro, a much younger man,
of being too friendly with Dominick's wife
and, though the boarder denied it—and it wasn't true—
Dominick told him to leave and said:
"Some day we'll meet again.
In my own house I'll do nothing to you
but the first time I meet you—."

Weeks later, a friend of Pietro told him
Dominick had just said that he would kill his former boarder on sight.
When Pietro heard this,
he took the loaded revolver another friend had given him
from the valise where he had kept it for a year or more
and carried it about with him.
On an evening, Pietro was in a saloon which he went to often,
drinking and chatting with friends at a table
when Dominick entered—
he had never been there before.
Pietro was frightened. He took a dollar out of his pocket
and calling to the barkeeper said,
"Give a drink to everyone here!"

Dominick drank half of his glass of beer and then left the bar
and coming up to Pietro as he was seated at the table
looked him straight in the face.
And Pietro knew by the way he was looking at him
that Dominick had come into the saloon to make trouble,
and Pietro wanted to leave as soon as he could.
He stood up
and Dominick was standing behind him
and said, "You are the fellow I'm looking for,"
and began to strike Pietro with his fists.

Pietro turned and, backing away,
drew his revolver
and snapped it three times
but it did not go off—
perhaps the cartridges were stale—
and Dominick ran out of the saloon.
Pietro followed,
and this time his revolver went off
and the second shot hit Dominick in the back of his neck
and he fell
to die in two or three minutes on the sidewalk.

9

A Negress, her two grown daughters, and some of their friends
were sitting in front of her house
in a narrow street known as "Bad Land Alley"
one hot evening in August,
singing plantation songs and drinking beer.
Ned, a Negro who lived in the house
with the elder daughter
came up to the group;
earlier, he had come home from his work in a steel plant,
washed up, had his supper, played cards with three friends,
and had gone out, and was now back—drunk.

He went up to a young Negro sitting beside the elder daughter—
a young man who worked on the boats on the river
and lived in the neighborhood—
and said, "What you doing, sitting here talking to my woman?"
The young man answered, "I wasn't talking to your woman: I was
    singing."
At that the younger daughter of the mistress of the house
went up to the man who lived with her sister and said,
"Don't start no fuss here in front of Mamma's door."
And the mistress of the house told the young man to get up
and go into the house next door for a while.

The young man—in his shirt sleeves—did get up
and put his hand in a friendly fashion on Ned's shoulder;
but Ned asked him what he had in his hand
and the young man answered, "I ain't got even a cigarette paper."
Ned stepped back
and began to pull out a pistol.
The pistol caught in his pants pocket
but he managed to free it
and as soon as he did
fired at the young man.

After the first shot, the young man turned
and ran down the alley
but Ned kept on shooting—
the last shot as the young man entered the doorway of a house.
Two of the shots struck him,
and the police found him in the house, mortally wounded,
crying and groaning.

10

In the winter Will, who had served in the Spanish-American War and
    been honorably discharged,
began living with Amelia as man and wife
in a room in St. Louis. She was then twenty-three and Will about the
    same age.

They had known each other as children
and had played together. Amelia's mother had died when Amelia was
 ten
and, after her mother's death, she had spent some time in a house of
 refuge;
when she was thirteen she married and was soon afterwards divorced;
and about sixteen began to live in whorehouses and to frequent
 winerooms.
This lasted two or three years. Will knew all about it.

In the spring they started west
with a horse, a covered wagon, and a camping outfit.
After almost a month of traveling,
they overtook an old man, his beard heavily sprinkled with gray
traveling by himself with a team of horses and a covered wagon
and going the same way;
they became friendly and went on together.

Two or three days afterwards, they camped early in the day a few miles
 west of a village,
and in the afternoon Will went hunting
and came back with two quail and a rabbit for supper.
In the meantime she had shaved the old man's neck and trimmed his
 beard.
After supper the three sat around the campfire
until nearly midnight. When Will began pulling off his shoes to go to
 bed,
she complained of a toothache
and asked Will to go to town and get some medicine for it;
but Will and the old man persuaded her to try smoking
to stop the pain. As she stooped to get a coal from the fire to light a
 pipe
she heard Will strike the old man on the head;
looked around and the old man was on his back.
He was raising his head when Will grabbed him by the throat with
 the left hand
and kept striking him again and again with the ax in his right.

When the old man was dead, Will took off the old man's boots, coat
     and vest, and went through his pockets;
then he wrapped a sack around the mangled head
and carried the body on his back to an abandoned well
in a field nearby; tied a rock weighing about thirty pounds around
     the body
with wire and a rope, and let the body down the well.
He then covered it again
with the old rails that had been on it
and with his fingers straightened out the grass around the well.
Next morning, Will took the old man's team, wagon and outfit,
his ax, bear hide and buffalo hide, his pillow, quilts, watch, gun and
     pistol,
and threw his bloodied cap over a fence;
and they drove on, Will driving the old man's team
and Amelia the one-horse wagon.

That summer they camped for several weeks in the backyard of a
     house in Topeka,
and here quarreled about money.
When Amelia said she knew something about him
that would put him behind bars for the rest of his life,
Will knocked her down—
the blow cut her lip and made her nose bleed—
and he would have stamped on her
if a bystander had not stopped him.
At that she left him for good.

11

A colored man who had been working in upper New York State
on the dams and reservoirs for a new aqueduct
was discharged on a Saturday.
When he came home that afternoon—
he and the colored woman he was living with
had a room in the house of another colored couple—
she asked for money for a pair of shoes
and he said he had none

and was planning to leave that part of the country
to find work in the Pennsylvania coal fields—
and she was to come along.

At that Captora, or Katie as she was called, said, "Leave me alone!
I don't want to go:
I am barefooted and have no shoes
and I'm hungry
and tired of following you.
I'm not your wife!"
The couple with whom they were living
just then asked for what he owed for their lodging
and when he would not pay anything
told him and Katie to leave.

When he had packed his suitcase that evening
and was ready to go
he took Katie by the arm and tried to pull her out of the house with
    him
but she would not budge and said,
"In the morning I'll go back to the city."
He left the house alone
and she quickly closed and locked the door.
But the couple with whom they had been lodging
again asked her to leave.
She wanted to go through the back door
but they would not let her
and made her leave by the front door.

In fifteen or twenty minutes, they—and others along the road—
heard screaming;
and Katie came to a hospital in the neighborhood,
bleeding badly.
She fell into a chair and in five minutes became unconscious
and was dead within the hour.
She had been cut by a razor on her right forearm and across the
    right shoulder
and again across the left shoulder,

from the left eye to the ear
and from above the right eye through the right ear
and, the worst cut of all, from behind the left ear
downwards across her throat
through all the blood vessels and muscles
down to the bone.

She had stopped at a neighbor's house
calling out that she had been hurt
and asked the woman of the house that her husband help her to
    the hospital,
but the woman answered that her husband was sick and in bed;
and in the morning the woman saw a lot of blood
on the stones in front of her door.

12

Brown was divorced by his wife
and she had the custody of their child
and went to live with her father.
On a Sunday in July, a month or so afterwards,
when she and the child were in the home of a neighbor,
Brown came there in a buggy, about nine in the evening,
and asked for his former wife and the child.
The neighbor's daughter saw that he had been drinking,
and told him that his former wife and their child
were at the home of his former wife's brother
across the creek. Brown drove there
but was told by his former wife's brother
that the woman and child were at the home of the neighbor.
By this time it was ten o'clock.

The neighbor was in bed in a front room of the house
and the former wife of Brown and their child—she was sick—
    and the neighbor's daughter
were in another room about to go to bed.
Brown knocked at the front door
and the neighbor's daughter asked him what he wanted.

He answered that he wanted his wife and baby
and told the young woman to open the door.
She answered that she was in her nightclothes and could not
and he said that she had better open up
and began rattling the screen door.

She went back and asked his former wife what she should do
and was told not to let him in,
for he was drunk;
and his former wife then hid in a closet with the child
and the neighbor's daughter went to the door,
unlocked it and opened it slightly—
the screen door was still fastened—
and Brown said again that he wanted his wife and baby
and added that he was going into the house.
She told him again that they were not there
and that he could not come in.
He said, "Damn you, I will kill you!"
At that she slammed the door in his face
and he answered with shots from his revolver;
three of the bullets went through the door.

He then went around to the back door.
It was kept closed only by a thumb latch and hook
and he burst it open. As he was about to go into the house,
the owner of the house was pointing a gun at him
and said he would shoot if he came in.
But the gun was not loaded and Brown shoved it aside
and sprang into the room,
swinging his revolver and demanding his wife and child.
The owner's daughter was about to go into the room
when Brown grabbed her by the waist and, pointing the revolver in
     her face,
said, "Death or the baby!"
She managed to get away but Brown followed
and raising his revolver said they would all die together
if he did not get his wife and child.
As he went about the house looking for her,

the owner and his daughter ran to a neighbor's house
to telephone the police.
The former wife of Brown had also escaped from the house
and hidden herself and the child in some weeds nearby;
and she could hear Brown in the house going about and calling her.

13

He was a plumber who did not earn much—
a widower with three small children.
When he was away at work
the children had to shift for themselves
and it would be better—everybody said—if he had at least a
    housekeeper
to care for them.
A woman who was among his acquaintances had him meet a young
    unmarried woman
who had a child of about two
and she agreed at once to become the housekeeper
and they began to live together—
as husband and wife, although they were not married.
And they were more or less happy
until the little daughter of the woman became one of the family.
The man her mother was living with did not like this at all—
perhaps because there was another mouth to feed—
and kept calling the child "brat" and "bastard,"
and now and then struck the little girl.

One night, when the man and woman had been out together visiting
and were back at midnight,
he asked her to go downstairs and get him a pint of beer
but she did not want to because she was afraid—
in that neighborhood.
He had taken off his shoes
and now struck her on the head with one
and went out. He was back in half an hour and asked,
"Where is that brat of yours?"
Told that she was in bed with his children,

he took her
and bringing her into the living room
threw her on the floor.
Her mother tried to keep him from striking the child with his fists
but he kept on
until she managed to snatch the child from him
and fled into the kitchen.
He followed and struck the child's mother with a plumber's tool
and then began hitting the little girl again with his fists—
until he and the child's mother saw that the child was dead.

14

He was seventy and homeless,
estranged from his wife who owned the farm
He would visit her now and then
and beg her to share some of her property with him
for his support—
visits wrangling and unpleasant
and bad for his wife who had heart disease.

His son was in a field nearby
stacking wheat—
for it was the harvest season—
and a boy, shortly before noon,
ran out to the field and told him
to come home at once:
his mother had fainted as a result of a meeting with his father
and was thought to be dying.
His son came at once
and sent to town for a doctor.
His father had left the house
and gone down the public road, slowly, leaning on his cane.

The old man found a battered tin can—it had been opened—
the top ragged and rusted,
and crept under a heavy, rank hedge on the side of the road
and cut his throat with the top of the can.

But he could not cut deeply enough to die quickly
and crawled to a well and drowned himself.

His son later went to the well
and found his father's body lying the the water.
At the funeral, his younger brother saw his grief and said to him,
"You need not be crying: you are glad of it—
and I am damned glad of it, too."

15

A colored man, just a farm hand, living in a village
in a small house on an acre or less of land,
had been married twice,
but his first wife was dead and his second did not live with him
nor did his son, Phil, by his first wife—as a rule.
He was living in his father's house just then—
and so were a young sister and the housekeeper—
because Phil was out of work.

There was ill will between father and son:
although the land on which the house stood
was owned by the young man's uncle, his dead mother's brother,
and the house itself had been built with his dead mother's money
and his father's second wife was not living with him,
Phil's father was unwilling to have his son
bring the young woman he wished to marry to live with him in his
        father's house,
and the young man said he had as much right to live there with his wife
as his father had with his.

Phil was not in the house
when the shot was fired from outside
that killed his father—
standing near the kitchen window.
The housekeeper, hearing the shot and the glass breaking,
went into the kitchen
and saw Phil's father on the floor

bleeding from a wound in his head
and ran to the door of the house shouting,
"Murder!"
Just then Phil walked up and asked,
"Is Pop shot?"
And the housekeeper answered, "Your father! Your father!"
The two went into the house
and Phil saw his father lying on the floor bleeding
and merely said he would go out and get help;
and the very next day after his father's death
he brought the young woman he wished to marry to the house to
    spend the weekend.

16

Father-in-law and son-in-law bought a farm together:
the son-in-law to do the work and have three-fourths of the crops
and his father-in-law the fourth.
But they quarreled about the management of the farm
and payments on the mortgage for the unpaid purchase price.

The crops that season were bad and the son-in-law troubled
about the payments on the mortgage; and his father-in-law told the
    hired hand—
at least that is what the hired hand told the son-in-law—
that he would make no more payments
and if his son-in-law could not meet them
and the farm had to be sold,
he himself would buy it in.

One afternoon, as they were walking from the house to the barn,
they began to quarrel again
and when they came to their wagon
the father-in-law sat down on it
and began to whittle at one of the uprights
with his small black-handled knife.
In a few minutes they were striking at each other
and the father-in-law slid from the wagon,

the son-in-law on top of him,
pounding him in the face with the end of the closed knife.

The hired hand caught the son-in-law's arm
and led him away;
and the son-in-law went to a tank nearby
and washed his hands,
for the right hand was covered with blood.
His father-in-law was lying on the ground:
nose broken—it lay on the side of his face—
the bones under his eyes crushed in,
and his eyes closed.

17

About four weeks before, her father ordered her out of the house
and she went to live with her grandmother and uncle;
and now, as she sat at the supper table,
she was crying.
Her mother had given birth the day before
and for two days her younger sister had been giving her mother
only toast and tea,
for there was nothing in the house to eat except bread.
But her father would go out
and buy himself steak and rolls and tomatoes
and sit down in the kitchen
and eat it all as his children watched.
"Then why not go home and take care of your mother?"
her uncle said. "I'm afraid," she answered.

They entered the kitchen together from the outside,
she and her uncle, and her father came in from an adjoining room
and seated himself in the rocking-chair near the kitchen table.
Neither her uncle nor father spoke a word to each other.
Then her uncle said to her,
"Stay here a couple of days and take care of your mother
and, if anything is needed or wanted,
I'll see that you get it."

At this her father said, "So you are the boss here, are you?"
Her uncle took off his glasses and put them on the table
and, going up to her father as he sat in the chair,
caught him by the throat with one hand and said,
"I'm not going to let you starve my sister!"
At this his niece cried out, "Don't, Uncle!"
and he dropped his hands to his sides.

Her father stood up and facing her uncle,
three or four feet away,
began speaking to him in French,
but in so low a tone she could not understand what her father was
      saying.
"Speak English!" said her uncle, interrupting her father twice.
Then her uncle turned towards the door to leave
and her father drew a pistol from his pocket
and fired at her uncle, killing him.

18

Johnny was an orphan. When he was ten
a farmer adopted him and took him from the orphan asylum,
but when Johnny was twelve he ran away
and went to the house of another farmer.
The farmer who had adopted him searched for him and found him
      there
and took him home;
but late that evening the boy ran away again.
The farmer looked for him at the place where he had found Johnny
      earlier that day
and was told that he was not there;
however, the farmer found him there the next day.

The farmer was carrying a heavy whip
called by some a "black snake."
He made the boy get behind him on the horse he was riding
and they started towards home, five miles away.
They had not gone far when the farmer told the boy to get off

and he was forced to run ahead of the horse
all the way;
and whenever he tried to stop or walk,
the farmer lashed him with his whip.
Johnny was barefoot
and part of the way was over stony ground;
one of his feet was badly bruised
and his back showed the marks and cuts of the whip.
They were still to be seen weeks afterwards.

19

Hattie was almost thirteen; an orphan,
she had been taken by Delia into her home
to bring up
and had been living with her two or three years.
On a Friday, Delia left her baby in Hattie's care
and told her to put some ironed clothes away;
but when she came back she found that this had not been done
and Hattie explained that the baby had been cross
and took up all her time.

Delia took Hattie into another room
and made her take off all her clothes
and lie down on the bed, face down.
Then from a drawer Delia took a cowhide whip
and began to whip Hattie.
She screamed and Delia, sitting on her head to smother her screaming,
told her that for every scream
she would burn her with the stove-lid lifter;
and kept on beating her.
Then Delia went into the kitchen
and came back with the hot stove-lid lifter
and burnt her on the chest and belly.

After Delia let Hattie up, she sent her to the corncrib nearby
to bring back some corncobs;
and a schoolgirl friend of Hattie's on the way from school

heard her crying and sobbing at the crib.
Hattie's teacher, next week, saw that she was not playing with the
    other children
and was trying to keep her clothes away from her body.
Later, more than ten burns were found on her chest and belly—
large and deep burns where the hot lid-lifter had crossed the ribs—

and some had become running sores;
many welts of the whip were also on her shoulders, back, behind,
    thighs and legs,
and in places the whip had broken the skin
and had drawn blood.

20

A young man and his wife, both in the late twenties,
with no children of their own
adopted a girl of ten or so as their daughter.
But they had trouble with her:
she signed his name to an excuse for absence from school,
and again she had not told him about money she had received for the
    sale of eggs,
and, finally, when she was twelve or thirteen
he missed a fifty-cent piece and charged her with stealing it.
She kept saying she had not taken it
and, to teach her not to be dishonest, he had her take her clothes off
and, as she stood naked before him,
whipped her with a riding-whip,
perhaps as many as seventy times—
too many times to count.
But so many that her body and legs were thick with marks of the
    beating—
afterwards blood oozed from some of them—
and still she said she had not taken the money.

Finally, he tied her hands behind her back
and kept them tied
that Friday afternoon until Sunday,

and gave her only bread and water.
But that Sunday, not to spoil the day for his wife and himself,
for it was August and the weather hot and unpleasant,
the two of them went off to the country.
The wife of a neighbor heard the naked girl's cries
and had the firemen of the neighboring engine-house climb to the
    window of the room
and free her.

21

After her husband left for work
and she had sent her two children off to school
her nephew—a young man of nineteen—
knocked at the door
and she let him in. He had lost his mother years before,
roomed here and there, and had worked as a messenger boy;
and would visit his aunt now and then
and she would give him breakfast
or whatever he wanted to eat.

When her children came from school
they found the door locked
and the elder—a boy—climbed from a neighbor's window
over the fire-escape
into his parents' flat.
His mother was lying dead on the floor of the kitchen,
her head in a pool of blood
and in the pool the two combs she used to wear in her hair.
Her earrings and the rings she had on her fingers were gone
and so was the change in the purse on the sideboard.

Her nephew had gone to a poolroom in the neighborhood
and there was a friend he used to meet
and they began playing pool together.
But he was not his usual self
and his friend kept asking him if anything was the matter
until he said, "Nothing is the matter!

Just let me enjoy myself today.
Come on and shoot pool!"

22

A young man of twenty-five or so, harnessmaker by trade,
came to the United States and, when he found a job,
left his cousin's home where he had been staying
and became a roomer in the neighborhood where he worked.
His room was the rear bedroom in the flat of an old woman
and there were no other roomers.

He was a heavy drinker
and that morning drank four or five pints of beer
but did his work as always
and when he came in with the beer
walked steadily and did not spill any.
At noon he told the man for whom he worked
that he wanted to go home and fix his bed—
it had broken down the night before, so he said—
and borrowed a heavy riveting hammer.

He also asked for a little money
to buy lunch
and his "boss" gave him a quarter.
He was back at half-past three:
he had changed his clothes
and showed the boss a ten-dollar bill and one or two one-dollar bills.
The boss said, "I thought you had no money."
"Well," he answered, "I always got plenty,"
and sat down to his work, had another pint of beer,
and began to sing.
At that his boss told him he was not wanted anymore
and he could have his tools when he brought the hammer back.

A week or so before, he had told his boss
that he knew where his landlady kept her money:
"under the stove where other people keeps wood."

A few days after his boss sent him away
a stench began to come from the flat where he had lived
and when the locked door was forced open
the old woman who had rented him the room
was found dead and decaying:
her body across her bed
with her legs hanging down
and a towel over her face—
bed and towel soaked with blood—
and the hammer with blood on it a few inches from her head.

He had broken her skull with the hammer
as she stood in the kitchen with her back towards him
and when she fell to the floor
struck her again and again.
But he found only a few pennies under the stove
until he saw the cord around her neck
and picking up the cord
there was a little pouch tied to it
and in the pouch a ten-dollar bill and two one-dollar bills.

23

Those who lived in that school-district called Dan "the little
    schoolteacher,"
and he said of himself, "I may be little
but I am the nerviest little man that ever came into the state."
And he was little—hardly five feet tall, if that.

He had been teaching for about seven weeks
and Olive's father had several children at the school,
among them his daughter who was sixteen.
One day, Dan accused Olive of breaking one of the rules—
whispering to someone seated near her,
although those seated near her said afterwards
that she was only reading in a whisper to herself—
and Dan tried to whip her.
But she would not let him,

hit him over the head with the poker as they scuffled near the stove,
broke his switch,
and left the schoolhouse.
As she left, Dan told her not to come back.

That evening her father said: he wanted his children to go to school
but if "that little schoolteacher" whipped his daughter,
or for that matter any of his children,
he would make him walk "a merrier gait than he ever did."
And next morning, Olive's father—
the largest taxpayer in the school-district as he was to tell her
    teacher—
went with her to school
and told Dan not to whip her again.
Dan answered that he was running the school
and told him to get out;
and just before the morning recess, Dan told Olive that she must take
    her punishment
and whipped her.

During the recess, one of her brothers hurried to his father
and told him that the teacher had whipped Olive
and that in the scuffle her clothing was torn.
Her father went to where his horse was tied
and, riding to the school, saw the children and their teacher coming
    down the road;
for it was the noon hour
and the children were going home to eat
and Dan towards his boarding-house.
Olive's father called out, "Hold on there!"
Dan stopped
and her father got down from his horse and said, "Why did you whip
    that girl?"
Dan answered, "Because she had broken a rule of the school,"
and added, "Go on and attend to your business,
for I want no trouble with you";
and Dan walked on.

He had not gone far before Olive's father picked up two stones
and threw them at Dan. He dodged one
but was hit by the other and began to run.
Olive's father followed
and when he was close to Dan pulled out a pistol.
Dan stopped and turned
and took hold of the pistol—pointed at him—to push it away,
and Olive's father fired.
Dan was shot,
staggered from one side of the road to the other
and then fell and died where he fell.

24

His mother had done some sewing for a woman
but had not been paid the dollar and a few cents due her;
so one evening Dick and his mother went to where the woman lived—
on the second floor of a house—
and found her and her husband at supper.

The woman for whom the sewing was done
said she was too poor to pay all of it at one time
but would pay it in two or three installments,
but Dick's mother would not hear of this
and soon the two women were quarreling.
The woman's husband then spoke up
and asked Dick and his mother to leave
and told his wife to push Dick's mother downstairs if she would not go.
Dick had a pistol with him—
he had taken in that day sixty or seventy dollars in his butcher shop—
and now he drew the pistol
to keep the woman from pushing his mother downstairs.
At this the woman's husband left, saying he would get a policeman.

Dick and his mother went downstairs and sat on the porch
waiting for the man to come back
but Dick, tired of waiting, went to a saloon across the street

and, while having two or three drinks,
told the bartender of his trouble with the man upstairs.
After a while the woman's husband was back
and told his wife—also waiting on the porch—that he could not find a
    policeman;
and Dick, back on the porch with the pistol in his hand, shouted,
"Now I've got you, you son of a bitch!"
The woman's husband tried to grab the pistol
and Dick fired twice and missed;
but the struggle went on
and Dick, backing down the stairs into the yard,
fired three more times
and the third shot killed the woman's husband.
Then Dick went back to the saloon,
laid his pistol on the bar,
and taking another drink said triumphantly,
"I got my man."

VI

NEIGHBORS

1

The Miller family and the Thompsons were neighbors.
Miller, his wife, and their grown son
were dealers in "junk"
and one day Miller and his wife hauled up a number of old fertilizer
    sacks
and unloaded them in their yard.
Later in the day they spread them out to dry
on the fence between their house and the house of the Thompsons.

Mrs. Thompson objected and when her husband came home
he asked Miller to take the sacks away
but Miller said he had to do what his wife wanted.
And when Thompson asked Mrs. Miller to have the sacks taken away

and added that if she would not he would knock them off
she asked whether he knew her son,
and when he said he did
she said, "He has killed one nigger and shot another
and when he comes home I'll have him fix you."
At this Thompson picked up a stick and punched some of the sacks off
    the fence
and Mrs. Miller went into her house,
brought out a shotgun,
and placed it where Thompson could see it,
and replaced the sacks upon the fence.

When her son came home late in the evening
she told him about her trouble with the Thompsons
and next day her son and Thompson were exchanging angry words
and her son said, "I have killed one nigger
and I guess you are his brother,"
and he jumped into the kitchen through the back door
and came out with the shotgun
and shot Thompson in the back. He died in a few minutes.
Miller and his wife were standing nearby
and Mrs. Miller said, "Yes, he is dead.
We live here and pay our rent
and if anyone fools with us
we will kill some more of the sons of bitches."
And her husband added, "If our son hadn't shot him, I would."

2

Two brothers, Wes and Sam, lived with their parents
several miles from town and Zack lived with the family
and worked on their farm. George lived with his mother in a village
the other side of town and one Saturday went to work as a farmhand
for a man whose farm was only a mile or two from the homestead of
    the parents of Wes and Sam.
On Sunday afternoon a friend of the brothers
came and told them about it.

Now Wes and Sam had been unfriendly with George for some time
and, as soon as they heard this, Wes said he was going over to their
    neighbor's farm to "get" George;
and his brother said he would go with him
for George might make a "knife play."
Zack thought it would be best to wait and some day "get" George on
    the road
but Wes said, "No, if I don't get him now, I may never get him."
"You will have to watch him," said Sam,
"if he is working with a hoe or scythe or something to cut you with";
and he added, "I will go with you and say to the man he is working for
    we'd like to borrow a lister."

Next day, after the morning's chores, Wes and his brother went around
    to the side of the house
where there was a pile of old iron
and Wes found a bar to take along and put it in his pocket.
The farmer for whom George was working had gone to town
and as Wes, Sam and Zack went away
Wes told Zack to go back and ask the man's wife where George was
    working.
He did and then the three crossed a wheat field and climbed over a
    wire fence
and entered the field where George was ploughing.
He saw them walking towards him
and stopped, leaning against the handles of the plough,
his arms folded and the reins about his neck.

Sam and Zack began to chat with him in a friendly way
while Wes slipped to one side and sneaking in back of George
hit him on the back of his head with the iron bar,
once, twice, and again.
George fell to the ground, face up, and Wes kept striking him—
a blow on the forehead just over an eye, another below the eye,
and still another just across the nose.
"Now I am even with you," said Wes.
George at first had tried to ward off the blows with his hands—
he was wearing leather gloves—

and, when Wes had ended striking George,
Sam said, "Let's turn the team loose and make people think the mules
    done it."

Just then one of the neighbors was passing through the field
and Sam or Zack called to him and he came over
and asked what had happened. Sam said, "They had a little scrap here,
    Wes and George."
George was sitting up, blood all over his face and in his hair,
the reins still around his body,
and his leather gloves lying on the ground before him.
Wes was standing a few feet away and said,
"He's been bullying around town long enough.
God damn him, let him bleed!"
But Sam said they should take hold of him and help him to the house.
George was not strong enough to walk
and Sam said they should unhitch one of the mules
and let him ride,
but he was not strong enough even to do that.
At the neighbor's suggestion, Sam unhitched both mules from the
    plough
and drove them to the house
and there he got a wagon in which George was placed.
But Sam would not lift him or help place him in the wagon
saying he did not want to get blood on his hands;
and, anyway, George died about the time they reached the house.

VII
PROPERTY

1

He had some logs in the yard of the sawmill
which he had brought there to have sawed
but changing his mind
came to the sawmill with two hired hands and a team
to take the logs away.

The owner of the sawmill said that he owed him money
and this would have to be paid before the logs were taken
and the sawmill owner's brother brought out the sawmill's books
and the three sat down on a log together.
The man who wanted to move his logs asked what he owed
and then asked to see the books
and said he owed only half as much—
somewhat more than a dollar.

The owner of the sawmill stood up
and facing the man whose logs were there
said again that he could not move them
until payment
according to the books of the sawmill;
but the owner of the logs said, "I'll move my logs."
The owner of the sawmill threw off his coat
and told him to be gone
or he would whip him.
At this one of the hired hands came between them and said,
"Boys, there's nothing to fight about."
But the owner of the logs drew a revolver from his pocket
and the brother of the owner of the sawmill drew his revolver
and facing the owner of the logs said, "Drop it!"
The owner of the logs lifted his revolver
and the brother of the owner of the sawmill fired twice.
The owner of the logs walked away
a few steps;
fell down
and was dead without another word.

2

The widow had carried a load of old fence posts to her home
from the railroad that ran through the village
and with the help of one of her little boys had piled up more beside the
        tracks
to take later. One of her neighbors, an immigrant from Germany,
would also take the old fence posts and ties to use as fuel.

No sooner did he come home from work that day
than he put down his dinner-pail, took off his coat, and called to his
        two boys to bring the wheelbarrow,
and the three went to the railroad.

They loaded the old posts on the wheelbarrow and wheeled them to
        the crossing
where they had to unload them to get the wheelbarrow over the rails;
and, impatiently, he took one of the posts on his shoulder
and started for home.
He passed a neighbor who was working in his garden
and the neighbor—a colored man—said, "Getting wood?"
And he replied, "Yes. Why don't you get some?"
Then the neighbor said, "The widow says it is her wood. I don't want
        any of it."
But he answered, "It's as much yours as hers."

Just then the widow saw him and said,
"I wish you would please leave that wood alone:
  it was given to me by the section boss of the railroad."
But he shouted, "Anybody can take this wood!"
The colored man left his garden
and coming out into the street—
although there had been some ill-feeling between him and the
        widow—
said, "I wouldn't take her wood. She is a poor woman."
However, he walked on and threw the post down beside his woodpile
and went back to his boys
who had, in the meantime, run the wheelbarrow across the tracks.

The boys were putting the posts back in the wheelbarrow
and their father took another post and was carrying the post to his
        house
when the widow's boarder came up to him.
The boarder was a newcomer in the street
but the neighborhood knew that he had been a performer in a circus,
had lived on an Indian reservation in the county,
and had been in the United States Navy for a while—

and in the state prison.
The boarder coming up to him said,
"Mister, you oughtn't to take the wood from that woman:
she is a widow and you are a man
and you can get wood better than she."
Shaking his fist, he shouted back,
"To hell with you!
Anybody can take this wood!"

On his way to the railroad again,
he saw the widow's boarder beside the wheelbarrow
throwing the posts on the ground
and shouted to his wife, "Get my gun! My revolver!"
She didn't, but he ran into his house through the back door
and came out with both shotgun and revolver.
The widow shouted to her boarder, "Come away! He'll shoot you!"
and the colored man shouted, "Put down that gun!
There's nobody done anything to you!
Put it down!"
He lowered his gun but shifted it to his left hand,
drew the revolver from his hip-pocket,
and kept going towards the boarder.

The boarder threw up his hands and cried, "Don't shoot! Please don't!"
But he fired.
The boarder staggered back two or three steps,
fell to the ground,
and died—as the colored man afterwards said—"without a word or
    groan."

3
Hood lived some sixty miles from the nearest railroad station
in wild country
and miles beyond the public highways:
his home reached only by traveling through forest
on rough roads used now and then by lumbermen.

He and a lumber company had claims to the same property
and soon there were legal actions against him—civil and criminal.
On a day in May two deputy sheriffs left the nearest railroad station
with a bench warrant to arrest him;
and, on the second day, they were only seventeen miles from his home,
but had still to go along roads that were seldom traveled.
They had spent the night at a farmer's house
and with them now were two men who worked for the lumber company
on their way back to the company's camp
and the farmer's hired man to take care of the farmer's team
now hitched to his wagon
along with a team of the lumber company.

The two men who worked for the lumber company took the driver's seat,
since they knew the way,
and one of them did the driving.
The two officers sat on bags of feed behind the lumbermen
and back of the officers sat the farmhand.
Both officers had guns but they were not loaded.
About three miles from where Hood lived,
one of the officers saw a man hiding behind a tree
not far from the road,
and as they drove on the man kept following them
still trying to hide behind the trunk of a tree.
The wagon had not gone far, however, before he stepped into the open,
lifted his rifle to his shoulder and yelled,
"Hands up, you sons of bitches!"
and began firing at once.
The lumber company's men knew him to be Hood
in spite of his blackened face and hat with its brim turned down.

Right after the first shot, Hood's companion, also with a rifle
stepped out from where he, too, had been hiding
and likewise began to fire at the men in the wagon.
However, at the first shot the four horses broke into a run
and the wagon was soon out of range.
But one of the bullets had gone through the farmhand's hat,
just above the hat band,

and in his fright he fell out of the wagon.
The others did not wait or go back for him.
Hood started off by a short cut he knew through the forest
to get another shot at those in the wagon, so he said,
but told his companion to make the farmhand go back
to the farm where he worked, and his companion did so:
forced the farmhand to run down the road
with a loaded gun pointed at his back
and now and then gave the farmhand a good kick
to hurry him along.

VIII
THEFTS—AND THIEVES

1

About nine o'clock at night, on his way to work,
carrying under his arm a pair of old shoes—
wrapped in paper—
he had passed the railroad tracks
when he heard someone running behind him on the sidewalk.
He turned to see who it was
and was struck in the mouth.
The man who struck him
grabbed him by the arm that held the shoes
and threw him down. He got up—
the shoes he had carried were gone—
and he went to a saloon nearby
to wash the blood off his face.

2

A young colored man went into the restaurant
and sat down at a table;
asked for corned beef and cabbage, ate it and stood up,
and walked towards the door.
The waiter asked him to pay for what he had eaten;

the price—ten cents.
The colored man answered that he had no money.

The waiter then said: "I guess you have ten cents.
I ain't going to be fooled by you;
you are the second one has done this today."
The colored man took a handkerchief out of his pocket,
from which he shook two nickels and two or three collar buttons on
    another table;
picked up the collar buttons
and brushed the two nickels on the floor.

The waiter stooped and picked up the nickels;
then rose and struck the colored man with his fist
and pushed him towards the door, saying,
"Get out of here!"
Pushed him again towards the door
and kicked him from behind as he went out.
The colored man did not fight back;
he went across the street into a store near the restaurant
and bought a five-barrel self-cocking revolver
for somewhat less than two dollars
and five cartridges for ten cents;
placed the cartridges in the revolver
and went back to the restaurant.

The waiter was standing behind the counter.
When he saw the colored man again, he said, "Get out of here!"
and began to come from behind the counter,
and the colored man fired two shots at him.
The waiter fell to the floor dead.
The colored man fired two more shots
and tried to fire the fifth shot but could not,
and ran out of the restaurant.

3
A number of Italians, working for a railroad,
were living together in a shanty

near the place where they worked;
and on an August evening
four others came to visit them—
so the four said—
and stayed until eight or nine o'clock
when the men who lived in the shanty went inside
to go to bed.

The four also went inside
and demanded money;
one stood at the door with a revolver
and another with a club

and said they would kill anyone who tried to get out;
and when the other two got his money from a man
they ordered him to bed.

But when they came to one of the men who lived in the shanty
he had only fifty cents
and kept saying he had no more:
and, if they would go with him upstairs where he kept his belongings,
he would show them that he had no more.
The two collecting the money did go upstairs—
wrangling and calling the man all kinds of names—
and, after a brief while,
the two downstairs began to shout,
"Stab him! Shoot him!"
And they did.

Then the four left the shanty together
and spent the night in the woods;
early in the morning
one of them went to a neighboring village
and bought new clothing and caps
and, after they had changed their clothing,
two of them went one way by train
and the other two another way.

4

Vito and Pete came from neighboring provinces in Italy.
Vito, about twenty-six, had been in the United States a number
    of years
and was living in a small village in New Jersey
working for the railroad: a hard-working and thrifty young man
but illiterate—could neither read nor write English or Italian.
Pete was living in the same village
and working on a canal owned by the railroad company
and the two became friends—close friends:
Pete knew what Vito earned and what he had saved and about Vito's
    search for his brother
who had come to the United States before Vito did
and Pete would write letters for Vito to relatives
and read him the letters he received.

One day Vito received a letter and Pete read it aloud:
it was from Vito's long-lost brother—so Pete said—
and the company for which the brother worked had established a
    branch in Yonkers, near New York City,
and he was a "boss" there;
he had found out that his brother, Vito, was looking for him
and it would give him great pleasure to see Vito again
and he could give Vito a good job, if he wished it,
and the letter ended with greetings from his brother's wife and
    children and a postscript:
"Come quickly, because it would give me great pleasure to see you"
and it added an address in Yonkers.
At about the same time Pete had mailed a letter to Vito.
The clerk in the post-office noticed that the letter had a red two-cent
    stamp,
instead of the green one-cent stamp enough for a local letter,
and wondered somewhat why Pete should write to Vito
when they lived in the same village and saw each other almost
    every day.

In a few days Pete wrote a letter for Vito
saying how happy he was to hear from his brother

for whom he had been looking for years
and he would go to his brother if he wished him to
but would rather that his brother came to him
for he did not understand just what kind of job his brother offered
and was uncertain about giving up the job he had,
and to the letter was added by way of postscript
that the answer should be sent in care of Pete—
and gave Pete's full name and address.

There were other letters
and, hardly a fortnight after the first,
Vito left the village with all the money he had:
what he had put into the local bank
and the pay due him from the railroad when he left his job,
and the hundred dollars he had lent a friend—
about three hundred dollars in all.
But before he left Vito told another friend that he was going to his
        brother in Yonkers,
and asked this friend to write his own name and address on a slip of
        paper
for Vito to take with him. At the railroad station Pete was waiting
to ride with Vito to New York,
for Pete had a pass because he worked for the railroad
and it would cost him nothing to go along
and he would read the street signs and other signs for Vito
and help him find his brother.
They came to New York at noon,
had lunch in a saloon in an Italian neighborhood
and saw a parade in honor of a saint
and then took the elevated train to the Bronx on the way to Yonkers.

That afternoon a man in a park between Yonkers and the city
looking for mushrooms in the woods
saw two men coming towards him—one he afterwards recognized as
        Pete—
and the other man, Vito, asked him the way to Yonkers;
and the man gathering mushrooms told them where they could get a
        trolley car to get there.

Next day the man they had met was again in the woods
to gather mushrooms
and he came upon the body of a man—
the very man who had asked him the way to Yonkers—
lying in a pool of blood
with arms outstretched.
He touched one of the man's hands. The man was dead.

He had been stabbed again and again
and the earth about him where he had struggled for his life
was torn up
and the weeds trampled.
In Vito's pocket the police found only a dollar or two
and the slip of paper with his friend's name and address
in the village from which Vito came. In Pete's pocket
when he was finally arrested in the same village
was more than he had in bank and pocket when he left with Vito
and a letter Vito had him write to his brother—supposed to be in
    Yonkers—
and, of course, never mailed.

5

Death of a Thief

He and his wife were sleeping in the front room
when he was awakened by his wife and told a thief was in the house.
He got his gun
and went outside and around to the kitchen door
and said loudly, "Come out!"
A foxhound jumped through a rent in the screen door.
He shot and killed it. The dishes on the kitchen table had been moved
    about in disorder
and the milk his wife had put in a crock on a shelf was gone.

IX

LABOR TROUBLES

1

Those at work in the stockyards in place of the strikers—
many of the "strike-breakers" colored and many of these women—
were taken to and from work in a special train.
That evening, a train of nine coaches loaded with "strike-breakers"
was passing through a street from the yards to the city;
and where this street crossed another
groups of men were standing at the corners.

A policeman brought five women to the crossing
to take the train
but the train was so crowded—even the platforms—
it was hard to get on,
and one of the women trying to get on
lost her balance and fell
just as the train started.
She screamed
and the women in the train also began to scream.

Shooting began at once from the cars
at the men in the street.
The switchman at the crossing saw a black hand holding a revolver
thrust through an open window—
the last shots fired—
and three of the men in a group at one of the corners,
one of them leaning against a telegraph pole,
were hit.
By this time the police had come
and someone in the train was shouting,
"Hide your guns!
They are searching the cars!"

2

A farmer, sick for years, was now going away for treatment.
He himself had been too sick to do any work,
and his daughter had made out time slips and given them to the hired
    hands
gathering the harvest.

He told the hands that he wanted to settle with them that evening
because he was going away early the next morning;
and, after he had his supper
and while most of the men were still at the table,
he went into the room used as his office.
Soon afterwards, one of the hired hands followed him
and, in settling what was due,
there was the difference of the fourth of a day
between the time as kept by the farmer's daughter
and that claimed by the hand.
As the difference was being talked over,
the hired hand said that others were making the same claim,
and the farmer asked, "Who?"
When the hired hand named them,
the farmer said of one of them, naming him angrily,
"He is the last man I would pay—because he shirked."
He said it loud enough to be heard by the man himself
who was still at supper, and the man came into the room saying,
"Old man, you don't know what you are talking about!"
And the farmer said, "Get out!
You have no right in here unless you are called in,"
and turned in his chair to get his pencil
to estimate how much he owed the hired hand he had been talking to.
As he did so, the hand who had just entered
jerked the chair from under him,
pitching him forward on the floor
on his hands and knees.

He looked up and the man was standing over him
with the chair lifted as if to strike.
The farmer had been packing his grip the day before

but had not quite finished,
and it stood open on the floor near the desk.
He had thrown his revolver into it
and now grabbed the revolver and fired.
But the hired hand came right at him
and he shot again twice—
and the hired hand fell.

3
In the evening, Mike and his friend left the boat on which they were
     working as firemen
and went to several saloons in the city
and finally into a saloon where they played three or four games of pool
with two men they did not know
who were part of a group in the saloon at the time.
There was then a strike of the union of firemen
and neither Mike nor his friend belonged to the union.

One of the two with whom Mike and his friend were playing pool
began to argue with them
about who should pay for the drinks they were having
and Mike paid;
and then one of the two
began to make fun of the way Mike or his friend was speaking Spanish
and said it was more like Mexican;
but neither Mike nor his friend said anything
that would anger those with whom they were playing pool
or any of the group in the saloon.

When Mike and his friend were leaving
one of the two with whom they had been playing
struck Mike in the face
and the other man began to strike Mike's friend.
Mike was knocked to the floor
and he heard one of the group—
a man who seemed to be their leader—
say, "Kill him!"

And then one of the two
kicked him and stamped on him
until he lost consciousness.
They lifted him, one on each side,
and dragged him to a vacant lot next to the saloon
and threw him into a hole
five or six feet below the sidewalk.

He was next seen,
a half hour or so afterwards,
in another saloon,
dazed,
his head covered with blood
and one of his ears torn off—
it was afterwards found in the hole into which he had been thrown.
In the meantime,
the group of men who had been in the saloon
left it
and went into the hall on the opposite side of the street—
headquarters of the union.

X

WHITES AND BLACKS

1

On a Sunday evening his body was found in a potato patch near a
        cornfield upon his farm
near the woods: four bullet holes in his body—
one in his back where the bullet that killed him had gone to his heart.
He had turned to run
from whoever was shooting at him; but there were no powder stains
        on his clothing
and the bullets had not been fired at close range.

He had been a well-to-do farmer, a man of fifty or so,
and his wife about fifteen years younger. "A very nice woman,"

the hired hand had said of her, but the farmer was "mean."
The hired hand was a young man of twenty, colored but almost white.
Four or five days before the farmer's death,
he had come into the house with the young man and the farmer had
    said to his wife,
"Our man is going to leave us and you had better watch him
and see that he doesn't take anything that doesn't belong to him."
At that the young man said, "You don't think that I would take
    anything that didn't belong to me, do you?"
And the farmer had answered, "I never saw a nigger yet that wasn't a
    thief."

When arrested for the murder, the young man said to the sheriff,
"I never shot him."
"Who did?
We have four or five witnesses who saw you going towards the
    cornfield that Sunday afternoon."
The young man hesitated a moment and then said, "His wife."
And still hesitating, "I had a date with her."
"Then you made this up between you?"
"Yes, but she plugged him before I got there," and he would say no
    more.
The undersheriff made believe that he was friendly and wanted to help
    him.
"If his wife shot this man," the undersheriff said,
"we've got to have the revolver. We want to convict her.
Tell us where to find it so that we can go and get it."
"She put the revolver and his pocketbook in my pocket
and told me to go back into the woods and hide them.
The revolver is by a beech tree in the first piece of woods beyond the
    cornfield";
and it was found there under a covering of leaves.

Then the undersheriff said, "We would also like the pocketbook."
"Why?"
"To get it into her bed or somewhere in her room
where it might be found." And the young man led them to a stump
not far from the tree where the revolver had been found,

and it was also hidden under dirt and leaves;
there were some papers in it but no money.

A couple of young women of the neighborhood had been with the
    farmer's wife all of that Sunday afternoon
and the young man was convicted of the murder.

2

In a neighborhood where both whites and Negroes were living—
and knew each other more or less by sight, if not by name—
a number of white boys were standing on a Sunday evening near a
    saloon,
when a Negro and a Negro woman passed.
Several white men who had been in the saloon
came out shouting, "Hurrah! Hurrah for McKinley!"
and the Negro turned, drew a pistol out of his pocket,
and rushed back to where one of the boys was standing
and thrusting the pistol into his face said, "You white bastard!
I'll make you respect my color!
You white son of a bitch, I'll make all of you white bastards respect
    me!"
The boy tried to back away from the pistol and said,
"Mister, don't shoot me! I done nothing."
But the Negro followed him, keeping the pistol in his face,
and said, "I think you are the one that hallooed at me!"
The boy kept backing away, all the while saying,
"Mister, don't shoot me! I never done nothing!"
And finally the Negro turned away and went back to his companion
    who was waiting for him.

Next day, shortly before sundown, the boy's elder brother met an
    acquaintance in the neighborhood
and they walked on together through an alley by way of a short cut.
Three Negroes came out of a gangway
that led into the alley and walked on ahead of them,
but when the boy's elder brother came out of the alley
one of the three was waiting for him.

The Negro aimed his pistol at him and said,
"I missed your brother last night
but you, you son of a bitch,
I'll not miss you!" and fired.
The young man was hit and staggered a few feet from the alley
and fell.
The Negro fired at him again
and, after firing three shots,
ran through the alley into a vacant lot overgrown with weeds
and was gone.

3

The white man washing dishes at night in the restaurant
had only one leg and a crutch.
A Negro—in the habit of eating there—
was sitting at the table in the kitchen
at which Negroes had to eat.
The dishwasher had a fit of coughing
and the Negro, to be friendly, said,
"What in the hell is the matter with you?"
The dishwasher answered, "I am not bothering you.
Leave me alone!"
"By God," the Negro said, taking him literally,
"I don't have to go out until I am ready."
And, thinking that most of the help in the restaurant were friendly
and that he himself was not a man to be trifled with,
added, "You don't know me."
"Yes, I do," said the dishwasher. "You are a nigger."
The Negro stood up
and the dishwasher, leaning on the table,
shoved the crutch at him to ward him off;
but the Negro took a pistol from his pocket, held it in both hands,
and pointing it at the dishwasher
shot him in the belly.

PERSONS AND PLACES

1

A man in his forties
going to work early in the morning
with his coat on his arm and a dinnerpail in his other hand
stopped for a moment
to watch two dogcatchers leave their wagon
trying to catch a stray dog.
Among those watching were boys
who began to make fun of the dogcatchers
by barking like dogs.

One of the dogcatchers—a brawny fellow—angered,
singled out the man as he stood near the others
smiling,
and struck him with his fist on the jaw
a blow that sent him to the brick sidewalk—
where he lay unconscious with a fractured skull.

2

Part of his work was the care of several horses.
As he was leading one of them into a shed
by a halter, the owner stopped him
and tried to wash a galled place on the horse's neck
with a medicine the owner held in a tin cup.
But the horse would not stand still
and a "twitch" was put on the horse;
but, after the "twitch" was taken off,
the owner saw another bruise on the horse's shoulder
and tried to wash this, too. The horse jumped aside
and struck him, throwing upon his clothes
the medicine he held in his hand.
Angered, the owner grabbed the "twitch"—
its handle a heavy stick—
and with it began to strike the horse.

The man holding the horse by the halter
urged him not to;
but the owner of the horse did not stop—
until his foot slipped
and a blow meant for the horse
struck the man holding the halter in the face
breaking the bones of his nose.

3

A carpenter by trade, now fifty-five, who had been steady and
        industrious
but had been hurt and had lost two or three of his fingers,
and was no longer able to work,
said to one of his neighbors, a woman his own age,
"I can't work any more. It's terrible."
"What will you do?" she said.
"Do? I will buy an organ and you can come along and dance;
I will sing and make my living."
She thought at first he was joking,
and then saw that he was in earnest:
he had lost his mind as well as his fingers.

4

Her uncle and aunt lived in a small house—it had once been
        a "wagon house";
and now it was divided into three rooms: a large room
in which her uncle and aunt had their bed
and a sofa on which the little girl slept,
and two small rooms.
One was used as the kitchen. The other room also had a bed
and this room was rented.

The little girl—she was not quite nine—caught cold
and her aunt thought it was because of sleeping on the sofa;
the weather had become bitterly cold.
It would be better, her aunt thought,

to have the little girl sleep on the bed in the little room.
The man who had rented the room, a man of forty-five or so,
like the little girl's uncle played the piano for his living
in saloons and "sporting houses"
and did not come back at night.
But late that night he did come back
and found the little girl sleeping in his bed.
"She can sleep there," he said
and assured her aunt he would do her no harm.

Her uncle and aunt heard her sobbing at night
and supposed she was sniffling because of her cold.
In the morning, her aunt saw the little girl's nightclothes stained
and the little girl crying and in pain.
But she said nothing to her aunt
because she was afraid to speak of what had happened:
the man had said he would "knock her block off"
if she did.

5

Mrs. Carr had been to her grandfather's funeral
in a small town in Kansas
and on her way back to Chicago
stopped in Kansas City to spend a few days with her aunt.
Mrs. Carr did not know her way about,
for she had not lived in the city since she was a little girl.

Saturday evening she and a cousin, also a stranger in the city,
went to Fairmont Park with two young men
and returning to the heart of the city had supper in a café,
and then all four went to where they could take a streetcar
to the home of the young women's aunt;
but by this time it was after midnight
and the "owl car" had gone.
Rather than wait an hour for the next car
the four started to walk. But when they were near the home of the aunt,
the young women were ashamed of the neighborhood

and the house in which their aunt lived—next to a livery stable—
and said they could go on alone
and sent the young men away.

The young women crossed the street,
went around a house and through an alley
to their aunt's home—so they thought—
but became confused
and went a number of blocks out of their way.
Then they noticed a young man following them and were afraid.

The street they were on came to a dead end at a bluff
and they had to turn
and came face to face with the young man
under an arc light.
Seeing him in the glare of the light—
dressed like a teamster but a very young man, perhaps no more than
    twenty—
they asked their way
and he answered he would show them if they would follow
and led them into a deep and dark ravine.

In crossing the ditch in the ravine,
Mrs. Carr's cousin fell
but jumped up and ran
and began to climb the hill towards a light.
As Mrs. Carr also tried to jump across the ditch,
the young man caught her around the neck
and threw her to the ground.
Her cousin heard her screams,
and at the first house up the hill
tried to wake up those who lived there
but she could not get them to answer her cries.
At the second house, she did wake the people in it
and told them what had happened in the ravine below.

When the police came,
she went with them to where Mrs. Carr was last seen

and they found her coming from the ravine,
crying and greatly excited,
her dress and underskirts badly torn,
her hat on the back of her head,
muddy and crushed,
and mud on her back.

6

Samaritan

In the evening driving from her home to town
she saw a man lying across the road
and stopped her horse,
got down from the wagon
and told the man to get over to the side of the road:
if he remained where he was
he might be run over;
and, on her way back,
she stopped to give the man a lift.

He sat down beside her
and she urged him to become a better man,
for she had seen him drunk several times.
They passed several houses
but when they were going through the woods
he grabbed her around the waist
and threw her down on the bottom of the wagon.
The seat fell on her
and she screamed,
but there was nobody near to hear and help.
She asked him to let her up from under the heavy seat
for it was hurting her,
and when he did she jumped from the wagon
and began to run down the road towards home.

He too jumped down and running after her
quickly overtook her

and threw her on the grass beside the road;
but, as she kept struggling with him and screaming,
a man came along
and she kept calling to him for help.

He did not heed her at first
but then came up
and soon began trading punches with the man with whom she had
    been struggling.
At that she jumped up and ran home—
all of two miles—
hair disheveled and down
and bruises on body and face.

7

A man in his sixties and his wife had been running their house as a
    place for prostitutes
and this was known in and about town.
One night several young men who had been drinking and were more
    or less "high"
went to the house, and three of them were let in through a rear door.
But when the man's wife took a good look at them
they were asked to leave as "too young to be in such a place."
They left laughing
and joined their companions on the sidewalk.

A little later stones were being thrown against the house.
The owner of the house was not well
and had gone to bed. Hearing the stones strike the house,
he got up and went out upon the front porch.
The night was dark and at first he could see no one.
But four of the young men went up to him as he stood on the porch
and he asked them if they had been throwing stones at his house;
they said they hadn't and one added: in fact, he had been hit by a stone.
The owner of the house then said he had a loaded shotgun in the house
and would use it on anyone throwing stones. With that, he went back
    to his room and bed.

Sure enough, more stones began to be thrown against the house
and the owner came with his gun
and went out on the porch again and then through the front gate upon
    the sidewalk.
The young men who had been watching him
began to run down the street
and the owner of the house followed
and fired. The buckshot struck one of them
and he fell on his face, gasping for breath.

The others stopped running and came back
but the young man who had fallen could not speak
and they carried him to a store and laid him on the steps.
The owner of the house put away his gun
and came up to the crowd.
Someone in the crowd asked, "Why did you shoot this boy?"
And the owner at first said he had not shot him ·
and then said, "I didn't aim to shoot him. I shot in the air."
Someone else in the crowd then said, "That's funny.
If you aimed in the air, how come you shot a man in the back?"
The owner of the house did not answer
and by this time the young man was dead.

8

In May she found that she was with child
and late in August went to a doctor—
a woman advertising in the newspapers
that she was taking care of "female irregularities"
painlessly.

The doctor placed her on a lounge,
after they had bargained about the price,
and began to use a surgical instrument on her.
She was on the lounge about twenty minutes
and then the doctor made her get up and walk around the room:
she was so weak

she could not walk much
and finally lay down on a bed.
The doctor began to use her instruments again
and Jill felt—so she said—that she was being "cut to pieces,"
but finally the doctor took the child away from her.
Next morning she visited one of her friends
and the woman she visited thought her "very happy."

On the morning of the fourth day
Jill was taken to a hospital in a carriage,
and late that afternoon
the doctor who had performed the abortion
was brought to her bedside.
Jill said, "What did you do to me?
Now I have got to die."
And the doctor answered, "What did you do to me?
See in what trouble you've brought me.
You promised not to say anything to anybody!"

9

He was sitting on a box in front of his drygoods store
talking to another man
when along came Mr. Ray.
Mr. Ray knocked his cap off, caught hold of his vest
tearing off a button,
and gave him two or three slaps on the head;
and, in a minute or two, came back,
took hold of him by the coat
and shaking him said,
"Now, you Jew, you can say to my face
what you said behind my back";
and struck him in the face so that he had a black eye.
By this time those nearby parted them.

The Jew went into his store,
felt again the pain in his chest and became dizzy—

he had been told by his doctor that he had a weak heart—
and when he came to
found himself lying on the floor of his store
with a doctor beside him.

The jury who heard the case
gave the storekeeper one cent in damages.

10

They were Jews, immigrants from Poland. Her husband became a
    peddler;
but her brother who lived with them
did not want to peddle,
although his sister and brother-in-law kept urging him to,
and he could find nothing else to do for a living
in the small town where they lived—
to the vexation of his brother-in-law
and the noisy vexation of his sister.
He became morose and surly
and spent much of his time in bed.

That morning, after his sister's husband had left for his peddling
and her children had gone to school,
she began her scolding again
and even pulled his beard;
and he struck her on the head with the flatiron she had been using
and had left on the ironing-board to cool;
struck her again and again
until she was silent—forever.

Some workingmen at a dam on the river
heard his cries
as he struggled among the floes of ice
and saved him—
to weep and sigh in a cell,
to be tried and condemned to die.

11

The youngest of six children, she came from a city in Turkish Armenia
where her parents were penniless.
She was only fourteen years of age
and good-looking—very good-looking—
and a fellow Armenian from the same city
leaving for America with his wife
thought she would make a good wife for their son in America.

Her parents let them take her along
and she left without money and [with] little clothing;
they went by caravan and sailing-ship and steamer and then—
because of delays and unexpected expense—
were stranded in Marseilles
waiting for money from the son in America.
There were other Armenians there
and one of them had an uncle in Boston looking for a wife
and just then the Armenian and his wife who were taking the girl to
          America
heard from their son that he did not want to get married.

Then the nephew of the man in Boston
told the girl about his uncle—
thirty-five or so, the nephew said, and well-established in business
and wrote the uncle of the girl's qualities
and her willingness to marry any good Armenian
who would make her a good home.
The Armenian in Boston cabled a couple of hundred dollars to
          Marseilles—
most of this kept by the man from the girl's city
for his expenses in bringing her to Marseilles—
and the rest went to the nephew
who took the girl to London:
there was just enough money for that.
They stopped at a cheap boarding-house kept for poor Armenians
until the man from Boston came to London himself—
an old man about sixty
who had lost an eye.

What could she do?
Without money or even decent clothing—
for what she had brought with her was now torn and hopelessly
    dirty—
among strangers
and unable to speak any language but Armenian;
it was her fate, she concluded,
and married him.

12

Years before, during a massacre of Armenians,
he had seen his mother and sister raped by the Turks
and he himself had been circumcised
and forced to become a Moslem.
He fled to the United States
and here he was a diligent workingman in a factory
but, although other Armenians could not help talking of the massacres,
he talked of nothing else.
At night his cousin would hear him talk in his sleep
of fighting the Turks,
and he would sometimes be lost in thought
and when he was asked what he was thinking of
would not answer.

He had come to New York to get contributions from rich Armenians
to help in a revolt against the Turks;
among others from an Armenian who, he had been told,
had refused to give anything
and had even, it was said, given the Turks names of those Armenians
    planning to revolt.
When he asked this man for a contribution
the man not only refused but said angrily
he would never give anything to "those brigands."
As the man asked for a contribution left his place of business,
the young Armenian shot and killed him;
and when arrested—the smoking revolver in his hand—
those who questioned him

noted how cool and calm he was
and proud of what he had done.

13

The murderer walked through the woods towards his victim
along logging paths no longer used:
rubbers on his feet to keep the mud from his shoes
and holding an umbrella in case it rained.

THE WEST

I

SOCIAL LIFE

1

The two had been companions for a long time,
had worked in the same mine,
and had roomed together.
They had just spent most of the night—Christmas night—
playing poker with a third man
in the card room of a saloon.
At six in the morning,
one of the two "called" his companion to name the hand he held
and when he did
threw his own hand on the table
to the third man—who was to deal next.

The man who had won pulled the money which had been lost
partly to his own pile;
and the man who had taken up the winning hand
was about to shuffle the cards for another deal
when the man who had lost asked to see the hand that had won.
Spread on the table,
there were six cards instead of five;
for the man who had picked it up, in taking the hand off the deck,
had—without meaning to—taken another card along with it.

Now the man who had lost charged the man who had won
with having six cards in his hand
instead of five
and reaching over the table
took back the money he had lost and put it in his pocket.
The winner demanded the money he had won:
the loser would not give it back—
and the game was over.

The three went into the saloon
where the winner again demanded the money he had won
but the loser again would not give it up—
and asked all who were in the saloon to have a drink with him.
But the man who had won the money—and did not have it—
would not drink.

The loser, after he had his drink,
went back into the card room;
and the winner took a drink by himself,
and, muttering something or other to the barkeeper,
drew his pistol
and also went into the card room.
Within a few feet of the man with whom he had been playing, he said,
"Give me the money I won or I'll shoot,"
and the other replied, "Shoot! You don't dare to."
But he did shoot,
once and again and again,
and the man who had pocketed the money died of his wounds within
        the hour.

2

A week before the shooting, Bill was heard to say,
"Ella won't let me go with her and, by God, no one else shall!"

When Ella's friend, Eliza, started for Sunday school,
he said to her, "Take a knife along.
I am going to raise such a smoke over the hollow
you will need a knife to cut it away."

After Sunday school,
the young men and women were walking up the highway to their
        homes,
laughing and talking; and Jess by the side of Ella,
carrying her Bible.
Bill was just behind them
and said, "Jess, I didn't know you were a preacher";

and then Jess asked what had become of the team of horses
Bill had when Jess had helped him load some telegraph poles,
and Bill said, "Do you want pay for your work?"
"No," said Jess curtly.
"You needn't get mad about it," said Bill.
"If you do, I can whip you where you are standing,"
and drew a pistol from his pocket
and fired into the ground.
At that Jess drew his pistol and fired at Bill;
the bullet passed through Bill's left arm and into the left side of his
    body
where his suspenders were fastened to his pants.
Bill then fired two shots quickly
and Jess fell to the ground.

Bill took off his coat
and folding it up
put it under Jess's head
and said, "Jess, you shot me first, didn't you?
You know I never would have shot you first, Jess."

II
DOMESTIC DIFFICULTIES

1

They had been married five or so years
and a son had been born to them;
now her husband was about to leave her.
After breakfast, he went into the kitchen
and discharged the Chinese cook
but she told the cook to stay.
Then he asked the nurse to pack his trunk,
and when the expressman came
his wife asked the man where he was going to take it
but the man would not tell her.

Just before the trunk was closed
she put in a shoe—
a little shoe, the first their baby had worn—
and put it on the tray of the trunk
and under the shoe a note:
"I married you for love;
I have lived with you for love;
and I would have clung to you forever for love";
signed it, "Your wife,"
and addressed the note, "My husband."

Then the nurse locked the trunk
and the expressman took it away.
But she did not hear from her husband.

2

He and his wife kept a lodging-house;
for a year they had been quarreling
and at last he stabbed her.
Perhaps he had been drinking too much
but, whatever it was, she was now at her mother's,
in bed because of her wound—
and suing for a divorce and having him prosecuted for the stabbing.

He came to see her with a friend
and brought her flowers.
His mother-in-law let him into the room where his wife was lying
and he kissed her
and asked her how she was feeling.
After a while, he said that though it was almost noon
he had had nothing to eat
and asked if the hired girl could not bring him some breakfast.
But his mother-in-law said that the hired girl had enough to do
without being bothered by him;
however, his mother-in-law did bring wine and cake—

his brother-in-law was also in the room—
and they all had some.

Then he asked the others to leave him alone with his wife
for a few moments
but her mother and brother would not leave
and his brother-in-law told him to speak out
and say whatever he had to.
He sat down on the edge of the bed—
his left side toward his wife because he had lost his right arm—
and leaning towards her whispering
urged her to stop the prosecution against him
and drop the suit for a divorce.
She was still afraid of him
and said she would think about it
and tell him her answer when she was better.

After a moment or two of hesitation, he spoke up and said that his
        brother-in-law would do all he could
to keep them apart.
At that his brother-in-law said angrily
that he was "a damn liar,"
and his mother-in-law asked him to leave
for the visit was already too long
and his wife had become nervous.
Starting to leave, he said to his brother-in-law,
"Never mind now! I don't want any more trouble."
"Yes," said his friend who had come along,
"don't have any trouble here. This is not the place for it."

But there was trouble,
and when his body was taken to another room
his brother-in-law had fired at least three shots from a revolver.

III

PROPERTY

1

Willie, a boy of fourteen living on a ranch with his parents—
his father the only man in the neighborhood who kept sheep—
was at the corral early one morning.
When Willie came to the gate,
about three-quarters of a mile from his father's house,
a man of forty or so was standing there barefoot,
aiming a rifle at him,
and Willie started to run for home.

The man was "a stock detective" who kept track of the cattle of the
        company for which he worked,
drove home the cows and calves he found belonging to the company
and now he was watching for the sheep of the boy's father,
for he had seen them on the pastures of other ranchers.
He had left his horse a long way off
and had taken off his boots—
"the only way to cover up your trail is to go barefoot"—
and he had a pair of field glasses with him
looking over the pastures—
and his rifle.

Secret work, riding on the range alone,
and he did not want to be seen.
Yes, he shot too much
but only to protect the cattle and grounds of the people he was
        working for,
and when he shot a man
would put a stone under the head of the body—
his sign to collect money for the job he had done.

Willie's body was lying on its back in the road
with the head turned towards his father's house.
The boy had fallen on his face
but the body had been turned over;

for the clothing was soaked with blood
and gravel was sticking to the face and clothing—
and underneath the head was a stone.

2

Fight for a Violin

While the ranchman with hired men was building a corral near his
     dwelling on the ranch,
one of the men who had worked for him—now and then—
rode up on horseback
with a rifle across the front of his saddle,
hitched his horse to the wheel of a buckboard,
leaned his rifle against it,
and, after some pleasantries between him and the ranchman and the
     men working,
asked if there was any mail for him;
and the ranchman said there was a letter for him in the house.
The visitor was now trapping and hunting wolves and coyotes
for the bounty on them,
and had left some of his belongings in the house when he quit work
     the last time.

The ranchman owed him some money for a wagon cover
and the hunter was reading his letter
when the ranchman came into the house and said he would give him a
     check for what he owed;
but the hunter would not take a check
because he said he would have trouble cashing it in that neighborhood,
     far from any bank or store,
and they began to quarrel, shouting at each other;
and the ranchman ordered the hunter to take his things out of the
     house—
to pack up and get out.

In the bundle was his violin
and the ranchman told him to leave the violin

and grabbed him
and tried to take it away.
The hunter jerked the bundle free
and started on a run to the buckboard where his horse and rifle were
and the rancher rushed back into the house
and came out with a loaded rifle,
looking about for the hunter.
He had dropped his bundle and was crouching behind the front wheel
    of the buckboard for shelter.
The rancher saw him and fired:
the bullet passed between the spokes of the wheel
and hit the hunter in a fleshy part of his hip.
He got up with his gun
and walking backwards, facing the rancher,
tried to get in back of a shed nearby;
but the rancher, after the first shot,
kept firing from a window—
until he hit the hunter again.

IV
THEFTS—AND THIEVES

1

The two were gold miners
living near each other on a creek
and acquainted.
In the forenoon of a spring day
the bones of one
were found in a burning heap of logs
a few feet from the right-of-way fence of the railroad.
Nearly all the flesh of the body
had been burnt away,
and only the skull was found,
together with the bone of the spinal column,
and the hip bones.

In the ashes where the hip bones were
was what was left
of his pocket knife
and near it the nails
that had been in the heels and soles of his shoes.
There were also dark spots of blood
on the grass, earth and stones,
and the grass was lodged
as if a body had been dragged over it.
His soft black hat
with matches stuck in the band—as always—
was also found
beneath a stump near the fire,
and in the brush
a leather belt
and his empty purse.

The other miner had borrowed a rifle from a neighbor
telling him he wanted to shoot a wounded deer he had seen,
and that Saturday morning
paid a bill which he owed a merchant in the neighboring town
with a piece of gold,
and returned the rifle
paying the man from whom he had borrowed it
for the cartridges he had used.

2

He had lived in a scow in the harbor
and had made his living catching and selling drift logs, digging clams,
    buying and selling fish,
and was last seen alive, one evening, in his boat
going towards a dock four or five miles away
from which, the next day, a lot of fish packed in boxes
was missing—
stolen the night before.

About ten days later his boat was found, overturned,
drifting on the waters of the harbor,
and a day or two afterwards his body,
lodged on a strip of land between the ocean and the harbor,
and a number of sea gulls about it.
The body was on its back behind a large log,
partly buried in the sand;
and the shirt still buttoned closely about his neck
but the flesh above the collar gone
and all the flesh of his face eaten off
by crabs and gulls.

One of the men who lived as he had
by catching and selling drift logs and buying and selling fish
said, as the man sat drinking in a saloon of the harbor,
that the dead man had drowned because in the rough weather
he just could not make it in his small boat
with all the fish he had stolen.
The dead man had asked him, the man drinking said,
to keep a light burning in his own shack,
because in the darkness of the night
he might go around the point of land where his body was found
and out to sea;
but he had also asked about coming back by way of a creek both knew.
And the man who was drinking said that he had kept his light burning
until after eleven that night
and had put it out because he had only a little oil

and, beside, he thought if the man who had drowned was not back by
    that hour
he had come back by way of the creek.
And the man who was drinking added:
he hated to stay in the neighborhood
and some night meet the dead man's face.

3

The sailor had just landed and had his money in his hip pocket,
rolled up in a handkerchief and tied with a string.
The whore got him to come into the house
and led him to a room upstairs.
The foot of the bed was within three feet of the door,
just far enough to allow the door to swing freely,
and the door itself was padded
so as not to make the slightest noise
when closed.
He did not take off his pants,
just let them slide down to his knees;
and when he was through
the woman held him tightly in a hug
two or three minutes.
When he pulled up his pants,
he found that his money was gone;
but the woman said she had not taken it.
While he was doing this, the woman who ran the house came in—
she had been in the next room—
and asked what they were making so much noise about.
The woman he had been in bed with said that the sailor claimed that
        he had lost some money,
and the woman who ran the house said,
"Why don't you look on the floor?"

Sure enough, he found some of his money on the floor,
lying on top of the handkerchief
and near it the string which he had used to tie up his money,
but there was less than a third of it left.

4

When the train passed another freight train on a side track
it slowed down to two or four miles an hour;
by this time it was almost midnight.
Shortly afterwards, four men climbed on top of the box car
on which a young man and his friend were riding

and one of the four, the shortest and heaviest,
went up to the young man and asked him for a match.
"I have no match," he said;
and then the man said, "Throw up your hands, you son of a bitch,"
and the young man did.
The four went through his pockets and those of his friend
and then told them to get off the train.

By then it was on a down grade and going from thirty to thirty-five
    miles an hour.
The young man was afraid to jump from the train going that fast
and clung to the ladder on the side of the car
begging to stay on the train.
But the short, heavy-set fellow and his companions
stamped on his hands
until he fell to the ground.

As he lay there, they kept shooting at him
and a bullet went through one of his lungs:
he knew it because the wound whistled when he moved.
He called to his friend—who had jumped first—to help him
but his friend was unconscious and did not answer.

5
The night marshal of the city was at a meeting of the council at the
    city hall
when he was called outside of the room:
going out he saw a woman with her baby.
She told him that her husband was away at work
and she wanted the marshal to see her home.
He told her of another man who could go with her
but she said she did not know the man
and that she wanted the marshal to go with her
because she was afraid to go home alone:
there were so many "hoboes" around.

He knew the neighborhood where she lived—
not many lived there—
and the road for some distance was along the railroad track
and the many side-tracks were crowded with freight cars.
The marshal, too, thought the neighborhood dangerous
for a woman to be alone at night;
and though he wanted to remain at the meeting of the city council
agreed to go with her.

The night was rainy and the road lonelier than ever.
As they walked along, the marshal wheeling the baby carriage,
she asked him if he had sold his livery barn;
he said he had,
and she asked if he got a good price for it.
"A fair price," the marshal answered.
She then asked him where he carried his gun
and he said in his right-hand coat pocket.
When they reached her home, she said she was afraid to go into the
    house alone.
Would he go with her? She opened the door
and he went in, taking the baby carriage up the three steps into the
    house.
She then asked him to sit down
but he told her he was in a hurry to get back.
Just then he heard the bedroom door open—
it had been ajar—
and her husband and a companion rushed into the room
and began punching him.

They held him while the woman put her hand into his coat pocket
and said, "Boys, I have his gun!"
Her husband, pointing the gun at him, said,
"If you make a move I'll kill you."
Both men went through his pockets
and then the woman's husband said,
"There's just one way for you to get out of this:
dig up two hundred dollars."
"I haven't got it," the marshal said.

"You went through my pockets and you see I haven't got it with me;
  but, if you will let me go downtown,
  I think I can get you the money."
"How?" the woman's husband asked
  and the marshal said he thought he could get it at a saloon both knew.

The three started downtown,
  the husband's companion holding the marshal's arm
  and the woman's husband walking behind the marshal.
"If you make a single crooked step," the husband said as they started,
"I'll kill you like I would a dog."
  And, as they walked along, he said,
"You sold your barn. Did you get a pretty good price for it?"
"Fair," said the marshal.
"Then why can't you give me a check?" said the woman's husband.
"I have no check," the marshal answered.
  Downtown, they went into the saloon the marshal had named
  and the saloonkeeper was surprised at seeing the marshal
  and asked him what the trouble was.
  The marshal did not answer but asked the saloonkeeper if he could give
        him two hundred dollars—
  and winked.

The saloonkeeper then said he must talk to the marshal alone in
        another room.
  As they came out of the room,
  the woman's husband and his companion saw by the look on their faces
  that the marshal had told the saloonkeeper what had happened—
  and ran out of the saloon.

6

Both were laborers, out of work and looking for a job;
  but Tony had a room in a lodging house in the city
  and shared it with Dino.
  Tony had more than a hundred dollars in gold
  which he carried about in a money belt
  but Dino had no money.

He would borrow small sums from Tony now and then
to get a shave or buy a meal.

One morning—Dino had just had his mustache shaved off—
he told Tony about a ranch on the other side of the river,
run by Italians, and said they should go there together
and perhaps get a job.
And so they crossed the river and were walking along the levee
when they were joined by two other Italians—
strangers to Tony. They had not gone far
when Dino suddenly turned on Tony
and demanded his money;
but Tony would not hand it over.

Then the two strangers held him each by an arm
and Dino, drawing a knife,
slashed him about the head and neck and across the body—
the wound across his body was from his spine on the left
to his spine on the right, cutting through his intestines
and almost cutting his body in two.
Then the three took his money
and carried him to the river
and threw him in.

Tony, still living, was able to drag himself to the bank.
Here he was seen by men on a passing steamboat
and picked up
to live a while longer—and tell what had happened.

7
He had only one leg and walked with a crutch.
Making his way across the country,
he was now lying down for the night beside a coal fire
among a pile of railroad ties.

Two Indians who had been drinking all day
at midnight saw the light of the fire

and climbing over the railroad ties
found him. One of them offered him half a dollar
to go and get them some whiskey
but he said, "I can't. I got one leg."
At that one Indian said to the other,
"I hold both hands and you cut throat,"
and gave the other Indian his knife.

The man tried to get up
but the Indian with the knife put his knee on the man's breast
and then tried to put his knife against the man's throat
but, drunk, first stabbed out the man's left eye,
and then cut a deep gash in the man's left cheek
before he cut the man's throat from ear to ear.
His companion kept saying, "Go ahead and cut him! Cut him hard!"

After they had killed the man they looked in the pockets of his coat
        and trousers,
and the Indian who had taken back his knife said,
"There's money in shoe sometimes,"
and cut the man's shoe from top to sole,
and still found nothing.

V

BUSINESS TROUBLES

1

The two working a ranch in partnership had hired a "handyman"—
about fifty-five or sixty, partially crippled—
to cook, take care of the chickens, mend fences,
and do other "odd jobs."
But one of the partners warned his younger partner
"not to bother or crowd him too much, or egg him on,
for he might shoot."

The two partners, one morning, rode out from their ranch house
to look after the fences

and a neighbor rode up and said he had told their handyman
about a break in a fence two or three days before
and the break was still there.
About noon the partners returned, put their horses in the stable,
and the younger of the partners
walked rapidly to the ranch house, flushed and irritated.
Entering it, he asked the handyman why he had not fixed the fence
their neighbor had told him about
and went on to ask why he did not get the cattle out of the horse
    pasture,
and had other complaints.

After the handyman's explanations and denials,
the partner said,
"You ain't doing a damn thing around here—
ain't doing any work at all
like you ought to."
With that he went down the walk that led to the gate
but, after going half way,
returned and said, "The best thing you can do
is to roll your blankets
and get off the ranch!"
The handyman answered, "All right, I can do that,"
and, getting ready to leave,
went into the room where the rifles and other weapons were kept
and put his own pistol in his pocket.

The partner who had discharged the handyman was soon back
and walking into the kitchen where the handyman was still at work
renewed his complaints
and ended up by saying, "You are a damn, lying, son of a bitch."
At this the handyman spoke up and said,
"Now cut that out—that 'lying son of a bitch'!
I may be trifling
but I am not a son of a bitch."
Later, picking up some potato peeling,
he went to the door that led to the back porch
to throw them into the slop basket,

and there was the partner who had discharged him
working the pump on the porch with his left hand
and holding a cup in his right;
and the young man began again:
he didn't see why the hired man could not find the hole in the fence
that had taken the partners only two minutes—
but before he could finish what he was saying
the handyman interrupted him and said
he was getting damned tired of his noise—
and shot him.
He left the dead body lying on the porch
with the head against the wall,
and going to the stable took a horse
and rode off.

2

Don went into a store selling secondhand goods and asked the owner,
	a Jew,
to show him something or other for sale
and, as the owner of the store turned to get it,
Don struck him on the head with a rusty gas pipe
wrapped in a newspaper. Don then ran out of the store
and left the owner of the store unconscious on the floor.

Next day another Jew was found in his store, about a block from the
	first,
lying on the floor, unconscious,
with a gas pipe of rusty iron wrapped in a newspaper
near him. A stepladder against the wall
and a suitcase on the floor
showed that the owner of the store had very likely been taking the
	suitcase from a shelf
when he was struck on the head. This man died of the blow.

That day Don was in a saloon in the neighborhood
when word was brought in that still another Jew had been struck
	down

by someone now called "the gas pipe thug";
and Don said,
"They ought to kill all the God damned Jews!"

A day or two afterwards, Don went into a tailorshop run by a Chinese.
Don had a rusty piece of gas pipe wrapped in a newspaper—
but not so well wrapped as to hide all of the pipe—
and asked to see an article on one of the shelves.
The Chinese owner of the store saw the pipe
and asked Don what he was doing with it
and Don answered that he was working for the gas company.
When the Chinese turned to take down the article Don had asked for,
Don struck him with the pipe;
but it was only a glancing blow and did not stun him.
Don ran out of the store with the Chinese after him—
and was caught. "You son of a bitch," he said to the Chinese,
"I thought I had killed you
as I knocked over a number of your kind."

VI
PERSONS AND PLACES

1

He had hated the old man a long time;
once, while skinning a live rabbit,
a man watching told him it was a cruel thing to do,
and he said he wished he could do it to the old man.
Now, while the old man was eating his evening meal
alone in his room—
a bowl of broth on the table, part of a loaf of barley bread,
a piece of it cut off
and a mouthful bitten out of the piece—
he struck him down,
gagged him with a knotted napkin
and drew a rope tightly around his neck,
tight enough to strangle him.

He hurried to the barber-shop
and, going to the back part, asked for a bath,
and stayed in the bathroom for fifteen or twenty minutes;
and when he came out asked for a quick shave.
He used to get shaved twice a week
and had been shaved only the day before,
and the barber saw that, for some reason or other,
he was greatly excited and sweating freely,
although it was a cool evening in October.
After his shave, he crossed the street to the cigar-store
and watched a game of cards being played,
still sweating and strangely excited;
and later that night when he was playing billiards in a saloon
the man he was playing with asked him why he was sweating so.

2
Death Valley

Jack and Walt, both prospecting for mines, were friendly
and when Jack was arrested for some crime or other
he asked Walt to go on his bail bond
and, if he did, promised to give him mining claims
which Jack said he had in Death Valley—and did not have.
Walt went on his bond and then wanted to see the claims.

They left on a freight train and at the station where they got off
had breakfast at a hotel run by a woman who knew them both;
borrowed a cart and mule from her
and went on to a ranch where both were also known;
sent back the cart and mule they had borrowed,
and borrowed another cart and mule at the ranch
and with provisions for their trip went on to Death Valley.

Next morning, one of the men working at the ranch
found the ranch's cart and mule standing outside the corral
but no one in charge; and the man who ran a hotel in the desert,

about a mile from the railroad station where Jack and Walt had left the
        freight train
saw Jack coming along on foot—alone.
Jack stopped at the hotel to pledge a revolver with the man who ran
        the hotel
for the loan of fifteen dollars—
this was the revolver Walt had carried with him—
and then Jack went on to the hotel where both had breakfast a few
        days before
and the woman in charge
saw how uneasy Jack was as he ate.

A week or so later, a cousin looking for Walt
found his body on the desert at the edge of Death Valley
a short distance from the road: wrapped in a blanket,
his clothing, hat, and pistol holster
under bushes nearby,
and two bullet holes in his head.

3

Great Salt Lake

The boy was about fourteen
and for three years had been working for five dollars a week
helping his widowed mother.
On a day in July, he and his mother went to the lake with some friends
and two of them, a young man and a young woman—as well as the
        boy—
bought tickets at the pavilion for bathing in the lake
and waded out;
about fifty or sixty people were bathing there.
The young man and young woman could swim
but the boy could not swim a stroke.
They floated together in "a chain":
the young man in the lead
with his feet under the boy's arms

and the boy's feet
under the young woman's arms.

They gradually floated out into the lake
into still deeper water;
the young man tried to touch bottom with his feet
but the water was too deep
and he suggested that they go back.
The slight breeze that had been blowing
had now changed into a high wind.

Now the young woman found it hard to breathe
for the water of the lake was heavy with salt;
and the boy, struck in the face by the waves,
also found it hard to breathe.
But the wind carried the three still farther out;
and the young man signaled to two men bathing near them for help
but the men did not understand his signals or call
and merely waved their hands in reply.

Finally, it was agreed that the young woman should make her way to
        the pavilion
and tell of the danger the young man and the boy were in.
It took her about an hour and a half to get to the pavilion
and the young man, because the boy could not swim or even float
        alone,
could make no headway back;
indeed, he and the boy were carried still farther out
as the wind grew stronger and the water rough.

It became dark and the lights on the pavilion went out.
The young man and the boy were being carried towards an island
and though the young man let himself down a number of times
he still could not touch bottom.
But he kept on floating and kept the boy floating too
until about two or three o'clock at night
his legs were suddenly seized by cramps.
He told the boy how to keep his body floating

and the boy drifted away.
At that the young man's feet touched bottom
and he knew he was in shallow water;
he looked about for the boy, but, even as he did so,
became unconscious.

In the morning, he came to
and saw the sun shining
and found himself lying on the shore of the island
with his feet and legs still in the water,
but the boy nowhere in sight.
A few days afterwards, the boy's body was found on the shore of the
     island.

PART FIVE   TESTIMONY

THE UNITED STATES (1911–1915)

RECITATIVE

THE NORTH

THE WOODPECKER'S REVENGE

On a morning in June
two black boys about seventeen or eighteen
together with a white boy about fifteen
were sent by the white boy's father
into his field to sucker his crop of corn.
After reaching the field the white boy and the two black boys
    quarreled
but all three went to work.

The black boys, however, were still angry at the white boy
and talked about clubbing him with the thinning sticks
they were using;
but they kept on working until noon.
Returning to work in the afternoon,
the white boy took along a shotgun to shoot a woodpecker
he had seen in the woods near the field.
He told the black boys to go on with their work
while he went into the woods.

He was soon back—
he had not found the bird—
and sat down under a tree
and gave the gun to one of the black boys
and told him to go into the woods and shoot the woodpecker.
The black boy did
and, coming back with the the dead bird, found the white boy asleep
under the tree
with his back towards him.
"Now is your chance," said the other black boy
and the black with the gun—
only three or four feet from where the white boy lay asleep—

aimed at the back of his head
and shot him.

The white boy was dead—he had not moved or even quivered—
and the black boys dragged him face downward
into the woods. One of the blacks went for a shovel
and they dug a hole in which to bury the body
and near it buried the gun.

But, finally, the dead boy's brother looking for him
came upon the mound of fresh earth
and taking away the loose earth with his hands
found the body.

II

The saloonkeeper came from the saloon with his bartender
at five o'clock in the morning
to the restaurant for breakfast.
The waiter who worked all night was still on duty
and the saloonkeeper and his companion sat down at the counter;
but something or other was said between the saloonkeeper and the
        waiter.
Whatever it was, the angry saloonkeeper reached across the counter
and took hold of the waiter;
and the waiter, trying to get away,
struggled along the counter.
There were groups of dishes on the counter,
sugar bowls, salt cellars, and the like,
and, whenever they reached a group,
the saloonkeeper would let go of the waiter with one hand
and throw whatever he could at him.
The waiter finally got loose from the saloonkeeper
and ran into the kitchen.

The saloonkeeper went to his overcoat,
hanging on a hook on the wall,

and took his revolver from a pocket;
and then went to the door of the kitchen looking for the waiter.
But the waiter had gone upstairs to call the owner
and the owner came down into the restaurant.
The other waiter was sweeping up the sugar, salt, and broken cups and
    saucers on the floor behind the counter;
and the owner of the restaurant asked what the trouble was.
The saloonkeeper said that he was not to blame but the waiter was,
and, talking loudly and angrily,
said that if the owner would not let the waiter go
both could go to hell;
and the owner, looking at the broken crockery, asked the saloonkeeper
    to leave.

The saloonkeeper did but, backing out of the restaurant door,
shot the owner.

III

A young woman, a Syrian who had been in the United States only
    about six months
and as yet could not speak English,
was traveling by railroad from town to town
peddling lace.
She should have left the train at a certain station
to change for the city she was going to
but was carried past the station
and could not leave the train until it reached another town.
By this time it was nine o'clock in the evening.
She went into the railroad station
and showed the ticket-agent her ticket and the note given her by the
    conductor of the train she had been on
asking that she be carried back to the station where she was to take the
    train for the city she was going to
and with the ticket or note the ticket-agent gave her she went into the
    waiting-room.

On the same train that had brought her to the town where she was then
was a young man with a quart of whiskey and a bottle of wine;
four or five of his friends met him at the station
and were in the station or about it
until the young Syrian woman was alone.
Then the young man went into the waiting-room
and, picking up the young woman's suitcase,
asked her if he could take her to a hotel.
She was sleepy and indeed asleep when he came up to her and woke her
and—he was polite and well-dressed—
she thought him a hotel porter
and followed him out of the waiting-room
towards what she thought would be a hotel.

They walked along the railroad tracks and then down a street
until they came to an alley
and here he turned and went into the alley.
His friends had followed them,
but not into the alley
and now waited in the deserted street.
In the alley the young man seized her.
Frightened, she tried to free herself
and began to scream;
and did free herself. But as she ran out of the alley
two of the young man's friends
knocked her down
and dragging her back into the alley
crowded a handkerchief into her mouth
and, holding her down on the ground,
two or three of them, including the young man who had brought
    her there,
raped her.

She had become unconscious because of the blow or fall
or perhaps merely out of fright
and, when she became conscious, took the handkerchief out of her
    mouth
and began to scream again

and cried for help in her native speech.
She managed to get to her feet
and, running to the nearest house,
the woman who lived there, awakened by her screams,
had opened the door
and now let her into the house,
while the young men gathered about the porch.
But they did not follow her.

The doctor found her right arm badly wrenched,
her breasts bruised,
her underclothing stained and soiled,
and her private parts torn.
A lesser matter was that her waist was torn
and a small bag in which she kept two gold coins hanging from her
    neck
was gone,
as well as the handbag which she had carried
and in which she had two or three dollars.

IV
SOCIAL LIFE

Two Italians, acquaintances if not friends,
met in a saloon
and drinking beer played cards for about three hours.
At five they left
and went to the house of another Italian
where they had supper
with others who joined them at the meal.

A young son of their host
was sent downstairs
to ask a neighbor if he would allow his room to be used for dancing
and would play for the dancers.
The boy came back

and said the neighbor would not play for them
because he was too tired from his hard work that day
and would have to begin again early the next day.
But one of the guests went downstairs to persuade the neighbor to
    play
and he then said he would
and the party went downstairs and began dancing
and the neighbor played upon his violin.
He sent out for beer
and now and then the dancers would stop to drink.

One of the two who had been playing cards that afternoon
became heated with dancing
and also stopped for a drink.
He asked his companion of that afternoon if there was any beer left
and the man poured out what was left in the pitcher—
less than half a glass.
He took it
and threw the glass back and what was in it.
The man who had poured the beer dodged and was not hit.
He then went up to the man who threw the glass
and told him in a friendly way
that he should not have done what he did
and at that the man struck him with his fists.

At this the man playing the violin came up
and told the man who threw the glass that they did not want any
    quarrel or trouble
and pushed him to a chair.
He sat there for a while
and then said to the man playing the violin
that he would like to get a handkerchief from the overcoat
hanging from a hook against the wall;
stood up
and reached for his overcoat
but took from a pocket a knife
and plunged the blade into the neighbor's belly.
It killed him.

V

FAMILY DIFFICULTIES

1

She was seventeen when they married
and her husband thirty-three.
They lived on a farm at first
but soon afterwards moved to a town where her parents lived
and her husband became a bartender.
But, about seven years after their marriage,
she left him and went to the home of her sister
in another town,
and took their child, a little girl now four years old,
with her.

She had written a number of letters to a young man in the town where
     she had lived
showing an infatuation for him
and their relationship had become, to use a legal term, "illicit."
Her husband found this out
after she had left him.
Although he could not read,
he demanded the letters from the young man,
got them,
and took the letters to the home of his wife's father and mother.
Although it was almost midnight,
her mother got up from bed and let him in,
and he threw the letters on the table
and told her to read them.
He called his wife "bad" names
and said he was going to have his little girl back
and asked where his wife was.
Her parents told him the city she said she was going to;
but he found out, elsewhere, that she had gone to her sister.

One morning, after taking two drinks of whiskey,
he left for that town
and took along a loaded pistol and a quart bottle of whiskey.

He reached his sister-in-law's house about noon
and found his wife doing the washing.
He asked her if she was not going to kiss him
and she said she had never refused
and kissed him,
and her sister said that if the two wanted to talk to each other
to go into the sitting-room.
He took the bottle of whiskey from his pocket
and put it on the table,
drank another glass of whiskey
and lay down on the couch.
He showed his wife the letters,
and said he had come for his "baby"
and his wife could come along or "go to hell."

After dinner, he came into the kitchen
and, taking another drink of whiskey,
drew the letters and his pistol out of his pocket and said to his wife's
     sister:
"Look what I got last night at the point of this gun,"
and added that his wife had written the letters and "gone to the dogs."
Her sister answered that if she had
he had driven her to it.
However, he wanted his wife to go back with him.

When the sisters were alone together,
his wife asked for advice about going back.
Her sister told her to do as she pleased
but added she would like to see her go back home
for the child's sake;
and the wife said, "I can go,
but I never expect to get there alive."
Her sister asked, "Why?"
And thinking that perhaps the wife was thinking of suicide
added, "You wouldn't do anything foolish, would you?
Think of your baby."
And the wife answered, "No, I wouldn't but he will."

Her sister said, "I don't think so,"
and the wife said, "You will see."

There was a train going back to their home town
and husband and wife started for the depot;
but her husband fell down the steps of his sister-in-law's house.
His wife helped him to his feet
and picked up his hat for him.
However, they were too late for the train,
and the train on another railroad was not leaving until evening,
and they went to a hotel to stay until it was time to go to the depot.

After they had been in the room a short while,
her husband ran into the hall
shouting to the hotel-keeper downstairs
that his wife had shot herself
and asked him to get a doctor.
The hotel-keeper and others hurried to the room:
his wife was lying on her back across the bed,
her feet hanging down from it;
her shirtwaist burnt where the bullet had entered
and she was unable to talk;
merely gasped a few times—
and was dead.

When her husband was asked
who did the shooting,
he said, "Ask the child";
and the little girl answered, "Mamma did it."
Someone among those present said afterwards,
"He told the child to say that, if asked."

2

Husband and wife, immigrants from Poland, and their boarder, a
    Lithuanian,
lived in a village, in a small house in a large lot

at the corner of two streets
with a pump near the corner.

That morning, the husband got up first, made a fire in the stove;
and about ten or fifteen minutes afterwards
his wife got up and went into the kitchen.
The boarder who lived in the only room on the second floor
came down a little later
and the wife got breakfast for both.
Then her husband took a pail
and went to the pump for water
but, soon afterwards, whistled for his wife to come out.

The pump was open to the streets
and used by others than the man and his wife:
an iceman, for example, would stop there earlier in the morning
to wash pieces of ice,
and the pump was used by boys and others—
it could be used by anybody from the street.
"Here is a box," he said to his wife.
The night before husband and wife had used the pump
to get water for their garden
and the "box" was not there.

It looked like a tin can, the kind used for tomatoes,
and was wrapped in newspaper
with a string around it.
"Don't take it in your hands," his wife said.
"Something bad might be in it."
And she touched it with her foot:
the package was heavy.
But her husband, picking up the package,
began to unwrap it—
and it exploded.
The explosion struck the wife in her face, blinding her,
and her husband lay badly wounded and died.

The boarder had often urged her to leave her husband
and go away with him.
He was often alone with her,
for her husband left earlier for his work in a factory than the boarder did
and came home later.
When the boarder first came to them,
he would usually sit with husband and wife
in the kitchen,
but that was only for a week or two.
Then one day he brought oranges and wine into their bedroom
when the husband had left for work
and the wife was still in bed.
She told him he should not have come in
but he tried to kiss her;
she turned her face away
and told him again to get out of the room.
Soon afterwards she had a lock placed on the bedroom door.

When she and her husband quarreled about their child—
a little girl of three—
the boarder heard them
and, after the husband left for work,
told her that when her husband got older he would get worse;
but if she would go away with him
it would be better for her
because her husband was a cranky man;
and she told him that she would not leave her husband and baby
for anything in the world.

Another time, as she was making dinner,
he took hold of her hand,
and she struck him with the dipper.
Once, when she sat working at the sewing-machine,
he stood beside her and again tried to kiss her
and she threatened to strike him in the face
with the scissors.
And still another time when he came home,

he went to the pump for water,
and, as he brought the water in, said, "Bringing in the water is worth a
    kiss."
She did not answer and he said, "Why are you so mad?
You used to speak pleasantly to me
and now you don't want to speak to me at all."
And she answered, "I told you once that you should behave yourself.
I don't want to speak to you.
Your business is to eat supper and go upstairs."
And he said, "I don't care if anybody is going to knock your husband in
    the head.
Your husband is to me like nothing."

And now she was sure that the boarder had placed the bomb by the
    pump.

3

The stepson was not quite sixteen.
He lived with his mother and his stepfather—
whom he disliked, in fact hated—
and, as he had been doing in spring and summer,
went into the country to work.
His mother had some property
which she had inherited from the stepson's father
and had given it by deed to her son and daughter
before her second marriage;
but her second husband kept urging the children
to deed it back to her.
This did not add to the stepson's love for his stepfather.

One day, that spring, the stepson came to town
to spend the weekend with his sister, who was married;
and, on Saturday, his stepfather and mother who had gone to their home
to move all they had there to his stepfather's father
where they were to live
found the evening too cold—snow and sleet falling—
and soon left.

On the way to the home of the stepfather's father,
they met the stepson;
his sister had gone into a store, still brightly lit,
and he was waiting for her outside.
His mother and stepfather greeted him and, as he turned away, his
    stepfather said,
"Your mother wants to talk to you."
He answered, "But I don't want to talk to her."
At that his stepfather said angrily, "Stop! Come back here!"
and he did come back
and, with his brother-in-law's revolver which he had in his pocket,
shot his stepfather.
His stepfather slumped to the ground—
and was dead.

4

As a girl during the Civil War
she had helped her mother nurse the sick and wounded
and remembered how her mother would quote the English clergyman
who, disposing of what he had,
left directions what should be done with any loose change that might
    be found in his pockets.
And now that she too was old, a widow of seventy,
she wanted to dispose of what she had—
what she had earned because of hard work during her lifetime.

She would leave just enough to keep her
as she was accustomed to live—
simply but with comfort
and generous in what she gave to relatives.
And she would leave as much but no more to her only child,
her son now forty,
without children and unmarried—
and she did not want him to marry
because early in life he had been mentally sick
and she did not think anyone who had been mentally sick
should marry and have children.

The rest she would give to those missions
who were helping the penniless in India, China, and Africa—
helping orphans and destitute girls.

But her son when he heard of her plans
brought suit
to have her declared of "unsound mind" to manage her own affairs
or leave a will.

5

A widow with three children
by her will left her daughter, Ann, a dollar,
and divided the rest of her property
between her two other children, Benjamin and Alice.

Before her death—
her son Benjamin was then dead—
she was living with Alice.
Her children, Benjamin and Alice, had urged her to make the will
in order to disinherit Ann;
for their mother had now several pieces of real estate
and personal property:
she had worked hard and had earned all that herself.

Ann, the eldest, had been a schoolteacher for about fifteen years
and when she was thirty-five had married;
but the rest of the family so disliked the man Ann married
that they would not even let her visit them;
and were bitterly against their mother visiting Ann,
although she lived only half a mile away.

Once, when a friend of their mother was visiting her,
already sick and weak and soon to die,
their mother, speaking of Ann,
said how she wished she could see her again and see Ann's children
but dared not ask her to come
because Alice so disliked her sister's marriage.

Alice, just then, came home
and, seeing her mother in tears, she asked,
"Why are you crying, Mother?"
and her mother answered, "I was thinking of Benjamin."

VI

MACHINE AGE

1

The "mangle" had a hollow cylinder, heated by steam:
above it,
three rollers with belts turning them.
The laundry to be ironed
was carried between cylinder and rollers.
Sometimes an article if not completely dry, passing under the third
        roller,
would stick to the roller and wind around it.
Then the machine would have to be stopped
or, generally, the article was just pulled loose
and then sent between cylinder and rollers a second time.

A girl of seventeen, working in the laundry,
in trying to pull a tablecloth from the third roller,
had a finger of her right hand caught between roller and cylinder
and, in her hurry, to pull her hand free,
the fingers of her left hand were also caught;
all the fingers drawn up to the knuckles
and the pressure such that the fingers were flattened
and the bones crushed.

2

All of sixteen she had worked in the laundry
almost two years
and that evening was at the steam-mangle:
the machine ironed sheets, pillow slips, and towels,

drawn in between a turning steam-heated cylinder
and the turning rollers.

But that night the machine was not working well:
would stop
and the laundry to be ironed bunch up before the rollers;
and she would have to pull it back
and start it through the rollers again—
until she cried impatiently,
"Darn it! I will make it go!"
and gave the pillow slip she was trying to iron
a shove.
And her fingers were caught
and her hand drawn in
between the heavy roller and the steam-heated cylinder.

3

Just seventeen, he was driving a buggy along a highway
that crossed a single-track railroad.
The evening was dark and a strong wind blowing.
On one side of the highway, before it reached the railroad,
there was an embankment about six feet high;
and on the other side several acres of elm trees—
the land on which they stood much lower than the highway—
and their branches between the highway and the railroad.

A locomotive had been pulling a stock train
but when it reached a station
the engineer found that he did not have enough water in the tank.
The conductor cut off the cars
and they were left on a siding;
and, after the engineer had reached a station where the tank was filled
    with water,
he began to return to the cars left behind,
locomotive and tender running backwards;
for there was no turn-table at the station where they had gone for
    water.

The fireman placed a hand lantern on one end of the tender,
but there was no light on the other end,
and no headlight on the locomotive.

As the driver of the buggy came towards the crossing,
he stopped to look about,
although he could see little because of the embankment and the trees;
and he did not see the single light on the tender nor hear the coming
      locomotive—
no whistle blowing and no bell ringing—
and no rumbling of a coming train;
and so he started the horse across the track,
just at a walk;
but at the crossing the locomotive struck the horse and buggy.

Later, the buggy was found smashed
and the pieces scattered about the track;
the horse dead nearby,
and the driver badly hurt.

4

The young fellow running the elevator was new at it
and had a stupid way of looking at those who spoke to him
as if he did not understand what was said
and a way of laughing
when there was nothing to laugh at.
He would often start the car
before fully closing the door
and would often open the door
before the elevator was level with the floor.

She was "head fitter" for the firm they were working for
and sometimes had to ride the elevator thirty times a day.
This time she had to go from the top floor to the first floor
to get a piece of satin;
and, after getting it, rang the bell of the elevator
to go up again;

and the young man in charge
came down and opened the door.

She put her right foot on the floor of the elevator
but before she could put her left foot on
the elevator shot up.
She found herself hanging below the elevator holding on to a bar
    attached to it;
but when the elevator got to the second floor
she could hold on no longer
and let go—
to fall to the bottom of the shaft
below the basement floor.

THE SOUTH

I
FAMILY DIFFICULTIES

That evening he said that he was going to a neighboring town
but was back about half-past eight
and found the lamp turned low;
his wife turning down the bedclothes,
and the man he suspected her of being intimate with
sitting down, his slippers untied.
The man left,
and the wife said she would pack up her belongings
and she, too, would leave.
"If Jim can't come into a house you pay rent for," she said,
"he can come into one you don't pay rent for."

II

One evening he was sitting on a stool at the counter of a restaurant,
near a railroad depot,
talking with the owner of the restaurant about the best way of making
    coffee—
a pleasant conversation—
when a stranger entered and sat down beside him
and, interrupting the conversation, ordered fish.
The stranger was shabbily dressed and somewhat drunk, perhaps,
and the man who had been talking to the owner of the restaurant
and still friendly and talkative said,
"If you want to catch fish in the country you must have a steel hook
but in the city you must have a silver one."
The stranger did not like this—
thinking, perhaps, that it was a sneer at his shabby clothing
or that he would not pay for the fish—
and answered angrily.

Before long the two were knocking each other's hat off
and, out on the sidewalk, fighting.

III

A woman, just over thirty and well overweight,
was about to get off the streetcar
with her valise, a basket in which was cake and a bottle of syrup, and
    with a bundle of sugar cane.
The car stopped
and she went out on the platform.
When she put her foot on the step below the platform,
leaving the valise on the platform until she was on the ground,
the conductor, inside the car,
gave the signal to start,
and the car started.

She shifted the basket from her right hand to her arm at once
and her right hand free
held on to the bar on the side of the car to help passengers on or off
but was thrown from the car
and swung around it.
She held on to the bar
to be dragged a hundred feet and more
before the car stopped.

The conductor came out on the platform.
"If I had been a white lady," she said,
"you would have given me time to get off

before you rang the bell."
And the conductor replied,
"Go on, nigger;
   you had time enough."

IV

RAILROADS

1

A young black, sixteen years of age,
earned a dollar and a half a day,
and gave almost all of it to his father
but kept the rest
to spend on himself:
buy tobacco, for example,
with which to make his cigarettes.

The train would stop for a while at the flag station
and he went into the car for colored people
where the "news butch" kept the newspapers, candy, tobacco, and
    whatever else was sold on the train
and the young black bought what he wanted,
and stood there talking to the "news butch" until the train was about
    to start
and then was walking to the platform of the car to get off.

Just then the conductor and the porter,
about to enter the car for white passengers,
saw him
and hurried up to him—
the train was now running pretty fast—
shoved him out of the door
and both threw him off the train.
"That damned nigger don't mind hitting the cross-ties," said the
    conductor,
as he and the porter turned back,
and the porter laughed.
The young black's body lay near the tracks,
his head one or two feet from the end of the railroad's cross-ties,
and his feet towards the ditch:
the head badly bruised on the side of the forehead
and the skull broken.

One of the passengers in the car for whites
saw what had happened,
but was advised by his friends
that the less he had to say about the matter
the better.

2
Dangers at a Crossing

Driving his buggy along the highway
he came to a railroad crossing:
a freight car was blocking it
and had been left there for days.
A showman had left it,
and the stench of the wild animals in it
startled the horse.

As the driver of the buggy tried to go around the car,
the noise of rabbits jumping about
in a wire cage left on the station platform
added to the fright of the horse;
and the buggy crashed against the embankment of the railroad
just above the crossing,
flinging the driver out.

V

NIGHTMARE

The two women were friends,
each living in a room next to the other
with a door between them.
One of them had been married
but was no longer living with her husband.
That evening both had visited her mother
and were back at midnight

and each went to her bed
leaving the door between them open:
and, as the married woman's friend did so,
she saw the married woman
kneeling beside her bedside saying her prayers.

About two hours later, the friend of the married woman was awakened:
the married woman was calling her.
The first thing she saw when she woke up
was the married woman standing at the foot of the bed
and she asked, "Were you calling me?"
"Yes," the married woman answered, "scream!"
And her friend said, "Scream?"
"Yes," said the married woman, "scream, scream!"
Her friend at that, jumping out of bed,
saw the married woman covered with blood:
the blood spurting out of her throat.
And her friend said, "My God, what has happened?"
She answered, "Husband . . . my husband did it . . . cut my throat."
Her friend caught her at once in her arms
and had her lie down on the bed;
but by that time she could no longer talk
and was just gasping.

VI

SOCIAL LIFE: A MERRY CHRISTMAS

Price lived on a creek and Porter on the same creek about a mile above.
A number of guests, including Porter's son-in-law,
were gathering at Porter's house to celebrate Christmas;
but Porter himself, at noon, was eating at Price's home
and afterwards invited Price to go home with him.
But Price and Porter's son-in-law had not been on good terms for some
    time
and Price had said to Porter's daughter, only the day before,
that he would kill her husband on sight.

When Porter and Price were near Porter's home,
Price saw the son-in-law standing in the yard
and told Porter he would not go in
because he and the son-in-law were not on good terms;
but Porter insisted that he should
and said that the house was his
and Price would not be troubled while there.

The house had a narrow porch along the front of it;
the entrance at one end.
Mrs. Porter and a guest had been sitting on the porch
plucking chickens for the Christmas dinner
and Mrs. Porter had asked her son-in-law to kill another chicken.
He had gone into the backyard and had shot a chicken;
and now, as his father-in-law and Price were crossing the yard
and beginning to go towards the house,
the son-in-law was standing on the porch, near the entrance,
twirling his pistol.

Price again said he would go no farther
and Porter again insisted that he should go into the house
and the two went on the porch,
Porter first and Price following.
There Porter met his daughter and, as they went into the house,
she began to tell him about Price's threat to kill her husband;
and Mrs. Porter, seeing Price, said she did not see how he could come to
         her house
after what he had said to her daughter
and added that he was not welcome.
Price answered, "I have always treated your husband right
and I would not have come if he hadn't invited me.
But I will leave—
and, if anybody wants anything, they can get it."
As he turned to leave, five shots were fired;
and when the smoke had cleared away,
the son-in-law was lying dead on the porch.
The son-in-law had fired first, aiming at Price;
but Price had knocked the pistol up with his right hand

so that the shot had passed above him,
and, drawing his own pistol with his left hand,
fired four times.

THE WEST

I

A sheepshearer, he lived in a sheepshearing camp
in which were twenty or thirty Indians and Mexicans.
When the sheepshearing was over,
he began to drink
and became quarrelsome.

He took his sheepshearing shears
and went to another tent
and challenged those within to come out and fight.
No one did
and then he took his rifle
and began shooting at a can on the ground
and said, "This is the way I'll kill one or two tonight."

He went back into the tent where he lived,
stumbled over some harness and fell.
When he got up, he asked who had pushed him
and was told nobody had
and then he said, "I'll go out and kill two or three."
He walked out and began firing his rifle again
and the third shot struck a fellow sheepshearer,
standing at the entrance of another tent a short distance away,
and killed him.

II
THE GOLDHUNTERS

A native of a foreign country, still in his thirties,
he found work in a town out west
and lived in a lodging-house kept by a man from his own country.
There he became acquainted with the man's mother,

a woman in her late fifties,
and the three became friends.

There was talk in the town of gold to be found nearby
and the lodger and the elderly woman
made up their minds to look for it together:
the man saying that he had some experience as a "prospector,"
and the woman that she had money to pay for the search.
The elderly woman took along a young woman as a companion;
and it was agreed that whatever was found
was to be shared equally among the three.
The elderly woman gave the man quite a sum—in those days—
to take care of it, buy supplies and pay the bills.

It turned out that the talk about gold to be found at the place they
        went to
was just talk;
but there was another place
where prospecting had been done and mining locations found
and the three went there,
part of the way by train and the rest by wagon;
and finally camped where the country for miles around
was a waste land of mountains and desert,
visited only now and then by prospectors.

The three had a tent
and the two women slept together in back of it
and the man at the entrance
with his pistol;
and they spent about six weeks prospecting in nearby canyons
without finding any gold.
Then another prospector came into the neighborhood
and settled down about two miles away
and the three visited him.
The two women were introduced by their companion
as his mother and wife—
not to embarrass them.
In their talk, the newcomer asked for salt,

if they could spare any,
and they said they would give him all the salt he wanted.

A few days later, the newcomer was coming towards their tent
when the companion of the two women saw him and called out,
    "Wait!
I'll bring you the salt,"
and he did,
and then said he would walk back with him.
The visitor was somewhat surprised at the greeting
but asked politely as they walked about the man's "mother" and
    "wife"
and was told—the man pointing—they were about a mile away
    washing their clothes.
But the visitor had just passed that very place
and saw no one there.
He did see how uneasy his companion was
and when the newcomer was left alone at the foot of a hill
he stood looking back from the top of it
and saw the man who had left him
walking quickly backwards and forwards with a bucket of sand
and scattering the sand about the tent.

The newcomer curious, if not suspicious,
went back a day or two afterwards
but found no one in the tent
or near it
and nothing in it at all but a pick and shovel.
Sand and gravel were strewn about the floor of the tent
and at a place near it
the ground had just been dug up.
He began to dig there with the shovel he had found in the tent
to see what was buried, if anything,
and had hardly dug a foot
when he found a blanket, tightly tied about with the cords of a
    hammock.
He cut the blanket open with his penknife
and there was a body—

that of the elderly woman he had met:
in her nightgown,
shot through the head.
And near her the body of the young woman, also in her nightgown,
wrapped in a mattress stained with blood.
She, too, had been shot through the head.

III

A man, tall and husky, came from a city to a neighboring town
on a Saturday
and went to a lodging-house for blacks.
He asked the woman in charge the price for sleeping there that night
and she said, "Twenty-five cents."
He answered, "I have no money just now but will be back,"
and went for a walk about town.

A Chinese, short and slender, ran a laundry there.
The building he was in had three rooms:
the front room where the customers left and took their laundry;
a room in back of it where he worked;
and back of that a smaller room, where he cooked, ate, and slept.
The back wall of the building had a hole in it,
instead of a door,
large enough for anyone to go in or out;
but the town had only a rainy season
and no cold weather generally,
and the laundryman had little need for a window or door
to keep the wind or cold out.

The man from the city went into the laundry,
just to look around he said,
and while he was there another black man came in, a customer,
and the three began to talk together.
"I wonder why you don't run a restaurant instead of a laundry,"
said the man from the city;
and the Chinese said, "I did run a restaurant in another town

but gave it up: no money in it."
"Where do you keep your money?" the man from the city asked.
"Do you send it back to China?"
The Chinese smiled and pointed to the calendar on the wall
with the picture of a bank in town.

Late Sunday night the man from the city
asked the woman in charge of the lodging-house
to wake him early the next morning
in time to catch a train back to the city;
and gave her fifty cents.
But she did not have to wake him,
for he was up before she was and when he left for the depot nearby
he was carrying a bag
in which she could hear a jingle
that sounded, she thought, like money.

That Monday a man who had come into the laundry
rang the bell in the room for customers;
but no one answered.
He went into the next room, thinking the Chinese might be at work
        and too busy to hear the bell,
and saw the Chinese lying on the floor:
he had only his undershirt and trousers on
and there were bruises about his face and head
and the queue which the Chinese had to wear in those days
was pulled tightly about his neck,
tight enough to choke and kill him.

The customer went for the town marshal
and the two went into the room where the Chinese ate and slept:
his two trunks were open
and all that had been in them was scattered about the floor
and even his bed clothes torn up,
as if whoever had killed him
had been searching for his money.

IV

MACHINE AGE

1

In places the highway through the canyon
became a "dugway";
that is, on one side of the canyon,
along or near its base.
At one such place
where the road was narrow and had many sharp turns
a man in a buggy, drawn by a team of horses,
saw an automobile
coming towards him.

The horses lifted their heads in fright,
shied,
jumping sideways and backing up.
But the driver of the automobile did not stop.
The horses turning away sharply—
the road was too narrow for the driver to turn,
even if he could manage the horses—
he was thrown from the buggy
and, holding on to the reins was dragged along the ground,
until he became unconscious.

2

Out of work, some of the men he knew were at work helping load the rock
for a jetty. The rock was carried in cars
to a trestle running into the river
and loaded from the cars on to scows
made fast along the trestle: put into a wooden "skip," as it was called,
weighing over a ton,
and then raised by a derrick, the boom of which swung in a circle,
and when empty
carried back over the cars;
held there until the man in charge showed where he wanted the skip
    lowered

and then one of the men on the car
signaled the engineer to drop the skip.

The man out of work asked the foreman for a job
and was told he had none;
but the man out of work stayed on the trestle—
to leave with some of his acquaintances
about to go off shift—
waiting on the offside of a car that was being unloaded.
The engineer on signal raised the skip
from the scow it had been loading,
swinging it over the car,
and, at the signal from one of those on the car,
lowered it:
it struck the man out of work on the forehead.

3
A young man of twenty or so had been hired through an agency to
        work in a millyard
but when he showed up for work was told by the manager that there
        was no work for him in the yard;
but, if he wished, he could work at a ripsaw in the mill.
He said he would and was asked if he knew about that kind of work
and answered that he did not
but would be glad to learn.
The manager then took him into the mill to a ripsaw and, showing him
        how to work at it,
took a board with his hand
and shoved it through the saw with a stick.
The saw was guarded by a board along the right side
and another board, over the top of the saw and at right angles to the
        first board,
was about three inches above the saw;
the saw itself projected more than two and a half inches through the
        table on which the boards were placed for sawing;
the front of the saw

and the left side above the table
were left exposed.

The young man began working at once as the manager had shown
    him:
starting the board with his hands
and then shoving it through the saw with a stick.
After he had been at work about an hour or so,
the foreman came up to him and, putting his hand on the young man's
    left shoulder,
shouted above the noise of the mill,
"This work has to be done fast."
The young man turned to see who was talking to him,
his hands about a foot in front of the saw;
he had the stick in his hands
and was beginning to shove the board through the saw,
his left hand forward on the stick.

He felt as if an electric shock ran through his arm
and looking at his left hand
saw it covered with blood.
Part of the forefinger was lying on the table;
the middle finger was almost cut in two
and his thumb was split.

V

The work was "driving" logs upon a mountain stream,
that is, freeing logs that had been lodged along the banks
so that they would float with the current
down to tidewater.
A boat, if not necessary, was at least useful
to carry the men from side to side
and, where there were no logs, downstream.

The man in charge of the boat—with another man to help him—
pushed it along with poles about twelve feet long.

The boat was leaky through a knothole in the side
and without oars or paddles
and meant for six or seven men at most.
Six men were in the boat when the man in charge, standing at
        the stern,
called to two men to join those in the boat.
One of them answered that the boat seemed to have enough men
        on board
but the man in charge said, "That's all right; get on!"
And they did. But the man who had said there were enough men
        on board,
looking down at the swift current,
said, "Boys, here's where we swim."
No one said anything by way of answer.

The boat went on downstream
and soon stopped in a quiet eddy
to loosen some logs and wait for a ninth man, the "boss."
He finally came downstream,
riding a log which floated into the eddy,
and stepped from the log into the boat.
Then the man at the stern shoved the boat into the current with
        his pole,
the prow pointing somewhat downstream.
However, there was a sharp bend in the stream at this point
and the current very swift.

The current caught the boat—
the water here too deep for the poles to reach bottom—
and the boat was carried sideways swiftly downstream,
until it struck two or three logs, partially submerged,
and capsized,
throwing all of the men on board into the water.
Two were drowned
but the rest managed to swim ashore.

A Note on the Texts of Parts Three, Four, and Five

Apart from minor regularizing of punctuation and typography to achieve a consistent book style and the correction of obvious slips and typographical errors, I have followed the texts of the published edition and the typescript exactly, with the following emendations.

Inconsistencies in the numbering of sections have been silently corrected. The typescript covering the the years 1901–1910 proved to be lacking a page of text, an omission that undoubtedly occurred during photocopying. The missing material was supplied from an earlier typescript in the Mandeville Department of Special Collections, University of California, San Diego. (My thanks to Michael Davidson, Curator of the Archive for New Poetry, for his assistance.) Finally, in two places in the unpublished typescript where sense and grammar seemed to me to require it, I have supplied in square brackets a word I judged to have been inadvertently omitted by the author.

SEAMUS COONEY (1978)

TESTIMONY
(1934)

By any account, 1934 was a bleak year in the United States and abroad. The economic disaster the Hoover Administration had optimistically dubbed the "Depression" as a means of differentiating it from earlier "Panics" was going into its fifth year, and showed no signs of remitting. The drought that would result in the decade's "Dust Bowl" had already begun to affect the Great Plains region the decade before. National labor unrest had culminated in a general strike of the West Coast Longshoremen's Union in San Francisco, resulting in violent clashes between strikers and police that left several dead. Newspaper headlines were dominated by the ongoing defense of the Scottsboro Boys, nine black youths facing the electric chair on trumped-up charges of assaulting two white women in Alabama in 1931, and by reports on the depredations of outlaws such as Charles A. "Pretty Boy" Floyd, Bonnie and Clyde Barrow, and John Harvey Dillinger, all of whom would be gunned down in spectacular fashion by year's end. With the "War to End All Wars" still very much in living memory, another global military crisis loomed; Japan had annexed three Chinese provinces in 1931, and fascist Italy under Mussolini would soon make its imperialist aspirations evident in Ethiopia. The Spanish Republic was finding itself challenged by a growing right-wing threat, and Hitler had ridden a tide of populist rage to power in Germany.

In the spring of that year, the newly christened Objectivist Press released its first three titles: William Carlos Williams's *Collected Poems 1921–1931*, introduced by Wallace Stevens; George Oppen's *Discrete Series*, prefaced with a statement by Ezra Pound; and a slim volume with an introduction by Kenneth Burke titled simply *Testimony*, by Charles Reznikoff, a thirty-nine year old New York poet who had studied law at NYU and passed the New York state bar. The Objectivist Press had been established by Reznikoff and Louis Zukofsky, who had guest-edited the iconic February 1931 issue of *Poetry* on Pound's recommendation to the magazine's regular editor, Harriet Monroe (who felt the need to disown Zukofsky's youthful arrogance in the next issue). Reznikoff was a decade older than Zukofsky, and had already produced seven books of verse (most of which he had printed himself on a hand press he had acquired), a handful of plays, and a raw realist novel of New York immigrant Jewish ghetto life titled *By the Waters of Manhattan*. (1934 was something of an *annus mirabilis* for Reznikoff: the press would release two more of his books of verse—*Jerusalem the Golden* and *In Memoriam: 1933*—later that year.) Zukofsky, the self-appointed spokesman for the loosely affiliated group of poets that also included Oppen, Carl Rakosi, William Carlos Williams, and the British poet Basil Bunting, would cite examples from Reznikoff's poetry to define the two traits that were to characterize the new style of writing he was then championing: "sincerity" and "objectification."[1] While anything like a shared sensibility was short-lived, and while the group's members generally rejected reductive classifications of their work as "Objectivist," the name—initially proposed by Zukofsky himself, at Monroe's insistence that his group have an "-ism"—has stuck.[2] It is within these overlapping contexts of the cultural despair of the early years of the Depression on the one hand, and the coterie of left-leaning, formally innovative New York-based poets gathered around Zukofsky on the other, that Reznikoff began work on *Testimony*. Sections of the work first appeared in 1932, under the title "My Country 'Tis of Thee," in two separate venues: the little magazine *Contact*, edited by William Carlos Williams and Nathanael West, and *An "Objectivists" Anthology*, edited by Zukofsky.

Employed beginning in 1930 by the Brooklyn-based American Law Book Company as a staff writer, a job he no doubt acquired based on his credentials as a lawyer, Reznikoff found himself immersed in the pages of the *Federal Reporter*, an ongoing series that reproduced reports from federal court cases with precedental value spanning back

1. Zukofsky first proposed this two-pronged program for "Objectivist" writing with reference to the work of Reznikoff, which he felt exemplified these characteristics in its "clarity of image and word tone" ("Sincerity and Objectification," in *Prepositions +: The Collected Critical Essays*, ed. Mark Scroggins [Hanover, NH: Wesleyan University Press, 2000], 193). Drawing examples from Reznikoff's poems, Zukofsky explores the ways in which writing—"audibility in two-dimensional print"—attains its physicality *as an object* through its unique combinations of connotative, sonic elements—"sincerity"—and the "rested totality" of its concrete formal characteristics—"objectification" ("Sincerity and Objectification," 194).

2. For an account of Zukofsky's work on the "Objectivists" issue of *Poetry* and his exchange with Monroe, see Mark Scroggins, *The Poem of a Life: A Biography of Louis Zukofsky* (New York: Shoemaker & Hoard, 2007), 104–19.

to 1789. Covering the mundane and the gruesome, the petty and the spectacular, the cases he encountered suggested a sort of alternate national history that departed from—and to some extent challenged—the schoolbook version of US history shaped by great men and great deeds. Kenneth Burke's Introduction quotes Reznikoff at length regarding his process in assembling *Testimony*: as he busied himself with the volumes of the *Federal Reporter*, "reading cases from every state and every year (since this country became a nation)," Reznikoff became absorbed by what he found—material that, to a less imaginative reader, might have proven rather dry. "Once in a while I could see in the facts of a case details of the time and place," Reznikoff claimed, concluding that "out of such material the century and a half during which the United States has been a nation could be written up, not from the standpoint of an individual, as in diaries, or merely from the angle of the unusual, as in newspapers, but from every standpoint—as many standpoints as were provided by the witnesses themselves" (534). Through assembling such material, Reznikoff thought, he might be able to offer a testimonial to "the life of a people, in mines and on ships, all the activities that the law itself covers, which is pretty nearly everything" (*ibid.*). In both technique and subject matter, *Testimony* marked a departure from Reznikoff's earlier work, as well as from modern poetry generally; in *Testimony*, Reznikoff doesn't so much write poetry as find the poetry implicit in legal briefs. *Testimony* thus adopts and adapts the collagist aesthetics of earlier modernist practitioners including T. S. Eliot, Ezra Pound, and Marianne Moore, yet *Testimony* takes this aesthetics to its outmost extreme, presenting its materials with a notable absence of any authorial commentary.

This notion of Reznikoff as "editor" is confirmed by his own prefatory note to the text, in which he claims to have "glanced through several hundred volumes of old cases—not a great many as law reports go—and found *almost* all that follows" (emphasis mine).[3] While

3. This reading of the poem is suggested by Michael Davidson, who describes Reznikoff's role in assembling *Testimony* "as editor—a witness of witnesses—whose arrangement of legal documents supplies a social narrative for acts of private observation" (*Ghostlier Demarcations: Modern Poetry and the Material World* [Berkeley: University of California Press, 1997], 151). In Davidson's reading, the narrative quality of Reznikoff's project in *Testimony* thus results not from the characteristics of any single vignette he includes but rather in the aggregate, in the vantage on nineteenth-century social and economic life the project constructs

Reznikoff's qualifying "almost" leaves open to question the extent of his authorial intervention, the availability of searchable electronic versions of the *Federal Reporter* makes it possible to locate at least some of Reznikoff's source material without spending hours searching through dusty volumes. In some instances, finding Reznikoff's sources can in turn have important implications for how we read the text. For instance, the text's final subsection, titled simply "*Depression*," opens with a fragment containing the following:

> In the middle of the night it was raining and thundering again. His wife woke up and found that he was gone. She didn't know where he could be. She got up and lit the lamp and waited an hour or so. At last she heard him on the attic stairs; he came into the room, dripping wet, the water running from his hair, and his nightgown pasted to his flesh. He had been up on top of the house. He said it was very nice on top of the house when it rained and the lightning flashed; he liked it. (pg. 580)

Searching the *Federal Reporter*, we find a case titled "Wolff v. Connecticut Mutual Life Insurance Company" from March 1879, in which the plaintiffs' claim on Henry Wolff's life insurance policy of $2000, rendered null by the insurance company due to Wolff's death by suicide, rests on their ability to prove his insanity. Quoted testimony by Wolff's wife reads:

> he got up in the middle of the night when it was raining and thundering. When I woke up he was off. I didn't know where he was. I got up and made the light and waited about an hour and then he came, and he had been up on top of the house and was all wet. I didn't know where he was, and I asked him and he said he had been on top of the house. He did that two or three times in one summer, the last summer of his life. He said it was very nice on top of the house when it rained; he liked it.[4]

---

in the fragments it shores. For accounts of Reznikoff's textual sources, see also Milton Hindus, "Epic, 'Action-Poem,' Cartoon: Charles Reznikoff's *Testimony: The United States: 1885-1915*," in *Charles Reznikoff: Man and Poet*, ed. Milton Hindus (Orono, ME: National Poetry Foundation, 1984), 309–26, and Linda Simon, "Reznikoff: The Poet as Witness," in *Charles Reznikoff: Man and Poet*, 233–50.

4. *The Federal Cases: Comprising Cases Argued and Determined in the Circuit and District Courts of the United States from the Earliest Times to the Beginning*

Reznikoff's text adds detail for dramatic effect—the water running from the man's hair, his nightgown "pasted to his flesh," the flashing lightning—yet the accounts are more or less the same in content. What Reznikoff's text does fail to provide, though, is precisely the kind of contextual information that would enable us to interpret the scene, or place it historically. In necessitating that the reader fill in the gaps, such omissions can have important consequences: rather than ending his text with a commentary on his Depression-era present, as the text's comparatively few critics have been led by the subsection's title to conclude, Reznikoff draws this material from the past, and more specifically, from the economic and personal aftermath of the Panic of 1873, which the text implicitly identifies as a precursor to the Depression of the 1930s.[5] This subsection's title—"*Depression*"—underscores the despair and anguish these passages of the text narrate; it also invokes the cyclicality of the boom-and-bust logic by which modern industrial capitalism functions, and thus the recursivity of history itself. In his original introduction, Burke describes the "Spenglerian despair" (pg. 533) casting its shadow over the text; it is perhaps more accurate to place *Testimony* within the historiographic tradition initiated by Van Wyck Brooks's 1918 call for a "usable past" from which the writers of the present might draw their materials. In its focus on anonymous, commonplace individuals as the agents of history, the text also bears comparison with the work of figures such as Charles and Mary Beard and Caroline Ware, who worked during the same period to establish the economic and cultural factors underlying national history.

The materials *Testimony* presents are gathered into three suggestively titled sections: "Of Southerners and Slaves," "Sailing-Ships and

---

of the Federal Reporter. Vol. 30 (Eagan, MN: West Publishing, 1897), 413. Accessed online at https://law.resource.org/pub/us/case/reporter/F.Cas/0030.f.cas/0030.f.cas.0413.2.html.

5. These critics include Matthew Sweney, who writes of this subsection of the text that "Reznikoff eventually delivers a verdict on his own period, the turbulent 1930s" ("Deposition: The First Testimony (1934)." *Sagetrieb* 13.1–2 [1992]: 217), and Michael Davidson, who claims that Reznikoff's use of the title "*Depression*" "extend[s]" his critique "into the economic hard times of the 1930s" (*Ghostlier Demarcations*, 160). Milton Hindus, too, notes that the "provenance of the initial volume of Testimony in the great Depression [*sic*] is quite clear" ("Epic, 'Action-Poem,' Cartoon," 322). It should be noted, however, that these critics are at least partially correct, in the sense that the "Depression" contemporary with Reznikoff's text serves as the immediate point of comparison for the material the text presents.

Steamers," and "East and West." Here the implication is that if planta-
tion slavery in the South, the shipping industry along the Eastern Sea-
bord, rapid industrialization in the North, and the nation's westward
expansion comprised the economic engines driving American mod-
ernization in the nineteenth century, these processes were not without
their collateral damage.[6] Where narratives of national historical prog-
ress gloss over the sordid details of anonymous personal suffering, the
vignettes presented in the text once again render such everyday forms
of misery legible: in *Testimony*, people are beaten, poisoned, stabbed
(and stab themselves), shot (and shoot themselves), flayed, whipped,
clubbed, torn apart by dogs, hacked to death with axes, drowned, dis-
membered, disemboweled, thrown from great heights. They contract
smallpox and yellow fever. They are abused and enslaved, held in
concubinage, conscripted, imprisoned, and forced to work against their
will. Yet for all its morbidity and despair, *Testimony* has its moments
of something approaching transcendence as well. *Testimony*'s most
potent effect is in the details: the burning book Jim dreams he holds in
his hands; the way the city glistens as Jacob, numb with cold, hobbles
ashore in New York as the good people, "stiff in their best," go about
their Christmas rituals; the way Frank Askin, "a handsome Irish lad
of seventeen," pleads for his life aboard an overburdened lifeboat in
the icy waters off Newfoundland, and the way his two sisters beg to
be thrown overboard with him when he is refused. The final subsec-
tion of "Sailing-Ships and Steamers," titled *"Rivers and Seas, Harbors
and Ports,"* stands out from the rest of the text; it is this section in
which, according to Burke's disparaging description, Reznikoff "give[s]
himself over to embellishment of the 'poetic' sort" (pg. 535), yet it is
this portion of the text, equally redolent of epic catalogue and of Walt
Whitman, where Reznikoff's collage is at its most seamlessly effec-
tive. In evocative prose paragraphs listing the names of ships and their
captains, the cargoes they carried, their far-flung destinations, and the

6. Simon notes that "Reznikoff's sources for *Testimony* were hundreds of volumes
in the *Reporter* series (these are published by region). . . . He looked particularly for
cases involving 'injury (death, assault, theft) due to primitive violence; injury due
to negligence, particularly those caused by machinery . . . , and unusual characters
or places—unusual and yet characteristic of the time.' These, he thought, would
illuminate the transition in America from an agricultural to an industrial society
and, presumably, the impact of that transition on particular individuals" (241).

conditions under which they sailed, Reznikoff's text effectively tells us more about shipping in the nineteenth century than reams of narrative prose ever could; here, too, the blood sacrifices presented in all their bare actuality elsewhere in the text are, if not redeemed, then at least accounted a place within a larger history.

Reznikoff would return much later in his career to the project he initiates here: subsequent texts bearing the same title and incorporating similar materials include the 1965 New Directions edition; a 1968 self-published edition; and the two volumes published by Black Sparrow in 1978 gathering these materials, and reprinted in this volume. (Reznikoff's 1975 long poem *Holocaust* would make use of a similar methodology in drawing on trial transcripts.) Despite its similarities to these texts in both process and content, and despite the fact that it shares its name with them, the 1934 *Testimony* stands on its own in terms of both the specific material it presents, which dates from a slightly earlier period, and its prose paragraph form; later instantiations of the *Testimony* franchise would lineate their materials. Perhaps surprisingly, then, given its centrality within Reznikoff's evolving oeuvre, as well as both "Objectivist" writing and Depression-era historiography, the 1934 *Testimony* was never reprinted, and thus critical accounts dealing specifically with it are few in number. In restoring the 1934 version of *Testimony* to print, the current edition thus makes the text available to scholars, students, and readers for the first time in eighty years. Readers conversant in modes of contemporary criticism including trauma theory and affect studies, and in Jacques Derrida's "hauntology" and Hayden White's ideas concerning the narrativization of history, will find resonances here; at the same time, the "conceptual turn" in experimental writing as practiced by Kenneth Goldsmith, Vanessa Place, and others will find an important precursor. *Testimony* is all of these things and none of them; its inconsistent, idiosyncratic nature betrays attempts to place it comfortably within established frameworks. It is precisely for this reason—*Testimony*'s ability to elude facile description—that the text will continue to find readers.

JUSTIN PARKS

Note

I glanced through several hundred volumes of old cases—not a great many as law reports go—and found almost all that follows.

C.R.

To Louis Zukofsky

CONTENTS

Introduction by Kenneth Burke

INTRODUCTION

The Matter of the Document

As the "scientific" quality of modern art came more and more into evidence, we began to note a progressive development of fiction towards the "case history." It is only recently that we have become aware of a complementary movement, the movement of the "case history" towards fiction. After having felt fairly well acquainted with the expressive maneuvers of the artist, I was nonetheless a bit uneasy on seeing two savants who, confident that their thesis was correct, but being asked to frame a popular presentation of it, patiently sat down to manufacture, out of their not very fertile fancies, the apt examples of Mr. X and Mr. Y and other hypothetical beings, with sparsely detailed lives sharply illustrative of what was to be demonstrated. Yet I had to admit that much the same principle of interpretation seemed to underlie both imaginative and "documentary" kinds of meaning.

The synthetic examples that were offered by the two savants served merely to make the position as clear as possible: they were "evidence" in the sense that a compelling metaphor is better evidence than a frail one. They were not concocted: they were "actual" experiences trimmed for the purposes at hand. They were deceptive, not in their general tenor, but simply in their "purity," their "efficiency." Being manufactured or refurbished cases, they could point more quickly and conclusively in the desired direction than fuller records could ever do, with all their ramifications and complications and "irrelevant" elements. In the end, any simplification of a human life is a fiction, and any case history is a simplification. And it is sometimes salutary for us to remind ourselves that even the vast "world-historical" perspectives of a Spengler may be at bottom but the "documentary substantiation" of an attitude as simple and moody as the lyric. Spengler is perhaps the ultimate instance of this process wherein a feeling or a metaphor is, by dint of industrious and ingenious selectivity, a tireless weighting of the evidence, given massive intellectual backing. His "morphology of history" is a poem, a pedant's dogged version of Shelley's Ozymandias, the *Stimmung* proper to one sonnet expanded into a life work, plus a military pessimism that led the author to interpret existence in terms of a struggle (misleadingly called *Werden*, or Becoming) which necessarily made good times look like a battlefield and peace like decay.

In these little pieces by Charles Reznikoff, which in their neatness and succinctness and swiftness of effect might at an earlier time have been called "vignettes," the scientific and fictive qualities of the "document" are both easily discernible. Mr. Reznikoff is a lawyer, and the genius of his calling is apparent in his work, correctly one of the first choices of a publishing venture which calls itself the "Objectivist Press." He gives us with great fidelity such a picture of the world as goes with the point of view of the law court. His profession itself providing the principle of selectivity, he could leave the matter of "truth" to the records as available.

"A few years ago," he has explained, "I was working for a publisher of law books, reading cases from every state and every year (since this country became a nation). Once in a while I could see in the facts of a case details of the time and place, and it seemed to me that out of such material the century and a half during which the United States has been a nation could be written up, not from the standpoint of an individual, as in diaries, nor merely from the angle of the unusual, as in newspapers, but from every standpoint—as many standpoints as were provided by the witnesses themselves." He felt that such material could encompass "the life of a people, in mines and on ships, all the activities that the law itself covers, which is pretty nearly everything." He felt that the work could fill "an entire encyclopedia," that "*Testimony* should be ten thousand times as large"; but in place of such a colossal undertaking, which would be as complex as the national life itself through all this period, he offers us this able distillation of his searches.

The result is worth much more than the "encyclopedia" would ever be. For I cannot imagine the more exhaustive project having the poignancy and the workmanship which run through the tales as here presented. In a direct style that frequently helps us to realize what Stendhal had in mind when expressing his enthusiasm for the Code Napoleon as a way of statement, he can contrive by a few hundred "factual" words to stir our feelings and our memories. And sometimes the bare recitals, devoid of "psychology," send us questing through our stock of psychoanalytic lore as no introspective accounts could do (though it must be recognized that Mr. Reznikoff here profits by the prior interpretative work of precisely those introspectionists whom he can abandon; to his externalities, we are equipped by other writers for supplying the internalities). In the large, however, his bare presentation of the records places us before people who appear in the meager simplicity of their complaints. They have grievances, they have brought these grievances before the law, whose abstract, forensic "justice" will often treat their problems in a manner wholly alien to the subjective quality of their distress. And one is made to feel very sorry for them, a humane response which far too much of our contemporary literature has neglected, with its overemphasis upon dominance, conquest, the attainment or frustration of "success."

At times Mr. Reznikoff does give himself over to embellishment of the "poetic" sort, as in his catalogue, "Rivers and Seas, Harbors and Ports." These efforts seem less effective in themselves, though they may serve to restore us for the pointedness of his more incisive manner. At other times his "objective" recital becomes a bit too artful in its understatement. And at still other times, he dwells on the gruesome aspect of his cases, though readers at home in our contemporary murder mysteries may not feel this as an objection. But again and again the most valuable quality of his work, his sensitiveness of appraisal, his deftness and accuracy in narrative, comes to the fore—and it is for this that I believe his "vignettes" should be received.

As for his hopes to present the material of life "from every standpoint—as many standpoints as were provided by the witnesses themselves," they raise an issue for not one critic, but many critics, to decide. I have suggested that the material is largely presented from but *one* standpoint, the standpoint of the law court, the "objectivity" of "the evidence," objective in the sense that the writer has given himself to the authority of the material which the court has furnished him, but "subjective," or "selective," or "interpretative," or "biased" in that the law court provides its own principle of selectivity. Whatever individual standpoints they may represent, be they plaintiff or defendant, interested or disinterested witness, slave or slave-owner, brutal sea-captain or recorders of his brutality, these bearers of testimony represent in the large the "law court point of view." In this respect Mr. Reznikoff's work embodies in miniature the problem of the "whole truth" as it arises in a civilization marked by many pronounced differences in occupational pattern. There arise the "doctor's point of view," the "accountant's point of view," the "salesman's point of view," the "minister's point of view," the "mechanic's point of view," and so on. Much of Mr. Reznikoff's "testimony" is clearly local to his profession; but the vein of sympathy that underlies his work is not similarly local. It is to this quality perhaps, and not to the documentary aspect of his work, that we must look for its measure of ultimate "truth," that is, its usefulness to living.

KENNETH BURKE

SOUTHERNERS AND SLAVES

OF MURDER

1

Dun had been down to a sunken boat, and was coming back in his skiff about dark when he met Broadus and Lucas. He got out of his skiff, and went with them in theirs. He came back at one o'clock and when he got into bed, asked his wife where Elizabeth was. She was in the other bed in the room, but asleep, said Dun's wife, because she had called her and she did not answer. Dun then told his wife that they had shot "Dutch," but had not killed him. "Dutch" was picking up wood when he was shot, and he ran and hallooed to those in the house, and cried out, "Boys, I am shot!" Broadus, the damned fool, ran and left his hat.

Elizabeth was "setting" in the gallery with Dun and his wife, Broadus, Lucas, and a man named Curtis. They saw John Williams coming up the road with a gun on his shoulder. When in sight of the house, he left the road and started across the field. Dun took his gun and ran across the field towards Williams. Williams ran also. After a short time Dun and Williams came back to the house together, and Dun said, "By God, boys, I got a prisoner."

Williams shook hands with the company and then called for liquor, and said he was never so frightened in his life as when he saw Dun coming after him. They all drank together. Lucas said to Williams, "I understand you have offered sixty dollars to know whose hat was left when 'Dutch' was shot."

Williams said, "I did."

Lucas then said, "Would you give it now?" Williams said no, for he had spent some of the money. Lucas then asked Williams what he would do if he knew who "done" it.

"I would bring them to justice."

Curtis said, "By God, Dun, he belongs to the strong party."

Dun said, "Yes, we must look out."

Lucas and Broadus then began to pick a quarrel with Williams, but he said he had never had a quarrel with any man, and hoped he never should, although he was no better to catch a load of shot than anybody else. Dun remarked, "You had better take care or you may catch one before you are ready for it."

After a while Williams said that he was going to Askew's for honey, bid them good day, and started up the road. Broadus took his gun and went off in the same direction. Elizabeth was standing on the back porch, and Broadus looking round saw her. He stopped, came to the house, went up on the porch, and beckoned to Lucas. Lucas took up Dun's gun. The gun was at the door of the bar-room; Dun was sitting on the counter, his face towards the door. Broadus and Lucas went in the direction Williams had gone, and, a little way from the house, both began to run.

Elizabeth heard a gun fire, and said to Dun, "They are killing that man."

Dun said, "No, they are only trying their guns."

Elizabeth heard another gun and again said, "They are certainly killing that man." Dun said, no, they were only trying their guns to let him know what they would do if he did not leave the neighborhood.

Broadus and Lucas were back in a short time. Broadus came dancing around Elizabeth, who was on the porch, and asked if she thought he would kill a man. She answered, yes, she believed he would and had. He said, no, he had not and would not. Broadus, Lucas, Curtis, Dun and his wife went into the bar-room. Elizabeth tried to go in too, but found the door locked.

Soon after, her father came for her. As she was about to leave, Dun came up to her and said, "Elizabeth, if ever you tell what you have seen and heard here this day, I'll hear of it and it will not be well for you." About half a mile above Dun's they saw Williams lying on the bank of the river, moaning and screaming.

Thomas Lacy had been working in his field when he heard the firing of a gun, but he paid no heed to it. In a little while, his neighbor, Pledger, called to him to come and see a man lying near the road and making a great noise. They supposed he was drunk until they lifted him and saw two bullet holes in his back and blood on his clothes.

Williams asked for water, which they gave him, and said he wanted to go to Mr. Dodge's, who lived below Dun's, and that he would give one hundred and fifty dollars to any one who would take him there in a boat. But this no one—several had come up—wanted to do.

Williams crawled down to the water, untied a canoe that was there, and got in. The boat drifted down the river until it was beached on a sand-bar along the other side, where no one lived, and Williams crawled out and died.

2

John Wilson and his younger brother, Cumberland, were cutting timber on a ridge in the woods when Ballentine came up. He had a rifle and a squirrel which he had shot, said that it was hot weather for cutting sticks, and left, going over the ridge. Later, he came out of the woods, and stood watching them.

John Wilson, sitting on the top log, turned his face to the team. The front pair of oxen had started, but the others were still standing. Cumberland Wilson was just rising to tell Ballentine good-by, when he saw him with his rifle up, the breach of it under his shoulder and the muzzle aimed at John. That instant Ballentine fired and Cumberland saw the smoke rising from Ballentine's gun. John Wilson put his right hand to his breast and said, "Lord of Mercy!" The blood gushed from his mouth and nose. Ballentine began to run away; he ran ten steps or so, stopped, and looked John Wilson in the face. The dying man bowed his head and Ballentine ran on.

3

Ely, his master's driver, had a fish-trap. Sunday afternoon, Cicero, a boy of fifteen, and Ely went to the lake together, and stayed there about half an hour, fixing the trap. On the way home, about a quarter of a mile from the lake, just as the negroes had passed a large tree, they heard a pistol shot. Cicero and Ely both looked back and saw Taylor, a fellow slave, one of the plowmen, coming from behind the tree, with a blue, double-barreled pistol. Taylor laughed and said he had scared Ely.

Taylor bantered Ely to wrestle with him. Ely would not, but Taylor gathered him around the body and threw him down. After wrestling for some time, Ely called to Cicero to get some switches and whip Taylor. Cicero caught hold of Taylor's legs to pull him off, but Taylor cursed him and kicked him in the belly. Ely took hold of a bush and pulled himself up. They kept on wrestling until they got down a hill, when Taylor threw Ely on his face and cried out, "Come on, I've got him!"

Ned, another plowman, now ran up with an ax in his hands. Ely cried to Ned not to kill him. Ned did not answer, but, holding the ax in both hands, struck Ely with the sharp edge across the upper lip. The ax broke the teeth and left the lip hanging at one end. Ned then turned the ax in his hands and struck Ely on the back of the head with the eye of the ax and broke his skull.

Ned took up the body by the head and shoulders and Taylor by the feet. Blood was still dripping from the head. They laid the body on a log beside the lake. They went along the shore for a boat; rowing the body out, they tied a bag of stones to it and threw it into the water. Then they washed the blood from the boat and the log, and covered up the blood on the ground with leaves.

4

Jim went to Ranty's to get a dram and found him in his garden. He asked Ranty if there was any liquor in the house for he had chills. Ranty had no liquor. Jim then said to Ranty, "If you've got a picayune, I have another, and we can go down to old Louis and get whiskey."

Ranty said that old Louis was saucy—said he would shoot Ranty if he caught him about the place again; but Ranty would get the whiskey. They took a jug and a spade. Jim walked behind Ranty stepping in his tracks.

Ranty went into the store and hit the old man twice on the head with the spade. The old man cried, "Oh, oh!" Ranty went out and got a knife from Jim to stab the old man saying he had done so much, he would do more and end it. He stabbed Louis three or four times and then got whiskey from the big jug, took some money from Louis' cap, and some from over the door, and some from under a mattress.

Ranty went through the marsh barefoot so as not to show his tracks. He stepped from turf to turf. Jim walked behind him stepping in his prints until they came to the "piney" woods.

When Jim was put in jail he dreamed a dream, and then he knew he would be hanged. He dreamed that his two hands were tied together, and were on fire; there was a book hung before them—it had a leather cover just like the one they swore him on at the trial—the book caught fire and all the leaves were burning.

5

The body was in a clump of post-oak bushes, ten or twelve feet from the road, the left foot over the right one. It was on its back. From the eyes down all the face was gone, the face bones were gone, and the brains had been eaten out of the skull by the hogs. The hogs were eating the body when it was found. There was plenty of blood under the head, in the clothes, and on the ground, but no other wounds on the body, except where the hogs had broken the skin of the fingers.

TWO LETTERS

1

Kelly's horses were conjured so that they would not plow. He could not fish much—the witches would not let him. His gun was bewitched so that he could not shoot a squirrel. But he made a good crop, working oxen, worked eight or ten hands, and made twenty-one bales or so of cotton. He never talked foolishly about business, but he blamed whatever went wrong on witches—sickness of negroes and bad stands of cotton. He would tell of being led out of his house backwards by the conjurers. Some of those to whom he spoke would try to persuade him that all the witches were put to death by Saul, but Kelly did not believe it: the witches that troubled him, he said, were descendants of the Witch of Endor.

He was said to be a fine historian: he had read the history of the United States and the history of the world. He could tell about King Richard—"how they used to do in their tournaments," about Richard III and Richard IV, Richard V and Richard VI, "big men and ruled over the people." Richard III, he said, rode in a tournament, but he was an old assassin, and had been the means of Queen Elizabeth's death. Kelly had fully half a dozen books. He had a Bible, but did not believe in it: said it contradicted itself about the river Euphrates.

He wrote to a friend: "The conjuring creatures have got me at such a pass that I can't go in my plantation. I have been plagued by one and overpowered by the other. Great God deliver this world of conjuring devils! You are old and heavy, but I want you to get some one to go over and see them people.

"We have a man in Granada teaching conjure school. They say he can make a man or woman puke at his pleasure. Some of the wags say it will be a fine thing for those who have scolding wives as they can now still their tongues.

"It is locked up in perfect darkness yet, and I expect that I have spent twenty years from then till now thinking about it. The last two years the bale worm eat up my cotton; this year the grass and drouth. But, alas! she won't let me alone now night nor day, and distance makes no difference. Are there no devils left in hell?"

2

"My dearest Uncle, I have formed a firm resolution, which I promise you I will do all in my power to keep. I know you will be rejoiced to hear it. It is, that I am not going to read another novel; and I trust in that power that doeth all things well. For I found that I cannot be a novel-reader and anything else. So great an influence have these ficti-tious tales on my mind, that I cannot be as a rational being under their influence. I would not be a novel-reader for the world. Such contempt have I for novel-readers, I intend reading all the histories that I can obtain and all valuable works of the distinguished authors.

"We have not had a great deal of fun this vacation; but, once in a while, we got a nice watermelon, and would slip off in the yard and eat it. Miss Swett does not allow us to buy things from the servants; and we have to steal off so she will not find it out. One evening we all went down to the farthest corner of the yard, where the grass is quite tall, and while we were giggling and eating three fine watermelons, we saw a snake crawling from under the dress of one of the girls. I guess we squalled then, and run.

"How my heart grows sick at the idea of leaving school in five months. Can it be possible that I am no longer to be a wild prattling school-girl? Yes, 'tis even so. I am to quit the old academy a young lady. A young lady, indeed. What foolishness is implied in that little word—*lady*. 'Tis all folly. Yes, all the world is folly and vanity. And all the human race are actors on the stage of life.

"I have a very dear friend here. She is a dear, sweet girl; the sweetest girl I most ever saw, and I love her better. She belongs to the Baptist Church. We are warm friends, always together. I was exceedingly amused today to hear some one hint that we must have brothers, and policy made us such friends. They are mistaken. She has only two brothers, both younger than herself."

OF SLAVES

1

Mosser, her master, seemed fond of the mulatto and was often in the kitchen with her when she was cooking, and she was often in his store. One morning, Martha Wood, the housekeeper, saw her come out of the store with some white homespun which she said her master had given her. Martha Wood went to the door of Mosser's room, and saw for the third time where two had been lying on the bed and two headings.

Martha Wood told Mosser that she was going away. He asked her what was the matter, and she answered that Holland, the mulatto girl, would not mind anything she said to her, and sometimes Holland would not speak to her, and when she said anything was so, Holland would say it was not so.

Mosser called Holland into the house, and asked her what was the matter between her and Mrs. Wood. She answered, "Nothing."

Mrs. Wood then said that when she said anything was so, Holland would say it was not so. Holland replied that she did not say so, and flirted out of the room with a great air.

2

Mr. Newton Smith had, a few weeks before, come from New Orleans were he had gone to buy a mulatto negress—good-looking and sprightly. (It was said that all his mulatto negresses were his concubines, and that one of them had threatened to poison his wife and had poisoned his first wife.)

Josephine had seemed unwilling to leave New Orleans. She had cried and "taken on considerably." Some of the negroes in the slave-yard, she said, had stolen her jewelry. However, she did not move about at Mr. Smith's house with the sprightliness she had shown in New Orleans.

One of Mr. Smith's negroes, George, had been sick for two or three years of a rheumatic fever. He did not work in the fields, but was set to do little jobs about the house and the yard. On Sunday, his master ordered the overseer to tell George to go to laying off corn-rows the next morning. When the overseer did so, George answered that he was sick and unable to work and that his master was tighter on him than ever before and that the overseer was the cause of it: he grumbled, but not more than negroes who have been indulged a great deal usually do—so the overseer thought, and he did not refuse to lay off the corn-rows.

About nine or ten o'clock at night, Josephine went to George's cabin to carry him supper. George said that he was sick and that the overseer had ordered him to lay off corn-rows next morning and that he could not do it, that his master had been getting tighter on him than he had ever been and the new overseer was the cause of it, that it was his master's day then but it would be George's after a while.

George got up and went to his chest to look for some tobacco he had there. After rummaging about for some time, he came from the chest with a vial in his hand, showed it to Josephine and said, "Here is some stuff, either ratsbane or strychnine—I do not know which."

Josephine said, "Let me look at it, Uncle George." A small part of the label was still on the vial and she tried to spell out the word on it; she could not make out all the letters but thought she could read "arsenic." George said he had found the vial with the white stuff in it on the road and had had it for a long time. He had shown it to Mr. Dixon who had been Mr. Smith's overseer and had asked him what he should do with it. It would kill rats, but he had no use for it.

"Give it to me," Josephine said, and with that put it into her pocket.

George was sick next morning; he had fever, and was not put to laying off corn-rows. A day or so after, he was at work fixing the palings around the yard, and the negroes who worked in the fields were planting potatoes up the river, above the garden. Josephine was in the kitchen—she had been the cook since she came.

Breakfast had been badly cooked, and Mrs. Smith talked mildly to Josephine about it, but she answered saucily. Mrs. Smith told her husband and he gave Josephine a slight whipping. Shortly afterwards, Mrs. Smith went to the kitchen and called Josephine. She did not answer, turned her back on Mrs. Smith, made a face at her, and knocked over a chair. Mrs. Smith then got the overseer to whip her. She was vexed and sulky afterwards, throwing her head around to her shoulder to see a cut made by the whipping. In an hour or two, Mrs. Smith went to the kitchen and asked Josephine to go with her to the smoke-house to get out dinner. This Josephine did, and then she seemed in good humor.

Mr. Smith, his wife, their little daughter Lucinda, about a year and a half old, his son by his first marriage, and a Mr. Forbes were having dinner. Josephine told Maria, the girl who helped her, to ask their mistress if she wanted tea. Mrs. Smith poured out a cup of the tea and handed it to Lucinda's nurse, and the baby drank of it. Mr. and Mrs. Smith had taken a few sups of the tea, when their little daughter began to vomit. Mr. Smith took the child into another room, and began to vomit himself. Mrs. Smith had a burning and cramp in her stomach, a retching in her throat and great thirst, but she kept trying to give her child oil and milk. The baby was so sick and vomited so much froth, she could swallow nothing, and was growing worse.

All their negroes were about the house and in the yard. The doors were open and towards evening fires were lit in the room. (Afterwards, the pieces of a vial were found in the fireplace in Mr. Forbes' room, the glass a little fused.) The negro women were bothering Josephine and charged her with the poisoning; they were asking her why she did it. At last she said, "For God's sake, hush! you all keep more fuss about it than the white folks. I am not the first that has done such a thing by ten thousand."

3

Sophia had been a good and obedient house-servant, devoted to her children. When her mistress gave her time, she would make clothes and knit for them. One evening, when Mrs. Rockett, who had just been married and lived twenty miles or so away, was about to leave her mother's house after a visit, she said to her mother, Sophia's mistress,

"Mother, I wish you would let me have one of those little negroes," pointing to Sophia's eldest boy, Douglass, and several other little ones.

Mrs. May answered, "Daughter, what do you want with it?"

"Why, it can pick up chips and be company for me," and she took Douglass away with her.

Sophia was no longer good and obedient, and her master sold her to a neighbor. Another neighbor, Mr. Gentry, found her one day in the woods. She had run away and he took her home. She walked slowly, but when he said he would whip her or she was afraid she would be ridden against by Mr. Gentry's horse, she walked faster. She said she had run away because she wanted to go to her children.

She would talk to herself and laugh without any one speaking to her as she worked in the fields. She was stubborn and unfriendly, and when she was scolded for it, said she wanted to go to her children; and she ran away time and again. At last her master sold her to Mr. Spencer, and she ran away again.

Spencer caught her and chained her. He asked her why she had run away, and she told him she wanted to go to her children. "I will show those legs," Spencer said, "they shall not run away from me." He had her stripped and staked down on the ground: her feet and hands spread and tied to the stakes, her face downward. Mr. Spencer was calm and took his time; he whipped her from time to time with a plaited buckskin lash about fifteen inches long. He drew some blood, but not a great deal, and then he took salt and a cob and salted her back with it.

4

Ranty had been caught without a pass by a patrol in the town of Camden, about a half-mile from his master's house, and Howe, under orders of the captain, had whipped him. The next morning, while Howe and two other white boys were going through the suburbs of the town, he passed Ranty. The slave greeted him rudely and followed the boys into town, talking loudly and insolently to Howe.

Howe told him to go away and threw a chip at him, but did not hit him. Ranty kept on talking angrily, saying among other things, "I don't see what business school-boys have to patrol, anyway," until Howe threw a piece of a wagon-felloe, about three inches long, at him, and then a piece of a buggy-shaft with a part of the cross-bar fastened to it, but did not hit him.

Ratcliffe, at work in his carriage shop as they passed, came to the door because of the loud and angry talking, and handed Howe a buggy whip, telling him to take it and whip Ranty. Ranty took up the piece of buggy-shaft, which Howe had thrown at him, and he and Howe started towards each other—then twelve or fifteen feet apart—and met about half-way. Howe struck Ranty around the body with the whip, and Ranty struck him on the forehead with the piece of buggy-shaft.

5

The negro had been chased for two miles in a summer day by negro dogs. He was found in the bayou, up to his chin in the water, with a scythe blade in his hand. This, at the bidding of the man after him, he threw to the water's edge, and came out. As he did so, the white man struck him upon the head with the heavy butt of a whip, and the dogs jumped upon him and began to bite him.

6

In the fall, Francis Troutman, who had been told that his grandfather's run-away slaves were in Marshall, Michigan, went there to find and arrest them. He had Dickson, a deputy sheriff of the county, come with him and his companions, Ford and Lee, to the home of the slaves. As they walked up the path to the door, Adam Crosswhite and his son Johnson, two of the run-aways, ran out. One went to the left and the other to the right, but they were followed, and, overtaken, came back to the house.

Francis Troutman went into the house and told the family he had come to take them before Squire Sherman to prove that they belonged to David Giltner. Hearing this, Adam Crosswhite tried to leave the house again, but Troutman blocked his way. He asked the family to get ready. Adam slowly put a cloak about his little girl, and said the weather was cold and the family could not walk to Squire Sherman's. Troutman answered that a wagon would be hired.

Adam, in Dickson's charge, went to see a lawyer in another part of the village, and Troutman stayed in the house. Before Adam was back, several men came in. Planter Morse, a negro, hurrying into the house said the family should not be taken; he pulled off his coat and said he would get into the fight. At that Adam came in and Morse told him not to go—he and others would stand by him and drive off the kidnapers. Adam went to a drawer and took out of it what Troutman supposed to be a knife and a powder-horn. Morse drew his knife and, making believe that he was using it on Troutman, said that was what he would do, if they tried to take the Crosswhites away.

Others were coming to the house. Hackett, one of the colored men, came up to Troutman, who was standing at the door, and asked what he was doing. He answered that he was doing what the law authorized him to do. Hackett said he would see about that and tried to get into the house. Troutman told him to stand back. Hackett's hand was in his pocket. Troutman again told him to stand back and drew a pistol, which he held in his hand but did not lift as if to fire, and Hackett stepped back.

Another colored man, James Smith, went towards them crying out, "Where are the Kentuckians who are trying to kidnap the Crosswhite family?" Troutman was pointed out to him, and Smith, with a lifted club, came within five or six feet of Troutman, saying that he would smash out his brains. Dickson took hold of him and, with the help of one or two others, led him away, Smith still saying that he would smash and welt the Kentuckians.

Then Charles Berger, a colored man, with a stone weighing from four to six pounds, said he would smash Troutman. Dickson took the stone from him and led him aside, though he still stayed about, holding a knife in his pocket, the handle of which Troutman could see. And still another colored man, William Parker, came up with a gun, shouting that he would risk his life that the Crosswhites should not be taken.

It was now about eight o'clock in the morning. One hundred or more men and boys had gathered, fifteen or twenty of whom were blacks or mulattoes. The white men and boys were talking and laughing, and egging on the others.

Gorham, a white man, said, "You have come after our citizens." Troutman answered that he had come as the agent of their owner to take them before a magistrate to prove the right to their services. Gorham said, "You can't have them—this is a free country and they are free." Gorham advised him not to take the negroes: "There is a great deal of danger in trying to take them"; and he added, "We will not allow them to be taken."

The wagon to carry the Crosswhites to Squire Sherman was driven near the house. Troutman announced that he was taking them before the magistrate. Combstock, a white man, shouted, "You cannot have the negroes!"

Troutman, looking him full in the face, asked, "Why not?"

Combstock, pointing to the crowd, said, "You see it will be dangerous," and then said, "You can't take them by moral, physical, or legal force, and you might as well know it first as last, and the quicker you leave the ground, the better for you."

Gorham took up Combstock's words and offered the following resolution: "Resolved, that these Kentuckians shall not take the Crosswhite family by virtue of moral, physical, or legal force." This was passed by acclamation and with much cheering.

Troutman, taking a note-book from his pocket, said that he wanted the names of all responsible persons who would stop him from taking the slaves. Gorham in a loud voice said that they came there by public sentiment to see that he did not take the slaves, that public sentiment was above the law, and that they would not let their citizens be taken away to slavery. He then gave his name and asked that it might be put down in capitals and taken back as a beacon to the land of slavery. Combstock also gave his name in full, Oliver Cromwell Combstock, Junior, adding the "Junior," he said, that his father might not be held for his acts.

Troutman then asked Dickson, the deputy sheriff, to summon Gorham, Combstock and others to help keep the peace, while he and his friends seized the negroes—some of the slaves were in the house, others among the crowd. But Dickson and Troutman's companions thought nothing more could be done.

Then Troutman turned to the crowd and asked if he might not offer a resolution: "Resolved that as peaceable citizens we will abide by the Constitution and the laws of our country and that I, Francis Troutman, of Carroll County, Kentucky, be permitted peaceably to take the Crosswhite family before Sherman, a justice of the peace, that I may make proof of property in the slaves, and take them to Kentucky." He heard only jeers and booing. He then said that if they let him take the slaves before the magistrate, and if he proved the right to their services, and got a certificate, he would give the citizens of the town time to raise money to pay a reasonable price for the slaves, and he himself would contribute more than any one.

Gorham replied, "You can't have a schilling for them!"

Two other white men, Herd and Easterly, who seemed to be the leaders although they had said nothing, and Gorham now talked among themselves a short time. Then Herd, standing outside the gate before the path to the house, said in a loud voice, "Resolved that these Kentucky gentlemen, if such they may be called, leave town in two hours."

Some one in the crowd added, "Or they shall be tarred and feathered and rode on a rail."

But Herd went on, "Or they shall be prosecuted for kidnaping or housebreaking."

Dickson flatly refused to execute the warrant and arrest the slaves. Troutman turned to Gorham, "You have the advantage of me now, but I can not tell how it will end."

Gorham said that he knew how it would end: the negroes would be gone and Troutman could never get them. Troutman and his companions walked away. It was clear now that Adam Crosswhite and his family would not be taken; the crowd stood about for a while, talking and laughing, and began to leave.

SAILING-SHIPS AND STEAMERS

WATER AND ICE

1

Jacob Robinson was the cabin-boy on a schooner. He had no mittens, neither woolen nor cotton, nor thick socks; he had a woolen shirt, but no heavy frock. Off the coast, nearing New York on the way from Curaçao, the weather became stormy. The cook was placed at one of the pumps and Jacob at the other. The waves burst over the deck and he was often knee-deep in the freezing water.

At dawn the schooner was in the bay. Jacob's feet were numb and he could hardly hobble about. As the ship went up the river to her wharf, the sky became clear and blue; and, except where the shadows of houses and smoking chimneys were on the snow, the white roofs and streets of the city glistened.

Jacob was left alone on the ship. Suddenly the church bells began to ring, for it was Christmas day. His sister's house, from which he had run away, was only a few blocks off. He hobbled and crawled—with bare hands in the snow—through the streets along which cheerful people, stiff in their best, were beginning to walk.

2

Holmes, a Finn by birth, was first mate on the William Brown. The ship made Liverpool without mishap, and left in March for Philadelphia. She had on board a crew of seventeen and sixty-five passengers, Scotch and Irish emigrants.

About two hundred and fifty miles south of Cape Race, Newfoundland, at about ten o'clock at night, the William Brown struck an iceberg and began to fill quickly. The long boat and the jolly boat were cleared away and lowered. The master, Holmes, and the second mate, seven of the crew and one passenger were in the jolly boat, the rest of the crew and thirty-two passengers in the long boat. In this was a Scotswoman, a widow, with her two daughters. As the boat was veering astern, it was found that another daughter, who was sick, had been left behind.

Her mother was calling, "Isabel, Isabel, come!" Holmes climbed up the ship's side, and, hoisting the sick girl upon his shoulders, ran astern and swung himself and her by the tackle into the long boat below.

The other passengers, thirty-one of them, were left on the ship. In an hour and a half she went down, settling towards her head, and those in the boats could hear across the water those on board shrieking. In the morning the men and women in the long boat found themselves alone on the sea, except for the iceberg which had sunk the ship, standing against the blue sky, dazzling white. The jolly boat had parted company with them in the night.

As soon as the long boat was in the water, it had begun to leak, and the passengers were set to bailing with buckets and tins. In the morning Holmes saw that the gunwale was five to twelve inches from the water, and that the boat might be quickly swamped. Luckily, there was little or no wind. The passengers were half-naked, crowded together, and a sudden movement by some of them might capsize the boat. Pieces of ice were floating about and if struck, the boat would go down.

The crew rowed and the passengers bailed. They had food and water for six or seven days—seventy-five pounds of bread, eight or ten pounds of meat, and six gallons of water. The passengers were almost benumbed with cold. Holmes gave one of the old women his woolen shirt, and had on only his undershirt and pantaloons. He asked the men of the crew what to do, and decided that he ought not to steer for Newfoundland; they would never reach it, but should go south—it would be warmer and they might meet with a vessel.

Next morning it began to rain. At night the wind began to freshen, the sea grew heavier, and the waves splashed over the boat's bows so as to wet the passengers seated there. During the day icebergs had been seen, and ice was still floating about. The boat had a great deal of water in it. At about ten o'clock at night, Holmes, who had been bailing for some time, gave it up and said, "This won't do; men, go to work." The men of the crew sat still. Holmes said, "You must go to work or we shall all drown."

The first man thrown out was one Riley. Holmes and the others told him to stand up. He did, and they threw him over the gunwale. Then they came to Charles Conlin, and he said, "Holmes dear, sure you won't put me out."

"Yes, Charlie," said Holmes, "you must go too," and he was thrown over.

Frank Askin, a handsome Irish lad of seventeen, offered Holmes five sovereigns to spare his life until morning, "when if God don't send us some help, we'll draw lots and if the lot falls on me, I'll go over like a man." His two sisters were in the boat and they begged for his life, and asked to be thrown over in his stead.

Holmes said, "I don't want your money, Frank," and took hold of him. He began to struggle, and the others thought the boat would be turned over. They threw him overboard at last.

His sisters began to beg that they might be thrown after him "to die the death of their brother." "Give me only a dress to put around me," said one, "and I care not now to live longer." They were lifted up and flung overboard.

After daylight, two men, stiff with cold, who had hidden themselves or crept under some clothes to warm themselves, were thrown over. In all, sixteen persons were put overboard, fourteen men and the two sisters of Frank Askin. Soon afterwards, the weather cleared, and early in the morning they sighted a ship.

Holmes saw the Crescent's mast several minutes before anybody else did, and raised a shawl at the end of an oar. The second mate of the Crescent happened to be aloft looking for ice. As the ship, in answer to the signal, put about, a cry of joy burst from those in the long boat. Some were crawling up the sides to see the ship coming towards them, and others, who had seemed frozen stiff, now stood up. "Lie down, lie down," said Holmes, "and be still. If they make out so many of us on board, they will steer off another way and make believe they have not seen us."

3

The largest ship afloat left Liverpool for New York with more than four hundred passengers and about four hundred officers and crew—engineers, firemen, servants, and others. Two days afterwards, she ran into a storm which swept away her paddle-wheels and several of her boats. Her screw or propeller, however, was unhurt and by this she made good headway.

That evening she fell into the trough of the sea and rolled so as to carry from side to side all that was movable on her deck and in her cabins. Much of the furniture was broken up and the luggage of the passengers was soaked and crushed into rubbish. At night it was found that her rudder shaft, which was of wrought iron, had been twisted off below the steering gear, and the ship, as if her rudder were gone, was helpless, rolling heavily with every swell.

The rudder shaft went through a compartment known as the "steerage deck." About the shaft, in this "steerage deck," was a ribbed iron cone, the base of which rested on iron balls—these ran in a groove, sunk in an iron plate which was the floor. The cone was fastened to the shaft so that the two revolved as one piece of iron, and a large nut, screwed down on the head of the cone, kept it in place upon the balls. The shaft had broken off just below the top of this nut, and the chief engineer was unscrewing it to fasten, if possible, a tiller upon the broken shaft.

His men had partly unscrewed the nut, though it was hard work, for the nut and shaft turned with every blow of the sea on the rudder blade, when a Mr. Towle, an American engineer on board, learned of what they were doing. Mr. Towle was afraid that if the nut were unscrewed, the rudder would be lost; and he made a sketch of his plan for steering the ship; but when he tried to speak to the chief engineer, he was ordered out of the "steerage deck."

Mr. Towle went to the captain. The captain had tried winding chains around the cone on the shaft; and he had rigged a spar over the stern of the ship, but this also did not work. By unscrewing the nut an inch the rudder had fallen half as far; and the chief engineer would be unable, so he said, to fit the tiller to the shaft under three or four days. The captain gave Mr. Towle all the men he needed.

They went to the "steerage deck" late Saturday afternoon, and screwed the nut back again after three hours. To do so, they hung from the upper deck by chains a spanner or wrench, weighing one hundred and thirty pounds, and held it to the nut, and as each blow of the sea on the rudder blade drove the shaft around, the nut was brought down on the thread.

They brought from the forward part of the ship a chain that weighed about sixty pounds to the link, and let it down into the "steerage deck" through a hole cut above it. Though the cone turned with the shaft and the swell of the sea kept the cone always turning, they managed to wind around it enough of the great chain to make a cylinder or drum. The links on the inner coil sank in between the ribs of the cone, keeping the chain from slipping and easing the strain on the lashings—the links were lashed to each other and to the base of the cone by smaller chains. The ends of the great chain were then carried to two strong posts or bitts which came up through the "steerage deck," a turn taken around each, and the ends joined to tackles. These were fastened to the sides of the ship and manned for taking up the slack and easing away as the wheel might turn the rudder shaft. Smaller chains, fastened between the bitts and the cylinder or drum, joined the great chain to the wheel—the size of the shackles such that a break would be in them, not in the great chain or its lashings.

The men worked during Saturday night and Sunday; and late Sunday afternoon, the ship was brought up to the sea and put upon her course.

4

The South Ferry boat left her berth at Whitehall between five and six o'clock in the evening for Atlantic Street in Brooklyn. She had on board five to six hundred passengers, besides as many teams as could be taken. The trip lasted, usually, seven or eight minutes.

The night was bitter cold. The East River was full of broken ice, carried by the flood tide against the Brooklyn shore. After the ferryboat had gone about two-thirds of the way, she found the ice so solid she could not push through to the Atlantic Street dock. She drifted with the tide up the river and tried to go into the Montague Street dock, but could not. She then went to the Fulton Street dock, but, on reaching it, two or three hours after she had left Manhattan, met with a large block of ice. The tide and the running ice swung her stern up the river, and brought it against the bow of a schooner, breaking the jib-boom and bowsprit.

COLLISION

1

The Almatia left San Domingo on August 31st with a crew of seven. The boy was not well when the schooner sailed, but he kept about until after they were over the bar; then he went to his bunk. When the ship was well outside and everything set, the master left the wheel and went below to see him. The boy seemed to have a fever. It proved to be yellow fever, and the boy died the seventeenth day out.

The ordinary seaman was taken down the evening after the ship sailed, and the master the next day. On the fourth day out both able seamen were taken sick, and the last seaman the day after the boy died. The mate was the only well man aboard.

By the night of September 22nd the ship was beating in to New York. The weather was fine and the moon shining brightly. The mate was alone on deck. All sails were set, except the outer jib, and the fore-sail had a reef in it. The mate had set the gaff topsail alone two days before. The other sails had been set a long time.

About three o'clock in the morning, the mate who had been on deck for thirty hours navigating the ship alone, went below and called one of the seamen, who seemed to be better than the others. He ordered the seaman to come up and steer, while he went into the cabin to get a little sleep.

The man had strength enough to keep the Almatia steady on her course, with the weather as it was, but could do little more. He was told to call the mate at daybreak, or before, if he saw anything, and to keep the course the ship was then on, steering by the wind.

The mate went into the cabin and lay down on the floor to sleep, about twelve feet from the man at the wheel. It was too cold to lie on the deck. The master was in his berth, unable to sleep because of his worry about the ship. After the mate had been asleep about half an hour, he was awakened by a faint call from the man at the wheel and went at once on deck.

The man at the wheel, too weak to speak, pointed to a ship near by. The mate went to the leeward, and, seeing the ship and her red light a few lengths away, ordered the wheel to port, and ran to help put it over, for the man was too weak to do it alone. The master had heard

the call from the man at the wheel and crawled on his hands and knees
to the deck, but was too weak to help or even sit up. As soon as the
wheel was over, the mate ran and let go the main sheet, but the Alma-
tia struck the other ship almost head on, at the mizzen rigging.

2

The day was clear. About ten o'clock in the morning, Jones and his
son were in a skiff. The steamer at the time was leaving the wharf,
loaded down with cattle, hides, and passengers. It had been lying stern
outward and had first to back out. The skiff was becalmed; Jones and
his son got their oars out to pull, and Jones called as loudly as he could,
"For God's sake stop the steamer—I can't get out of the way!"

One of the passengers called to the pilot, "Stop the boat; there's a
little boat right ahead!"

A voice from the pilot-house answered, "Damn the little boat!" The
bell, however, was rung to stop the engine. Several of the passengers
called to those in the skiff to jump overboard. The steamer could not be
checked from striking it; the skiff filled with water and sank. Jones and
his son were drawn toward the wheel which was still slowly turning.

3

The master of the flat heard the noise of the Choctaw below them, a
mile or so away. They stirred up the fire and roasted pine wood near
it so that the wood might blaze quickly. As the steamer came around a
point, about a quarter of a mile away, the master lighted his pine torch,
and placed himself in the front of the flat.

The moon was rising in the tops of the trees behind the steamboat
so as to throw their shadows ahead. The Choctaw made a sheer toward
the flat, the master and crew shouted, but the steamboat kept on and
the barge at its side struck the flat. It was swung around and hit again
by the bow of the steamboat, stove and broken. The master and crew
jumped on the Choctaw. All of the flat did not sink; one side of it
stayed above the water and it floated down the river.

HANDS

1

On the way home from Calcutta, Cresswell, while reefing a topsail at night, was thrown from the yard by the sudden motion of the sail in a gust of wind and broke both legs below the knees. The master, with the help of the first mate and one of the crew, set the bones and secured them by bandages and splints as well as he could. Cresswell was then placed in his hammock in the forecastle. This was on the 30th of March. The ship did not come to Boston until the 10th of June. All this while Cresswell lay in his hammock, helpless, swinging in the unceasing motion of the ship, and for a time in great pain. He was left to the chance care of the crew.

The ship came to anchor on the afternoon of a Thursday and hauled into the wharf on Friday. The crew were discharged and left the ship. The forecastle was in confusion—the crew making ready and taking away their luggage and stowing away rigging. The master left on Saturday and did not come back until Monday. No one stayed by the ship but the first mate, who paid no heed to Cresswell except to send him food from shore. It began to rain Friday and rained Saturday and Sunday. When the master came back on Monday, he had Cresswell carried to the hospital. His left leg was found to be somewhat twisted, but the right was much worse—the foot was turned out at right angles from the way it should have been.

2

Tomlinson, a seaman on board the steamship Pacific, was sick of the smallpox. The ship was then on the Umpqua River. The captain told him he had seen to it that he would be taken care of at a village about fifteen or twenty miles up the river, where there was a doctor, and he had a boat ready to take him there. Tomlinson went into the boat and was rowed to the village. He asked the man who rowed him where the doctor was and was told there was none in the place, or nearer than Oakland, sixty miles or so away.

The sick man went to the store—the principal building of the village—and the storekeeper also told him there was no doctor there. The sight of Tomlinson, with smallpox broken out on his face, frightened every one. The storekeeper advised him to go back and, down the river, about six miles below the steamer, he could get a horse to take him to Coos Bay.

They reached the steamer about nine o'clock at night. The boatman called to the master and asked if he should take the sick man down the river. The master, angered and cursing, answered that he might put him ashore anywhere. Tomlinson was landed at dead of night and began to crawl over rocks and driftwood to the only house for miles around. He reached it late at night and found a young man who, unaware of his sickness, let him sleep in the house, and in the morning gave him a horse to ride to Coos Bay. (The young man was dead of the smallpox in a few weeks.)

Toward night, Tomlinson came to the river across which the town is reached by a ferry. Here, as directed by a man he met on the road, he tried to get to the flag-staff and raise the flag as a signal for the ferry-boat, but, worn out, he fell from the horse in a faint. The man, shortly afterwards, came back and, keeping safely away, told Tomlinson that he would cross the river in his boat and tell the authorities about him.

This was Sunday night. Until Tuesday morning Tomlinson lay upon the beach, blind, unable to move, without anybody coming near him to give him even a cup of water.

3

The ship was bound on a secret voyage—in the shipping articles, "a voyage to a port or ports easterly of the Cape of Good Hope or any port or ports to which the master should see fit to go to procure a cargo." Ten hands would have been enough to navigate the Sam Slick to the East Indies, but the master was hiring twice as many, half of them green.

The vessel was going to the island of Ichaboe for a cargo of guano, but the owners, to hinder competition, kept it a secret and made it known only to the captain and the mates. The guano on Ichaboe was dug in pits, dug through from one side of the island to another. When a ship had a place where loading was easier, the crew of a second-comer would often help that they might have the place when the first should be loaded. Upon making Ichaboe, the master called the hands together and told them to go to work loading another ship.

They helped load the ship and then loaded their own. They were at work about ninety days. The ships that came for guano were anchored in a roadstead open to every wind and the waves, always in danger of dashing against each other or upon the rocks. The island was barren and uninhabited. The work on the guano was unpleasant because of the smell and the dust that choked them and irritated their eyes and the skin of their faces and hands. They were also in danger of the pit caving in, for the walls were in places forty feet high and only ten apart.

4

The Arab was bound for Desolation Island to take sea-elephant or walrus oil. The sea-elephants were killed by spears here and there on the island. The blubber was taken from the animals wherever killed and carried by the men on their backs over blocks of ice to their hut on the shore to be tried into oil. The land was one of fog and clouds, snow and ice; they saw the sun seldom, and upon the sea on all sides the floating ice.

5

About five o'clock in the morning, while the Amsden was at anchor in the harbor of Toledo, the mate called the crew and they turned to; he kept them at work until five in the evening. The master was away much of the time. At five o'clock a tug came alongside with an order from the master to get up anchor and lay the schooner alongside an elevator. They did so and made the ship fast, but the elevator was not ready for the cargo. The work on the Amsden went on until about eight o'clock in the evening. At that time the elevator began taking the schooner's grain; and it was not until past one in the morning that the last of it was delivered. The mate and the caw had been kept on duty. They then cleared up the decks of the ship, hoisted in the boat, put the hatches down, got the tow-line on board—ready for moving in the morning. At about two o'clock, the mate told the crew they might turn in and went to his berth.

He had been asleep but a short time, when the master of the tug rapped on the cabin door. The mate woke at last, and told the master not to trouble him until daylight. The master said the day was dawning, but went away. In a little while he was back and woke the mate again telling him to call the men and get the ship under way. The mate answered that he had worked them all night and that he could not get up until daylight. The master turned out some of the men himself, cast the lines off the dock, and started the schooner toward Erie.

6

As the Arab sailed from Desolation Island the first mate told Captain Cushman that Ryan had again been afoul of the rum. The master called Michael Ryan, the steward, out of the cabin and asked him, "What have you been doing with my liquor?"

Ryan said he had not taken any of the liquor at all. The master told him not to lie: he had taken the liquor and given the cook some. The master said two or three times that Ryan was not to lie to him and that he knew a damned sight better—Ryan had taken the rum. Ryan said he had not: the rum he had drunk did not belong to the master, but was some he had got on shore. The master with his right fist struck Ryan above the left eye and cut a gash over it, and at once with his left fist struck Ryan on the right ear so that the blood ran from it, and he was knocked down upon the deck. "What is this for, Captain Cushman?" cried Ryan.

Captain Cushman said, "I will let you know what it is for," and kicked Ryan and beat him with a rope. Ryan rolled and crawled away from him. The master had him lashed to the rigging, his trousers stripped down, and lashed him with a cat upon the naked buttocks until Ryan could not help letting his dung fall. At this Captain Cushman had Ryan cut down and told him to get a shovel to clean it away. But he did not find the shovel as quickly as Captain Cushman thought he might and he cut Ryan across the legs and arms with the cat and ordered him to the masthead. There he was kept for nearly four hours in the cold and rain until he was so benumbed with cold he could hardly keep himself from falling.

7

As the cabin-boy of the bark Massassoit was shaking the table-cloth over the side of the ship, the cloth slipped from his fingers and was lost. The cooper advised him to tell it to Pettingill, the steward, a green hand, and ask him to tell the master. Pettingill told the cabin-boy to tell the master himself, but the boy answered that he was afraid he would be flogged and begged the steward to do it for him.

The master answered roughly. Pettingill said that he would pay for the cloth. Captain Maxwell replied that he wanted no other pay than what he could get from his hide, and knocked him down, and while down shook him and brought his knees and feet upon the steward's breast and took him by the hair with such force as to pull out a handful.

8

Butler, while on the Argo in the harbor of Matanzas, Cuba, was sent with another of the crew for the master. Captain Brewster had been spending the evening on board the Eastern Star—also from Portland— lying in the harbor.

As the boat was coming alongside the Argo, Captain Brewster called out to unrow or take in the oars. Butler, who sat in the after seat and held the weather oar, doing so, turned the blade aft. The spray was blown upon Captain Brewster sitting in the stern.

In a loud and angry voice he called Butler a rascal and asked why he did not turn the blade forward. Butler said that the ship was so near it was impossible. The master answered that if he did not turn the blade forward he would beat out his brains with the tiller, and gave Butler two or three blows with his fist. Putting his arm up to ward them off, Butler knocked the master's hat into the water; it drifted away and was lost in the darkness.

Captain Brewster went up the steps of the ladder first, and as soon as he was on deck, stripped off his coat and took a rope. As Butler came up, the master made several passes at him. Butler dodged and ran along the deck. Captain Brewster went after him and Butler, hitting his leg against the windlass, fell. The master sprang upon him and holding him down kicked him about the head and breast.

9

Roberts was troublesome. He had been a prizefighter and was not unwilling to try himself with his fists. He had great faith in his strength and skill, and his bearing was such as might be looked for from such a man. He had been set to caulking the forecastle. Fairfield, the mate, was near him. Roberts asked for a caulking mallet. Fairfield told him to work with the serving mallet he had. He answered in a surly tone that he could not work as well with that as with a caulking mallet.

Captain Skolfield heard him and came forward with the master of another ship in port, who happened to be on board. Both fell on Roberts, the mate standing by. Captain Skolfield knocked Roberts down with his fist and both seized him by the hair or collar, as often as he tried to rise, and threw him down again, and for some time they struck and kicked him on his head, face and shoulders.

Captain Skolfield, soon after, left the ship. Roberts kept on him with his work and asked the boy to bring him some oakum. His face was bloody, the upper lip cut; he was holding his handkerchief, clotted with blood, to his face. The mate told the boy not to go and to let Roberts get it himself. As Roberts came back with the oakum, Fairfield met him and taking a slingshot from a pocket struck Roberts twice with it on the face and once on the back of his head. For two days the blood oozed from the wound on his nose.

10

Captain Pride had once beaten a sailor until he was flat on the deck. When he got to his feet, he began to run forward; he was brought back by the mate, upon Captain Pride's order, and beaten again until he was all bloody. This time he was tied to the rigging by his hands, and as the master beat him he sank down lifted up only by his hands.

11

William Freeman, master of the brig Floyd, had in his crew a young man, David Whitehead, who had not been to sea long. Captain Freeman called on Whitehead often, cuffed him, and pulled him by the hair. Once he sent him up to scrape the main topgallant mast, and went up after him, complaining of the way he was scraping, and took hold of the rigging and shook it, as if to shake him off, while Whitehead was holding on to the mast with one hand and scraping with the other.

One day in April Whitehead was sent up with another hand to let a reef out of the foretopsail, and he left one point untied, which, in hoisting the sail, split it. When Captain Freeman came on deck and saw the hole he shouted at Whitehead, beat him with his fist and a piece of rattling stuff, and kicked him.

The next day the master lashed him to a ring bolt. Whitehead's hands were tied behind him with a spunyarn, and he was lashed around his middle with a rope to the ring. The weather was bitter cold. After several hours, Captain Freeman asked him if he wanted a dram. Whitehead said he would like one. The master put two doses of tartar emetic into a glass of New England rum and gave it to him, and Whitehead vomited and vomited.

Then Captain Freeman unfastened the spunyarn about Whitehead's wrists and the rope from the ring bolt, and tied Whitehead to the rail with an inch-and-a-half or two-inch rope so that he stood in the middle of the deck with nothing to lean against, and set him to watching the seagulls. The rope was tied by the master as tight as he could draw it; Whitehead's hands became swollen and black as a hat. Captain Freeman took a stick from the tar bucket and put it between his lips, and then laughed at him and asked him where he had been stealing molasses.

For a day and a night, until he was set free, Whitehead had nothing to eat and drink but half a biscuit and about a pint of water. The biscuit was broken up and laid upon a cask, and he had to eat it like a beast.

The hands were called to hand the main sail; five went on to the yard. Whitehead was then scrubbing. His hands were still stiff and swollen so that he could hardly close his thumb and forefinger. Captain Freeman asked the mate why he did not send "that damned soldier" aloft. The mate answered that Whitehead was not able to go. The man at the helm added that so sure as that man went aloft he would never come on deck again alive. "Damn him, send him aloft!" cried the master, taking up a piece of rigging. He struck Whitehead with it, saying, "Damn you, start along now! Damn you, away with you aloft!"

Whitehead crawled up the rigging slowly, and reached the yard. He went upon the lee yard, and got to the end of it. The man next to him said, "Davey, come try and hand me in the beck if you can." He tried to get hold of the beck of the sail, and, not able to hold on any longer, fell, struck upon the rail, and fell overboard.

12

In making up a crew the shipping master heard of four Norwegians, decent men, who were on their way to California, where gold had just been discovered. They were engaging a direct passage to San Francisco. The shipping master called at their boarding-house and offered them wages to go as seamen in the Loo Choo; they had better earn wages to Valparaiso and could always get a passage from Valparaiso to San Francisco. The Norwegians went to look at the Loo Choo and, after talking it over among themselves, decided to go in her.

The shipping master took from his pocket the shipping articles for them to sign. The men hesitated, and then would not sign unless a stipulation was put in that they should be discharged at Valparaiso. The shipping master told them they were green and they would surely be discharged there. They answered that they knew they were green, but they were afraid of trouble if the articles were not plain about their agreement. The shipping master then said he would write it in the articles if that would satisfy them, and, taking a pen, wrote upon the paper.

During the voyage there was nothing but good feeling between them and Captain Allen. When the ship made the harbor of Valparaiso, the Norwegians helped moor the Loo Choo and make everything snug on board. They then packed up their clothes, dressed themselves, and respectfully asked the master for their discharge and wages. Captain Allen would not discharge them.

They reminded him that such was their agreement and asked for the articles. They showed him the clause written against their names; this read: "monthly $14 and to have $15 if they perform the voyage and return the ship to Boston." Still the master would not discharge them. They then asked to see the consul. Captain Allen brought them the consul's clerk, for the consul was away.

The clerk read the articles to the men, and when he came to the written clause said, "Captain, I can do nothing with these men; you have got two rates of wages in the alternative in your articles." Yet, he added, the master had power to discharge them if he would. Then, saying that he would not do anything officially, he told the men they had better stay with the ship.

They would not, and Captain Allen would not discharge them. The clerk then asked if he could be of any service to Captain Allen and what was he going to do with the men. The master asked the clerk to have them put in prison.

The Norwegians would not do another thing on board, and were sent to prison. For one day each was kept by himself in a cell, and then they were put in a room, about thirty feet long by twenty wide, with two grated windows, opening upon a brick wall, and a grated door. Here were criminals of all kinds, many of them sick and some with loathsome sicknesses, never less than one hundred and sometimes more than two hundred. Then they were so crowded as to be unable to lie down. There were no berths, beds, or bedding.

The food was bread and a mixture of Chili beans, peas, barley, and Chili pepper. Once a day, in the morning, each prisoner was given bread, as much as a sea-biscuit, with water, and nothing else. In the evening the pepper mixture was served in iron kettles, each holding about a gallon. One was given to ten prisoners. There was nothing with which to scoop the food out, and nothing to eat with but their hands.

The four Norwegians could not eat the pepper mixture. At last they became so weak on the bread alone, that they tried the mixture again. As soon as they did so, all but one were made sick.

After they had been in the room for more than a month, Captain Allen called for a moment at the door. He said something to one of them, which he could not understand, and left before the others could make their way to the grating. In a day or two they were taken out, covered with lice, hardly able to stand, blinking and squinting in the sunlight. They asked to see the consul and were not allowed to see him, but still they would not go with the Loo Choo.

They were put in irons, their arms hung from a rope about a stanchion between decks, and kept without food for almost two days. Then they said they would turn to, and did their work as well as they could, until the ship was back in Boston harbor. Here Captain Allen took from their wages the cost of keeping them in prison in Valparaiso.

13

While Martin was in the forecastle one day at dinner time, one of the crew found fault with some of the food as not fit for a man to eat, and put it into Martin's dish. Martin said, "You say yourself that this is not fit for a man to eat; why do you put it into my dish?"

At this James Collins, another of the seamen, said, "It is good enough for a Frenchman," and spat into Martin's face. He sprang up, but some one from behind caught him by the throat until the blood gushed from his nostrils, and he was pulled back upon the bench.

PASSENGERS

1

The City of Boston was lying at the dock, with steam up, ready to start. A detachment of United States soldiers, about sixty of them, with several non-commissioned and two commissioned officers, went on board. Fourteen or eighteen of the soldiers were armed with muskets, loaded and capped, bayonets fixed; the rest were unarmed.

From the train came a large number of passengers. Among these were about one hundred and fifty United States soldiers in a detachment, rationed and equipped for field duty, under the command of officers; they were marched on board at the forward gang-plank. The first detachment had been placed on the main deck, forward of the engine room, and armed sentries were set to keep them there.

As the boat, heavily laden, went slowly through the night, a number of soldiers were in the dense crowd, some armed, some drunk, quarrelsome, cursing and speaking indecently, scuffling with each other and jostling the civilians. One of the soldiers with arms went up to a civilian and with a blow of the fist struck his hat down over his eyes.

2

A number of Irish emigrants made up with a Mr. Brennan, a ship agent at Cork, for the passage to New York. The ship to carry them not ready for sea as soon as they wished, Brennan charted the "between decks," as it was called, of The Flash, then in port and bound for Philadelphia. He gave each a certificate, in the form then usual, partly printed and partly written, by which he engaged that upon the ship's arrival they would be forwarded to New York, free of all expense.

When the ship made Philadelphia, it was found that Brennan had no one there to act for him; and neither the master nor the consignees of The Flash recognized any obligation to receive or forward the passengers. As soon as the ship had been fastened to the wharf, the master stopped the rations and the fires for cooking.

Two days afterwards, the passengers were talked into leaving The Flash and bringing their baggage ashore by the assurance that a ship was waiting to take them to New York. It was in July; the sky was blazing. They carried their bundles and chests for a mile or more along the wharfs to the one to which they had been directed, and found that the ship was gone. In fact, no passage for them had been arranged.

3

At night the deck was cleared and those who had no cabins had to stay in a space under cover. From this a large door with glass panels led to the forward part of the deck, taken up with freight, cattle and horses.

The boat went swiftly along in the dead of night. The weather, though it was August, had become chilly. Bridget Nine had a big cloak about her and sat on her trunk. Two men stood near her, talking to each other briefly between puffs at their pipes. She could tell by their brogue that they were Irish.

When one went away, Bridget asked the other, after a while, how far it was before they got to the place where they took the train for Boston. He didn't know exactly. Then she asked if he lived in Boston and he told her yes; he had been in the country four or five years. She asked what kind of a place Boston was about serving girls. He told her the price and asked if she had any friends there. She said that her husband was in Boston and had been for four or five years. He asked in what street did he live. She named some place he didn't know anything about. Then he asked her what did he do. She said he worked along shore. He asked her how long since she left Ireland. She said, "I was in

Ireland thirteen weeks ago." At that he heard the child she held under her cloak cry.

"What! have you got a baby?" said he.

"It's none of your damn business," said Bridget, and she walked out into the forward part of the deck trying to quiet the child. Some of the passengers gathered at the door to see what she was out there for, among the horses and cows. She walked to the very bow and stared over the bulwark at the black water.

RIVERS AND SEAS, HARBORS AND PORTS

The sloop Hamlet, heavily laden with stone—a fair wind, but light and unsteady—running down the river on the morning of a clear day, the tide young flood. The channel of the river half a mile wide, with wide flats each side of it, covered with water. The Paul Jones going up the river, the water curling white at its bow. The pilot could see the stones on the Indiana shore. Bright moonlight; the steamboat, Lamar, going up the river with the flood-tide, two tow-boats with her; the steam "checked down," for the water was shallow on the bar. When the Lamar had passed it, the captain called for headway. The channel of the river ran as close to the landing as a steamboat could go, to keep clear of some sunken flats. The bank high and shaded by trees, in the back a brick-kiln; here the river was darkest and without moonlight;

The ships: Harvest Queen, the brig Torrid Zone, Clara Clarita, Five Boys, Seaflower, Seagull, Sparkle, Black Squall, Sea Nymph, Silver Spray, the sidewheel steamer Comet, Fair American, the hermaphrodite brig Androdus, the bark Storm Bird, the steamer Golden Age, the sloop Jewess, The Gentleman, Gold Hunter, the sloop Gold Leaf, the brig Susannah, the brig Laurel, Mist, Fawn, Serpent, Sam Slick, the poleacre Jerusalem flying the Greek flag; Polly and Sally, newly coppered to light watermark and sheltered above with leather to the wales; Live Yankee, the brig Sea Horse, Polly and Kitty;

The men: Captain Proud, Captain Lorillard, Captain Percival, Mr. Appleton Oaksmith the mate, Captain Ivory, Thwing, James Fortune, John Jarvis, John Law, Job Mewster, Merry, Hugh Grimes, Heartwell, and Benjamin Chew; drinking houses and tippling shops; the women: Kitty Pad, Sally Williams, Mahala, Polly Robinson;

The ship chock and block full of bags of wheat; a cargo of yellow pine lumber, barilla, and pipes of wine; bales of lambskins and cases of manna; cases of essence of bergamot and boxes of lemons and oranges; ten tons of brimstone; a cargo of white ash, white oak, walnut and black walnut; sugar in hogsheads, tierces, barrels, and boxes; a keg of doubloons; bags of San Domingo coffee; sugar in casks, in boxes, in bags or mats; a cargo of sandalwood at the Fiji Islands and at Guam a quantity of beech de mer, betel nuts, and deer horns; ivory rings for martingales; a cargo of copper ore, shipped in Chile; sperm and whale oil, sperm candles and whalebone; pigs of copper; six seroons of indigo; pigs of lead, moys of salt, and frails of raisins; seal skins, prime fur and pup skins, from seals taken at the Falkland Islands; a cargo of tea, fresh, prime, and of the first chop, quarter chests of tea, hyson skin and congo, with the present of a shawl from the hong merchant in Canton; cases, trunks, bales, casks, kegs, and bundles;

The Chincha Islands; Savannah la mer; Jamaica; the island, a coral reef around most of it, a fine harbor, half a mile from the reef to the island, at high water the reef not out of water, but at low water the natives walking on the reef—no better harbor in the South Seas; a low sand island, but a few feet above the water, three miles or so around, without a tree or shrub on it and all about it shoals, rocks, and coral reefs—on one side stretching away for twenty-five miles; Rattlesnake Shoal, Pelican Shoals, Flapjack Reef; the ship aground all of the night, chafing and grating upon the sand, the weather dark, threatening to be worse, dark and stormy, spitting rain; the schooner under full sail with a fair wind running upon a bar of mud in Mobile Bay, thumping upon the bar heavily, the water calm but a very heavy surf;

Standing at the helm as the ship goes up the river in the evening, between daylight and candlelight, gawking at the town; a cask of wine brought alongside, slung in a lighter to be hoisted on board, the mate himself at the tackle-fall, and then at the point of passage over the waist of the ship, which is high, the cask suddenly turning athwart-ships, slipping out of the slings, stoven, and the wine lost; messes of salted halibut and rice or beans, a helping of duff, coffee or tea morning and evening and a weekly allowance of spirits; jogging at the pump, pulling the ropes, going aloft;

A slight haze upon the water, the wind blowing freshly, the lake somewhat rough; clear starlight; the night clear and bright moon-

light; the ship pitching and rolling heavily in the head sea, the wind
driving the rain inboard and the spray from the waves beating against
the bows, the ship reeling and plunging in the head sea; a clear star-
light morning and the wind moderate; the night dark and hazy, the
morning dark and misty, the brig sailing close-hauled, with a light
breeze, just enough to move her through the water, all her sails set,
going about half a mile an hour; the night dark, somewhat foggy,
and ice floating in the bay; one o'clock in the morning, the moon just
setting, the sky overcast, at first flying clouds, sometimes darkening
the moon and sometimes leaving it bright, but, afterwards, the clouds
becoming dense and heavy; a steamer passing and the yawing of the
ship in the following sea and with the free wind; the wind not a breeze
but enough to make the boat flank somewhat; a fair day, a whole-sail
breeze blowing; the day bright and clear; the night clear and the moon
shining brightly; the night the darkest ever from clouds and fog—lit-
tle wind, the water smooth; the night dark and thick and the sea high,
and the wind a gale; wet, dark, and thick weather, the stars to be seen
from time to time, the wind from the southwest and the sea high, light
drizzling rain, a dirty foggy night raining a drizzling rain the whole
night; a clear cold night, the moon having set just after midnight; the
wind blowing a stiff breeze from about southwest; the loud whistling
of the wind through the rigging; the wind fresh from the south and
the schooner beating against the wind, the night clear and starlit; the
wind southwest blowing free; the night hazy, the moon at times dark-
ened by clouds, the wind fair for Boston; squalls of wind and rain, high
confused sea flooding the decks at times, hail and rain, the sea flooding
the decks fore and aft; squalls taking off but still a heavy sea; heavy
seas, heavy swells, causing the ship to pitch hard, ship pitching heavily,
heavy head sea, causing the ship to go bows under, ship driving heav-
ily, rolling heavily, ship going bows under, filling decks fore and aft;
the weather misty and a drizzling rain, and during the afternoon the
weather more and more boisterous until the wind is blowing a gale;
the wind east and light, the night dark and without moon; the night
dark and cloudy with a fresh wind from the southwest, showers and
some mist, the sea heavy and confused, running from the northwest
and from the southwest; the night dark and then a drizzling rain, the
sea heavy and the ship pitching a good deal, misty, a pretty thick night,
small thick rain;

The sound calm and the night starlight; the vessel anchoring in the bay about nightfall, the snow turning into rain, the wind, about midnight, coming out of the northwest and blowing heavily on shore, the weather growing cold; the ship moored in the channel, the moon shining through a slight haze, on the easterly side a high bluff jutting into the sea, to the west a low sand-spit, in front of the sand-spit the shore line of the bluff curving into a bight; bays, inlets, rivers, harbors and ports.

EAST AND WEST

UPSET

The driver took the box at Farmington, ten miles east of Uniontown. He stopped at Snyder's, three miles from Farmington, and was drunk when he came into the house. He asked for liquor and was refused. Two miles further he stopped at Downe's tavern. Here he was overtaken by another stage-driver. By this time he was staggering. Each took a turn watching the horses while the other went in to drink. It had become dark, for it was five or six o'clock of a winter evening.

The second driver told him to drive slow. He answered, "If you are going to keep up with me, you must drive damned fast," mounted his box, cracked his whip, shouted, and in three minutes was out of sight.

Here the way down Laurel Hill began; the ride became rough and rapid. They came down the hill, however, went along the level below, went up a little hill, went down it at a trot, and near the bottom struck a log and were upset. The log was lying over the summer road, reaching nearly, if not quite, to the macadamized part of the turnpike.

HOLD-UP

The mail-coach left Reading at half-past two in the morning. As it crossed Turner's Lane, a man darted out, got the off leader by the head, and turned him around to the right. Two men then stepped up, one on each side of the box, and, both pointing pistols at the driver, one cried, "Stop, stop, or we blow your damned guts out!" The driver threw his whip across the horses and tried to get on, but could not. They then struck the stage's lamps with their pistols, broke them and put them out. The lamp on the right did not go out at once. The man who was holding the horse's head let go, put a handkerchief around his face and struck out the lamp with his pistol.

Pye got Adams to go with him to a stable where, Pye said, he had a coat which he would sell Adams cheap. It was almost Christmas and the weather had become cold and raw.

No sooner had they walked into the stable than Jefferson Roach came in. After some talk with Pye, Roach took out a pack of cards and the two began to play. They tried to get Adams to join the game, or make a bet, but Adams would not, for, he said, he knew nothing of gambling. Roach then asked Adams for a loan to make a bet with Pye. After much urging, Pye promising him the coat if the money was lost, Adams lent Roach four two-dollar orders of the Baltimore and Ohio Railroad Company. Roach and Pye at once made a bet, which Roach lost, and he handed over to Pye the money he had borrowed from Adams, and said to Adams, "He has won all my money and yours too, now what am I to do to pay you?"

Adams said, "Gentlemen, I hope you did not bring me here to rob me, instead of selling me a coat?"

Pye answered with an oath that he would keep the money, and went away. Roach went out with Adams after Pye, but took him into a street other than that down which Pye had gone.

Pye at first had put the "rails-money" into his trouser pocket, in which he had a five dollar note of a broken bank and a few coppers, but now he put it between his drawers and his legs, tying the drawers about his ankles with string.

GUNSHOT WOUNDS

1

In gunshot wounds the edges are sunken; in wounds made with a knife the edges are smooth and the lips of the wounds stick out.

2

Costello was working a mining claim near Gold Hill. Three men, Murphy, Blanchfield, and Carver, owned the claim next to his. Costello worked his claim by means of a ditch used to take water from the main mining ditch of the place. Murphy and his partners said he was running tailing down on them, and at last they went upon Costello's ground to fill up the tail-race and ditch. He stopped them that day.

Next morning, Douglas, a hired man of the partnership, went to Costello's cabin and told him they were going to fill up the ditch that morning, but he hoped that Costello would not think hard of him, because he was only a hired man. Costello had a loaded gun in his cabin and told his man to put it at a place near the ditch.

When Costello went to his ditch, he found Murphy and his men filling it up. Costello said he would leave the matter to a miners' meeting to arbitrate, but Murphy told him he could go to law. Costello then said he would cut another ditch, but Blanchfield said it would not do. Costello then said he would clean up his tail-race, into which they were shoveling dirt, and if it did not pay much, would quit and go away; but if it did pay, he would work so as not to do Murphy and his partners any harm. Murphy told him he had had time enough to clean it up, and dared him to put a pick in the ground. In the meantime, Carver was shoveling dirt to Murphy, who was treading it into the ditch.

Murphy had an overcoat, folded up, lying close by him, and he moved it about with him. Costello knew that it hid a pistol. After nothing that he could say would stop them, Costello left, but in two or three minutes was back with his gun, and called out, "Leave my claim, you have damaged me enough!" He leveled his gun at Murphy. Murphy, Blanchfield, and Douglas ran, but Carver ran towards the coat. Costello called out, "Don't touch that!" and brought his gun round on Carver, and as Carver put his hand on the coat, fired and shot Carver in the back of the head.

3

Georgia Travis and her brother Wirt were at a meeting of the Blue Ribbon Club in its hall at Petaluma. While they were seated there, Hill came in and seated himself near them. Miss Travis rose at once and went out of the hall.

Wirt followed her and when outside asked her why she had left her seat. She said that Hill had slandered her and had tried to "scandalize" her and she wouldn't stay near him. Wirt saw their brother John near at hand and told him that their sister had left the hall because Hill was there and asked John to go home with her. He would not and said he was going to the Blue Ribbon meeting himself. Wirt then went back to the hall followed by his brother.

Both went towards Hill; Wirt took a seat about eight or ten feet from where Hill was sitting and John went to a chair nearly in front of Hill. As he was about to sit down, John suddenly reached over the head of a man who was seated between Hill and himself and struck Hill a blow on the head with his fist, because, as he said, Hill was making a face at him. Hill rose to his feet, facing John Travis—Wirt Travis at his back—and moved backwards a few steps. As soon as Hill rose, Wirt sprang to his feet and pulled a pistol out of his pocket. He went forward towards Hill, put his pistol within five or six inches of the back of Hill's head, and fired.

4

A German, known as Dutch John, lived in a cabin in the mountains. He owned about five hundred sheep and three hundred lambs. With him lived an old man, a Mexican, named Juan. On a day when Juan was alone at the cabin, Jose Maria and Pacheco, two Mexicans, came there about noon. They stayed a short while, then saddled their horses and rode away. In the afternoon they came back, unsaddled their horses, and Pacheco said to Juan, "My friend, gather your things and leave at once; we are taking a bad step."

Juan was gathering up what he had, when Pacheco said, "Stop, John is coming."

But before the German reached his door, Jose Maria, with a pistol in his hand, stopped him, and told Pacheco, "Go and tie him." Pacheco tried to catch him, but John would not let himself be caught; so, when Pacheco had gone to one side, Jose Maria shot the German, the ball hitting him in or near an eye. He staggered and fell, rose and was going towards the cabin when Jose Maria shot him in the back.

Pacheco then went to help Juan catch his horse. The old man heard another shot from the cabin. Pacheco said to him, "Hurry! Catch your horse and don't be afraid: we are not going to hurt you. God will kill you soon enough. But you mustn't say anything, otherwise we will kill you." Juan caught and saddled his horse, and rode away.

Not far from the cabin was a large white oak that had been cut down for some time. It was lying near a picket fence. It had been a tall tree and about ten feet from the butt it branched in a fork.

The day was dark and foggy. Two boys, passing by, saw a fire not far from the cabin. In a few days the boys, Cyprian and Eulario, passed that way again. The oak tree had been burned, with its branches, and several lengths of the picket-fence, and some fence posts. The posts had been pulled up. Wire had been used on the fence, and they found several pieces curled together where the fire had been. In the ashes were a few pieces of bone.

Pacheco at that time was living with a woman called Rosa Smith. He and Jose Maria had left her house before noon on the day Jose Maria killed Dutch John, telling her they were going to a dance. They came back the next morning. Pacheco told the woman they had bought some sheep. Another time he told her that Dutch John had given him the sheep to take care of.

They left the sheep up the mountains. Soon after, Jose Maria and Pacheco sheared them, and hauled the wool to Salinas, where they sold it for over two hundred dollars. They divided the money. Jose Maria at once lost forty dollars at cards.

Pacheco was down-hearted and said he was sick. He gave away some of the sheep.

MISTRESS

A few years before, Glervina had been living with a Captain Lyle as his mistress. He died without making any provision for her, and she became one of the women in a brothel in Portland.

Thomas Ford was one of the well-to-do citizens of Portland. He owned a number of lots and blocks of land in the city and had quite an income in rents. He was in his late forties. The youngest of his children was grown-up; his second wife—not the mother of any of his children—was an ailing woman, and at last she died. Before that, however, he had taken Glervina out of the brothel, and kept her as his mistress in a house that belonged to him, near his home.

Upon the death of his wife, Ford left Portland on a voyage to New York, and Glervina, after a while—so they had made up between them—went to San Francisco to meet him on his way back.

She had asked him to visit her father in the East and tell him that they were going to be married—her family had not heard of her for years. Ford wrote her several letters: two from San Francisco as soon as he came there, two from on board the steamer Sonora, and one from New York. In the letter from New York he wrote that he had forgotten the kind of goods she wanted for her wedding-dress, but would get something. He had not the time to visit her father in Ohio, but had written him and enclosed the answer.

The letter from her father was written at Felicity, Ohio; it acknowledged the receipt of a letter from Ford with twenty dollars "for which you will please accept my thanks. You also desire my consent to a union with my daughter. Upon this delicate question I hope my consent is given to a gentleman of honor, of kind and tender feelings, and that the result will be for the good and happiness of you both."

Ford and Glervina came back to Portland together and lived together in his home. Ford spoke of her as his wife and told his friends that he had spent more happy hours in the last six months than for twenty years before. Glervina, when in the brothel, had been known as Clara to his friend, Doctor Davenport. When he asked Ford how to address her, Ford said, "as Mrs. Ford." Ford asked another friend, Boyd, what he thought of his marriage. Boyd, trying to pass it off, said he knew nothing about it. Ford asked him again what he thought of it. Boyd answered that he had heard gossip about it, but had never believed it. Ford asked him yet again what he thought of it.

Boyd then said, "It is in very bad taste."

When he was fifty years of age, Ford died suddenly. Glervina was then nearly forty. Ford left no will.

The day after the funeral, his eldest son and the husband of his eldest daughter called upon Glervina. They spoke about the right to administer the estate—it was worth about one hundred thousand dollars—and said that if she had a certificate of marriage with their father, her right would not be questioned.

At first she said she had a certificate, but had promised the dead man never to show it to anyone. They talked some more about it; the court would have to see it, they said. She then burst out crying and said she had no certificate and had not been married and that this was the second time she had been fooled. She wanted to go to her father, near Cincinnati, and would they give her the money for it, for she had nothing.

Yes, they would help her leave the state quietly, for their father's sake, without stirring up comment on her living illicitly with Ford and others; she would not be turned away penniless as "a cast-off wanton," but would be paid $500 in cash in Portland and $500 in a note, payable in ten months, at Wells Fargo and Company's in San Francisco.

MACHINERY

His work was to carry rolls of wet cloth from a machine called an "extractor" to a hoist outside the building. On one side of the passage-way to the rolls of wet cloth were the "extractor" and the shaft propel-ling it and on the other a fan and the shaft upon which it turned. The fan was used for drying wool and turned about seven hundred times a minute—so fast that it looked like an object at rest. The "extractor" was not so swift as the fan, but ran with much more noise, so that one would be likely to keep farther away from it. The passageway was about four and a half feet wide. As he walked along, his hand-barrow under his right arm on the side next to the "extractor," and in his left hand a handful of ropes used in binding the rolls of cloth together for hoisting, a rope caught and wound around the shaft of the fan.

THE WILL

The old man got into his sleigh and went ten or twelve miles to Hoyt's home. He came there about dusk. It was cold and snowy, and the wind was high. As he came into the house, he said he was afraid the storm would spoil his new blue horse-blankets.

He asked the girls for pen and ink, and that one of them witness his will. There were gold pens and quill pens on the stand, and he tried several to get one to suit him. He could write better than any of them, he said, and he would take pains with so many ladies looking on.

When he turned to them to witness his will, they demurred. He

said, "Any young lady might consider it an honor to witness my will."
At last he turned to one and said he had a fancy to her name, for it was
the same as that of his dead wife. Asked point-blank, she could not say
no and witnessed the will.

Mr. Hoyt said that he might have left them something, but he
answered that they had enough.

DEPRESSION

1

It had stopped raining. He was walking home with his brother. There
was a puddle of water on the sidewalk, shining in the afternoon sun-
light, and when he came to it, he slapped his brother on the arm and
said, "See, there is money, can't you see? I will make money out of
that. That is the biggest thing in the world to make money out of."

In the middle of the night it was raining and thundering again. His
wife woke up and found that he was gone. She didn't know where he
could be. She got up and lit the lamp and waited an hour or so. At last
she heard him on the attic stairs; he came into the room, dripping wet,
the water running from his hair, and his nightgown pasted to his flesh.
He had been up on top of the house. He said it was very nice on top of
the house when it rained and the lightning flashed; he liked it.

2

Frederick Wholgemuth had retired from business with a dwelling
house, a stable, a one-horse carriage; he had fitted out his son as an
apothecary, and had been worth, perhaps, $16,000.

He was writing a letter to his son. He would write a little, and then,
in a day or two, write again. He wrote: "Dear Karl, if God calls me
away from you and Mother, you must do the best you can. You know
that I have always tried to do the best I could, but oftentimes, when I
thought I could make something, I lost. Don't do as I have done; don't
let people talk you into anything, to go security, to endorse notes to
the banks, and all sorts of such things. Whatever you do, don't let
people lie you into things as they did me. Do the best you can, but

never go security for anybody, nor even endorse a note for no man, no matter who he is.

"Keep out of these companies, for it is worth nothing to be in these large companies. Be very careful that you don't get cheated so much, and don't let people talk you into all these things. If anything should happen to me, sell my interest in all those iron mines or ore leases; it is too expensive and very risky business; and don't listen to what other people tell you, and tend well to your store. Stay out of these companies, never go in a company of no kind, for it is worth nothing to be in these companies; it's very risky business, 'lottery business,' as Mr. Jacob Kempf said. This mining is very risky business; don't spend any money on them leases that I hold.

"I insured so much that all my debts can be paid. Pay all my debts, and be a man, so that nobody can say they lost money on your father. But when you get the money out of the insurance companies, if it ever should happen so, don't think you would keep the money and not pay the debts."

He went to see his widowed sister. After some talk about garden seed, he said that he had seen their parents in a dream. Both were silent for a while, and then he said he was going to New York to a doctor about his hearing. If anything should happen to him, his wife and son could help themselves. There were no tears in his eyes when he said good-by, but when he got into the street the tears came into his eyes.

When he got to New York, it was raining. He had no umbrella and bought one. The train pulled in from New York about ten o'clock at night. It was very cold. When the three or four other passengers had gone their ways, no one was in the street. A man had been murdered in this neighborhood a day or two before. If they found his body too, they would think, God willing! that he had been murdered.

He unbuttoned his overcoat, his coat and vest. He opened the knife he had bought in New York and, still holding the new umbrella open in his left hand, closed his eyes and pushed the blade into his belly near the navel. It was only a scratch; he would have to go deeper if he was to die.

He stabbed again upwards and again downwards. That was deeper. He threw the knife away and buttoned his overcoat. It was very cold. He walked up and down the street. He was not bleeding much. He was not dying, at least not for a long time, and in the morning would have to face everybody. He walked to the station and reached the bridge over the shallow creek, twenty feet below. It was pitch black. He could not hear the water among the stones—perhaps, because he was growing deaf. If he jumped down, the water might be frozen; he would not drown, but only hurt himself.

3

Selim Jones was in his office on a lounge, his left hand lying on his belly, and his right on the floor of the room. His hat and coat were on a chair. About eight or ten inches from his right hand was a pistol of two barrels, one of which was empty. There was a hole in his right temple and a bulge at the left of his head that the bullet inside had made. Blood was running down on his right shoulder from the wound and then down his right arm to the floor. His set of false teeth had fallen out and were lying on his shirt, near the right shoulder.

4

As the case was turned over upon the wharf, a rattling was heard inside. The looking-glass was broken. The pieces were wedge-shaped; the cracks radiated from a center, as if the glass had been struck by a pointed instrument.

18   The railroad company's depot was between two streets:

75   The railroad crossed the highway nearly at right angles

385 The railroad was running an excursion on a Sunday in July from the city

373 The rendering plant making fat into tallow

62   The rest of the family did not like him.

344 The river was at a high stage with a rapid current

161 The road ran beside the river

465 The sailor had just landed and had his money in his hip pocket,

482 The saloonkeeper came from the saloon with his bartender

228 The savings bank failed; almost all of its deposits

234 The sawmill, run by steam, was lit by electric lights at night

387 The seamstress, a woman of sixty and deaf, had been working for a family in the village that day

137 The sheriff and his posse were about to remove a Negro prisoner

95   The shovelers, unloading a ship lying at the wharf

41   The "show" consisted of some stuffed snakes

80   The steam planing-mill used the shavings and sawdust

243 The steamboat was lying at a wharf in Cincinnati

492 The stepson was not quite sixteen.

232 The stone-cutting machines of the marble company

375 The storm came up suddenly

106 The stranger had come into town that day:

200 The street ran beside the railroad tracks; a hundred trains and more

42   The three had met at a singing society

314 The trouble began at a bawdyhouse on Gas House Alley.

399 The two families lived next to each other in a town near Kansas City

455 The two had been companions for a long time,

348 The two policemen on duty at the Union Depot began to talk about two Negroes:

462 The two were gold miners

502 The two women were friends

470 The two working a ranch in partnership had hired a "handyman"—

74   The wagons of fruit and vegetables

158 The weather had been the coldest in years;

348 The white man in the waiting-room of the railroad station had been drinking,

442 The white man washing dishes at night in the restaurant

426 The widow had carried a load of old fence posts to her home

513 The work was "driving" logs upon a mountain stream,

394 The young colored woman said: "My huband Tom and me was in town on Saturday night

497 The young fellow running the elevator was new at it

198 The young man and his wife were separated

195 The young man had been at work during the day

338 The young man's parents lived in the country

452 The youngest of six children, she came from a city in Turkish Armenia

279 Their bodies were found about a mile apart:

315 There was a dance at a house in town, and one of those at the dance

139 There was a fair—a "festival," as they called it—

372 There were about a hundred dead horses and cows—with maggots and flies—

275 There were four machines for making horseshoes in the shop

23 There were three on the locomotive:

193 They had a farm of almost two hundred acres:

457 They had been married five or so years

362 They had been stealing his corn

44 They had come, man and wife, together from Italy.

24 They held the light very close to him,

163 They were coming back from a "church sociable"—

451 They were Jews, immigrants from Poland. Her husband became a peddler;

436 Those at work in the stockyards in place of the strikers—

94 Those drills, in the right man's hands,

419 Those who lived in that school-district called Dan "the little schoolteacher,"

354 Three young white men were on their way from a prayer meeting in a church,

50 Tilda was just a child

91 Toller was a surveyor

56 Tully had gone to Reilly's in the morning;

423 Two brothers, Wes and Sam, lived with their parents

485 Two Italians, acquaintances if not friends,

320 Two men were neighbors and lived on opposite sides of a creek.

49 Two streetcars coupled together were coming along,

42 Van Nicely with his warmest smile—

301 Vic had been mining coal since he was fourteen;

433 Vito and Pete came from neighboring provinces in Italy.

270 Watson was a mechanic, a hard-working man

380 When Ben was all of thirteen

197 When his wife would get the house cleaned

377 When Lea was twelve she became a "doffer" in a spinning-company's mill:

378 When Susan was about eleven, she worked in a cotton mill:

151 When the headlight is beaming, the earth between the railroad ties

465 When the train passed another freight train on a side track

90 When they told her husband

198 When Willie, Jenny's bastard, was about two years of age she married;

7 While Berry was dancing

461 While the ranchman with hired men was building a corral near his dwelling on the ranch,

163 While the services were going on

152 Whipple lived about ten miles from the railroad

68 Williams—a Negro—Davis, Sweeney, and Robb

460 Willie, a boy of fourteen living on a ranch with his parents—

126 Wisdom and his wife and three or four other Negroes

54 Woods, a colored man, was a laborer

109 Work was scarce and the weather bad.

33 Years ago, a company procured a body of land

453 Years before, during a massacre of Armenians,

13 "Yellowstone Kit," as he was called,